Cultivating Consciousness

Cultivating Consciousness

An East-West Journey

K. Ramakrishna Rao et al.

GITAM University Press

DK PRINTWORLD
Publishers of Indian Traditions

Cataloging in Publication Data — DK
[Courtesy: D.K. Agencies (P) Ltd. <docinfo@dkagencies.com>]

"Cultivating Consciousness for Enhancing Human Potential, Wellness and Healing" (Conference) (1991 : Durham, England)
Cultivating consciousness : an East-West journey
K. Ramakrishna Rao et al. — [Rev. ed.].
p. cm.
Includes bibliographical references (p.) and indexes.
ISBN 9788124607176
1. Consciousness — Congresses. 2. Parapsychology — Congresses. I. Rao, K. Ramakrishna. II. Title.

DDC 153 23

ISBN 13: 978-81-246-0717-6
First Published in USA in 1992
Revised edition published in India in 2014

Published by:
GITAM University Press
Rushikonda, Visakhapatnam – 530 045 (A.P.)
Phone: (0891) 284 0312; *Fax*: (0891) 279 0037
e-mail: director_cgs@gitam.edu
Web: www.gitam.edu
and

D.K. Printworld (P) Ltd.
Regd. Office : '*Vedaśrī*', F-395, Sudarshan Park
(Metro Station: Ramesh Nagar), New Delhi - 110 015
Phones : (011) 2545 3975, 2546 6019; *Fax* : (011) 2546 5926
e-mail : indology@dkprintworld.com
Web : www.dkprintworld.com

Printed by:
D.K. Printworld (P) Ltd., New Delhi

To

Dr. Karan Singh

Statesman–Philosopher and Fellow Traveler

Preface

THIS volume is an expanded and revised edition of *Cultivating Consciousness*, published by Praeger in 1993. This book has been out of print for several years now. Following the demand for it in India and considering the need to include the Indian perspectives on cultivating consciousness, Part II is added. All the chapters in the first edition are included in Part I. In Part II, we added four more chapters. They are again revised version of three chapters from my book *Consciousness Studies: Cross-Cultural Perspectives* published by McFarland & Co. Jefferson, NC in 2002. The last chapter "Two Faces of Consciousness" is a revised version of the paper published with the same title in the *Journal of Consciousness Studies.* I thank Praeger, McFarland & Co. and the *Journal of Consciousness Studies* for making this expanded version of this volume possible. I am also thankful to Prof. D.P. Chattopadhyaya, Prof. Bhuvan Chandel and the Centre for Studies in Civilizations for allowing me to use some materials published by them in my book *Cognitive Anomalies, Consciousness and Yoga* (Rao 2011).

I gratefully acknowledge the help and support of several others in publishing this volume. First, I thank the then Board of Directors of the Foundation for Research on the Nature of Man (FRNM) and the Chairman, Russel Moores, who enthusiastically supported this project to honor the Birth Centenary of Dr. Louisa E. Rhine. Second, I am grateful to the Fetzer Institute and its President Rob Lehman and the Institute for Noetic Sciences and its President Willis Harman, who evinced keen interest in this project and provided grants to organize the Conference on Cultivating Consciousness where the chapters that are printed in Part I of this volume were first presented. Third, my grateful thanks go to all those who contributed chapters to this volume and to those who travelled long distances to participate in the consciousness conference. Fourth, I acknowledge my appreciation to the following organizations which as co-participants supported the conference: American Society for Psychical Research, Archaeus Project, Atlantic University, Center for Frontier Sciences of Temple University, Consciousness Research and Training

Project, Human Potentials Foundation, Isthmus Institute, Institute of Transpersonal Psychology, International Society for the Study of Subtle Energies and Energy Medicine, Parapsychological Association, Parapsychology Services Institute, Society for the Anthropology of Consciousness, Society for Scientific Exploration, and the West Georgia College Psychology Department. Fifth, I thank all my colleagues at FRNM who helped me in various ways, especially Rick Steeves, Administrative Assistant, Anne Carroll, Business Manager, and Pat Spivey, who was of special help in editing the Part I of this volume.

I am happy to include in the revised edition four additional chapters discussing the subject of consciousness from the perspective of classical Indian tradition. Together the two parts give us a more wholesome account of consciousness from two distinct traditions. I express my thanks to Dr M.V.V.S. Murthi, President, GITAM University and Shri Susheel K. Mittal of DK Printworld for undertaking the publication of this volume. I would consider this effort worthwhile if this volume could help to spur interest in the study of consciousness by philosophers and psychologists in this part of the world.

Visakhapatnam **K. Ramakrishna Rao**

23 June 2013

Contents

Introduction

In a significant sense, consciousness is the defining characteristic of the human condition. Yet, the currently dominant scientific paradigm virtually ignores consciousness and renders our deeply-held values irrelevant to our existence. This state of affairs has led some who believe that advances in our knowledge will lie in the area of consciousness to raise significant questions about the nature of science and its role in society. Again, those who see the incompleteness of the physicalistic worldview, the reality of anomalous phenomena such as extrasensory perception (ESP), and the intrinsic difficulties in casting consciousness in a sustainable deterministic and reductionistic mold have started to look into alternative paradigms or radical extensions/modifications of existing theoretical constructs. All these attempts portend exciting times ahead, where a clash of paradigms appears imminent.

This book gives us glimpses of the nature of things to come, the controversies and questions about assumptions, concepts, methods, and possible outcomes. In this unique collection of scholarly articles contributed by eminent researchers involved in consciousness studies, the authors discuss from a transdisciplinary and intercultural perspective the nature of consciousness, the methods of studying it, its relevance to our values, and its role in enhancing human abilities and wellness.

The birth centenary of Louisa E. Rhine was the occasion for the first edition of this volume, which incorporated the papers that were presented at the conference, "Cultivating Consciousness for Enhancing Human Potential, Wellness and Healing", held on 8-10 November 1991, in Durham, North Carolina. Author of six books and numerous research papers, Rhine was the first lady of parapsychology for half a century. Her vast collection of spontaneous "psychic" experiences, the largest in the world, is a veritable gold mine. Her motivation in collecting these cases was not merely to document cases suggestive of psi occurrence in the human condition but also to explore the extent of human potential and the outreach of consciousness to encompass those aspects of our nature that are simply inconsistent with mechanistic and materialistic conceptions of our being. As I have pointed out elsewhere (Rao 1986), Mrs. Rhine's studies (Rhine and Rhine 1978) led her "to challenge the concept of physical determinism into which the sciences had all allowed themselves to slip" (pp. 195-96) and to believe that "there is at least something beyond physics" that "profoundly changes the picture of man's nature" (p. 196). Both the conference and this volume are dedicated to address this challenge and to discuss consciousness as an aspect of our being that goes beyond the mechanistic perspectives provided by those disciplines that ignore or deny the existence of consciousness.

The purpose of this book is to call attention to the importance of consciousness research and its implications for improving the human condition. The contributors come from a variety of disciplines, reflecting the transdisciplinary character of consciousness research. The diversity of topics represents the richness and broad scope of consciousness studies. In my opinion, the conference was an important event. I know of no other occasion when so many organizations with scholarly and scientific interest in the study of consciousness participated in a conference of this kind and thus provided a unique opportunity for a frank exchange and clarification of ideas from several perspectives.

In a book like this, it is customary for the editor to present brief synopses of the contributions. I wish to do something different, for I do not believe that a short summary can adequately address the richness and complexity of the issues and problems dealt with by the authors. Instead, I will give a brief account of the accomplishments of L.E. Rhine, to whose memory the conference was dedicated, and at the same time attempt to bring out the relevance of the Rhines' work to consciousness research and vice versa.[1]

L.E. Rhine

Born on 9 November 1891, on an island in the Niagara River to Christian Weckesser and his Mennonite wife, Louisa E. Rhine, ever since she could remember, "wanted to amount to something, something that most people never even heard of, something original, something different". This ambition was fulfilled when she and her husband, J.B. Rhine, decided to devote their professional lives to a scientific study of psychic phenomena — a career that lasted for almost sixty years, first at Duke University and later at the Foundation for Research on the Nature of Man in Durham,

1. For a more complete account see Rao 1986.

North Carolina. Throughout her long career, Mrs. Rhine's commitment to things she believed in was always tempered by her concern for objectivity. Her mind was an exemplary blend of laboratory precision and experiential richness. With her husband, Louisa Rhine helped to bring legitimacy to the study of psychic phenomena, a field previously shrouded in mystery. While her husband designed simple laboratory experiments to test the possibility of psi abilities, she collected and analyzed thousands of real-life psychic experiences and laid the groundwork for a taxonomy of psi.

Even though Mrs. Rhine is rightly recognized as the foremost researcher of spontaneous psychic experiences, her contributions to the experimental study of psi are also considerable. Apart from her day-to-day involvement with the experimental research carried out at Duke University, Mrs. Rhine did several experiments on her own, which are still cited in current publications.

Rhine's major contribution to parapsychology, however, was her study of spontaneous cases. Her collection is the most extensive in existence. She began her study with a research strategy somewhat different from that of her predecessors. Her focus was not to prove the existence of psi (the extra-sensorimotor ability involved in phenomena such as ESP) but to see whether the cases would throw any light on the psi process and provide ideas that might form the basis for research under controlled conditions. As she put it:

> It was partly in a search for clues for new insights by which to guide the framing of experiments that attention was turned to personal experiences. . . . But besides that, another reason for the study was to get a more rounded, full-bodied conception of the effects trapped so laboriously in the laboratory. — L.E. Rhine 1961: 8

Therefore, the Duke collection, unlike the British SPR collection, for example, did not involve any effort to authenticate the cases. The only consideration for inclusion was that the case must seem to involve some form of psi and "state explicitly what the experience was like, and also, just as clearly, the real happening and attendant circumstances" (ibid., p. 10).

With the overall objective of understanding the basic psi process, Mrs. Rhine attempted to classify and analyze her cases, to identify the main forms in which psi is expressed in consciousness, and to understand the extent of knowledge conveyed by them. Between 1951 and 1967, she published eighteen separate research reports, vastly adding to our understanding of spontaneous psychic experiences. The most important of her findings was the observation that psi seems to manifest in real life in the form of intuitions, hallucinations, unrealistic dreams, and realistic dreams. Other surveys (Haight 1979; Sannwald 1963) revealed a comparable distribution of cases into these forms.

Three of Mrs. Rhine's studies had to do with apparition cases, a subdivision of hallucinatory experiences that by earlier accounts had a bearing on the survival hypothesis. "The result of all three studies," according to her, "was to show that if apparitions had any bearing on the survival question, it cannot be because of the hallucinatory *form* of the experience. That, it was shown, is one of the basic ways in which psi is expressed in consciousness" (L.E. Rhine 1977: 72).

Her studies led her to emphasize the unconscious and dynamic aspects of psi (L.E. Rhine 1965). Following up on Tyrrell's suggestion, she hypothesized that psi is a two-stage process. Although we hardly know anything about Stage I, where psi interaction takes place and paranormal information is received, she suggests that the process by which the unconscious psi information finds its way into overt behavior may be understood to be the same in psi as it is in other psychodynamic functions. The four types of psi experiences revealed by her vast collection of spontaneous cases seem to fit neatly into the hypothesis that they are the "mediating vehicles" that bring the information received at Stage I into Stage II. Also, her analysis of cases with incomplete and distorted psi information suggests that these cases are better understood in terms of the two-stage hypothesis and that the incompleteness, distortions, and imperfections in overt psi responses seem to be traceable to known psychodynamic factors. She also suggested that psi-missing is due to blocking and repression of Stage I information from reaching Stage II awareness.

Her first book, *Hidden Channels of the Mind,* published in 1961, incorporated the results of her study of spontaneous cases. The *New York Times* described it as a "classic source book", and the *Los Angeles Times* called it "a voyage of discovery". The book addresses such questions as: Who has ESP and how common is it? Do sane, healthy people have it? Are women more "psychic" than men? Can foreseen dangers be avoided? What is the effect of time and space on ESP?

In *Mind Over Matter,* Rhine (1970) presented a history of psychokinesis research, from the first impromptu dice-throwing experiments to the recent and sophisticated work, and discussed their meanings in the context of such strange events as hauntings and poltergeists. Her *ESP in Life and Lab* (1967) is a significant contribution to the reconciliation of laboratory research and real-life experience. *Psi: What Is It?*, published in 1975, is still used as a standard textbook in many parapsychology courses for young adults. Her 1981 book, *The Invisible Picture,* provides us with a grand overview of her work. In her last book, *Something Hidden* (1983), she recounts with "extraordinary grace and openheartedness" the story of her life, marriage, and career with J.B. Rhine.

At 91, Louisa Rhine was active and alert both physically and mentally. In 1980 she served as president of the British Society for Psychical Research. She also acted as editor and consultant to the *Journal of Parapsychology.* From the time of her husband's death in 1980 until her death on 17 March 1983, she served as the Executive Director of the Foundation for Research on the Nature of Man.

The Rhines' Work and Consciousness Research

"The question involving the total nature of man and his relation to the universe," wrote L.E. Rhine, "is not the easiest, for although it has probably been asked the longest and by the greatest number of people, it is still unsettled" (1967: 8). It is to this unsettled question that the work of the Rhines was directed. Even though the discussion of consciousness as such did not figure significantly in Mrs. Rhine's extensive writings, it is clear that many of the gaps in her discussion of psi function are a consequence of our lack of understanding about the nature of consciousness. For example, her speculations about the two-stage psi process require that we know more about the unconscious and its relationship to consciousness before we can raise meaningful questions about the manner in which unconscious psi inputs may manifest as conscious response outputs.

The Rhines repeatedly observed that psi is an unconscious process. But they meant by unconscious more than a mere lack of subjective awareness. As J.B. Rhine put it:

> Psi is profoundly unconscious. It is not merely one of those transiently subconscious processes that go on practically all the time in everyone, mental activities that can be consciously recovered if one tries and knows how to do so. It is not even one of those more hidden kinds which the psychiatrist can bring to the surface if, because of an unhealthy attitude, control over them has been lost. Neither is the psi experience similar to

> the dissociated or submerged section of consciousness which can be allowed to operate by itself during sleep, as in dreams; rather, psi is simply not capable of being dragged into consciousness unconverted and direct.
> — 1953: 108

Therefore, he goes on to emphasize:

> The operation of psi is *really* unconscious [Rhine's emphasis]. It is unconscious in a different degree or way from experiences that are merely forgotten or repressed or left out of consciousness by the shift of attention or preoccupation with an object of concentrated interest. The operation of the psi function is, so far as the researches can indicate to date, irrecoverably unconscious.
> — pp. 203-04

The emphasis on the "really unconscious" operation of psi takes into account the general notion that consciousness is simply sensorial awareness. Conscious awareness is invariably associated with one of the sensory modalities. All conscious mental life, as J.B. Rhine says, "is compounded of derivatives of what were originally sensations" (1953: 118). To the Rhines, the really unconscious represented mental activity, such as psi, which is not mediated by sensations or their derivatives. Real unconscious mental activities and their outcomes are in principle beyond awareness. They are "irrecoverably unconscious". The unconscious mental inputs, however, may be converted into sensory derivatives and thus may manifest in awareness. They enter into consciousness only in a converted form. Mrs. Rhine's analyses of her cases revealed to her that there are essentially four different forms in which psi manifests itself in our awareness. They are (a) realistic dreams, (b) unrealistic dreams, (c) hallucinations, and (d) intuitions. The realistic experiences are in pictorial form and occur mostly in dreams. On rare occasions, however, someone may see something in his or her "mind's eye" that is later found to correspond to an actual event. The unrealistic experiences contain imagery that is fictitious or symbolic, and they seldom occur with realistic elements. Hallucinatory psi experiences are vivid, sensory-like experiences and occur when one is awake. These are least frequently observed. Unlike the other forms, intuitive experiences do not involve imagery. An intuitive experience is a hunch, a sudden "just knowing" feeling. The vehicles by which psi is mediated are thus *"normal, ordinary,* and *familiar* forms of mental life. . . . *ESP has no distinctive form of its own"*(L.E. Rhine 1961: 68, her emphasis).

The Rhines speculated that psi is primordial in nature and primitive in its evolutionary origins. They felt that psi is a function "submerged and overlaid by the development of the association network deriving from the sensory functions on which consciousness depends" (J.B. Rhine 1953: 119). It is clear that the Rhines considered consciousness as sensorially mediated awareness, and unconscious to be as nonsensory consciousness. That extrasensory awareness is possible is the central theme of their research endeavors. It is important to note, however, that extrasensory awareness is not, according to them, a non-natural phenomenon. Instead, it is an empirical phenomenon that is "energetically real". It follows, therefore, that extrasensory awareness may involve energies that are insufficient or inappropriate to evoke sensations. Because *extrasensory* has a narrower connotation, it is perhaps best to describe unconscious as an implicit awareness that includes extrasensory and other non-conscious phenomena such as subliminal perception. The Rhines felt that the apparent independence of ESP from time–space constraints suggests that the energies involved in psi may indeed be qualitatively different from those of sensory experience. It is, of course, entirely possible that the same energy at different levels of intensity may have properties and produce effects that are qualitatively different. For that reason some may argue that extrasensory and other kinds of non-conscious awareness may involve the same but different energy levels. Whether ESP may result from a flow of extremely low energy, perhaps at micro levels, between the organism and the environment can be a subject of future research. The Rhines believed, however, that the energy involved in psi is non-physical in the classical sense. But quantum physics may render that distinction between physical and non-physical somewhat misleading (see Walker 1972a, b).

Recent research in the area of subliminal perception, another controversial area in consciousness studies, has produced some interesting results of possible relevance. There is impressive evidence that stimuli presented at low energy levels, or in masked forms so that they cannot be recalled, recognized, or discriminated from other similarly presented stimuli, can nevertheless produce detectable cognitive, affective, or other behavioral effects. For example, subliminal (4 ms) exposure to the message "Mommy and I are one" is shown to have beneficial effects on those undergoing psychotherapy (Silverman and Weinberger 1985). What is even more interesting is that the effects obtained under subliminal conditions are greater than those obtained when the subjects report seeing the stimulus message (Bornstein 1989). In a study by Spence and Holland (1962), the subjects were presented with a list of twenty words to memorize. Ten words had remote associations with the word *cheese,* whereas the rest were neutral. One group of subjects were presented the word *cheese* subliminally; another group saw the word supraliminally. The third group was exposed to a blank. The results showed that the subliminal presentation group recalled more words associated with cheese than did the subjects in the group who actually saw the word or those in the blank group.

There are interesting parallels between psi and subliminal perception research that suggest we may be dealing with similar, if not the same, unconscious processes. As Dixon (1979) pointed out, a number of variables like motivation, memory, altered states such as dreams, hypnosis, and relaxation, as well as right-hemispheric mode of functioning, appear to have a similar influence on both subliminal perception and ESP. These similarities encourage us to consider that subliminal perception and ESP may be two species of implicit awareness. Such a consideration is further strengthened when we begin to appreciate the controversial nature of these fields and to consider why there is a general reluctance to accept them. For example, the following statements were made by a respected researcher writing about subliminal perception. "Apparently there are those who will never accept the idea that behavior can be influenced by stimuli of which we are unaware" (Masling 1992: 263). "It is not easy to obtain an effect from subliminal stimulation, and some of those who failed to obtain results may not have known how to find the phenomenon" (ibid.: 268). Those observations are just as true for ESP as they are for subliminal perception.

One may, however, point to an important difference between an ESP target and a subliminal perception stimulus. The latter is considered to be in sensory contact with the subject even though at too low an intensity level to cause explicit awareness, whereas the subject in ESP tests is presumed to be completely isolated from the target with no possibility of any sensory contact whatsoever. This difference may indeed be crucial if the subliminal target is in fact in sensory contact with the subject whereas the ESP subject is in complete isolation from the target. Such assumptions, however, are by no means obvious. In what respect does an ESP card concealed in an opaque envelope differ from a masked stimulus the subject is unable to recall, recognize, or discriminate from other similarly masked stimuli? Is it not possible that some energy, perhaps too weak to be detected with current instrumentation, is also involved in ESP function?

It is difficult to conceive that a subliminal stimulus presented at or below objective threshold, where the information is actually discriminated at no better than chance levels (Cheisman and Merikle 1985), is in any kind of sensory contact with the subject. In subliminal perception, sensory contact is inferred from the observed behavior of the subject because it is assumed that such a contact is necessary. In ESP, however, though similar behavior is observed, no sensory contact is inferred because it is not believed to be necessary. In neither case do we have a clear understanding of the process by which the subliminal stimulus or the ESP target causes these behavioral effects from which we infer subliminal or extrasensory perception.

Even granting that there is sensory contact between the subject and the subliminal stimulus, we are left with the problem of explaining how such contact, which causes no explicit awareness, has an influence on the behavior of the subject. This problem appears to be the same as the one that relates to the second stage of psi process in Mrs. Rhine's theory. It is clear that subliminal perception, like ESP, presumes some kind of dissociation between conscious and unconscious processes, in so far as the stimulus (target) information being unavailable to consciousness in both. Therefore, the question of how the unconscious information comes into consciousness, how the implicit becomes explicit awareness, needs to be answered in subliminal as well as ESP research. This common problem provides a clear connection between the two fields and suggests at the same time how each of these areas can benefit from learning from the other.

Regrettably, however, with few exceptions, researchers in subliminal perception have shown no interest in psi; and parapsychologists by and large have carried out their experiments, benefitting little by the advances in subliminal studies. As mentioned before, subliminal perception research has shown that subliminal stimuli can have behavioral effects even when subjects are unable to detect them (fail to guess in a forced-choice test whether a subliminal stimulus is present at better-than-chance levels). Parapsychologists, however, continue to use detection criteria instead of the semantic or psychodynamic activation effects that seem to occur even in the absence of detection. It does not seem to me at all unreasonable to expect that test procedures such as those used to study subliminal exposure effects (Kunst-Wilson and Zajonc 1980), subliminal semantic activation (Cheisman and Merikle 1984), and subliminal psychodynamic activation

(Silverman 1983) may enable psi researchers to obtain more consistent and reliable effects.

The need of the day in consciousness research, I am persuaded, is greater coherence and mutuality among those who are coming from a variety of disciplines and are engaged in studying different aspects of consciousness. Such a coherence will be possible only when proper communication exists between them. Desired communication can be facilitated by a discussion of the conceptual issues, as well as the methodological, that often divide researchers. In order that we can have a basic understanding of these issues, we also need to have a critical appreciation of the metaphysical foundations of science. The conference on cultivating consciousness was convened to discuss all these issues, theoretical and empirical, conceptual and methodological.

The chapters in Part II discuss consciousness from an altogether different perspective. The perspective they portend could be seen as a forerunner of a more inclusive paradigm that could expand the scope of consciousness research to include those grey areas such as anomalus phenomena and other hard problems of consciousness for a fuller understanding of human nature. This could also be an important bridge between East and West which are often seen as two mutually exclusive traditions.

Part I

1

Does Further Progress in Consciousness Research Await a Reassessment of the Metaphysical Foundations of Modern Science?

Willis W. Harman

A cartoon shows a woman driver attempting to deal with a police officer who has accosted her for driving the wrong way down a one-way street. "Officer," she says, "did it ever occur to you that maybe the *sign* is wrong?"

It seems clear in retrospect that the relatively unfriendly reception of the scientific and medical communities to research in psi phenomena, dissociative states, altered states of consciousness, and other areas related to consciousness in some of its non-normal forms has come about mainly because the meaning and significance people tended to attach to these experiences seemed to clash so directly with prevailing assumptions about the nature of scientific reality. But perhaps, like the one-way street sign, it is our "official" concept of reality that is wrong.

The Broader Challenge

These other states of consciousness and paranormal experiences to which I refer are not the only areas that challenge the worldview of modern science. Among the areas where there are major failures of the prevailing scientific worldview to accommodate well-substantiated evidence are the following:

1. The fundamental inquiry within physics into the ultimate nature of things does not appear to be convergent. The search for fundamental particles seems to lead to still more fundamental particles; the search for the ultimate reductionist explanation seems to point to a wholeness that defies explanation. It is a fundamental initial assumption of physics, which has influenced every other area of

science, that ultimate reality consists of fundamental particles, separate from one another and interacting through mechanisms (especially fields) that can be discovered and specified. With Bell's theorem, however, quantum physics now displays an inherent contradiction; particles originally assumed separate turn out, apparently, to be connected.

2. There appears to be evidence for a fundamental *self-organizing force in living systems,* from the smallest to the largest conceivable organisms, which remains unexplained by physical principles. Living systems exhibit a tendency toward self-organization (e.g. homeostasis; intricate patterns in flowers, butterfly wings, etc.); toward preservation of integrity (e.g. healing and regeneration; ontogenesis from a single fertilized egg to an adult organism); toward survival of the organism and the species (e.g. complex instinctual patterns for protection and reproduction). The evidences of acumulative effect, over time, of this self-organizing tendency in evolution cast doubt on the adequacy of the neo-Darwinist orthodoxy.

3. There is a persistent puzzle of "action at a distance", or *nonlocal causality.* This shows up, as we have already observed, in the far reaches of quantum physics. It also appears in the area that John Beloff (1977) calls *meaningful coincidences,* referring to two or more events where there appears to be a meaningful connection although there is no physical connection. Here, *meaningful* may refer either to the subjective judgment of the observer or to a judgment based in historical data (as in the case of astrology or the I Ching). The term *meaningful coincidences* includes Carl Jung's "synchronicity" (Peat 1987) and most of the range of the "paranormal". Examples include apparently "telepathic" communication, seemingly clairvoyant "remote viewing", and the "coincidence" between the act of prayer and the occurrence of the prayed-for, such as healing. Another example is the feeling of having a "guardian angel" when a person feels warned about a danger or provided with a particularly fortuitous circumstance in life. A host of historical and anecdotal examples fall into the categories of "miracles" and "psi phenomena".

4. Our scientific knowledge about the universe appears to be incomplete in that there is no place in it for *the consciousness of the observer* — or, in general, for volition (free will) or any of the other attributes of

consciousness. Nobel laureate Roger Sperry (1987) insists that no science can be complete if it does not include "downward causation", from the higher level of consciousness to the lower, physicochemical level.

5. One of the most challenging aspects of the consciousness puzzle is *the concept of the self.* The conscious self is ineluctably involved in observation; yet the science constructed from those observations contains no place for the self. Psychologist Gordon Allport wrote in 1955, in a little volume entitled *Becoming,* "For two generations, psychologists have tried every conceivable way of accounting for the integration, organization and striving of the human person without having recourse to the postulate of a self." The battle is still going on.
6. Related, but worthy of separate mention, is the area of *altered states of consciousness,* including particularly those states traditionally sought out in a spiritual or mystical context.

Reviewing the Nature of Scientific Inquiry

To understand what it means for science to be presented with such a broad challenge, we need to review some basic aspects of scientific inquiry.

Quine's "Theoretical Network" Argument

W.V.O. Quine (1962), a major figure in recent philosophy of science, argued that the scientific explanation for any phenomenon is embedded in a theoretical network that involves multitudinous assumptions, including:

a. assumptions involved in "observations" of the phenomenon;
b. hypotheses about the context of the phenomenon;
c. underlying theoretical hypotheses;
d. "basic laws" of the pertinent area of science;
e. the accepted nature of scientific methodology;
f. epistemological assumptions underlying scientific inquiry;
g. ontological assumptions about the basic nature of reality.

When there is an "anomaly", or a failure of observations to conform to scientific expectations, it means that *somewhere* in that network there is a falsity. There is no way to tell just where in the theoretical network the falsity lies. Thus, in the face of an anomaly we must consider revising any or all elements of the network. There is ultimately no such thing as a "crucial experiment" to "prove" a scientific hypothesis. Hypotheses and conceptual models are useful or not useful — not "true" or "false".

When experience contradicts scientific theory, the theory must be changed, but there is no infallible logic for determining exactly *what* to change. Karl Popper's insistence that theories are never proved, but only falsified or not, seemed at one point an important insight; in today's science, to talk of "verification" or "falsification" of theory sounds naïve and simplistic. We must, says Quine, give up any idea that we can use experience *either to confirm or to falsify* particular scientific hypotheses. A consequence of Quine's view is that even our epistemological convictions about how we acquire knowledge, and about the nature of explanation, justification, and confirmation, are subject to revision and correction.

It is precisely to that point that present-day scientific paradoxes seem to have brought us. Most scientists today would assert that science has moved away from the strict determinism, reductionism, positivism, and behaviorism of a half-century ago. But it appears that more subtle forms of "isms" remain, and it is not at all clear what scientists are moving *toward.*

Three Aspects of Scientific Inquiry

In arguing that the areas of human experience just listed comprise a fundamental challenge to the adequacy of present science, we are in no way attacking the fundamental spirit of scientific inquiry. We are, rather, suggesting the timeliness of science taking a major step in its own evolution.

This point can be made more clear by considering the three basic aspects of scientific inquiry (Rubenstein et al. 1984):

a. *Constructing, testing, and using conceptual models*: Creating, testing, and applying conceptual models comprise the chief *activity* of scientists. It is not unique to science; the main ways in which little children learn about their environment are by creating mental models and testing them by experience. The uniqueness of scientific inquiry lies in the other two aspects.

b. *Distinguishing values*: Chief among the distinguishing values of science are the openness of inquiry, healthy skepticism, and public validation of knowledge.

c. *Adopted assumptions*: Modern science tends to be characterized by certain basic ontological and epistemological assumptions that are the result both of long-standing characteristics of Western culture and of the tension between science and the Catholic Church around the seventeenth century. It is in these basic assumptions that the present form of science is most vulnerable to challenge.

The Metaphysical Foundations of Modem Science

Among the metaphysical assumptions that have been assumed intrinsic to modern science, perhaps the most important are:

Objectivism: The assumption of an objective world which the observer can hold at a distance and study separately from himself.

Positivism: The assumption that the real world is what is physically measurable.

Reductionism: The assumption that we come to really understand a phenomenon through studying the behavior of its elemental parts (e.g. fundamental particles).

These are essentially the assumptions of *logical empiricism.* By the middle of the last century there was almost complete consensus that these are the proper foundation assumptions for science. They amount to the premise that the basic stuff of the universe is what physicists study: namely, matter and physical energy — ultimately, "fundamental particles", their associated fields and interrelationships.

To be sure, these underlying assumptions have been modified with the advent of quantum physics, particularly by the indeterminacy principle and the inherent statistical nature of measurement of the very small. What we want to suggest here is the possibility of an even more fundamental change — change at the level of underlying ontological and epistemological assumptions.

Underlying these (modified) classical assumptions is *an ontological assumption of separateness*: Separability of observer from observed, of man from nature, of mind from matter, of science from religion; separateness of "fundamental particles" from one another; separability of the parts of a system or organism to understand how it "really" works; separateness of scientific disciplines, of investigators, competing over who was first discoverer.

The assumption of separateness leads to the hubris that humankind can pursue its own objectives as though the earth and the other creatures on earth were here for its benefit; to the myth of the "objective observer";

to reductionist explanations; to the ethic of competition. It implies the locality of causes; i.e. it precludes "action at a distance", either in space or in time. It implies the epistemological assumption that our sole empirical basis for constructing a science is the data from our physical senses.

Scientists typically take these ontological and epistemological assumptions to be inviolate, to be an inherent and ineluctable part of the definition of science. But it is precisely here that we are likely to find the resolution of some of the most fundamental puzzles in science. This resolution would come through extending the accepted "separateness science" (based on the ontological assumption of separateness and the epistemological assumption that all knowledge is based on physical sense data) to a "wholeness science" (based on an *ontological assumption of oneness, wholeness,* interconnectedness of everything).

Toward a More Holistic Science

There is increasingly widespread agreement that science must somehow develop the ability to look at things more holistically. In a more holistic view, where everything, including physical and mental, is connected to everything, a change in any part affects the whole. Only when a part of the whole can be sufficiently isolated from the rest that reductionistic causes appear to describe adequately why things behave as they do, do the ordinary concepts of scientific causation apply. In general, *"causes" are limited explanations that depend upon context.*

In his book *Unconditional Life* (1991), Deepak Chopra describes an incident in which the doctor (Chopra) made a remark that, because it was misunderstood by the patient, triggered a rage resulting in stabbing chest pains and collapse. All attempts at resuscitation failed, and the patient died. Autopsy revealed that the heart had literally torn itself apart along the line of an earlier damage to the heart muscle. The coroner's report simply stated: "Cause of death: myocardial rupture". As Chopra observes, "If the report had read: 'Cause of death: distorted perception of the situation,' we would have come closer to the truth" (pp. 25-28).

The mistake of modern society has been to assume that, ultimately, reductionistic "scientific" causes should explain everything. One should not expect reductionistic science to comprise an adequate worldview. The context of reductionistic science is the desire to gain control through manipulation of the physical environment. Within that context, its description of "causes" works amazingly well. Our problems arise when we change the context and attempt to elevate that kind of science to the level of a worldview. That is when we generate conflicts like "free will versus determinism" and "science versus religion".

One of the main implications of "wholeness science" is the epistemological assumption that *we contact reality in not one but two ways.* One of these is through physical sense data — which form the basis of normal science. The other is through being ourselves part of the oneness — through a deep, intuitive "inner knowing". In other words, there is a basic epistemological issue involved: namely, whether our encountering of reality is limited to being aware of, and giving meaning to, the messages from our physical senses (sometimes referred to as "objective") or it also includes a subjective aspect in an intuitive, aesthetic, spiritual, noetic, and mystical sense. (It should not escape our notice that an intuitive and aesthetic factor already enters into normal science in various ways — for example, the aesthetic principle of "elegance"; the "principle of parsimony" in choosing between alternative explanations.)

Relationship to the "Primordial Tradition"

If this subjective aspect of knowing is to be taken seriously, it necessarily leads to a new openness regarding what might be learned — and how it might be learned — from knowledge systems that start from a different perception of reality, such as Chinese medicine, Tibetan Buddhist psychology, or Native American relationship to nature.

The central finding of the study of comparative religion over the past half-century or so has been that within any of the world's spiritual traditions there are typically various *exoteric* or public versions and an "inner-circle", *esoteric* version. The latter, which tends to be more experiential and less sacerdotal, usually involves some kind of meditative discipline or *yoga*. Although the exoteric versions may vary greatly from one another, and from one tradition to another, the esoteric versions are essentially the same. This "primordial tradition" or "perennial wisdom" (Huxley 1945) is to be found in every religion and can be owned exclusively by none.

> The Primordial Tradition is not merely an ancient system of belief and practice. . . . It is, rather, a whole set of archetypical realities waiting to be discovered, at the highest reaches of the human consciousness, by all people.
>
> — Rossner, 1989, p. xvi

The "perennial wisdom" tends to include convictions such as the belief that nature is directed from within by a higher intelligence or mind; that all minds in the universe are linked by participation in one universal mind or source; that various mental or physical rituals can sometimes effect what they symbolize or set the proper conditions in motion for the desired events or result to occur; that prayers, thoughts, and mental projection might directly aid in the healing of sick and diseased persons through the release of powerful, life-giving energies; that all individuals have a powerful, if hidden, motivation to discover and identify with a higher self that is, in turn, in immediate connection to the universal mind. Since this "perennial wisdom" has been distilled from inquiry persisting over a far greater span of time than the duration of modern science, it can hardly be simply set aside as inconsequential.

Characteristics of a Wholeness Science

These arguments suggest the need for an "extended" science which would include present science as something useful but having limited application. Present science, tremendously effective in its chosen context, is based on (a) an ontological assumption of separateness, and (b) an epistemological assumption of physical sense data as the sole empirical evidence on which the scientific picture of reality is to be based. The prospect of an extended science would build upon (a′) an *ontological assumption of oneness, wholeness,* interconnectedness of everything, and (b′) an *epistemological choice to include "all the evidence".*

By "all the evidence", we mean to include all of the following (Baars 1988):

1. Those data admissible in the strict logical empiricism model — namely measurements of physical parameters.
2. Data depending on the connoisseurship of expert judges, such as those on which systematic (taxonomic) biology is based.
3. Data that is essentially self-reports of subjective experience, obtained in an environment that promotes high levels of trust and candor, subjected to sophisticated skepticism because of our known capability for self-deception and checked in other ways wherever possible.
4. The subjective self-reports of trained "inner explorers" of various cultures.

In none of these categories, of course, are data to be accepted without some sort of careful consensual validation.

Once we recognize the non-necessity of the separateness assumption, there is no reason to assume that the biological and cognitive sciences can be reduced to the physical sciences (materialistic, reductionistic, deterministic), let alone to physics. The biological sciences involve more holistic concepts (e.g. organism, function of an organ) that have no counterparts at the physical sciences level. Similarly, there is no reason to assume that the characteristics of consciousness are reducible to biology. In other words, although theory reduction (as, for example, the laws of optics explained through electromagnetic theory) will be welcomed whenever it proves to be possible, it is not a dogma of extended science that it must be, in general, possible. This extended science will be concerned both with "downward causation" (Campbell 1974; Sperry 1987) and with the reductionistic "upward causation" that presently dominates the scientific world. The presence of teleological factors in the biological realm presents no problem once there is releasing of the insistence that biology be reducible to physics and chemistry. We observe teleology in ourselves; why do we not, then, observe it in the larger system of which we are a part? Neither consciousness nor the concept of the self presents any fundamental problem to the extended science. As we have seen, the "perennial wisdom" seems to recommend an inner search involving some sort of meditative or yogic discipline and discovery of, and identification with, a "higher" or "true" Self. Science in the 1990s appears to have a new fluidity and humility that make admission of such an extension of science seem far more possible than would have been the case earlier in the century. Because scientists are no longer concerned with sounding the death knell of the medieval worldview; hierarchical, essentialistic, and teleological connotations are not so threatening. In fact, explicating in these terms frees these concepts from their former association with medievalism.

Combining Separateness and Wholeness

Certain aspects of the unity that is the whole will continue to be quite profitably studied by means of separateness science. That kind of science, however, would — as only part of a more extended science — no longer have the authority to insist that we are here, solely through random causes, in a meaningless universe; nor that our consciousness is "merely" the chemical and physical processes of the brain.

Wholeness science would include and emphasize more participative kinds of methodologies; it would assume that whereas we learn certain kinds of things by distancing ourselves from the subject studied we get another kind of knowledge from intuitively "becoming one with" the subject. Openness to alternative theories and explanations and healthy skepticism are at least as important as they have been in the present separateness science. Consensus validation also remains of central importance, but it will be accomplished in a somewhat different way.

Many of the questions about a wholeness science are taken up by Lincoln and Guba (1985) under the definition of "naturalistic inquiry". The purpose of naturalistic inquiry, they insist, is *understanding,* not prediction and control. They emphasize the human as instrument, tacit knowledge, and qualitative inquiry.

Goodwin (1987) describes aspects of a "science of qualities". It shares many of the aspects we have been considering. He urges that we "return to the vision of the Renaissance magi, in which subject and object, known and unknown, can relate and participate in an appropriate unity, made possible by the fact that reality is a single coordinated domain".

Some of the more radical implications of a wholeness science are not immediately apparent. Imagine starting from the holistic assumption that everything — not only physical things but all things experienced, including sensations, emotions, feelings, motivations, thoughts — is really part of a single unity. If things are so interconnected that a change in any one can affect all, then *any accounting for cause is within a specific context, for a specific purpose.* In the broadest sense, *there are not cause and effect; only a whole system evolving.* What normal science does, in this view, is to study relatively isolable systems where causal factors can be considered limited and, in particular, where no volitional factors need be taken into account. (To recall how special this is, note that the judicial setting comprises another special case, wherein volition and motivation are considered central.)

Starting from the holistic assumption, there is no separation of observer from observed. "Action at a distance" does not pose a particular problem; we do not even have to hypothesize "fields" or "particle exchanges" to account for it. We do not find volition, other states of consciousness, teleological influences, meaningful coincidences, and so on to be anomalous. To re-emphasize the point, none of present science is invalidated in the limited domains where it was generated. However, some of the common extrapolations of scientific findings into the area of human affairs become questionable.

Indeed, it turns the prevailing scientific concept of causality on its head. Whereas the ultimate reductionistic causation is taken to be in terms of fundamental particles and consciousness evolved out of matter, in the "oneness" view ultimate causation is in terms of the universal consciousness-continuum within which all that is exists.

Further Characteristics of a Wholeness Science

An inquiry that starts from the presupposition of wholeness implies that the basic method of observation is much more participatory — observation through identification *with,* rather than separation *from.* Strict interpretations of objectivity and of reliability through replication are inappropriate in participatory research. But if they are, there must be other criteria something like these that *are* appropriate. Something like the Buddhist ideal of non-attachment might come to replace the concept of strict objectivity. And something like trustworthiness (perhaps based on multiple imperfect tests) may replace strict replicability of controlled experiments as the basis for judging reliability. Lincoln and Cuba (1985) have proposed four criteria to establish trustworthiness in what they term "naturalistic inquiry" — credibility, transferability, dependability, and confirmability — and suggest tests for each.

Heretofore, science has started with a limiting set of assumptions and has then found it necessary to deny the validity and even the possibility of a host of reported phenomena that will not fit within those limits. A tremendous amount of effort has gone on within science defending the barricades against, or explaining away, these outcasts — not only "miraculous" healings and "psi phenomena" but also more ordinary experiences such as volition, selective attention, and the hunger for meaning.

Rather than having to defend against the anomalous, wholeness science permits the assumption that any class of inner experiences that have been reported, or of phenomena that have been observed, down through the ages and across cultures, apparently in some sense exists and has a *face validity* that cannot be denied. We seek, in other words, a science that can accommodate *all that exists.* (There are many subtleties, of course. Whole societies can perceive things that observers from other societies do not, so it is necessary to be very cautious about claiming that some class of experiences is universal, even in potential. There is a tendency among some persons today to regard it as a mark of New Age distinction to be willing to believe almost anything. Total gullibility is not our objective.)

In addition to what has already been said about the role of the observer in participatory research, one other important point should be noted — the fact that in such research the experience of observing brings about sensitization and other changes in the observer. *A willingness to be transformed* himself or herself is an essential characteristic of the participatory scientist. The anthropologist who would see clearly a culture other than his or her own must allow that experience effect change so that the new culture is seen through new eyes, not eyes conditioned by the anthropologist's own culture. The psychotherapist who would see a client clearly must have worked through personal neuroses that would otherwise warp perception. The social scientist who would use a participative approach to understanding and guiding organizational arrangements and processes will almost certainly be changed through personal involvement. The scientist who would study meditative processes and those other states of consciousness so treasured in the various spiritual traditions has to be willing to go through the deep changes that will make him or her a competent observer.

The time is ripe. Development of the sort of "extended" science that I have described (summarized in Table 1.1) would tend to stimulate research in the entire spectrum of states of consciousness. These include "religious experiences"; experiences of "mystical" states of consciousness, of "other dimensions of reality". These experiences have been at the heart of all cultures, including our own. They have been among the main sources of the deepest value commitments. They cannot be ignored; yet modern science has denied their significance.

A great deal of cultural change has taken place since the early attempts to deal with these areas within the framework of science. The new emphasis on wholeness and the legitimating of "intuition" and related aspects of inner knowing, have brought us a completely new climate. Richard Tarnas, in *The Passion of the Western Mind* (1991), has impressively documented the evolution of the Western mind from the Greeks through to modern times, concluding that we are due for a more holistic and participative science, not as a challenge to Western consciousness but as fulfillment of it. I believe the time is ripe to insist upon a reexamination of the metaphysical foundations of modern science. Until this is done, research on consciousness will continue to miss the mark because it will continue to be distorted by the misguided attempt to fit it into a basically reductionistic and positivistic framework.

Table 1.1: Assumptions, Corrolaries, and Characteristics of Two Sciences: A Comparison

Separateness Science	*Wholeness Science*
1. *Basic ontological assumption*: The universe is made up ultimately of fundamental particles and quanta which are separate from one another except in so far as there are specifiable connections (such as fields).	1. *Basic ontological assumption*: The universe is basically a single whole within which every part is connected to every other part. This wholeness includes every aspect accessible to human awareness — the physical world as discerned through our physical senses, and all the contents of consciousness.
2. A scientific explanation of a phenomenon (understanding of causes in a scientific sense) consists in relating the phenomenon to more general and fundamental relationships or "scientific laws". The ultimate scientific explanation would be made in terms of the motions and interactions of the fundamental particles and quanta involved. (This desideratum is approached, for example, in thermodynamics or physical optics.)	2. Pragmatically useful scientific explanations enhance under-standings of phenomena by relating them to other phenomena and relationships. Because things are so inter-connected that a change in any one can affect all, then *any accounting for cause is within a specific context, for a specific purpose*. The search for ultimate reductionistic cause is futile; *there are not cause and effect but rather the evolution of a whole system*. Order is observed in the physical world, but it is never free from the possibility of "downward causation" (from consciousness "down" to the physical).
3. All scientific knowledge is ultimately based on data obtained through the physical senses. Such information is, then, ultimately quantifiable.	3. Reality is contacted basically in two ways. One is through physical sense data. The other is inner, through being ourselves part of the oneness — through a deep intuitive "inner knowing". Our encountering of reality is not limited to being aware of, and giving meaning to, the messages from our physical senses

Table continued

Separateness Science	Wholeness Science
	(sometimes referred to as "objective") but includes also a subjective aspect in an intuitive, aesthetic, spiritual, noetic, and mystical sense.
4. The truest information about the objective reality is obtained through the observer being as detached as possible. There is an ultimate limit to objectivity, in that there is inevitably some "observer effect" in any observation.	4. Understanding comes not from being detached, objective, analytical, or coldly clinical but rather from *identifying with* the observed, becoming one with it. (This is not to deny the usefulness of objective knowledge but only the recognition that it leads to a *partial* understanding.)
5. The universe is scientifically understood to be ultimately deterministic.	5. The concept of a completely deterministic universe (even in a statistical sense, as in quantum physics) stems from the "separateness" assumption; there is no reason to expect it to be borne out in experience.
6. The material universe evolved to its present state from the "big bang" by random physical process and, after the advent of life, mutation and natural selection. Consciousness (whatever it is) is a product of material evolution.	6. There is no a priori reason to assume that "scientific laws" are invariant; rather, it seems more plausible that they too are evolving. Hence extrapolation to the "big bang" may be suspect. Evidence seems to point to consciousness either evolving along with, or being prior to, the material world.
7. There is no evidence for mysterious "drives" or "purposes" in evolution. What appears as a "survival instinct" is merely the result of natural selection; organisms that did not have such a drive were selected out. There is no scientific evidence for anything in the universe resembling "purpose" or "design". The	7. Because we humans are part of the whole and experience "drives" or "urges" such as survival, belongingness, achievement, and selfactualization, there is no a priori justification for assuming these are not characteristics of the whole. Similarly, because we experience "purpose" and "values", there is no

Table continued

Separateness Science	*Wholeness Science*
biological sciences use teleological language for convenience, but what it really means is that those structures and behaviors that contribute to survival survived.	valid justification for assuming these are not also characteristics of the whole. In other words, the universe may be genuinely, not just apparently, telic.
8. The wide range of more-or-less commonly experienced phenomena known as "meaningful co-incidences" (including the great preponderance of so-called "anomalous" phenomena) — where two or more events appear to be meaningfully connected but there is no discernible physical connection — must ultimately be shown either to have a physical connection or to be, in fact, merely coincidence.	8. "Meaningful coincidences" are not to be explained but rather are instances of apparent separateness. In other words, the question is not "How can we explain apparent telepathic communication?" but rather, "How can we explain why our minds are not cluttered by all that information in other minds?" Not "How can we explain apparent psychokinetic phenomena?" but rather, "How should we best understand why our minds have such a limited effect in the physical world?"
9. Non-normal states of consciousness, dissociation, and so forth are phenomena to be studied largely in the context of the pathological and in terms of their effects on behavior.	9. The entire spectrum of states of consciousness is of interest. It includes "religious experiences", experiences of "mystical" states of consciousness, of "other dimensions of reality". These experiences have been at the heart of all cultures, including our own. They have been among the main sources of the deepest value commitments; they may be an important investigative tool, a "window" to other dimensions of reality.
10. The explanations of ontogenesis, morphogenesis, regeneration, and related biological phenomena are to be sought in terms of coded "instructions" in the genes and similar mechanisms.	10. The ultimate explanations of ontogenesis, morphogenesis, regeneration, and related biological phenomena will probably turn out to have to include something in consciousness analagous to "image" or "idea".

2

Getting Clear about Wholeness
A Critical Response to Harman

Stephen E. Braude

I heartily echo Willis Harman's desire to overturn many of the misguided assumptions pervading current scientific thought. And I very much sympathize with his choice of targets — in particular, the familiar forms of atomism and mechanistic reductionism one finds in most areas of science. However, I would like to challenge Harman's diagnosis of the situation. Although Harman points his finger at scientific reductionism and the hypothesis that items in nature are separate from one another, the real problem is that scientific theories tend to be *mechanistic*. Because Harman fails to identify the most serious errors of mechanistic theorizing, his own position (ironically) is as deeply defective as the views he hoped to avoid.

In that respect, Harman's suggestions remind me of Sheldrake's hotly debated — and considerably overrated — theory of morphogenetic fields. As I noted some time ago (Braude 1983), Sheldrake presented his theory as an alternative to mechanistic analyses of certain organic phenomena. But because Sheldrake (like many others) apparently misunderstood what lies at the root of mechanistic science, his theory differed only trivially from those he opposed. The only notable difference between traditional explanations of morphogenesis and those couched in terms of morphogenetic fields, morphogenetic germs, and so forth is a relatively insignificant difference in hardware. In fact, Sheldrake simply replaced one sort of mechanism with another. Hence, his view commits all the classic mechanistic errors having to do with the structure of nature and the relationship between structure and function.

In a similar vein, many mistakenly think that in order to oppose traditional mechanistic theorizing in science, it is sufficient to offer a *non-*

physicalistic alternative — for example, a theory couched in Cartesian terms rather than in the language of physics. (In fact, that seems to be one reason why Harman claims that science must accommodate both physical and non-reducible mental phenomena.) But mechanistic theories need not be physicalistic; indeed, even dualist and idealist theories can be mechanistic. Here, too, what matters is not the hardware — for example, whether the *things* or objects referred to in the theory be physical or not. What matters is the *form* of explanation in which those objects play a role.

Now this is not the place to launch into a full-scale attack on scientific mechanism. Fortunately, since Harman's proposals seem to rely more conspicuously only on certain mechanistic assumptions rather than others, it will be sufficient to concentrate on those.

* * *

Harman sees what he calls separateness science as resting on a basic ontological assumption — namely, that "the universe is made up, ultimately, of fundamental particles and quanta which are separate from one another except in so far as there are specifiable connections (such as fields)". Harman wishes to replace this with a basic ontological assumption of what he terms wholeness science — namely, that "the universe is basically a single whole within which every part is connected to every other part".

Although Harman never really explains what sort(s) of deep connectedness he has in mind, certain tacit features of his position are clear from his objectives. One thing Harman wants to do is to find a way to accommodate what to separateness science would seem to be intolerable cases of nonlocal causality or action at a distance. Harman believes that his version of holism renders these cases tolerable. Because all parts of nature are connected (whatever that is supposed to mean), there is simply no problem of action at a distance if we fail merely to find familiar sorts of (presumably) physical connections. In Harman's view, the connections are there; the mistake of ordinary science is that it looks for connections of only a very limited sort.

But there are a number of serious problems with this maneuver. To begin with, Harman's version of holism apparently retains a crucial explanatory feature of traditional separateness science — namely, a fundamental reliance on efficient causality. Ostensible cases of action at a distance (as in telepathy and psychokinesis (PK)) seem to pose a problem for traditional separateness science because it appears that there are no causes spatiotemporally contiguous with the effects that one wants to explain. Harman thinks he can handle this by proposing a wider (but unspecified) assortment of connections between items in nature — and also a wider range of scientifically allowable objects in nature. But this is not a particularly deep rejection of the sorts of causal explanations favored within separateness science. In fact, it may indicate only that Harman's view of efficient causes rests on a somewhat revised conception of the importance of spatiotemporal contiguity. In order to handle cases of apparent action at a distance, Harman could say either (a) that causes need not be spatially contiguous with their effects although they must at least be temporally contiguous, or else (b) that in wholeness science the concept of space gets transformed into something less traditionally topological, so that objects count as spatially contiguous so long as they bear the right sort of "connection" (in Harman's sense) to each other.

Hence, Harman's reliance on a wider network and variety of connections does not seem to be a particularly radical proposal. So long as events get explained in terms of simultaneous or immediately preceding causes, efficient causality (of some sort) still reigns. But more important, like any red-blooded mechanist, Harman wants to explain observable phenomena generally by *going beneath them* — i.e., by analyzing them in terms of some even more basic set of underlying phenomena. Granted, Harman endorses what Sperry (somewhat naïvely) called "downward causation" from the mental to the physical. But in Harman's view, the analyses of both downward and upward causation rest finally on appeals to underlying sorts of connections between things in the world (wherever they might be located in space or — as in the case of mental states — even if they have no spatial location). Perhaps Harman thinks that apparent cases of action at a distance cannot be explained scientifically *except* in terms of lower-level processes or state of affairs. Many people do hold such a view, either wittingly or unwittingly. But that position rests on serious confusions about the nature of explanation and understanding generally; I return to those issues shortly.

Before that, however, we must consider another crucial mechanistic assumption that Harman seems unwilling to abandon. Harman thinks that in order to overturn the atomism of separateness science, one must reject the assumption that nature's elements are profoundly separate and thereby embrace his rich form of holism. But that strategy fails to strike at the heart of the problem. The alleged separateness of nature's elements is not a particularly profound or pernicious feature of traditional science. It is merely an elaboration on an even deeper conceptual blunder —

namely, the assumption that nature is intrinsically divided into elements or (to put it another way) the assumption that there is a preferred or perspective-free inventory of things in nature, quite apart from whatever parsings of nature we find useful and illuminating. Hence, to reject what Harman regards as the basic ontological assumption of separateness science, one needs only to reject the claim that nature has atoms or any other structural feature inherently. It is not necessary to take a stand in advance about what sorts of objects exist and which things in nature are connected.

Of course, there is nothing wrong with providing an alternate ontology. But Harman adopts a position that is recklessly gratuitous at best and obviously false at worst — the claim that "the universe is basically a single whole within which every part is connected to every other part". In fact, for reasons outlined later, one would think that Harman's holistic assertion cannot possibly be true. Actually, I suspect Harman would have been content with a more cautious claim that might easily be mistaken for the one he advances. But although the mistake may be innocent, Harman's holism displays the same sort of professional or perspectival chauvinism that condemns separateness science.

As I see it, one deep problem with standard mechanistic reductionism is the assumption that there is a context-independent preferred descriptive scheme or way of talking about nature (usually that of the physicist). That assumption entails that there be an inherently or absolutely preferred (or final) inventory of events, objects, qualities, and relations in nature that science (or physics) will lay out for us when (or if) it finally gets things right. But it is preposterous to suppose that nature has a preferred description. On the contrary, it may be parsed in numerous ways, spanning a continuum running from the fine-grained to the coarse-grained. And it may be characterized on different levels of description, each of which recognizes certain kinds of things (but not others) as objects, certain descriptive categories (but not others) as appropriate to those objects, and certain sorts of connections (but not others) as possible.

It might help to think of levels of description or sets of descriptive categories as *conceptual grids* through which we view reality.[1] Different grids will parse reality into different kinds of objects and thereby enable us to recognize distinctive sorts of connections or regularities. Of course,

---

1. I owe this useful metaphor to my colleague Bruce Goldberg.

some grids will stand in lawlike relations to others. For example, a grid through which we identify audible sounds will be nomologically related to one that parses reality into waveforms, amplitudes, and frequencies. But some grids reveal objects, properties, and relations that have few (if any) lawlike connections to the sorts of things countenanced by other grids. The diagnostic grids of Western and traditional Chinese medicine are incommensurate in this way, as (I would argue) are the grids of so-called "folk psychology" and contemporary neuroscience. Moreover, although some conceptual grids may be more illuminating or useful than others relative to a background of interests or purposes, none is justifiable — much less correct — apart from any contextual guidelines. But even more important, no parsing of nature or conceptual grid is inherently more fundamental than any other. In fact, that is true even among those standing in lawlike relations to others, because ultimately it is we who decide what counts as a law and which assumptions should be taken as basic.

This last observation deserves additional comment because many think that some kinds of laws (say, the laws of physics or logical laws) are inherently more fundamental than others or that within a given domain (say, logic or physics) certain laws are *inherently* fundamental. Although a cursory survey of radically different axiom systems in logic (or, e.g. alternate axiomatizations of Euclidean geometry) affords clear examples of how the primitiveness and lawlike connections between statements are simply a matter of convention, the following brief example should help illustrate the point in a rather different way.[2] This example shows how the acceptability — indeed, the very *meaning* — of a logical law hinges on a larger network of commitments. Whether we accept the law of identity, "$(x)(x = x)$" (roughly, "anything is identical to itself"), depends on numerous other considerations. If we allow, for instance, that "Zeus = Zeus" is true, then in many systems of deductive logic containing the otherwise unobjectionable rule of Existential Generalization, we can infer that Zeus exists. To many (but by no means to everyone), that result is intolerable. But one can handle it in several ways. One can stipulate that "Zeus" is not a genuine name and that genuine names pick out only real existent individuals (and not, say, mythical or fictional individuals). Or, one can reject the rule of Existential Generalization and endorse a so-

[2] This example also illustrates the sort of point Harman associates with Quine's "theoretical network" argument — which, incidentally, should more properly be attributed to the turn-of-the-century pragmatic philosopher C.S. Peirce.

called (existence)-free logic. Or, one can adopt a substitutional interpretation of the quantifier, according to which the troublesome statement"$(\exists x)(x = z)$" apparently asserting the existence of Zeus no longer has existential import. The reader need not understand all these options. What should be clear, however, is that the law of identity — like logical laws generally — is not simply true *no matter what*. Its truth turns on a number of other decisions as to which logical laws or principles are acceptable, and the whole package of decisions can be evaluated only on pragmatic grounds.

Now none of this forces us to conclude, counter-intuitively, that nature has no structure or no atoms. On the contrary, nature has as many structures (and *kinds* of structures) as we can properly and usefully identify. In other words, we can acknowledge that parsings of nature are perspective relative and still accept some form of scientific realism (roughly, the view that true scientific theories actually describe the world). The view I am articulating asserts only that no structure properly attributable to nature is intrinsically deeper or more fundamental than other such structures and that no structure in nature is identifiable except against a background of interests and purposes (i.e. a context of inquiry). And clearly, if parsings and descriptions of nature always presuppose a perspective or point of view from which they are appropriate, then no description of nature is *true* independent of some associated perspective or point of view — the specific, but contingent, background against which we understand our utterances and assign truth-values to them. No statement is true either inherently or absolutely. So, there *are* atoms in nature (assuming that physics is more or less on the right track). But there are also persons, pigs, loveseats, desks, manipulativeness, and compassion — not to mention the old standbys, memory, volition, ESP, and PK. But these count as things in nature and can properly be said to *exist* only with respect to a set of descriptive categories and a corresponding way of dividing nature into parts. And those sets of categories (those conceptual grids) are human constructions that are always subject to revision or rejection on purely pragmatic grounds.

Curiously, Harman sometimes writes as if he is endorsing a modest plurality of acceptable perspectives on nature, as if the conceptual frameworks of separateness and wholeness science each have some utility. But in the end, he endorses one such framework as fundamentally correct — namely, that in which nature is seen as a whole, every part of which is connected. And to make matters worse, he writes "this wholeness includes *every* aspect accessible to human awareness" (italics added). But that claim is clearly unacceptable. To suppose that every part of nature *could* be connected is to make the same mistake that Harman finds intolerable in old-fashioned reductionism. Both positions miss crucial points about what it is to divide nature into parts and to apply descriptive categories to those parts (Braude 1986: chapters 1.3, 4.4). First, any parsing and description of nature is an act of intellectual abstraction, and all such acts necessarily ignore certain aspects of nature in order to single out others. Second (or perhaps the first point viewed from another angle), every division of nature into objects limits the range of predicate and relational expressions at our disposal — namely, those appropriate to the kinds of objects we identify. And third, our choice of parsings or descriptive categories inevitably reflects the *contingent* and ever-shifting background of needs and interests relative to which those choices are appropriate.

To illustrate the point, let me briefly offer an example I discuss more fully elsewhere (Braude 1986). Consider: how many things are in this room? The important fact to observe here is that this question has no single correct or best answer. How many things there are depends on what counts as a *thing*, and that (in turn) depends on who is asking and why the question is being asked. If the question arises in a technical discussion among a group of atomic physicists, it would probably be appropriate to say the room contains billions of things. But to household movers, interior decorators, or insurance adjusters, the inventory of things in the room might be dramatically smaller.

Moreover, our decision to parse nature a certain way (i.e., to regard certain things, but not others, as objects) helps to fix an appropriate range of descriptive terms. Physicists will assign to their things a range of properties (e.g., spin, ground state, nuclear density, anti-strangeness) not ascribable to the objects identified by household movers, and so on. Similarly, such terms as "bulky", "fragile", "expensive", and "garish" do not apply to atoms and their constituents.

All Harman needed to endorse (and perhaps what he really wanted to assert) is the classically mystical view that no parsing or description of nature is preferred or perspective-independent. But that does not mean that nature is a whole, all parts of which are connected. As I have indicated, not only is that view gratuitous, dogmatic, and as perspectively chauvinistic as the one it opposes; it is also blatantly false. What I think Harman should have said is simply that nature is *intrinsically undifferentiated.*

In that sense, it is a whole, a single thing that we can divide up any number of useful ways. But it is no more ultimately a whole than it is a collection of things. When we view nature as an undifferentiated whole, we simply adopt one of various coherent and pragmatically illuminating perspectives on it. Moreover, when we take nature to be made up of parts, there is no final or all-inclusive answer as to what its parts are, no perspective-free warehouse of ontological furniture. To suppose otherwise would be to reason like a cartographer who thinks that state and county borders on a map must correspond to natural divisions of the land. And clearly, this modest view avoids the error of supposing that every reasonably discernible part of nature can be identified through a single conceptual grid or subsumed *and connected* under a single set of descriptive categories. That error, however, is one of several fatal similarities between Harman's position and traditional separateness science.

* * *

Let us now consider Harman's apparent reluctance to abandon explanations of psi phenomena (and other cases of ostensible action at a distance, such as memory) in terms of more primitive sorts of processes, state of affairs, or (as he puts it) connections. At the root of this, I submit, is an unwillingness to reject a widespread but unjustified assumption whose abandonment would lead to a truly radical (but nevertheless sensible) change in scientific theorizing. I have called this the *small-is-beautiful assumption* (Braude 1986), and it is one of the cornerstones of traditional mechanism. I have written about this many more times than I would have liked; but apparently the community that I am addressing cannot get enough of a good thing.

Most scientists assume (explicitly or otherwise) that observable facts or phenomena (including lawlike regularities) always have analyses in terms of underlying processes or state of affairs. Of course, scientists will generally concede that some facts or phenomena in nature will be basic or unanalyzable. They recognize that explanations by analysis — i.e., in terms of lower-level processes — cannot continue indefinitely and that sooner or later we must arrive at a point where such vertical explanations can go no further. At that point we will have identified genuinely primitive phenomena, whose primitiveness is reflected in the fact that there will be no answer to the question *how* those phenomena occur. The universe simply works in those ways, and no appeal to constitutive processes will explain why. Now *that* position is quite reasonable. But most scientists assume, further, that wherever explanation by analysis stops, wherever these fundamental phenomena occur, it will always be on the level of the very small — for example, the neurological, biochemical, atomic, or subatomic level. Hence, they assume that there are no primitive phenomena at the observable level — e.g. at the level of behavior. That is the *small-is-beautiful assumption.*

Now first of all, notice that this is only an assumption, not an empirically established fact. Moreover, anti-mechanists have mounted a strong case against it. Because space does not permit a detailed assault on the assumption, I shall content myself with sketching the strategies by which one may expose its defects. First, one may show how the assumption fails in particular sorts of cases. For example, one can argue that analyses of most cognitive phenomena (e.g. memory and volition) in terms of lower-level processes or mechanisms presupposes one or more deeply unacceptable theses. The most glaring of these are (a) the Platonic or essentialist view that the relevant classes of observable phenomena (e.g., mental or psychological kinds) can be specified by some set of necessary and sufficient conditions, (b) the view that specifiable kinds of microstructures (e.g. brain states) can be functionally unambiguous — i.e., that structure determines function, and (c) the view that a brain state (or some other kind of microstructure) can be intrinsically isomorphic to the state of affairs it represents or produces (see Braude 1979; Bursen 1978; Goldberg 1982; Heil 1978, 1981, 1983; Malcolm 1977, 1980).

Consider the phenomenon of memory, for example. Rather than accept the possibility that my ability to remember a person or event has no analysis in terms of underlying processes, psychologists and others posit the existence of memory traces whose purpose is to provide a spatiotemporal link between the thing remembered and the act of remembering that thing. But it turns out that no analysis of that phenomenon is possible. To begin with, it is not possible to state necessary and sufficient conditions (say, a structural characterization in terms of brain states) for the relevant memory types. Second, one cannot explain how memory traces trigger the right memory except in one of two ways, each of which is fatal. First, one may appeal to structural isomorphism between the trace and the thing remembered. But that requires adopting views about the nature of similarity and the relation of structure to function that are literally nonsensical. Moreover, because one cannot count on exact matches between memory events, the things remembered, and the memory triggers, the only alternative is to posit a lower-level memory (or recognition) process that explains why it is that appropriate things trigger the memory and how only the proper memory trace is activated. But that explanation is clearly circular and leads to a vicious regress of memory processes (for details, see Braude 1979; Bursen 1978; Heil 1978). For these sorts of reasons, it is far more plausible to regard memory as a phenomenon that is literally unanalyzable. Similar arguments work for volition and for cognitive phenomena generally, including psi phenomena (see Braude 1979, for their application in the case of telepathy, and 1986, for their application in the case of PK).

Another way to expose the poverty of the *small-is-beautiful assumption* connects with points made earlier. That assumption is one form of the view that nature has a preferred (or inherently fundamental) level of description, a level at which we can identify absolutely primitive phenomena and their basic properties. Most supporters of that view would maintain that the preferred level will be described in an adequate theory of physics. But no matter what the preferred level of description is taken to be, the *small-is-beautiful assumption* is committed to the view that statements true of observable phenomena are inherently superficial and that only statements true of the microcosm can be statements about primitive phenomena.

But that position is quite bizarre. For reasons hinted at earlier, it is preposterous to claim that one way of characterizing nature is preferred, final, and inclusive of everything worth describing. Moreover, since no set of descriptive categories is justifiable independent of a background of interests and purposes — or a *perspective* on nature — the *small-is-beautiful assumption* is committed to the view that some perspective on nature is inherently preferred or deeper than all alternatives. That is why most adherents of that assumption would have to say that the physicist asks deeper questions than the psychologist, or interior decorator, or simply the average human being engrossed in everyday matters of psychological survival. Again, this point could be elaborated and criticized much more fully (see Braude 1986); for now, I'll simply note that this is what I earlier identified as perspectival chauvinism.

* * *

So what happens if we reject the *small-is-beautiful assumption* and wholeheartedly embrace the possibility that some observable phenomena (including practically all cognitive or intentional phenomena) have no analysis in terms of underlying processes or mechanisms? How, for example, would it affect the study of psi or the study of memory if we abandoned the search for vertical explanations of the phenomena and really accepted them as primitive and unanalyzable? One consequence, I suspect, which would undoubtedly seem professionally threatening to many, is that research into those phenomena would take off in rather different directions. And to many, I suspect, those fields would seem to take a giant step backwards. Both psychology and parapsychology would probably return to less experimental and mechanistically analytic, and more naturalistic and descriptive modes of inquiry.

These days, of course, that is quite out of vogue in psychology as well as in the philosophy of mind, action, or language. The fashionable approach today is to try to explain particular behaviors or mental events by specifying behavior — or cognition-emitting mechanisms — for example, the internal states that allegedly cause them, or else some other set of conditions purportedly necessary and sufficient for their occurrence. I submit that these programs are profoundly futile and that we should replace them with a much different sort of explanatory project in which we attempt to understand behavior and cognition against a background of actual and possible behaviors and experiences, of the agent in particular and of human beings in general. To understand what a person said, did, meant, experienced, intended, decided, and so forth, we must know what else the person (and others) *might* have done or experienced instead and how the behavior or experiences of the person (and others) might have been different if the circumstances had changed. Hence, by rejecting vertical explanations for these phenomena, we stop trying to understand them exclusively in terms of their *source.* To borrow some useful phrases from my colleague Bruce Goldberg, we must be able to position a person's behavior, and so on, within an appropriate *action space* or *counterfactual space.*

An example should help clarify this point. Suppose we want to explain why Jones said "That's a nice dress" to his friend. And suppose our explanation is that Jones hoped that a compliment would help ease the bad feelings caused by an argument the two had been having — i.e., because Jones wanted to improve the conversational atmosphere. Now the reason that explanation succeeds is that it helps us to identify Jones's behavior as part of a larger and illuminating pattern of behaviors. We then see it as part of an action space of things Jones might have done instead (e.g., things he would not have said to *this* person but could have said to someone he knew more intimately, or things he might have said in private rather than in public). We also see it as part of a larger action space of things persons generally do to be complimentary or to improve a conversational atmosphere. But no state within Jones, and no other kind of behavior-emitting system, can offer that degree of explanatory systematicity.

Incidentally, this shift in explanatory strategy is a shift to a kind of holistic explanation. That is, rather than trying to explain human behavior and experience in terms of sources for them or systems that emit them, we understand these phenomena against a larger counterfactual background of behavior and experiences. We understand specific episodes in terms of the way we position them against a larger whole. And when we start to take that seriously, we eventually come to appreciate what is wrong with individualistic theories in psychology — for example, the view that thoughts are simply "things in the head". Needless to say, this is nothing like the sort of holism Harman endorses. On the other hand, it has the virtue of being both defensible and intelligible.

At any rate, we can now see that the failure of vertical explanation does not mean that the phenomena in question are totally inexplicable. It means simply that the phenomena cannot be explained in the way heat is explained as molecular motion. Other sorts of explanation — say, explanation by analogy, covering law explanations, and the looser sort of holistic explanation just sketched — might still prove useful. And that situation is no more cause for alarm than it is in other branches of science where unanalyzable phenomena are countenanced as a matter of course. In fact, in most branches of science, it is considered a victory of understanding to determine which phenomena and regularities should be treated as primitive.

Now if the study of human beings were to change in the way I have suggested, it would force a radical shift in priorities within psychology and parapsychology. I suspect we would see a greater emphasis placed on the importance of perceptivity and observational skills rather than on a mastery of experimental procedures, statistical analysis, and specialized technical vocabularies. And I suspect (and certainly hope) this change would lead to the predominance in those areas of the sort of research exemplified by William James's *Varieties of Religions Experience* (1902), Jule Eisenbud's *Psi and Psychoanalysis* (1970), and, of course, much of the work of Louisa E. Rhine. Strange as it may seem, behavioral scientists might once again be required actually to understand something about real human behavior, as opposed to the contrived and straight-jacketed performances elicited in most laboratory studies.

I should emphasize that the shift away from vertical explanations would not mean that no mechanisms mediate our behavior and experiences and that there are no causally relevant underlying processes to study. For example, human vocal and auditory mechanisms play a role in verbal communication; and neural, biochemical, and muscular processes undergird volition, even though volitionary acts and instances of successful communication have no analysis in terms of those lower-level mechanisms and processes. The failure of vertical explanation in these cases means simply that critical features of the phenomena are inexplicable in terms of underlying mechanisms. For example, in the case of volition or in cases of verbal (or telepathic) communication, semantic or representational properties of mental states are unanalyzable. There is no specifiable set of states (hardware or software, internal or external) that uniquely determines what a mental state means or represents (i.e., what it is about) (Braude 1979, 1986). Hence, even if certain lower-level processes contribute causally to the occurrence of, say, a certain kind of psi or memory event or an instance of successful communication, no set of such processes will be either identical with that event or causally both necessary and sufficient for its occurrence.

Let me now comment on yet another sort of change that should follow a rejection of the *small-is-beautiful assumption*. This change, however, is as much political as it is conceptual. I think we might see the end of a pitifully widespread kind of idolatry presently existing both inside and outside the academic community. To put it bluntly, many people engaged in the study of the mind could stop genuflecting in the presence of physicists and so-called cognitive scientists. Laypersons and behavioral scientists tend to be too easily impressed and intimidated by the physicist's command of imposing formalisms, as well as the cognitive scientist's similarly formidable reliance on the technical language of the computer scientist and electrical engineer. This phenomenon is virtually identical to one witnessed all too often in my own field of philosophy, where perfectly competent professionals have been unjustifiably cowed by colleagues who rely heavily on the language of formal logic. Apparently, many regard these specialized forms of expertise as surefire marks of high-powered profundity. But what they often illustrate instead is how technical facility can be a smokescreen for work that in other respects is shallow and conceptually unsophisticated. In my view, the physicist's knowledge and skills are generally irrelevant to the study of consciousness, and the cognitive scientist's reliance on technical jargon is often little more than a trendy and fancy method for obscuring elementary philosophical errors.[3]

One final point is in order concerning the extent to which primitive observable phenomena pose a threat to physics (or any other established science). Apparently, some think that psi phenomena (or the phenomena of memory) would *violate* our scientific laws if they cannot be analyzed in terms of underlying processes or mechanisms. That seems to be why many have glibly asserted that psi phenomena are proscribed by the laws of physics. But that position is egregiously confused. One can argue that certain observable phenomena or regularities are primitive and unanalyzable without rejecting the laws of physics or any other well-entrenched scientific law. Of course, some think this demonstrates merely that physics is incomplete and that an adequate future theory would countenance those phenomena. But (quite apart from specific anti-mechanistic arguments to the contrary) that is clearly little more than a manifesto of blind reductionism. If primitive macroscopic phenomena or regularities exist, the most sensible explanation is simply that they fall outside the domain of physics. Analogously, the fact that adding 7 cc of alcohol to 5 cc of water yields less than 12 cc of liquid does not show that 7 + 5 = 12 is false. It shows merely that there is a problem in applying formal laws of arithmetic to that domain. Similarly, the failure of standard deductive logics to deal successfully with subjunctive conditionals shows merely that the laws of deductive logic apply only to some domains of discourse.

In general, there is no reason why any cognitive or intentional (or, for that matter, organic) phenomenon should pose a threat to physics — or at least to the laws of physics. There is, however, a sense in which the *status* of physics would be threatened, but once again the problem is as much political as conceptual. The only way in which the unanalyzability of cognitive or organic phenomena threatens physics is that it challenges physics' (already spurious) claim to be the fundamental branch of science. The change in thinking that this should bring about is the abandonment of the view that *any* branch of science is fundamental. Physics would be seen as neither more nor less fundamental than psychology or biology, or any other successful systematization of a broad domain of nature. So, although this change might alter some persons' faith in the reducibility of

3. For example, Karl Pribram's attempt to analyze memory in terms of holographic representational states of the brain is as simplistically mistaken as Plato's suggestion that memories are analogous to impressions in wax.

all other sciences to physics, the laws of physics themselves would not need to be discarded on that account.

What is needed, then, is not an all-encompassing holism, either of Harman's sort or of the less sophisticated variety one finds in much New Age quasi-philosophizing. That approach is as wrongheaded as the general claim that all science reduces to physics or the more specific claim that some particular theory (e.g. superstring theory) will account for all the forces of nature. What we need instead is a healthy scientific pluralism, recognizing and valuing the distinctive methodologies and perspectives of different scientific disciplines. We must recognize that nature has many different aspects and that no single approach to describing nature *can be* complete. And once we do, we will see that the various sciences, taken together, form not a hierarchy or a single unified body, but a genuine community of equals.

3

Facilitating the Study of Consciousness
Emerging Themes on the Frontiers of Science

Thomas J. Hurley III

THE development of modern science during the last 400 years has played a significant role in the transformation of the world. Prior to that, the truths of religion permeated human understanding and aspiration. Today, it is the assumptions guiding scientific inquiry, and the results of that inquiry, that powerfully shape our beliefs about nature — including human nature — our commitments as a community, and our interpretations of experience. Significantly, the modern scientific worldview has virtually no place for consciousness or for the values that give our lives their deepest meaning. Critics have thus begun to question the nature of scientific inquiry, its fundamental assumptions, and the role of science in society.

There is a particular reason to be interested in science in relation to consciousness. In *Staying Alive: The Psychology of Human Survival,* psychiatrist Roger Walsh pointed out that a striking feature of most contemporary problems — from ecological degradations and the threat of nuclear annihilation to poverty, homelessness, and hunger — is that they are "human-caused". This suggests that they can be understood as "symptoms of our individual and shared mindset" (1984: 1) and that we are not likely to resolve them without better understanding their roots in our deeply embedded values and beliefs. A disciplined study of the nature and developmental potentials of human consciousness would significantly contribute to such an understanding and is thus essential at this time in history.

Historically, of course, science and consciousness have existed in an uneasy, ambivalent relationship. This dates to the dawn of modern science, when science was developed to wrest the secrets of the material realm from nature but left the realm of the mind to priests and philosophers.

That division of labor was suspended by the development of psychology and psychiatry, but in a century of development, these fields have yet to produce a meaningful science of consciousness. One reason for this failure is "physics envy". To achieve scientific vigor and respectability, we have characterized first behaviorism and then cognitive psychology by reductionistic, mechanistic, and objective paradigms modeled on those of classical physics. Although such approaches can help us understand some aspects of mental functioning, they are not well suited to a comprehensive study of consciousness and human experience. In particular, they are inadequate for illuminating the nature or significance of meaning, values, and purpose — dimensions of experience arguably at the heart of what it means to be human.

Hence, the question that we at the Institute of Noetic Sciences have posed in our program "Causality Issues in Contemporary Science": Does further progress in consciousness research await a reassessment of the metaphysical foundations of modern science? I will argue that it does and that we can already discern some of the key features of emerging scientific paradigms that will be more conducive to the study of consciousness. It is not, however, only the challenge of understanding consciousness that now draws attention to the foundation assumptions of modern science. New theoretical and methodological paradigms being developed in response to other scientific puzzles are also helping to reshape the scientific landscape. Before considering these, however, I shall comment briefly on some of the key philosophical foundations of science and why they are problematic for the study of consciousness.

Metaphysical Foundations of Science

Modern science developed in response to the sterility and intellectual oppressiveness of medieval scholasticism. The architects of its philosophical and methodological foundations held that laws governing the physical universe could be discovered empirically and that human reason, guided by an experimental methodology that controlled for individual bias and suggestibility, could achieve objective knowledge of reality. Initially, the principles at work in the domains of mind and spirit were not considered amenable to the same forms of investigation and understanding (Toulmin 1986). Gradually, however, belief in the existence of an independent realm of mind eroded as leading thinkers reached "the strange conclusion that, if the realm of objects in space and time is the only area that yields objective knowledge, then the only reality is made up of objects in space and time" (Polkinghorne 1986: 18).

By the end of the nineteenth century, scientific thinking was characterized by naturalism, empiricism, and positivism. Logical positivism was essentially an attempt to formalize a method for achieving scientific truths; its proponents argued that scientific observations could be independent of theory, that scientific inquiry could be value free, that tests of knowledge claims must be restricted to publicly observable phenomena, and that scientific research findings were generalizable to all times and cultures (Borg and Borg 1989). These assumptions still underlie most research in the social and behavioral sciences despite the fact that they are philosophically bankrupt and have not produced much useful knowledge (Baumrind 1980; Hales 1986; Stigliano 1986).

Other key philosophical characteristics of modern science include an abiding faith in reductionism and a commitment to objectivity.

Reductionism involves the idea that explanation invariably consists in understanding a structure or process in terms of its constituent parts (the smallest, most fundamental parts would presumably be quantum particles). Naïve reductionism is inconsistent with a rigorous study of consciousness and human experience as both a methodological and a conceptual orientation. Methodologically, the strategy of analyzing a complex natural phenomenon such as consciousness in terms of its component parts (assuming you define consciousness in such a way that you can identify component parts) often trivializes that phenomenon and will always miss its nature and significance as a whole. Methodologically, the belief that a "real" understanding of consciousness or the mind can be achieved only through brain research or that the meaning or significance of particular subjective experiences somehow resides solely in the physiological processes that are correlated with them, simply explains away the conundrum of consciousness while denying, by definition, its potency as a causal reality.

Commitment to objectivity in science involves assumptions that an observable reality exists independent of the observer and that only a detached and impartial observer can discover the truth about this reality. These notions have been undermined by a number of developments. One, often cited, is the statement within physics of the uncertainty principle. Initially formulated to account for limits of the precision of quantum measurements, the uncertainty principle in its most general form states that the observer is always a part of the system he or she is observing and that the act of observation — or measurement — changes that system in unpredictable ways. Objectivism has also been made untenable by research in both the neurosciences and psychology, where the world we experience is shown to be a construction whose features necessarily reflect the influence of biological, psychological, socio-cultural, environmental, and historical factors (Goleman 1985). All knowledge is invariably a social and historical product. Even the simplest sets of observations are conditioned by the observer's background, interests, and frames of reference. Bias is therefore unavoidable in science, and pure objectivity is a chimera.

With the realization that objective, certain knowledge is unattainable in principle there has come a recognition that the "transituational, transhistorical verities" (Sampson 1986: 34) sought within the positivist paradigm take us further away from — not toward — a meaningful understanding of human phenomena, including consciousness. One implication of this insight is that the search for a basic human nature independent of context may be misguided. Rather than taking what is most real about people to be what is abstracted from the particulars of a given situation, we must take most seriously those "surface features" that uniquely define personal identity and action (Stigliano 1986).

Certain methodological predispositions of modern science also impede the study of consciousness and objective experience. For example, experimental methodologies — the benchmark of scientific practice — are based in part on the attitude, first articulated by Francis Bacon, that nature must be vexed or disturbed if knowledge about it is to be obtained. The manipulative rationality that informs this approach is ill-suited to the study or appreciation of more subtle, qualitative, and relational aspects of nature, life, or human experience. Thus, despite the assertion by historian-psychologist E.G. Boring that "the application of the experimental method to the problem of mind is the great outstanding event of the study of the mind" (cited in Hearst 1979: 3), a growing number of scientists and philosophers contend that the experimental method is handicapped as a tool for investigating important questions of human concern and for providing meaningful knowledge about fundamental characteristics of the human realm. A comprehensive science of consciousness will almost certainly require the development of empathic, organic, and relational approaches to inquiry based more on participation and "reverential thinking" (Skolimowski 1984) than on classical modes of objectivity.

I noted earlier that the foundation commitments of science — which include materialism, determinism, positivism, reductionism, and objectivism — are being challenged by research in a number of areas. Let me mention a few of these in order to highlight some of the emerging features of the contemporary scientific landscape.

Enduring Scientific Puzzles

In physics, despite our having had some seventy years to wrestle with it, quantum mechanics still presents deep challenges to established ideas about causality, objectivity, and the nature of exploration itself. I have already noted that discoveries in this field played a decisive role in undermining the assumption that an observational space exists between the observer and the observed. Quantum mechanics also troubles adherents to a deterministic paradigm by virtue of its probabilistic features. For example, its implications led Einstein to argue that the theory must be incomplete because it allowed for a fundamental indeterminism in nature. Even today, the quest continues for a "hidden variables" theory that will remove that indeterminacy from our understanding of physical reality. Were such a theory to be developed, quantum mechanics would be recognized as an astoundingly successful tool for calculation but not as an actual description of reality.

Einstein also expressed unease with another implication of quantum theory, which he termed "spooky action at a distance". Quantum theory states that two particles simultaneously produced by a single source will remain correlated with each other regardless of the distance between them. The results of a measurement made on one particle will depend on the results of an apparently independent measurement made on the other, even though there is no way for the particles to interact with one another. Unfortunately for Einstein, recent experiments to test Bell's theorem have convincingly demonstrated the existence of such nonlocal interactions. The quantum realm is characterized by a fundamental interconnectedness for which there is no parallel in classical physics, although what this means for the macro-world is still unclear.

In biology, the neo-Darwinian paradigm of evolution is being challenged on a number of fronts. For example, there are challenges both to the contention that evolutionary change is gradual and to the notion that every feature of an organism is a naturally selected adaptation for a particular function (Gould 1982). In the attempt to account for evolutionary change, there is a growing recognition of the need for a plurality of explanatory principles — principles pertaining to a plurality of hierarchical levels including genes, organisms, populations of organisms, communities of diverse populations, and ecosystems (Grene 1987). There is an emphasis on the reciprocal relationship between organism and environment, as in the Gaia hypothesis, so that it is the whole system that is understood to be evolving (Ho et al. 1986). There are challenges to the notion that evolutionarily significant mutations must be random. For example, research by John Cairns and his colleagues suggests that in some situations bacteria can direct their own evolution by "choosing" which mutation to produce (Cairns et al. 1988). And, there is increasing conviction that spontaneous self-organization, the tendency of dynamic systems to fall into ordered states even in the absence of external selective pressures, figures centrally in evolution. An important feature of self-organizing systems is their tendency to produce novel, unforeseeable, emergent features. At some points in the development of such systems, predictability breaks down and "the system becomes enormously sensitized to minute fluctuations. It is as if the system had a 'free will' to choose between different paths of evolution, to explore new possibilities" (Davies 1987: 43).

Self-organization also plays an important role in morphogenesis, the development of biological form. Morphogenesis has been one of the thorniest problems in the history of biology, and despite the spectacular success of molecular biology during the last thirty years, there is growing recognition that not all the keys to biological organization and development will be found encoded in the genome. Genes and gene products are clearly necessary for development, but understanding morphogenesis will require that we learn about the dynamic non-material principles of organization that give rise to form and to the transformation of form. These principles are embodied in the spatial and temporal properties of the morphogenetic field and have to do with the network of relationships that constitutes the organism, in which the organism is embedded. Morphogenetic research also highlights the need for a science more sensitive to the distinctive characteristics of *living* systems. Consider the following description by biologist Mae-Wan Ho of an insight she experienced while using a non-invasive technique to study a developing fruit-fly embryo:

> It was as though the embryo was revealing to me its intimate life history in the most exquisite language and music. I was put in touch with the organism as never before. It made me acutely aware of how much violence

> we routinely do to organisms, including ourselves, based on our mechanistic conception of life processes. Most conventional techniques kill the organism and break it down to pieces until no trace remains of the living organism that is supposed to be the object of our investigation. The need for a new conceptual framework impressed itself upon me with renewed urgency. At the same time, I am convinced that the conceptual revolution in science must be accompanied by an appropriate methodology that enables us to study the organism sympathetically, as it is living and developing. — 1989: 7

The mechanistic and reductionistic paradigm of life that has dominated biology has also ruled the medical profession. During the last decade, however, both healing research and greater appreciation of alternative healing traditions have matured to a point where we can see how limiting this paradigm has been, both with respect to the methods considered legitimate to aid healing and with respect to the intrinsic, self-healing capacities of the person as an integrated whole comprising mind, body, and spirit.

One area of research that will powerfully impact both biology and medicine is the study of bioelectromagnetic and other subtle energies in living systems (Becker 1990). This work encompasses traditional research on electrical and magnetic fields of the body, as well as studies of acupuncture, homeopathy, and other complementary healing systems. Another potentially revolutionary research area has to do with spontaneous remission. Under Brendan O'Regan's leadership, the Institute of Noetic Sciences has compiled what we believe to be the world's largest database of medically reported cases of spontaneous remission — over 3,500 reports from more than 850 medical journals. These are full of provocative clues to important dimensions — and possibly triggers — of the healing system. As to psychological factors, for example, there are cases such as that of the woman who suddenly recovered from cervical cancer after "her much-hated husband suddenly died" (Weinstock 1977). As to potential physiological mechanisms, there are numerous cases in which remissions have occurred following an unrelated infection. More startling still are cases of spiritually mediated healing, such as those reported at pilgrimage sites like Lourdes. An international medical commission investigating purported cures at Lourdes has certified approximately sixty-five cures (out of some 6,000 claimed) as miraculous, meaning that the condition was not one known to remit spontaneously, the healing was exceptionally rapid, and no known mechanism exists to account for the recovery. Such cases illuminate the farther reaches of our healing potential and hint at the complex interaction of physical, emotional, mental, social, and spiritual processes in our lives (O'Regan 1987).

Several aspects of consciousness research are problematic from the perspective of positivistic science. One, of course, is our experience of consciousness as a causal reality. Roger Sperry (1987, 1991) has been the most prominent proponent of the need for a restructuring of science to accommodate "downward causation", but a diverse group of other scientists and scholars joins him in arguing that consciousness is not completely reducible to brain function and that higher order processes are emergent phenomena that involve wholly new principles of organization and activity beyond those characteristic of physiological functioning. Assuming such is the case, different modes of inquiry and analysis are clearly required to understand consciousness, including the refinement and extension of phenomenological and noetic methodologies.

A second area of consciousness research that is problematic from a mainstream point of view is the study of exceptional states of awareness and exceptional abilities (Hurley 1988; Murphy 1992). Here I include research on dissociative processes such as hypnosis and multiple personality, study of contemplative states, and research on paranormal or anomalous experiences, among other areas. Such states and experiences have been ubiquitous throughout human history, and have, in fact, contributed significantly to human achievement in many fields of endeavor. They have profoundly transformed individual lives and contributed to the deepest value commitments of most cultures. Yet from a scientific standpoint they are poorly understood and are likely to remain so until our models of consciousness and unconscious processes advance beyond the reductionistic formulations now current.

A related category of experiences, also poorly understood, involves transformational life events. Some life-transforming events, such as near-death experiences, have received a great deal of attention in recent years. Others, such as those involved in the altruistic transformation of some of our great humanitarians, have received much less attention. Study of such transformational experiences and life events may tell us a great deal about the developmental potentials of consciousness and the pathways by which to realize those potentials.

Finally, there is the inquiry into the nature of consciousness itself. Is consciousness an emergent property of the brain, or is it better understood as a deeper, more fundamental dimension of reality that is omnipresent in the universe? These are more than academic questions. The views of consciousness and human nature that inform our research also influence which human capacities will be cultivated, how they will be cultivated, and to what end.

If modern science has not been conducive to the study of consciousness, what kind of scientific paradigms would produce more accurate and empowering pictures?

Emerging Themes

I have briefly surveyed some of the enduring puzzles in physics, biology, and the human sciences because, in addressing them, researchers are gradually developing more holistic frameworks for thinking about nature. By examining the models and concepts emerging at the frontiers of science, we can identify several trends suggesting that a restructuring of some of the deep foundations of science is under way, albeit in an early and still fragmented way. Consciousness will be more at home in this new scientific landscape and may even become the acknowledged ground of scientific inquiry, in the sense that the cultivation of critical self-awareness by scientists is seen as an essential aspect of scientific training and practice.

The first of these trends is an emphasis on complex processes, self-organization, and natural causality. Until recently, scientists did not have the theoretical or methodological tools to study complex systems. This has changed dramatically with the advent of chaos theory, self-organizing systems theory, and allied disciplines. Reductionism has been a prominent causality, because the properties of complex self-organizing systems as wholes cannot be deduced from their component parts and because causality in such systems typically involves upward, downward, and horizontal influences. Moreover, self-organizing systems may give rise to emergent properties that increase the system's capacities for self-determination and hence its evolutionary potentials. Self-organizing systems theory thus provides a rich set of models and concepts for understanding consciousness in the context of physical, biological, and human evolution; and the sciences of complexity provide a powerful set of tools for understanding the structures and processes of our mental life in dynamic terms. In effect, we recognize that human structures of experience, thought, and knowledge are not separate from nature but expressions of nature's evolving capacities.

Concurrent with the growing interest in self-organization is the reconsideration of purpose and self-determination within science. For example, a key dimension of the postmodern challenge in biology is the reconceptualization of evolution in terms of the interaction of purpose and chance, or chance and self-determination (Birch 1988). This carries with it the radical implication that evolution is essentially the evolution of subjects — i.e., of internal relations as well as external relations — and that subjectivity is a characteristic, in some sense, of all nature, not just human beings and higher animals. If we adopt this view, a radically different approach to science is called for and a more empathic, co-operative ethic becomes imperative.

A third trend is the prevalence of holistic models, concepts, and methods that emphasize relationship, connectedness, and context. This is evident in an insistence on systems approaches, in recognition of wholes as more than the sum of their parts, in an emphasis on integration over fragmentation, and, again, in the need for empathic and caring methodologies that do not disrupt or destroy the subject of the study. The work of Barbara McClintock, awarded a Nobel Prize for her research on "jumping genes", illustrates how powerful a relational approach can be. McClintock intuited the complex, nonlinear aspects of gene activity at a time when a linear, hierarchical model of the gene was dominant. She did so because she developed a "feeling for her organism" from her focus on relationship and process rather than on simple mechanisms of control (Keller 1983).

In the human realm, relational approaches figure in a compelling challenge to the myth of the separate self on which psychology and Western culture are based (Noddings 1984; Sampson 1988). They have also given rise to formulations like that of Gregory Bateson, who argued that

> The individual mind is imminent, but not only in the body. It is imminent also in the pathways and messages outside the body, and there is a larger Mind of which the individual mind is only a subsystem . . . that is still imminent in the total interconnected social system and planetary ecology.
>
> — cited in Hayward 1987

Systems approaches naturally encourage the development of much more dynamic models of causality than do those characteristic of reductionistic approaches. There is a growing recognition of the need to appreciate upward, downward, and horizontal influences on any system of interest, leading to a new concept of causality as mutual simultaneous shaping (Lincoln and Guba 1985). In these models there is much more room both for the study of consciousness as a causal influence in its own right — in both its normal and paranormal manifestations — and as a phenomenon or process influenced by other factors.

Another trend is the interest in qualitative aspects of reality. In calling for a "science of qualities", biologist Brian Goodwin (1987) urges "a return to the vision of the Renaissance magi, in which subject and object, known and unknown, can relate in an appropriate unity, made possible by the fact that reality is a single, coordinated domain". A science of qualities may necessarily be, to a large extent, a science of subjective experience. Clearly, it directs attention to the potential development of more subtle capacities of consciousness through which qualitative and subtle aspects of reality can be encountered.

A fifth feature of the new scientific landscape has to do with the rediscovery of time. The experience of time is a fundamental feature of human experience, yet modern physics tells us that the passage of time is illusory. Today, given the work of Ilya Prigogine (1980) and others, change and evolution, not permanence, must now be seen as both fundamental features of our world and as limits on our ability to know that world. Rather than view this as a setback, however, we may, by bringing time back into science, help bridge the gap between science, the humanities, and religion; illuminate our understanding of human freedom; and integrate our understanding of the qualitative and quantitative features of reality (Griffin 1986). Moreover, the challenge of understanding time links the study of mind–brain interactions and consciousness with the fundamental concerns of physics.

I have already noted that consciousness becomes a foundation element in science through recognition of the role of the observer in all observation. The observer brings his or her biases to the process of observation and enters into a relationship with the subject of his or her study. Participation is unavoidable, not optional; and we can expect to see increasing attention given to the values that shape the way research is conducted, to the philosophical assumptions that structure inquiry and interpretation, and to the uses to which knowledge is put. There is also considerable interest in the expansion of science to accommodate or cohere with other ways of contacting reality. A characteristic feature of modern science, at least in the context of verification if not the context of discovery, has been a reliance on a single species of reason as the standard for knowledge. A key feature of various alternative paradigms now emerging is their recognition that multiple modes of knowing are valid and useful, including cognitive, esthetic, kinesthetic, noetic, and mystical modes. The insight and understanding we gain through deep intuition, reflecting our essential connectedness with and participation in all life and being, are as important as the insights and understanding we gain through our physical senses allied with our intellect. In research on consciousness, these diverse modes of knowing become subjects for study as well as means for investigation and experience.

A final feature of many of the new initiatives in science is an explicit acknowledgment of the sacred. I do not want to imply that the tension between science and religion no longer exists. One has only to look at the creationist debate, on the one hand, or on the other, at simplistic attempts to equate the insight of mysticism and quantum physics to see the dangers in this area. But there is a growing awareness of the larger reality in which we all live, grow, and experience a "beinghood" that we share with others. Sperry (1991), for instance, tells us that in his model "a changed sense of the sacred is centered in the natural world . . . and is held to be consistent with a reconceived cosmology of science". Thomas Berry is well known for his attempts to articulate a contemporary cosmology — a "new story" — grounded in science yet not bereft of its transcendent, awe-filled, and mysterious dimensions. In terms of research, we see this openness to the sacred in attempts to better understand spiritual experience in its own terms and to develop models of human development that present open-ended possibilities for psychological and spiritual growth. Throughout our world the resacralization of nature is recognized as an essential balance to the material fixation of contemporary culture and modern science.

Considering all these features collectively, Willis Harman (1991) has recently begun to speak of the need for a science explicitly founded on an assumption of wholeness and interconnectedness rather than the ontological assumption of separateness, which he sees as the root of modern science. Some of the features of such a "wholeness science" are mentioned in his article in this volume; Harman lists others. Notably, such a science might be more open to the insights from other systems of knowledge that are based on different sets of assumptions about reality. It would rely to a much greater extent on participatory methodologies, would encourage the broadest possible investigation of subjective experience, and would include the recognition that science itself can be a transformational process for those engaged in it.

Of course, holism is not a panacea, either conceptually or existentially. The development of more holistic paradigms does not automatically validate particular beliefs about consciousness or reality. It is no more legitimate to define paranormal experiences (to take one example) into existence than it is to define them out of existence. Moreover, we must recognize that the phrase "every thing is connected to everything else" is at once a potent insight and a trivial observation. It does not make the analysis, critical thinking, or the careful delineation of relationships any less necessary.

Nevertheless, as committed individuals work with care and creativity to build new sciences founded on connection with, rather than separation from, nature, sciences grounded in the primacy of consciousness, we may expect more meaningful descriptions of the full breadth and depth of human reality to emerge — descriptions at once richer, more compassionate, and more empowering than those we presently endure.

4

What Is Consciousness and Why Is It So Problematic?

David R. Griffin

CONSCIOUSNESS has been extremely problematic, especially in the late modern world. By "problematic" I mean, in the first place, that thinkers have held diametrically opposed opinions about it and that there seems to be, within the hitherto accepted terms of the debates, little hope for consensus. Three of the disputed questions are (1) Does consciousness exist? (2) If so, does it have much, if any, power to produce changes in the world? (3) Is consciousness a blessing or a curse? In this chapter, I suggest that an unusual way of understanding what consciousness is — a way different from the more well-known ways, at least in the modern West — can be illuminating in itself and can also help us understand why consciousness has been so problematic. Furthermore, by showing that each of the opposing opinions on these three questions contains an element of truth, this new way of understanding what consciousness is can overcome the problematic nature of consciousness.

In suggesting that the problematic nature of consciousness can be overcome by a better way of thinking about it, I am using the term *problematic* to mean *intellectually* problematic. The last of the three questions, which suggests that consciousness may be a curse as well as a blessing, points, however, to another meaning: consciousness may be *existentially* problematic. If it is, merely understanding what consciousness is will not overcome its problematic nature (even if it may somewhat alleviate it). Overcoming an existential problem inherent in the very nature of consciousness, at least in its presently prevalent form, would require that something be done to consciousness — that it be somehow transformed. This concern probably lies behind the notion of "cultivating" consciousness, around which the present volume is based.

My discussion directly addresses this issue of the transformation of consciousness only minimally. I primarily deal with what I take to be three prior questions, namely, what consciousness is, how much power it has, and in what ways it is existentially problematic. The third question is the most closely related to the transformation or cultivation of consciousness. I suggest that consciousness in its presently prevalent form is existentially problematic because particular dimensions of experience are typically submerged, or "uncultivated". To cultivate those dimensions would accordingly make conscious experience more unambiguously a blessing.

The basis for my discussion of all three questions is the idea, derived from the philosopher Alfred North Whitehead (1861–1947), that *consciousness is the subjective form of an intellectual feeling, which arises, if at all, only in the late phase of a moment of experience.* This definition, which at first sight will surely seem not only strange but unintelligible, provides a basis, I suggest, for a view of consciousness that overcomes some of the theoretical impasses modern thought about consciousness has reached and shows some of the reasons why consciousness is existentially so problematic.

Does Consciousness Exist?

The first theoretical impasse regarding consciousness involves the question of whether it even exists. At first glance, this may seem a silly question, because the existence of consciousness is self-evident. Are we not more certain of our conscious experience than of anything else? Was Descartes not right in saying that our present consciousness is one thing we cannot doubt without self-contradiction, because its reality would be implied by the very act of doubting it?

Modern philosophers have, nevertheless, doubted its existence. They have at least denied what Descartes affirmed. In affirming the existence of consciousness, Descartes was affirming it as the essence of the human mind, which he regarded as a conscious substance, a substance whose very essence involved, and in fact consisted of, consciousness. Furthermore, in affirming the existence of consciousness in this sense, he was contrasting it with physical substances, said to be totally devoid not only of conscious experience but also of all experience whatsoever. What the modern thinker who affirms consciousness typically affirms, then, is the existence of minds that (1) embody experience and perhaps consciousness as their very essence, (2) are understood to be actual things, and (3) are different in kind from physical things.

The main reason why other modern thinkers deny the existence of consciousness in this sense is the problem of dualistic interaction. That is, if we have minds that are different in kind from the things of which our physical bodies are made, how could mind and body interact? On the one hand, how could the body produce, or otherwise affect, our minds? On the other hand, how could our minds affect our bodies? Descartes and other early modern thinkers could answer this question by appealing to the omnipotence of God: being deterred by nothing but logical impossibilities, if even them, God could make conscious and physical things interact (Reid Descartes) or at least appear to interact (Geulincx Malebranche). But later dualists, not being able to make this appeal to supernatural agency, have not been able to explain how mind and body, understood as ontologically heterogeneous actualities, could interact. This problem has led the majority of philosophers to reject dualism in favor of some version of materialism, according to which the only actual things in the world are physical things.

Materialistic philosophers must still, to be sure, give some account of consciousness (because, if for no other reason, they are presupposing that they and their readers are conscious). They do so, however, by denying that consciousness is something actual, on a par ontologically with the matter–energy that is embodied by physical things. Consciousness is said by some materialists to be an "epiphenomenon" of matter, which means a non-efficacious by-product. For most materialists, however, even this idea gives consciousness too much reality. More customarily, consciousness is said to be a "function" of the brain, perhaps in some sense even "identical" with it. What all these views have in common is the denial that "consciousness" refers either to some full-fledged actuality or to the "stuff" of some full-fledged actuality (namely, the mind).

The classic problem of mind–body interaction is not the only reason for choosing materialism over a dualism that would give consciousness full-fledged existence. A second reason is provided by the evolutionary form of this problem, which is: How could a conscious entity *emerge* from the evolutionary changes in purely physical atoms? As J.C.C. Smart has phrased it:

> How could a non-physical property or entity suddenly arise in the course of animal evolution? . . . What sort of chemical process could lead to the springing into existence of something non-physical? No enzyme can catalyze the production of a spook! —1979: 168-69

Smart's conclusion is that what we call consciousness must in reality be something physical.

A third reason for denying the full-fledged reality of consciousness is that it would constitute the great exception. The premise of this argument is that, with the possible exception of the psychological states of sentient beings, everything is in principle fully explicable physicalistically. Given this assumption, it is, as Michael Levin says, "simply more reasonable to think that the properties expressed by psychological predicates will turn out to be physical" (1979: 87).

We seem to be at an impasse. On the one hand, the reasons for denying the existence of consciousness in the Cartesian sense are formidable; belief in consciousness in that dualistic sense is deeply problematic. On the other hand, the materialistic way of making this denial is equally problematic. While claiming to be empirical, for example, the materialist denies the full-fledged actuality of the reality that we know most immediately, our own conscious experience. Denying the full-fledged actuality of conscious experience, furthermore — to anticipate the next section — means denying that it has any causal power and that we have genuine freedom, which also flies directly in the face of our immediate experience. Finally, materialism does not really avoid the problems it charges dualism with. For example, materialism still has conscious experience somehow "emerging" out of totally insentient matter. The fact that materialists say that consciousness is "really" something physical hardly lessens the mystery of how such emergence could occur: How an enzyme could catalyze the production of an actual spook is no more mysterious, if an enzyme and all the other bodily parts are purely physical, than how it could catalyze an *apparent* spook.

What led us to this impasse was the twofold idea that, on the one hand, consciousness is the "stuff" of which our minds are constituted and that, on the other hand, the so-called physical world is made of things that are devoid of experience altogether. The way out suggested by Whitehead is to think of all things — or, more precisely, all individuals — as experiencing. The most individual things are experiential events, which Whitehead calls "occasions of experience". Each occasion is a creative synthesis of feelings (or prehensions) of prior events. The process of creative synthesis involves several phases, in which the received feelings are integrated into a more-or-less sophisticated prehensive unity. Consciousness arises, if at all, only in a late, derivative phase of the most sophisticated occasions of experience. Accordingly, says Whitehead, "consciousness is the crown of experience, only occasionally attained, not its necessary base" (1978: 267). The "stuff" of the mind is hence creative experience, not consciousness. Another way of stating this point is that "consciousness presupposes experience, and not experience consciousness" (Whitehead 1978: 53). Consciousness, if it occurs, lights up experience that preceded it, a level of experience that can exist without consciousness.

This point is crucial in overcoming mind–body dualism. Of course, this point has in many respects already been widely accepted. Through the influence of depth psychology, it has become commonplace to say that most of our mind's activity is unconscious, that consciousness is merely the "tip of the iceberg". The thought still seems widespread, nevertheless, that the human mind is *essentially* conscious, that unconscious experience is somehow weird, aberrant. The thought remains that unconscious experience is, as Freud suggested, the result of repression, that fully healthy experience would be fully conscious. Conscious experience is taken to be the norm, not the exception. And this view, that unconscious experience presupposes conscious experience, leads to dualism. Most people would not, to be sure, agree with Descartes in limiting the capacity for consciousness, and thus experience, to human beings. Surely dogs and cats and other higher animals have experience! Most people do, however, draw a line somewhere (often at the level of animals with central nervous systems), whether explicitly or only implicitly, below which they assume that there is no experience whatsoever, but "mere matter". It may be an active, energetic matter; but the energetic activity involves no inner reality, no experience. And drawing such a line is fully reasonable if to have experience requires the capacity to be conscious: There is no reason to suggest that DNA molecules, let alone silicone molecules, are conscious. Drawing such a line, however, leaves us with the problem of dualistic interaction: How can experiencing and non-experiencing things causally influence each other? If we, however, fully accept the idea that experience is an activity that is not essentially conscious, that *conscious* experience is a great exception, then it will be easier to think of the actual world as a whole, and hence of our bodies, as constituted by experiences of various types and levels.

Given this "pan-experientialist" view, problems do not arise through which we will be tempted to deny that consciousness exists, in the sense of seeing it as reducible to physical processes. In the first place, the relation of mind and body is not a unique relation, creating a unique problem of causal interaction. The mutual interaction of mind and body is simply a special form of the universal causal relation, which involves the sharing of feelings. (This statement explicates the earlier assertion that *no* things or processes in the world can be adequately described in physicalistic terms.) The mind–body relation is different, to be sure, from causal relations between equals, such as two brain cells, because the relation between the brain cells and the mind is a relation between middle-level experiences and a very high-level experience. This relation between unequals has many other parallels, however, such as the relation between the brain cell as a whole and its macromolecules. In the second place, the emergence of the mind as a full-fledged actuality in the evolutionary process is not seemingly impossible, as if it had emerged out of purely insentient stuff. In the third place, although consciousness is still a great exception, it is an exception not to a world that is otherwise fully explicable physicalistically but only to a world that is otherwise explicable in terms of non-conscious experience. Consciousness is only an exceptional form of experience, not exceptional *because* it is a form of experience.

None of the reasons that arose from the dualistic worldview for denying that consciousness exists, accordingly, remain within this pan-experientialist worldview. In those rare cases when consciousness does occur, as in one's own experience, its existence can, without contradicting one's worldview in general, be fully acknowledged. One can, furthermore, accept at face value its appearance as something that not only exists but also exerts power in the world — a subject to which I now turn.

Does Consciousness Have Much, If Any, Power?

Probably no subject in contemporary culture evokes stronger disagreement than that of the power of human consciousness. Everyone *in practice* presupposes that it does have power, at least power to move its body through the body's motor-muscular system, and some scientists and philosophers attribute at least this much power to the psyche in their theories. Some scientists and philosophers, citing psychosomatic evidence, attribute even more extensive powers to consciousness. Evidence for psychokinesis leads a few thinkers to attribute even greater power to human consciousness. Some thinkers, indeed, regard human consciousness as the most potent force on the planet. The dominant position in intellectual circles, however, has been the view that human consciousness is completely impotent. It is generally regarded as being simply a product, a function, of the processes of the brain. Even if it be allowed some modicum of power to determine itself, it is not allowed any power to affect its body (and hence, through the body, the world beyond). The central tenet of the materialistic worldview, in other words, is that conscious experience has no capacity to exert "downward causation".

The centrality of this tenet is illustrated by Keith Campbell in *Body and Mind* (1984). Earlier in his career, he says, he had rejected dualism in favor of materialism because of the problems of dualism — namely, how spirit and matter could interact, and how spirit could emerge out of a wholly materialistic universe. Later, however, he came to reject materialism as well, because he could not regard phenomenal properties, such as pain, as properties of a material object (ibid.: 38, 48, 105-09). This problem led him to "a new epiphenomenalism". This view not only means a return to the causal relation between matter and spirit, which has been a reason to reject dualism. It also involves arbitrariness, because it "rejects only one half of the interaction of matter and spirit" (ibid.: 132). That is, epiphenomenalism affirms "the action of the material on the spiritual" while denying "the action of spirit on matter" (ibid.: 131). It allows no downward causation from mind to body, only upward causation from body to mind. The motive for this arbitrariness is that it allows one to "preserve the completeness of the physical accounts of human action" (ibid.: 125). That is, if we were to allow downward causation from the spiritual mind to affect the physical body, we could no longer hope to give a physicalistic, deterministic description of human behavior and therefore of the world in general.

The extent to which the scientific and philosophical communities have been reluctant to allow any downward causation from mind to brain is also illustrated by Roger Sperry's awareness of novelty in asserting such causation. Having once denied, with scientific orthodoxy, any downward causation from the mind, Sperry now says that mind and consciousness control physiological, physical, and chemical processes more than the latter direct them (1983: 31, 79). His new position has been regarded as revolutionary, even though Sperry's break with the dominant viewpoint has been extremely modest: his "neomaterialism" (ibid.: 102) denies that the mind is a "first cause" or "prime mover". This denial implies that what comes down from the mind has been previously pushed up from the brain. He therefore still regards the mental as causally reducible to the physical and still affirms causal, predictive determinism (ibid.: 40, 89-91, 96).

Part of the stir created by Sperry's position may be caused, to be sure, by the fact that he sometimes speaks of "self-determination", "freedom", "free will", "will power", and "responsibility" (ibid.: 39-40, 112, 120-21) and sometimes describes his position as non-deterministic and non-reductive (ibid.: 4, 27, 65, 79, 81), thereby obscuring the extent to which his position *is* deterministic and reductionistic. Nevertheless, Sperry himself, who does realize how deterministic and reductionistic his position still is, regards his affirmation of downward causation as the beginning of a new era in science. (He refers to the old science as "pre-1965 science" [ibid.: 114], pointing thereby to the fact that his affirmation of downward causation was first made in 1965 [ibid.: 4, 79-81].)

Sperry's position, although important in terms of its significance for the scientific community, provides no help for the philosophical issue. In the first place, his position is dualistic, affirming "the interaction of such different things as mental states and physical events" (ibid.: 80). His position on this issue is confusing, too, because he sometimes says that he rejects dualism (ibid.: 38, 41, 60, 68-69). This rejection, however, hinges on defining dualism in these contexts as the belief that consciousness could exist apart from the brain (ibid.: 78, 82, 92, 113). He clearly is, nonetheless, a dualist in the Cartesian, ontological sense. He specifically rejects panexperientialism (for which he uses the older term *pan-psychism* [ibid.: 70, 113]) and says that "subjective qualities are . . . of very different quality from the neural, molecular, and other material components of which they are built" (ibid.: 100; see also ibid.: 83, 85, 93). Sperry claims that "no logical flaw . . . has yet come to light" in dualism in this sense (ibid.: 89), but this statement ignores a long discussion in scientific as well as philosophical circles. In any case, Sperry has provided no help in understanding how mind and body *could* interact.

In the second place, even aside from this problem of dualistic interaction, Sperry's position does not affirm "downward causation" in the sense needed to affirm genuine human freedom. We are free only if our minds exercise self-determination in the moment — i.e., if they in each moment make decisions that are not fully dictated by prior events (meaning the whole past universe, including the prior states of both the brain and the mind). Unless there is this self-determination in the moment — so that the mind is, *contra* Sperry, a "first cause" or "prime mover" — the affirmation of downward causation from mind to body just adds mind as one more link in the deterministic chain. In this case, even if one speaks of a "new science", this new science is scarcely more adequate than the old to our presupposition that we are partly free and therefore partly responsible. In fact, unless there be an element of self-determination in the moment by the mind, it is a misnomer to speak of the mind as a "cause" and hence of "downward causation".

Mortimer Taube (1936) has cogently defined an efficient cause thus: "An event A causes event B, when B results partly from some activity or influence originating from A" (p. 17). In other words, if an event in the life of my mind helps bring about an event in my body, I cannot accurately refer to my mind as a cause upon my body unless the bodily event resulted partly from some activity that originated in the mind-event itself. If instead, as Sperry says, the mind-event was totally determined by the prior state of the body, combined perhaps with the prior state of the mind (which had in turn been determined by still earlier states of the body, and so on), then the mind-event cannot be called a cause. In terms of our question, then, Sperry has not really, despite appearances to the contrary, attributed any power to consciousness. Sperry's position, seen in this light, is not as different from standard materialism and epiphenomenalism as he suggests.

The positions of Campbell and Sperry illustrate the major assumption of modern thought that prevents the ascription of power to consciousness. This is the assumption that what is usually called "nature", or "the physical world", is constituted by things, processes, or events that are devoid of spontaneity, in the sense of the capacity for self-determination. This assumption leads, in the first place, to the expectation that nature or the physical world should (aside from some possible lack of complete determinism at the quantum level) be subject to a scientific knowledge involving, in principle at least, complete predictability. Given that assumption, scientists and science-based philosophers will be loathe to attribute to human consciousness the power to upset this ideal. The assumption of determinism in nature leads, in the second place, to incredulity at the idea that conscious experience could involve any self-determining power that it could inflict upon the physical world. In a worldview in which the elementary units have no spontaneity, the idea of an emergent mind with self-determining spontaneity just does not fit. People *are* somewhat forced, as the case of Campbell shows, to conclude that insentient things must have given rise to sentient minds because their own sentience is so abundantly self-evident. They are not equally forced, however, to believe that these sentient minds are partly self-determining and that they influence their bodies on the basis of this self-determining activity. Although they do presuppose these things in practice, they can convince themselves in theory that these ideas are illusions, that in reality the mind's seeming self-determination and efficient causation are simply non-efficacious concomitants of purely physical, deterministic processes.

The acceptance of a panexperientialism in which experience and spontaneity are accepted as fully natural, hence as characteristic of all individuals at all levels, would thereby seem to be a necessary condition for the widespread and wholehearted acceptance of the idea that consciousness has power, the twofold power to exercise self-determination and to exercise causal influence upon one's body and other things.

As important as such a change would be, nevertheless it would by itself go only part way toward providing a basis for consensus on the power of consciousness. Thinkers who had previously rejected the idea of downward causation might, on the basis of panexperientialism, now agree that the mind does influence the body. They might, however, hold this power to be relatively insignificant compared with the power of the body to influence the mind. This view would put them at the opposite end of the spectrum from those who, perhaps on the basis of psychosomatic and parapsychological evidence, think of the mind as extremely potent. The various positions on this issue can be illustrated in terms of a spectrum of interactionist positions.

Amount of Power of Mind Compared with That of Body

Epiphenomenalism				Interactionism				Hypophenomenalism		
0%	10%	20%	30%	40%	50%	60%	70%	80%	90%	100%

Epiphenomenalism and hypophenomenalism are the two absolutist positions. Epiphenomenalism holds that the mind exerts no power on the body, so that 100 per cent of the power in the relation belongs to the body. Hypophenomenalism (e.g. Christian science) holds that 100 per cent of the power in the relation belongs to the mind. Between these two extremes, there can be a wide range of interactionist positions, according to which mind and body both influence each other. Some interactionists might, I am suggesting, be close to the epiphenomenalist end of the scale whereas others might be close to the hypophenomenalist.

Both groups can cite empirical facts to support their views. Those near the epiphenomenal end of the spectrum can point to the inability of most people through "will power" to change habits and overcome addictions and to the fact that the mind's ability to affect its body is, at least for the most part, limited to the motor-muscular system. Those at the opposite end can point to psychosomatic phenomena — both ordinary phenomena, such as ulcers and the placebo effect, and extraordinary phenomena, such as stigmata and sudden cancer cures — as well as to large-scale psychokinetic effects. The near-epiphenomenalists can reply by doubting these large-scale psychosomatic and psychokinetic effects or by setting them aside as "anomalies". They can add that, even if these macroeffects were accepted, they would hardly point to the power of conscious (as distinct from unconscious) experience. After all, the effects are sporadic: only one person in a million can produce them, and even these people cannot produce them at will throughout their lives. Some of the effects, such as stigmata and most "poltergeist" effects, furthermore, are not consciously willed at all.

The Whiteheadian version of the mind and consciousness may be helpful in bringing about greater consensus on this issue. The mind, on this view, is a serially ordered society of occasions of experience (with perhaps between ten and twenty occasions occurring per second). Each occasion of experience has three or four phases, with consciousness arising, if at all, only in the fourth phase. During this process of development, the occasion is a subject. When an occasion of experience reaches its conclusion, its subjectivity perishes, and it becomes an object, or superject, which means that it then exerts causal influence on subsequent occasions of experience — for example, the next occasion of the mind and the next occasions of the cells constituting the brain. The question at hand is this: How much power does consciousness, which arises in a late phase of an experience, have to exert upon brain cells and — for those who believe in psychokinesis — other, non-contiguous occasions of experience?

My suggestion is that consciousness has very little power directly to exert upon the body and other things. This would be the truth in the position near the epiphenomenalist end of the interactionist spectrum. Consciousness in itself *is* virtually epiphenomenal, being a nearly non-efficacious by-product of non-conscious experience.

Note that in distinction from virtual epiphenomenalism in the customary sense, according to which consciousness is a virtually non-efficacious by-product of the *brain*, my suggestion is that consciousness is a virtually non-efficacious by-product of the *mind* — i.e., of the mind's unconscious experience. Far from thinking of the human mind as epiphenomenal, or virtually so, in relation to the brain, furthermore, I endorse the view that the human mind as a whole — with its unconscious depths as well as its conscious surface — is the most powerful actuality on the face of the planet. In terms of the interactionist spectrum diagrammed above, however, I would not endorse a position close to hypophenomenalism even for the mind as a whole, because the body does exert powerful influence upon the mind. I would, rather, suggest a position somewhere near the middle of the spectrum, according to which the mind exerts about as much power on the brain as the brain does upon the mind. (Because there are billions of brain cells, this view would mean that the psyche is billions of times more powerful than a single brain cell.) Actually, the truth is probably that people differ with regard to their psychic power. It may be that some people have relatively weak psyches, so that a position somewhere near the 40 per cent level might be true for them (meaning that they would have relatively little power to influence their bodies, for good or ill, psychosomatically), whereas others have relatively strong psyches, so that something like 60 per cent of the power in the ongoing mind–body relation would be on the psyche's side. This difference could account for some of the difference in opinion about the power of consciousness: each side could be stating the truth about a certain portion of the population.

In any case, after the unconscious portion of the mind has been distinguished from the conscious, the question is how to think of their respective roles in downward causation so as to explain the great differences in opinion about the power of consciousness (to explain, i.e., the differences that would remain once the purely philosophical objections to downward causation had been set aside), differences reflecting diverse data. My suggestion is that most of the power of an occasion of experience, meaning here the power to exert causation upon other things, lies in the first phase of an occasion of experience (what Whitehead calls its "physical pole"), which lies in the mainly unconscious depths of experience. The conscious decision or "willing" of an occasion of experience can significantly affect its brain (or directly affect some other portion of the body, or the world beyond), then, not directly, but only indirectly, *via* a subsequent occasion of experience in the life of the mind. That is, the consciousness of Occasion A can directly exert very little power on the brain cells (or anything else); it can directly exert significant power on the brain cells (or anything else) only by persuading Occasion B, especially in its unconscious depths, to effect its desires.

On this theory, the crucial issue with regard to downward causation from mind to body, or to things outside the body, would be the degree of "attunement" between the conscious and unconscious portions of the mind. That is, the conscious portion of the mind would be able to effect its wishes, indirectly, to the extent that the conscious desires of one of its occasions of experience can activate the unconscious portion of its subsequent occasions of experience. Those with minimal attunement — those people who in the modern West are considered "normal"— would be able, for the most part, consciously to affect their bodies only through their motor-muscular systems. Those with somewhat greater attunement would through conscious effort be able to do such things as increase their heart rate and raise the temperature of their feet. Those with still more attunement would be able to heal bodily ills. Those with even greater attunement would be able to move ping-pong balls and influence plant growth. And so on. Accordingly, although consciousness in itself — i.e., in terms of its *direct* effects upon the physical world — would be relatively impotent, as near-epiphenomenalists say, consciousness would *indirectly* be capable of exerting a considerable range of power, depending upon the power of the mind and the degree of attunement between consciousness and the unconscious portion of the mind, where most of the power is.

This theory would seem to be consistent with a wide range of evidence. Allusion has already been made to some of it — that the ability of people consciously to bring about psychosomatic and psychokinetic effects varies greatly and that the most powerful psychosomatic and psychokinetic effects seem to be produced unconsciously (as in stigmata and poltergeist phenomena). This theory would also be consistent with certain hypnotic phenomena, as when persons are given post-hypnotic suggestions that they will not be able upon awakening to raise their arms: Although in the post-hypnotic state they consciously try to raise their arms, they cannot because (by hypothesis) their consciousness works on the body only through the unconscious, and this portion of the mind, which hoards the power, is convinced that the arms cannot be raised. A similar explanation would fit for cases of trauma-induced (hysterical) invalidism: The fact that the person may consciously want to walk (or talk, or see, or hear) is practically irrelevant if the unconscious portion of the mind does not want to, so that the conscious portion of the mind cannot activate the unconscious portion to carry out its wishes.

In such ways, I suggest, this view of consciousness — as an optional, derivative feature of experience, appearing if at all only in a late phase of a moment of experience and acting upon its body primarily through the unconscious portion of subsequent occasions of experience — can reconcile the evidence typically drawn upon by those at opposite ends of the interactionist spectrum. We can see, from this perspective, why human consciousness by itself is fairly epiphenomenal, even though the human mind or psyche as a whole is the most powerful of all earthly creatures.

Is Consciousness a Blessing or a Curse?

Whereas the first two questions dealt with ways in which consciousness has been theoretically problematic, the present question deals with the fact that human consciousness can be considered existentially problematic — as a curse as well as a blessing.

That the human form of consciousness is a blessing may seem obvious. The fear of death is largely the fear that death will mean the permanent loss of consciousness. Most people probably think that a subhuman form of existence, however pleasant, would not be worth living: Sages have said that it is better to be a human being in misery than a hog happily rolling in the mud. Human consciousness is the precondition for all the achievements that have been widely regarded as the glory of the human race: the facility with logic and mathematics; the creation of artistic masterpieces; the development of post-tribalistic, universalistic religious outlooks and moral codes; the progressive understanding of the universe and the concomitant ability to control diseases and other natural threats to human life. Some thinkers, like Carl Jung, have even said that human knowledge of the world is the very meaning of human existence because it is the way in which the deity itself becomes conscious of its creation (Jung 1963: 338-40).

There are, nevertheless, numerous signs that human consciousness is deeply problematic. While some hold on to life tenaciously, others commit suicide. The regular heavy use of drugs and alcohol is often a way to deaden or obliterate consciousness. Many religious rites are ways to move into a greatly altered state of consciousness. Early Cynics suggested that human consciousness, with its self-consciousness and moral inhibitions, is a disease and that the only way to live authentically is to recover the instinctual spontaneity of animal life. Recent romantics, like Blake, Wordsworth, Melville, Conrad, and Jeffers, while generally not going that far, have struggled with the question of whether rational consciousness is worth the price it exacts or have at least protested against the claim of rational consciousness (Blake's "Urizen") that everything must be justified in its light. The emergence of "axial existence" in the millennium prior to the Common Era has been portrayed as a shift in the seat of existence from the unconscious to the conscious portion of the psyche (Cobb 1967), and the rise of this form of existence, with its individualism, is seen by many as the "fall", even if a "fall upward". This individualism has meant not only a loss of the earlier sense of community with other human beings but also a loss of belonging to what we now call "nature", a loss that is widely seen to be at the root of the ecological crisis. The Enlightenment demand to judge all things in terms of "clear and distinct" deliverances of conscious experience has led, furthermore, to what Max Weber called the "disenchantment of the world", meaning a world perceived to be without divinity and objective values (see my discussion in Griffin 1988b: 5, 10). Philosophers carrying through this Enlightenment project have even been led to a solipsism that denies knowledge of an actual world beyond their own consciousness — a solipsism that provides no basis for commitment to justice, peace, or sustainability. These and many other indictments of human consciousness raise the question of whether its advantages make up for its disadvantages: Does a house with hot running water compensate for a universe without meaning?

This way of posing the issue begs, of course, another question: Are the downsides of human consciousness inevitable concomitants of the upsides? Or could the seeming inevitability of a tradeoff be overcome? Is there a way to regard or transform human consciousness so that the positive achievement of human consciousness can be preserved while transcending the negative side effects? Can we overcome the human disease without destroying humanity itself? This goal, of course, lies behind many of the philosophies, theologies, psychologies, and therapies of our time. This goal probably lies, more or less explicitly, behind the topic of the present volume: ways to cultivate consciousness. The idea that it should be cultivated (not deadened) suggests that, on the one hand, human consciousness is a good thing whose positive benefits we want to retain but that, on the other hand, something is problematic about its presently dominant form, so that transforming it could lead to a healthier way of being human. In any case, I mean my reflections in the remainder of this chapter to be a way of supporting this enterprise.

Any proposal for how to overcome the disease of the presently prevalent form of consciousness requires, of course, a diagnosis of the source of the disease. The key notion for my diagnosis is, again, the idea that consciousness is a subjective form that arises in an occasion of experience, if at all, only in a late phase. The reason this idea is so crucial for the issue at hand is that consciousness, arising near the conclusion of a moment of experience, fails to shed its light upon the origins of that moment and thereby its basic ingredients. In Whitehead's words:

> Consciousness only arises in a late derivative phase of complex integrations [and] primarily illuminates the higher phase in which it arises. [Accordingly,] consciousness only dimly illuminates the . . . primitive elements in our experience.

Whitehead even refers to this point as a "law" — "that the late derivative elements are more clearly illuminated by consciousness than the primitive elements" (1978: 162). I will call this *Whitehead's perceptual law.*

This perceptual law takes on a tragic character once one sees what the "primitive elements in our experience" are. They include (1) the existence of other things that are as actual as one's own present existence; (2) the causal efficacy of these things for one's own experience; (3) the value-laden character of these things; (4) the existence of a Holy Reality; and (5) the objective existence of values, such as truth, beauty, and goodness. Before discussing the existential consequences of the dimness of our perception of these primitive elements, I will explain more fully why they are generally perceived so dimly.

Whitehead's perceptual law depends upon a distinction between two pure modes of perception, a distinction that is one of Whitehead's most significant, if not yet widely recognized, contributions to philosophy and psychology. This distinction involves an inversion of the normal assumption about what our primary mode of perception is. Modern epistemology has been "sensationist", assuming that sensory perception is our primary (and in fact our only) mode of perceiving anything beyond our own experience.

Whitehead rejects this sensationist assumption, maintaining instead that sensory perception, with its clear and distinct sensory data, is a secondary form of perception. It is derivative from what he calls "perception in the mode of causal efficacy", or simply "prehension" — which I, for the sake of added clarity, will refer to as "nonsensory prehension". In this truly fundamental mode of perception, we directly grasp (prehend or feel) other actual things (which is why we know that other actual things exist) and directly experience their causal efficacy upon us (which is why we know that causal relations exist). The part of nature that one perceives most clearly in this nonsensory mode is one's own body. What is meant here is not looking at one's body or touching one part with another part, but the psyche's direct prehension or feeling of its body from within. We are most aware of feeling our body in this internal, nonsensory way when we feel pain in, say, the hand or the stomach. We are thereby aware of the causal efficacy of the hand or the stomach upon our experience. Even in sensory perception, however, as when we see a tree, we are slightly aware that we see the tree *by means of our eyes:* we perceive the causal efficacy of the eyes for our experience. This example shows that this nonsensory prehension, or perception in the mode of causal efficacy, is more fundamental than sensory perception, because sensory perception presupposes it. Without my direct, nonsensory prehension of my bodily parts, I would not enjoy sight, sound, touch, smell, or taste.

Sensory perception involves the other pure mode of perception, which Whitehead calls "perception in the mode of presentational immediacy". He uses this name because in this mode various types of sensory data are immediately present to my consciousness, and these data in themselves tell no tales about where they originated — whether from the outside world, from my brain, or from my psyche itself. These sensory data, such as colors and shapes, do not necessarily give us, therefore, any information about the world beyond our own bodies, or even beyond our own minds.

The widespread tendency among modern philosophers not only to equate perception with sensory perception but also to equate sensory perception with perception in the mode of presentational immediacy, as in David Hume and George Santayana, leads to the denial that we have any direct experience of causal influence and even to the solipsistic denial that we know of the existence of an actual world beyond our own experience, which is a denial of the first two items on the above list of the primitive elements in our experience.

In Santayana (1955: 14-15), this solipsism became "solipsism of the present moment", according to which we also have no real knowledge (only "animal faith") that there has been a past and will be a future.

Such a position undermines reverence for forms of existence that have been developed over eons in the past and for commitment to the welfare of human beings and other species of life in the future. Indeed, Santayana's "solipsist of the present moment" is very similar to Christopher Lasch's "narcissistic personality" who, wrapped up in concern for immediate gratification, has no interest in posterity (Lasch 1979).

Most people and even many philosophers, of course, are not solipsists, even if they equate perception with sensory perception. This is because, as Whitehead suggests, sensory perception is really a mixed mode of perception, which combines the two pure modes. Whitehead calls it "perception in the mode of symbolic reference", because data from one mode (usually presentational immediacy) are used tacitly to interpret the data from the other mode (usually causal efficacy). The data from perception in the mode of causal efficacy, dimly present in consciousness, lead us to say that we see a "red chair", not simply a "red shape". Perception in the mode of causal efficacy also teaches us, as the term indicates, what causal influence is. In any case, solipsism and denials of causation as real influence are not serious cultural problems. The serious existential problems involve the dimness in consciousness and consequent denials of the three other primitive elements of experience mentioned above.

Before dealing with these existential consequences of Whitehead's perceptual law, however, I must explain more fully its relation to his distinction between sensory perception and nonsensory prehension. Why should sensory perception generally be lit up by consciousness so much more fully? The reason is that the nonsensory prehension of other things takes place in the first phase of an occasion of experience, whereas sensory perception occurs in a late phase — *as does consciousness.* The mind or psyche, it will be recalled, is (by hypothesis) not an enduring substance (or even stream), numerically one through time, with consciousness as the stuff of which it consists. *Consciousness is not, accordingly, simply waiting there, as it were, to be filled by this content or that.* If it were, then we would expect it to light up early arrivers as clearly as latecomers. The mind or psyche is, instead, a serially ordered society of distinct (but intimately interconnected) occasions of experience; and consciousness is a subjective form that arises, if at all, only in a late phase of these occasions. It is not lying in waiting but must be provoked into existence. What now needs to be explained is why this provocation can occur only in a late phase.

Consciousness, suggests Whitehead, is provoked into existence by, and only by, the right type of datum, and this datum is what he calls an "intellectual feeling" (1978: 241, 277, 344). This is Whitehead's way of agreeing with a point many philosophers have made, that consciousness is associated with *negation.* Experience is present whenever there is any awareness of *what is;* but we should not speak of *conscious* experience, Whitehead proposes, except where there is also an awareness of *what is not:*

> Consciousness is the feeling of negation: in the perception of "the stone as grey", such feeling is in barest germ; in the perception of "the stone as not grey", such feeling is in full development. Thus the negative perception is the triumph of consciousness. — 1978: 161

More precisely, consciousness is the awareness of the *contrast* between what is and what might be but is not, between fact and theory. Consciousness involves awareness both of something definite and of potentialities

> which illustrate *either* what it is and what might not be, *or* what it is not and might be. In other words, there is no consciousness without reference to definiteness, affirmation, and negation. . . . Consciousness is how we feel the affirmation–negation contrast. — ibid.: 161

Without this affirmation–negation contrast, there is no intellectual feeling, and without this feeling, no consciousness. But when this feeling does arise, so does consciousness.

Because an intellectual feeling is a complex feeling involving the integration of feelings arising in earlier stages, it can arise only in a late phase of an occasion. And because consciousness, therefore, can only arise in a late phase, it illuminates most clearly those feelings or prehensions that arise in late, derivative phases and least clearly those that arise in the first phase. This means that our nonsensory prehensions tend to get left in the dark: "consciousness only dimly illuminates the prehensions in the mode of causal efficacy, because the prehensions are primitive elements in our experience". By contrast, "prehensions in the mode of presentational immediacy . . . are late derivatives"; they, accordingly, "are among those prehensions which we enjoy with the most vivid consciousness" (ibid.: 162). Sensory data, in other words, are prominent in our conscious experience not because they are our basic way of perceiving things but precisely because they are *not*.

This technical discussion provides Whitehead's explanation of an intuition that has been shared by most profound thinkers about perception and reality — namely, that consciousness tends to be highly misleading, even illusion-producing, as to the nature of reality, including the true nature of our own experience. Having given this explanation, I return to some of the negative existential implications of the illusions consciousness tends to promote.

Whereas the first two illusions, already mentioned (namely, that we have no direct experience of an external world and of causality), usually afflict only a highly intellectualized minority, the other illusions are more widespread. One of these is the tendency to regard "physical things" as devoid of value for themselves. This view implies that they are not fitting objects of moral concern, that we can treat them purely as means to our own ends, not also as ends in themselves. The reverse side of this implication is that we, with our value-realization, are aliens in the world, not really belonging. The consequence of this twofold attitude is that although distinctively human consciousness makes possible an unprecedented joy in communion, human existence, especially in the post-Enlightenment world, tends to be based on an unprecedented delight in destruction.

Although the issue of why human beings are so destructive is extremely complex, surely involving an intricate interweaving of numerous factors, one of the deepest factors, the preceding analysis suggests, is Whitehead's perceptual law. In nonsensory prehension, or perception in the mode of causal efficacy, we directly perceive the values inherent in other things. This is clearest, by far, with regard to our own bodies. In feeling our bodily pains, we are feeling, with sympathy, the pains being experienced by our bodily cells. Likewise, when our bodily parts are enjoying themselves, as when enjoying good food, drink, sex, or exercise, *we* feel good, because we feel the body's pleasure with sympathy. Whitehead, in fact, sometimes refers to the first phase of an occasion of experience as the "conformal phase", because it repeats as its own the subjective forms of the prior occasions that it prehends: "The primitive element is *sympathy,* that is, feeling the feeling *in* another and feeling conformally *with* another" (ibid.: 162). Because of a nervous system that has evolved precisely to heighten our sensitivity to our bodily feelings, our nonsensory prehensions of some of those feelings often rise to consciousness. But — aside from exceptional, paranormal experiences — this is not the case with our nonsensory prehension of the rest of the world. This we usually perceive consciously only in sensory perception.

In conscious sensory perception, our nonsensory perception in the mode of causal efficacy, which is sympathetic and therefore heavily emotional in character, is overwhelmed by perception in the mode of presentational immediacy, in which this emotional character is largely absent. In the movement from nonsensory to sensory perception, the emotional data prehended in the first phase are transmuted into definite sensory data perceived as qualifying external regions. In this transmutation, a reversal of emphasis occurs (ibid.: 114, 119, 169; see also Whitehead, 1967: 215). In nonsensory prehension, the emotional character of the data is prominent, while the spatial location of their origin is indistinct. In sensory perception, by contrast, the spatial location of the origin of the data is clear and distinct: I see the tree right over there. But the emotional character of the data is virtually lost: I can scarcely realize that what I call "green" was received by me as a particular emotion, quite different in emotional impact from the datum that in conscious sensory perception I call "red".

Because we consciously perceive most of the world — all except our own bodies — only (at least most of the time) in the derivative mode of sensory perception, so that we do not directly *feel* its values, we tend to *think* of the world as not realizing values, as being insentient stuff. Through generalizing we tend even to think of our own bodies in this way too, so that we smile if someone suggests that, in feeling pain, we are feeling sympathetically the pain felt by our bodily cells. We come, accordingly, to see our conscious experience as the one great exception in an otherwise valueless world. The result is that the most powerful, dangerous being ever evolved feels a lack of kinship with all other beings.

A fourth primitive element in our experience is the experience of a Holy Reality. This Holy Reality exists (by hypothesis) as the all-inclusive Whole in which we exist. Being in our immediate environment, it is prehended nonsensorily all the time. Besides the other effects that this primitive experience has on us (some of which are mentioned in the fifth point, below), it gives us a sense that life is ultimately meaningful. Because this primitive experience is usually not lit up by the searchlight of consciousness and is in fact usually left even more in the dark than the other primitive elements, however, we can deny in the conscious portion of our minds that life does have any ultimate meaning.

Our nonsensory experience of the Holy Reality *can* become conscious. Just as our constant (by hypothesis) nonsensory prehensions of other *finite* actualities can occasionally rise to consciousness, leading us to speak of "telepathy" or "clairvoyance", so our constant nonsensory prehensions of the infinite actuality can occasionally rise to consciousness, in which case we speak of a "mystical experience", or an "experience of the Holy". In most people, however, this seems to happen at most only once or twice in a lifetime. Accordingly, the awareness of a Holy Reality, and with it the sense that life is ultimately meaningful, can remain submerged, so that "belief in God" becomes a purely conscious belief based on rational inference or authority, not on direct experience. We can even come to deny that there *is* a Holy Reality, thereby becoming nihilists at the conscious level of our minds, saying that life has no ultimate meaning (even though in practice we reveal that, down deep, we still presuppose that it does). We become in our conscious experience aliens — now not only in relation to nature but in relation to the cosmos as a whole.

A fifth illusion that can result from the tendency of consciousness to illuminate the self-produced elements more than the primitive givens of our experience is the idea that values are not given. By "values" here I mean not, as earlier, the values that have been achieved by prehended experiences but values in the normative sense. One of the main questions of the twentieth century has been whether objective values, such as truth, beauty, and goodness, somehow exist in the nature of things and can be known by us. The transition to seeing the world as not embodying such values has been called "the disenchantment of the world" by Max Weber. The existential implication of this disenchantment — stressed, indeed, by existentialists — is the relativistic belief that values are created, not discovered. The political implication is that "might makes right" (Griffin 1988b: 9-10).

This illusion that we do not perceive values is closely related to sensationism: because values are not the kinds of things that can be detected by means of our physical sense organs, the belief that we can perceive only by means of our senses can persuade us that we do not perceive values. This illusion is also, however, closely related to the previous point about the usually unconscious nature of our prehension of the Holy Reality. It is by prehending the Holy Reality (by hypothesis) that we prehend normative values, because the Holy Reality envisages these values with appetition that they be realized in the world. Because our prehension of the Holy Reality is generally at the fringes of the conscious portion of our experience, so is our prehension of normative values. This fringiness of values does not mean that they are absent or secondary in our experience. The exact contrary is the case: they are secondary or tertiary in consciousness because they are primary in experience. But this primacy does not prevent them from being denied, especially in a culture that not only equates priority in consciousness with priority in experience but also tends to deny the empirical nature of anything not experienced with clarity, distinctness, and regularity, and, indeed, anything not measurable.

I conclude by suggesting what "cultivating consciousness" might mean, given the foregoing analysis of why consciousness is existentially problematic. In suggesting a remedy, Whitehead himself did not speak of a "cultivation of" consciousness but of a "self-correction by" consciousness. What he had in mind can be made clear by quoting the entire passage in question, which also nicely summarizes his point about how consciousness obscures at the same time that it illuminates:

> Philosophy is the self-correction by consciousness of its own initial excess of subjectivity. Each actual occasion contributes to the circumstances of its origin additional formative elements deepening its own peculiar individuality. Consciousness is only the last and greatest of such elements by which the selective character of the individual obscures the external totality from which it originates and which it embodies. An actual individual, of such higher grade, has truck with the totality of things by reason of its sheer actuality; but it has attained its individual depth of being by a selective emphasis limited to its own purposes. The task of philosophy is to recover the totality obscured by the selection. It replaces in rational experience what has been submerged in the higher sensitive experience and has been sunk yet deeper by the initial operations of consciousness itself. The . . . conversion of the intellectual insight into an emotional force corrects the sensitive experience in the direction of morality.
>
> — Whitehead 1978: 15

As this passage shows, in speaking of a "self-correction by consciousness" Whitehead meant philosophical reflection. Indeed, in his analytic table of contents this passage is summarized as "Subjectivity and the Metaphysical Correction" (ibid.: xvii). He, of course, meant his own metaphysical philosophy to be supplying that self-correction. This type of self-correction is indeed extremely valuable, as I hope my discussion in this section illustrates. We can still ask, however, whether it is sufficient. Can the solution to an existential problem be purely intellectual? Should the self-correction not also involve actual practices in mind training, in which the mind seeks to become conscious, on a somewhat regular basis, of those primitive elements in experience, just discussed, of which we are normally, perhaps especially in modern Western culture, only dimly conscious? We would "cultivate" consciousness by widening it to include elements that are usually unconscious or at the border between conscious and unconscious. This suggestion, of course, is in harmony with the recommendations of a long line of thinkers, including Myers, James, Freud, and Jung, who have seen our salvation to lie, at least in part, in raising certain elements of our unconscious experience into consciousness. The present suggestion differs from theirs, however, with regard to the elements of our unconscious, or semi-conscious, experience for which this salvage operation is envisaged. In any case, I suggest that this is one of the ways, perhaps the most important way, in which we need to promote a transformation of consciousness in our time.

5

Some Epistemological Problems Inherent in the Scientific Study of Consciousness

Eugene Taylor

CONSCIOUSNESS, the great enigma! It is all about us, pervades all that we see, motivates all our thoughts, words, and deeds, and yet remains illusive. We cannot ever seem to measure it in its totality. When we grasp it concretely it seems to fade into insignificance because our new measurement appears unmoored to anything else. There is hardly ever any agreement among philosophers and scientists about what it is. Meanwhile, it is the central fact of our immediate existence.

Within a Western scientific frame of reference, we seem to be remarkably naïve about the subtleties of conscious experience. We stay closely anchored to the phenomena of waking consciousness, revealed to awareness primarily through sense perception and analytic reasoning. We ignore true state changes as demonstrated naturally by sleep and artificially through hypnosis. With the exception of psychotherapy, artistic creativity, and some forms of religious discipline, we largely ignore the reality of the unconscious. Indeed, Western medicine has a long history of equating any kind of inwardly-oriented creative genius with insanity.

Non-technological cultures, on the other hand, unfettered by the obsessive drive toward quantification, have at least preserved some semblance of respect for the long heritage that describes consciousness in narrative terms more directly useful to our immediate experience. The projective symbol, the poetic metaphor, and the archetypal myth all continue to live in vital relation to the normal discursive waking state, giving us access to alternative dimensions of awareness. Within this tradition, various languages of inner experience have described consciousness and its transformation with some subtlety and sophistication. But it is extremely difficult to present any of the major ideas from these traditions to a Western audience for several reasons, not the least of which is a possible misunderstanding of context. All too often, inner events expressed in symbolic form are removed from their proper interpretive frame of reference and analyzed according to a foreign, externally oriented and preconceived rational standard.

Some years ago I had occasion to address a distinguished gathering of the American Society for Psychical Research. Dealing mainly with a passage from the Yoga texts, I tried to discuss the idea that supernormal powers are epiphenomena in the process of self-realization. In yoga this means that the goal to be attained is the transformation of consciousness. The capacity of intuition is to be developed as a way to generate insight; and though the content of the insight is important, the real focus of the training is on the illuminating quality of insights as a way to direct attention to consciousness and its purification. The practice of yoga and meditation help to burn out the seeds of past karma and produce thoughts of a spiritual nature that create no further karmic consequences of their own. The isolation (*kaivalya*) of consciousness from matter takes place, and the eventual liberation of personality from karmic attachment is the result.

Now within this process, the texts say that supernormal powers, what we would call clairvoyance, telepathy, telekinesis, and so on, are a natural by-product of the cleansing of consciousness. They are guides or signposts along the way, meant only as indications of progress. Such powers are not the ends in and of themselves and should not be developed for purposes of self-aggrandizement. To egotistically identify with them is karmic-producing behavior that has to be lived out, thus delaying the main process.

My purpose was to apply this thoroughly yogic idea to an analysis of contemporary scientific research in psychic phenomena. Reproducing psychic events in the laboratory under measurable conditions, it seemed to me then as now, does produce small effects in an extremely large number of trials. Yet, although the methodology of such experiments is becoming even more sophisticated, the community of other researchers in the natural sciences remains unconvinced by the data, declines to take parapsychology seriously, and continues to refer to the field as pseudoscience.

If, as Charles Tart has said many times, there are already over 200 experiments indicating the reality of psychic phenomena, then why haven't the other scientists been convinced? My answer to this question was twofold: First, if scientists cannot accept the data, then it is possible that their denial might be based on epistemological grounds, i.e., on a metaphysical philosophy beyond argument. Second, it is possible that the parapsychologists are studying the wrong thing. In my address some years ago, I suggested that instead of trying to reproduce individual psychic events in the laboratory, psychical researchers might focus on the underlying process of personality transformation, which, the Asian texts clearly say, is the more consistent source for the production of the kind of events they seek.

My conclusion was that by taking up the psychology of character development and personality transformation, parapsychologists might well be correcting the misguided direction that academic psychology has taken in its own century of scientific experimentation. By such a radical change, parapsychology could initiate a revolution in the wider domain of psychology, particularly because the production of self-knowledge is so relevant to the phenomenology of the science-making process. If psychology, in turn, could ever make a contribution to understanding this process, it might yet stand at the forefront of some future transformation of the social and medical sciences and, perhaps, of the natural sciences as well.

My audience was made up of hands-on practitioners of the paranormal, clinicians in psychology and medicine, and scientists investigating paranormal events in the laboratory. All, I believe, had at least two things in common: one, a belief that human personality is endowed with paranormal abilities that are developed to one extent or another in each individual; and two, a belief that to counter the overarching influence of scientific materialism in modern culture there must be a reinstatement of the person at the center of our quest to understand reality.

But beyond these points of general agreement, the audience in the room was sharply divided, particularly over the question of whether a science of the paranormal was even possible. Some asserted that scientific knowledge is the only way to legitimize psychic phenomena. Others advocated a clinically-oriented paranormal depth psychology. Still others represented the view that direct experience of psychic phenomena was its own sufficient proof.

Although the scientific view held the floor, the laboratory investigators did what they have always been forced by history to do, namely, to preach to the converted. This means that because scientists from mainstream disciplines ignore their work, experimental parapsychologists are left to address audiences who already are convinced of their conclusions, even without the supporting empirical measurements. The urge is very strong to create a science of consciousness that justifies paranormal investigations, but for the bulk of clinicians and practitioners who already believe in psychic phenomena, this is just window dressing. The main function of such a science, for them, is to gain adherents from the wider world of reductionistic skeptics.

There seems to be in this an unwarranted certainty in affirming the reality of an *outward* science of *inner* events. Can empirical methods of exact measurement be applied to symbolic events? Here we have, in miniature, the unceasing great war between biological, psychodynamic, and existential ways of approaching the problem of consciousness. Consciousness is, for one camp, nothing but a by-product of physiology. For another, consciousness is a mere reflection of the unconscious. For yet a third, we are surrounded by a larger spiritual reality, which expresses itself to the individual only by the powers of cognition, emotion, and intuition. It should be duly noted, however, that in contrast with the classical systems of Asia, in modern Western culture the scientific and therefore biological model always defines the interpretive frame of reference, and hence the outline of the ensuing discussion.

The problem I take up in the present context is the epistemological one I raised earlier; namely, what is the relation of these models — the biological, the psychodynamic, and the existential — to each other. Is there one that is more true? After all, the presuppositions of each seem at least to partially exclude the reality of the others. Or is it fair to attempt to treat them all as equally valid? Are they all the same? Or are we confusing our own immediate phenomenological experience of sameness for our lack of ability to perceive their ultimately unreconcilable differences?

I confess, since I am no advocate for the unity of science, that I have absolutely no idea how these three models are to be ultimately integrated within the objective scientific domain.[1] I cannot present data any more real for the one view of consciousness than the other. I myself remain completely baffled, not by the glut of theories but by something basic, what Melville has called "those greatest of all mysteries, facts". No so-called fact can exist without a context, and contexts for me keep shifting.

---

1. See Taylor (1988a) for a discussion of 150 years of American interpretations of Asian ideas as compared to the way selected traditions in Asia have viewed themselves. This was, however, a historical and not a scientific analysis.

I cannot assert a fact based on my authority as a distinguished scientist, a decorated war hero, a Nobel laureate in the humanities, or a canonized saint. I wish only to give you my own opinion as a "literary psychologist" (as B.F. Skinner once derisively called it) concerning what I take to be the problem of consciousness.

I believe that the scientific study of consciousness and our direct experience of it should be considered as two distinct realms of inquiry. Consciousness as a phenomenon in nature to be studied is not the same as self-knowledge, because the function of acquiring scientific information is external control whereas the function of self-knowledge is the internal transformation of personality. The epistemological foundations of these two realms are radically different.

I do not plan to elucidate the entire history of epistemological theories about reality. To address the question and my answer to it, I plan only to present my own theory, which is actually quite simple.

An Experimental Case Study

My understanding of the problem is based partly on a study I did some years ago designed to look at the process, rather than the content, of consciousness (Taylor 1973). In that experiment, I took 250 subjects through a sensory deprivation experience for varying lengths of time in different numbers. I took measures of heart rate, blood pressure, and time estimation; and I collected detailed introspective reports. The experimental environment was a specially constructed anechoic sound chamber, which had been built by a group of physicists for purposes of studying sound waves under echo-free conditions but which I adapted into a comfortable meditation environment. The chamber was deep in a basement in one of the buildings at Southern Methodist University. It had been constructed on its own independent foundation and had sides several feet thick. The walls, floor, and ceiling were covered with wedge-shaped acoustical baffling. Over the set of baffles on the floor was a set of suspended wire springs, on top of which I threw a large, thick oriental rug. Here the subjects sat, on the average for a half-hour, but sometimes longer, with plenty of ventilation but in complete darkness.

The subjects were all self-selected. My method was to take a small group of volunteers through the experience, which they all felt was wonderful. I then locked the door and made myself somewhat difficult to find. When the word got out that I was looking for subjects, throngs came, and those who were able eventually to find me were the ones who got in. The literature was full of sensory deprivation studies done only under stressful conditions, with the resultant conclusions that isolation was bad for health. Thus, the point of this study was to optimally bias experimenter, subject, and environmental variables to see what effects on consciousness, if any, would emerge.

The physiological measures taken were consistent with those seen in most successful meditation studies. That is, heart rate and blood pressure decreased with a pleasant experience. There was also a trend toward wildly over- or underestimating the time spent in the chamber when the experience was judged more emotionally positive, compared to consistent time underestimation, as with most sensory deprivation studies, when subjects reported persistent boredom.

But more important for our present discussion, I want to focus for just a moment on the conceptual results of the detailed introspective reports. What the subjects described was an orderly progression of attention through a series of transitional states of consciousness ranging from the waking state to a profound state of quiescence, which I have called psychological suspended animation. The transition states we defined in the following way:

1. *Exploratory Awareness of External Stimuli*: Here, consciousness stays with an awareness of purely external events — sights and sounds in the environment, particular smells, perception of movement, etc.
2. *External Bodily Awareness*: Awareness of stimuli in the immediate external environment gives way to awareness of the physical body, particularly the placements of hands and feet in the complete darkness, feeling the placement of the facial muscles, comfort of the sitting position, air against the skin, and so on.
3. *Internal Bodily Awareness*: Attention soon shifts to activities such as the flow of air in and out of the nostrils, swallowing, sounds emanating from the digestive tract, ringing in the ears, feeling of the heartbeat, concentration on the expansion and contraction of the chest cavity.
4. *Internal Cognitive and Emotional Awareness*: Awareness suddenly shifts to the cognitive flow of thoughts and the rise and fall of accompanying emotions.
5. *Visual Translation and Projection*: Consciousness of the flow of thoughts and feelings becomes visible to the mind's eye in the form

of mental images, oftentimes colorful and in three dimensions, as in the experience of a waking dream. Sometimes the subjects experience this as if they were watching an animated cartoon sequence. Other times the projection of mental images out onto the darkness may be experienced as a stream of insights. What usually emerges from the stream of visualizations is the identification with some deep symbol or mythic image reflecting aspects of both personal and collective destiny.

6. *Awareness of Transitive and Substantive Alteration of the Stream of Consciousness*: Here, consciousness splits, and two halves share the field. One is an intuitive mode, where the subject becomes increasingly aware of longer and longer periods of no mental and emotional activity. The other, which is interspersed in between, is a rational, analytic mode, made up of long chains of thought with accompanying images and feelings.
7. *Psychological Suspended Animation*: Here, by ignoring the flow of thoughts and seeking out only the longer and longer periods of quiet, consciousness reaches a resting state where the subject merely witnesses that nothing is happening. Prolonged immersion in this quiet condition was often reported. The subjects told us of extreme relaxation, profound stillness, the complete absence of cognitive thinking, the feeling of great serenity and peacefulness, and a secure sense of well-being.

Finally, there was an eighth stage, the return to waking reality. There were many ways in which the subjects psychically decompressed from their inner subjective experiences and made a successful transition back to the waking, material condition. Two phases occurred, one was the immediate experience of return on coming out of the anechoic chamber. The other was what might traditionally be called long-term follow-up, an analysis of the effect of the isolation experience on subsequent functioning as reported by a selected cohort of subjects, in some cases as long as a year afterwards.

Though there is much more to say about what happened, my purpose here concerns what this demonstration tells us about the function, rather than the content, of consciousness. When we focus our attention on the outer, material world of objects, the structures of the mind and personality (the kinesthetic memories of body image, the habitual ways of seeing wired in by our inheritance, the unconscious attitudes built up by experience, and the analytic categories that appear to be permanent fixtures of our unique worldview), all become relatively stable. As long as attention stays anchored to the external world of objects, these categories of our internal existence are continually projected outward. This is my explanation for all science, all mathematics, in fact, all forms of objective knowledge; namely, the superimposition, and hence marriage, of the mind with material reality.

When consciousness turns inward upon itself, however, all these internal forms start moving around and begin to alter their previous, relatively fixed position in terms of one another. Some are more enduring, but ultimately all are susceptible to change and restructuring. Dissolution is a fact of personality, in psychopathology, in transcendence, and in death.

By turning within, we are confronted with the apparent chaos of subjective experience, and to understand where we are, we construct a phenomenological language of inner experience.

A Psychology of Inner Experience

The idiosyncratic language that a person evolves to comprehend his own inner experiences, oftentimes only to himself, is rich in personal symbols. Although these symbols are the products of personal insight and intuitive development, they are constructed as cognitive conceptualizations, which the person communicates in metaphoric terms. The symbols are highly projective. And even though they are described in a personalized language of inner experience, they are nevertheless resonant with the comparative idiosyncratic cartographies of other inwardly-oriented persons.

The ability of many individuals to resonate projectively with highly energetic symbols has led me to think in terms of an inward visionary tradition. For each individual, the inward doors of perception have either been thrown open or they have not. If you have turned within, you have seen what I am talking about. If you never have turned within, you hear what I am saying as if listening to a foreign language. There are plenty of litmus tests. Ask people what they think about their dreams. If they say they have never considered their dreams, they are probably not a part of the visionary tradition. In modern culture, it is sufficient to simply bring up the subject of Tibet and watch for either a dead-panned or an animated reaction. In scientific circles, merely the mention of the word *consciousness* is enough to make the naysayers squirm.

Such an idiosyncratic language of inner experience might be illustrated by the following propositions:

1. Immediate experience is the only reality we can directly know. This means that representational knowledge, like model-building or theories about reality, is secondary to immediate apprehension. Even in the individual scientist, phrases such as "an elegant theory" or "robust data", mean that the scientist is still using his or her own inner experience as an ultimate referent for how good these things feel.
2. It is possible for consciousness to alter normally unconscious physiological processes.[2] This means that it is possible for the normal powers of cognition to gain control over unconscious bodily functions. The adept must adopt the attitude of passive volition to succeed, however, a condition inimical to the rationalist who must maintain control at all times.
3. When consciousness becomes conscious of itself, it becomes something else. This means that when consciousness turns inward and uses some medium, such as dreaming or mental imagery, to see a reflection of itself, it immediately becomes fluid. This is the basic mechanism of all successful psychotherapy.
4. In the normal but undeveloped individual, consciousness remains an ultimate plurality of states. This means that the experience of unity comes only by transcending the limits of the waking state. No single thread ties the whole together for the person who has not had a unitive experience. But after such an experience, everything seems connected to everything else in some way.
5. The higher unity of different levels of consciousness is achieved through transcendence, but at the risk of being captured by the demonic. This suggests that turning within does not automatically confer sainthood on the person. The journey is fraught with dangers, the worst of which is that personality can become mired in its own psychopathic and lower nature.
6. The locus of psychological healing is always within ourselves. This refers to a unique interpretation of the successful interaction between patient and therapist. It suggests that once the patient has exposed

---

2. See Taylor (1988b) for an account of recent scientific evidence supporting behavioral interventions such as yoga, meditation, biofeedback, hypnosis, and psychoneuroimmunology.

his pain to the therapist, the therapist, already an inveterate seeker after self-knowledge, is confronted with the inner problem of his own wholeness. In this encounter the therapist must find healing at some inner level of personality, depending on the subtlety and progress of that particular healer's own life journey. This sets the conditions for the patient to be healed in the therapist's presence by a kind of spiritual resonance, but only by harnessing the patient's own powers to heal. We do not heal; rather, others are healed through us.

7. Supernormal abilities, such as clairvoyance and telepathy, are an epiphenomenon in the process of self-realization. This means that the purification of consciousness, which is the primary and unwavering goal of all inward development, is always accompanied by the occurrence of paranormal events. They are to be ignored, however, as only signs or guideposts along the way. If the ego identifies with them, the person wanders from the path, perhaps for eons in psychic time.

8. The truth of ultimately transforming experiences can be tested only in terms of their fruits for life. This means that the validity of profound inner experiences is always tested not by where they came from but in terms of their effect on enhancing the moral and aesthetic quality of daily life. We do not need a world catechism, where everyone believes the same set of teachings, but rather we need an increased appreciation of religious diversity that leads to commonality of action and behavior in the way we treat each other.

The Search for External Corroboration

This exercise merely suggests some of the dimensions of a language of inner experience that may generalize from the individual to the collective. Such inward experiences often lead one to those outward sources within one's culture that contribute to further understanding of what has happened internally. Usually, after investigating the complete lack of understanding by scientists for these inner events, the seeker after inward knowledge moves on into the domain of literature, the arts, and religion for corroboration and for further clues. In these sources, we have numerous maps presented to us, from the world's religious literature to the latest issue of the *Journal of Transpersonal Psychology*, all of which suggest that there is a cartography of inner experience.

The language is stated in terms of levels or dimensions of consciousness. There are prescribed techniques. There is a substantial literature on the nature of the ultimate experience and the type of personality that emerges. It is here in this domain that, in my opinion, only in the subjective experience of transcendence will the neurobiologic, the psychodynamic, and the existential models seem to overlap and become one. The difficulty is that the previous collective consensus called objective information has got to become personalized. For it to be true or real for me, I must be the one who owns it. Thus, whatever else scientific control of consciousness may achieve, it does not become relevant to the individual until it is translated into narrative, symbolic, and mythic modes of personal experience. Yet, here we have reached an epistemological dilemma, because the narrative language of the self and the meaning-frames it points to that are pregnant with possibilities, yet beyond words — the energic power of the very symbols that would transform us — become a private, albeit projective, language and are no longer susceptible to numerical quantification and the rules of logical discourse.

The Epistemological Dilemma

The essential problem of consciousness, as I see it, refers to how the normal everyday waking condition can become aware of states other than itself. It is the case of the fish who has never been out of water and so cannot know about the experience of air or the drunk looking for his keys under the lamp-post because the light is there and nowhere else. When the rational mind wants to know about some inner event, it always takes it out of context and tries to make something physical and material out of it. To prove that psychic phenomena are real, one must today have produced them in a laboratory. To the asylum psychiatrists, religious ecstasy in the context of an in-patient hospital ward looks just like any other symptom of psychopathology. To the behavioral psychologist, meditation looks like nothing more than relaxing and doing nothing. So you can see that according to this perspective by confusing inner events for outward realities, by artificially superimposing one upon the other, all of science, it seems to me, leads only to a gigantic elaboration of the ego.

On the other hand, proponents of a science of the spirit maintain that all religions are one, that all the highest states of consciousness refer to the same place, and that science both can and will soon be able to measure *chi*, subtle energies, *prāṇa*, and a host of other metaphors taken raw and purportedly measured directly from the heights and depths of transcendental consciousness.

I feel that both approaches to understanding the problem of consciousness are profoundly naïve and that we must evolve an entirely new set of criteria, new methods, and new ways of thinking that are far more sophisticated than these if we are to attract the best minds and hearts to the endeavors outlined by this conference.

Thus, I believe that the construct of a "science of consciousness", by its very nature, is a contradiction. Logically, the program is either utterly impossible, because consciousness cannot be objectively considered when it is an object of itself, or else the program implies nothing less than the complete overhaul of science into some form radically different from what we now know, followed by an equally radical transformation of our worldview concerning the way human beings conceive of themselves. The idealistic side of my personality absolutely subscribes to this latter goal. Yet the realistic side hints that it may not be attainable in my lifetime.

What, then, are we to do in the meantime? As an alternative plan, suppose that we give up the attempt to squeeze a phenomenological psychology of personality transformation into the outmoded corset of reductionistic science. The attempt always seems to produce the same results anyway. One invites scientists and spiritual seekers to the same conference. The seekers want to hear about everything from transcendent insights to empirical facts, while the scientists try to intimidate everyone with their rhetoric and want to see only the hard data.

Instead, I propose that we work on the development of a psychology of transformation based on the philosophical metaphysics powerful enough to critique the mathematical and logical foundations upon which the sciences are presently conducted. History, philosophy, the humanities, language, literature, the arts, the world's religious literature, as well as our own insights, could be our tools. Economics, which will surely define the battleground, could be the short term *raison d'être*, personality and consciousness the conceptual platform. With the new revolution in the neurosciences currently under way, historical conditions are at present in our favor. The problem is that we are not yet prepared even to begin the dialogue with the bench scientists.[3]

---

3. See Taylor (1991, 1992) for a review of some of the history and prospects for this dialogue. An important blueprint for how such a dialogue might be launched between science and religion comparable to the unprecedented interdisciplinary communication now going on in the neurosciences is given by Schmitt (1992). See also Schmitt's (1990) more detailed autobiographical account.

Only by fashioning some such strategy like the one I have proposed can we hope to meet the scientific mindset of radical materialism on equal terms. Only then, in my opinion, will science begin to evolve to its next level. Only then will science be able to help us develop an environment clean enough for our children, an educational system that fosters transcendence, or a Manhattan Project for health. Only then can a true science of consciousness finally emerge.

6

Cultivating Consciousness
Some Conceptual and Methodological Issues

K. Ramakrishna Rao

WHAT is consciousness? How do we cultivate it? I wish to address these two questions with a view to exploring the nature of consciousness and the strategies for studying it.

At the outset, let me make clear my own biases and presuppositions. I believe consciousness as empirically given is real. Its existence in the human condition cannot be denied without contradiction. It is utterly unimaginable for me that I stand before a group to speak, for example, without assuming that I am conscious. I believe also that consciousness is autonomous and that my freedom to choose and act is a consequence of that autonomy. In other words, being conscious is what distinguishes me from the machine, which I consider to be devoid of consciousness and self-determination.

Even though consciousness is assumed to be autonomous and irreducible to mechanical and deterministic processes, I am convinced that it is open to scientific study and empirical investigation. Because consciousness is experienced in real-life events, it should be possible to study and understand its operation in those experiences in a systematic fashion and to thereby obtain insights into its nature.

The preceding presuppositions render it irrelevant for us to consider esoteric notions that hold consciousness to be beyond the reach of science. Similarly, we will part company with (a) those who deny that there is any such thing as consciousness (Watson 1928), (b) those who regard it as an epiphenomenon of matter that has no causal efficacy of its own (Skinner 1974), and (c) those who see no more in consciousness than the neural events in the brain (Feigl 1967).

Conceptual Questions

What Is Consciousness?

Consciousness in several of its senses seems to refer to awareness of two sorts. First, it denotes a *state* of awareness. For example, we say that we are conscious when we are awake and unconscious when in deep sleep. Consciousness obviously refers to something more than alertness. Sometimes it is taken to mean the total description of all mental experience. It is the unity underlying the discrete sensations that gives us awareness, as well as the subjective feeling of awareness. Such a unity may be regarded as an enduring self or a stream of experience. In all these senses, awareness denotes a state of being. It does not refer to awareness of something. Awareness in this sense is a *subject* or function rather than a *predicate* of something. This type of awareness, which does not refer to the phenomena of the natural world but to itself, may be termed *subject consciousness*, or *S*-consciousness.

Second, we also use awareness to mean awareness *of* this or awareness that such-and-such is the case. We may call this type of awareness *predicate awareness*, or *P*-consciousness. When we think, doubt, remember, or perceive, there is always something to which our thoughts, memories, and so forth refer. We remember or see something. The British philosopher John Locke (1894), for example, regarded consciousness as the perception of what passes on in one's mind. We reflect and are aware. There can be no such thing as non-conscious awareness, according to Locke. But on occasion we may not be aware of what passes on in our minds. Yet we may engage ourselves in purposive and discriminatory behavior indicating our awareness of the event, even if we are unable to recollect awareness relative to the event. Thus, awareness and reflective awareness may not be the same. If we allow for subliminal mentation, then we must assume not only awareness but also awareness of awareness. G.E. Moore (1922) argued that awareness of awareness is not an inference derived from self-consciousness but an element given in the sensation itself. The sensation of blue, for example, has two elements, the sensation of the blue object and the awareness of the blue object. Although it is difficult to discern the element of awareness in the experience of the blue object, Moore believed that if one could look "attentively enough" one could "see" the consciousness of the blue object.

We may also speak of self-awareness as awareness *of* one's self, or *I*-ness. According to some thinkers like René Descartes, self-awareness is implied in all awareness. This possible reflexivity between me and my consciousness makes it difficult to classify self-awareness either as *S*-consciousness or *P*-consciousness. It seems to fit into either of the two categories, depending on how we understand it. Consciousness in this sense indicates its self-manifesting function. Awareness function implies not only the potential to be aware of an object or event but also awareness of itself. In other words, in being conscious *of* something, I am also conscious of my consciousness as well as myself. Thus we are led to postulate not only conscious images and states but also consciousness as such, as a self-manifesting function or being.

Consciousness as awareness phenomena may be depicted on two bipolar dimensions. First is the horizontal dimension *P*- and *S*-consciousness. The second is the vertical liminal–subliminal or explicit–implicit dimension. This categorization leaves us with basically four kinds of awareness, all of which in one sense or another refer to consciousness. On the side of *P*-consciousness, we have reflective and subliminal or implicit awareness, where awareness is always awareness of something. The *S*-consciousness includes consciousness as such, which is presumed to be the source for manifesting consciousness in the variety of forms we have of it. The distinction between consciousness as such and awareness phenomena of consciousness is similar to the distinction Jung makes between the archetype as such and archetypal images. Self-awareness, unlike consciousness as-such, is liminal in that it has phenomenal existence.

Conscious and Unconscious

Although Locke and Brentano might have been justified at the time in their attribution of explicit awareness to all mental phenomena, the work of Freud and those who followed him has revealed how complex thought processes can occur at the level of the unconscious as well. The notions of subliminal mentation and unconscious motivation are no longer questionable assumptions. Freud also spoke of the preconscious, which contains memories and images that can become conscious when needed, unlike the unconscious material that is ordinarily inaccessible to attentional control.

If psychoanalysis, with its discovery of unconscious processes, shows that the unconscious is not merely the absence of consciousness but has a domain of its own, C.G. Jung, in showing the relative quality of consciousness, further blurs the distinction between consciousness and the unconscious. We may recall that the unconscious, according to Jung, is not the dung heap of repressed thoughts and infantile sexual fantasies that Freud described. Rather it is a consummate source of our collectivity and creativity. The collective unconscious "is an image of the world which has taken aeons to form. It consists of the sum of instincts and their correlates, the archetypes. Just as everybody possesses instincts, so he also possesses a stock of archetypal images" (Jung 1919: 138). In his later years, Jung was led beyond archetypal images to the concept of the archetype-as-such and the psychoid level of the unconscious. The archetype-as-such, a transpsychic concept, is an a priori ordering principle by virtue of which we experience synchronistic events that suggest an "acausal orderedness". This advance in Jung's thinking from subjectively experienced archetypal image to archetype as an a priori ordering principle obscured his earlier distinction between consciousness and the unconscious (Frey-Rohn 1974). Consciousness was originally associated with a certain degree of brightness and luminosity. Jung increasingly saw that this luminosity is not limited to what is called consciousness but is also to be found in some of the unconscious contents. Jung thus came "to the paradoxical conclusion that there is no conscious content which is not in some other aspect unconscious" (1954: 185).

We can no longer regard non-conscious mentation as merely speculative. Advances in cognitive psychology suggest that information processing occurs by primarily non-conscious operations. Max Velmans's (1991) review of literature led him to conclude that consciousness in the sense of being introspectively aware does not enter into the processing of information at any level, including the organization of complex activity that requires planning, reflection, or even creativity. There is also increasing evidence that not only mental *processes* but also a good deal of mental *content* is non-conscious. Studies of "blindsight" (Weiskrantz 1986) and implicit memory (Schacter 1987), for example, clearly establish the reality of non-conscious perception and memory. Also, there is impressive experimental evidence for subliminal psychodynamic activation (Silverman and Weinberger 1985). A survey by A.G. Greenwald (1992) of those active in research on unconscious cognition revealed that more than 50 per cent of the respondents endorsed the view that four types of unconscious cognition are empirically established. For example, 93 per cent of the respondents believed that the phenomenon of subliminal semantic activation (indirect evidence for analysis of semantic content of words presented under subliminal conditions) is established.

The discussion of consciousness is rendered at once complicated by the realization that thought processes such as perceiving, believing, willing, and so forth, once considered as the functions and criteria of consciousness, are also found at the unconscious level, that some perceptions and memories can be "implicit" in that we have no awareness of them, and that the line between consciousness and unconsciousness is not as sharp as once believed. The commonsense simplicity of conceiving consciousness as awareness becomes deceptive and sterile. If we can meaningfully refer to conscious as well as non-conscious awareness, the usefulness of awareness as a descriptor of consciousness becomes problematic. How can we speak of consciousness as awareness and at the same time hold that awareness can be either conscious or unconscious? Either we mean by consciousness something different from awareness or the distinction between the conscious and the unconscious is spurious.

Some Philosophical Approaches

The discussion of consciousness gets complicated further when we note how philosophers, and even psychologists, have written about it. Some hypostatized it as an entity or substance, while others regarded it as a process, function, state, or quality of experience. Primarily, in philosophical discussion for example, we find the source of difference in the approach one takes, whether it is an ontological or an epistemological one, whether one is concerned with being or knowing.

René Descartes

René Descartes, as I mentioned earlier, thought that consciousness is the essence of mind and that the mind is different from the body, including the brain and the nervous system. There are in existence two kinds of radically different substances — the extended physical substance and the thinking mental substance. The latter in principle is irreducible to the former. Consequently, mental phenomena are those for which there can be no physical explanation. It will be of interest to note in this context that Descartes denied consciousness to animals because their behavior can be explained in essentially physical terms. Even in human beings, Descartes thought, such activities as digestion and muscular reflexes do not involve mind because they can be explained by purely mechanical principles. It is the essential non-corporeality of the mind that Descartes saw as its distinguishing characteristic.

Even though Descartes deduced his certainty of the existence of consciousness or mind on rational rather than empirical grounds, i.e., from the indubitability of its existence inherent in the very nature of consciousness, its self-revealing characteristic, his conception of consciousness may be seen to have an empirical dimension as well, for he assumed conscious phenomena to be essentially devoid of any corporeal quality. If, for example, all the mental phenomena can be accounted for in physical terms and if the presumed activities of the mind, thought, volition, and so on are shown to be governed solely by mechanical principles, as Descartes recognized in the case of reflex actions, there will be hardly any empirical justification for assuming that humans, unlike animals, have mind or consciousness. When we consider also the logical weakness in Descartes' assertion that one's inability to doubt his ability to think is sufficient ground for believing in the independent existence of mind (although it is self-evident that you cannot doubt your doubting, it is not so evident that you can do the doubting independent of the body), the importance of attesting for the existence of what he called "ideas of pure mind" that have no corporeal base becomes more important.

We therefore find that those like D.M. Armstrong who espouse a materialist theory of mind argue that there is nothing in conscious experience that cannot be accounted for in strictly physical terms. The experience of consciousness, according to Armstrong, is no more than one part of the brain scanning another. "In perception," he says, "the brain scans the environment. In awareness of the perception another process in the brain scans that scanning" (1968: 94). The inner sense that gives us introspective awareness is simply another brain process, and therefore it is no reason to hypostatize the existence of a process that can function independently of the brain.

It is again not surprising that empirically-oriented dualists like Sir John Eccles argue that some mental phenomena can be shown to have separate and independent status beyond what goes on in the brain and nervous system. As a physiologist, Eccles (Popper and Eccles 1977) finds it difficult to account for the unity of conscious experience in terms of heterogeneous, discontinuous, and spatially discrete neural events. Similarly, self-consciousness and human will require for their explanation an agency independent of brain processes. Phenomena such as "antedating", where conscious experience does not immediately follow stimulation but is referred backward in time, do not fit with the hypothesis of psychoneural identity. Again, we do not know the precise physiological process involved in the synthesis of perceptual experience. Finally, Eccles argues that the surface-negative potential in the cerebral cortex preceding simple voluntary movements, called the "readiness potential", takes considerable time to develop and is distributed widely over the cortex. This phenomenon, according to Eccles, suggests the action of the self-conscious mind upon the specialized modules in the cortex that are critically poised at a special level of activity to produce conscious-willed actions. Eccles explains:

> The willing of a movement produces a gradual evolution of neuronal responses over a wide area of frontal and parietal cortices on both sides, so giving the readiness potential. Furthermore, the mental act that we call willing must guide or mold this unimaginably complex neuronal performance of the liaison cortex so that it eventually "homes in" on the appropriate modules of the motor cortex and brings about discharges of their motor pyramidal cells. — 1976: 117

In his address to the Parapsychological Association (1977), Eccles termed this action of mind on brain cells *psychokinesis* and called on psi researchers to focus on the mind rather than the brain. He also suggests that the dominant hemisphere may be the "seat" of the conscious self because the persons in whom the corpus callosum is surgically severed do not report any conscious awareness of actions programmed from the minor hemisphere.

Other contemporary defenses of dualism from an empirical perspective also attempt to show the inadequacy of materialistic explanations to account for certain kinds of mental phenomena. John Beloff (1989), for example, argues that physicalism is in principle inconsistent with parapsychological phenomena like ESP and PK.

Edmund Husserl

Phenomenologist Edmund Husserl, like Descartes, believed in the self-revealing character of consciousness, that consciousness cannot be denied without contradiction, and that its non-being is utterly unimaginable. Taking an epistemological rather than an ontological approach, Husserl, however, avoids Cartesian dualism without compromising on the unique nature of consciousness. Consciousness is seen by Husserl (1964) as a function rather than an entity. Like Brentano before him, he emphasized the intentional nature of consciousness. The external object, the content of consciousness, and our awareness of it are directly related by the intentionality of consciousness. Our knowledge of the world is not via sensations we receive but is a consequence of the logical process of intention. The common world we share with each other is made possible not by the sensations that tend to be discrete and private and cannot therefore reveal the universal and unitary character of their objects, but by a "constitutive function" of consciousness that intuitively grasps their essence. The constitutive function of consciousness lies in this intuiting of the essence of objects so that we may understand their significance and meaningfulness to us. The unitary character that objects have as phenomena of our experience can be understood only in terms of their essences and not as a summation of their shifting qualities.

It is important to note that this constituting function of consciousness is not psychological and subjective but logical and objective, because we are dealing here with the essences of subjective experience and not the fleeting impressions we have of the objects. Husserl proposes a "transcendental" mode of analysis in which the natural world of scientific inquiry is deliberately "bracketed" (i.e., put aside) so that we can closely observe the experience itself. When we do this and consciousness reflectively considers its own cognitive acts, we find the emergence of what Husserl calls "the transcendental ego". The transcendental ego is "the principle of subjectivity". It may not be confused with any capacity of the mind or the contents of consciousness. It is simply the principle that governs the functioning of conscious awareness so that one is conscious of himself. It is "transcendental phenomenological self-experience". Transcendental ego, unlike the empirical ego, is consciousness of itself and not consciousness of something else. It is the characteristic function of consciousness that it is aware of itself as well as the world. Our transcendental self-experience consists in our ability to function as a being who is self-consciously aware. It is clear that Husserl's transcendental self-experience is what we have referred to as subject consciousness in its most abstract form, consciousness as-such.

Jean-Paul Sartre

Existential philosopher Jean-Paul Sartre questions the Husserlian method of transcendental reduction, "bracketing", which puts aside the transcendental world in order to deduce the transcendental ego as a consciousness function. No such ego is phenomenologically apparent. Nor is it logically necessary to account for the unity of experience. Arguing with Brentano that consciousness is always consciousness of something,

Sartre points out that both consciousness and the objects of our consciousness are the two facts given in experience. They enjoy two distinctive kinds of reality. Since the very nature of consciousness is intentional, that it is always directed to something, the essential characteristic of consciousness is the *revelation* of the thing to which it is directed. Its reality is functional and not substantive. Therefore, it cannot be described as this or that. It is not a thing; nor is it a container into which the phenomena of our experience are deposited. Its sole reality consists in its revelatory function. For this reason, Sartre characterizes consciousness as signifying "nothingness". But by "nothingness" he clearly does not mean complete void but merely lack of content or corporeality. It signifies the contrast with the objective world that is "being". By "being", Sartre does not mean the phenomena of our experience that derive their significance by virtue of their appearance in consciousness. *Being* refers to "the in-itself", whereas *consciousness* is a "for-itself".

The nothingness of consciousness may be understood only in the sense of lacking content and not as being unreal. "The existence of consciousness," says Sartre, "comes from consciousness itself" (1956: lxvi). There is non-being in its being, for it can transcend itself and intend an object. That is why consciousness, unlike objects of experience, is a being for itself.

The concept of nothingness may be better understood in the context of Sartre's psychology of imagination. Where we imagine, for example, a book, we do not, according to Sartre, form an image of the book in consciousness. Consciousness is not a container, not a canvas on which the images are imprinted, and not a stage on which objects are played. Both in imagination and in perception, the object always remains external to consciousness. The difference between the imagination of a book and the perception of it consists in the manner in which we intend the book. When we imagine something we have imaginative consciousness of it, which reveals at once its non-presence. In perceptual consciousness of the book we intend its presence. Therefore, the image, perceptual or imaginative, is not an entity but merely a function of consciousness. Consciousness in signifying "nothingness" is beyond being. Inasmuch as we can go beyond being in our imagination, we are able to grasp the synthetic unity and totality of the world.

In Sartre's discussion of consciousness, one may find several contradictory statements. Sometimes he speaks of consciousness as if it is not an autonomous something but dependent on the objects it reveals. On other occasions he asserts that consciousness is absolute and autonomous whose being a for-itself cannot be derived from that of objects, the in-itself. When he asserts its autonomy and freedom, consciousness becomes the principle of subjectivity as in Husserl. In his introduction to *Being and Nothingness,* Sartre describes consciousness as "the first being to whom all other appearances appear . . . it is subjectivity itself, the immanence of self itself" (1956: lxvii). Sartre here uses self and consciousness interchangeably.

When Sartre criticizes Husserl, it is apparent that he falls back on the more restrictive conception of consciousness as being not absolute but dependent on objects. But he himself finds it necessary to use consciousness in a broader sense. The transcendental ego, distinguished from the empirical ego, is the principle of subjectivity and consciousness in Husserl's philosophy and is not very different from Sartre's conception of consciousness in its absolute sense. Again Sartre's *revelatory* function of consciousness is similar to Husserl's *constitutive* function. In both, it is the intentional nature of consciousness that is stressed as its essential characteristic. Both Husserl and Sartre find it logically necessary to postulate consciousness as a principle of subjectivity to account for the manifest unity and significance of the phenomena of our experience, even though Sartre's view of consciousness as "nothingness" goes beyond the epistemological to an ontological understanding.

Consciousness As-Such

From the preceding discussion, admittedly selective and brief, the following points may be made. First, consciousness refers to some processes and phenomena beyond explicit awareness. Awareness can be explicit or implicit. The distinction between "conscious" and "unconscious", useful no doubt in some other contexts, is inappropriate for our purpose inasmuch as mental activities and phenomena seem to manifest even when individuals are not aware of their occurrence. Second, consciousness or mind is used basically to refer to two sorts of things — consciousness as such (*S*-consciousness) and consciousness of something (*P*-consciousness). Subject consciousness refers to a state of being, whereas predicate consciousness is awareness of something, that such and such is the case.

Opinions may differ as to whether there is anything one can refer to as consciousness, whether it is a fact of its own, autonomous and irreducible, apart from certain cortical states. Accepting that there is indeed something that can be referred to as consciousness, one may consider it a substantiative entity or an autonomous function. We thus have fundamental dualism as in Cartesian philosophy or functional dualism as in Husserl. Fundamental dualism is ontological; functional dualism is an epistemological doctrine. But as we have seen in Husserl, once we consider consciousness as autonomous and irreducible, whether it is a function or an entity, we are invariably led to the domain of consciousness as-such, the principle of subjectivity and autonomy.

At this point it may be instructive to see the respects in which a conscious person differs from a machine. It is argued that contemporary advances in neuroscience, computer simulation, artificial intelligence, and cognitive psychology increasingly threaten the concept of mind as involving processes beyond the brain. Recent attempts to design representational schemes by which computers may be able to generate global understandings have left many with the belief that the human mind may be no more than an information-processing machine. The distinction between conscious experience and the brain may be the same as the logical-structural distinction in the Turing machine.

What then are the functions that we attribute to consciousness? Or what are the criteria by which we identify the presence of consciousness? I think we can all agree that some kind of discriminatory and purposive behavior is involved in most conscious activities. Our ability to react, reflect, possess images, and use them as representations, to control and plan programs of action, to project into the future, to use language, process information, and to perceive our own state are the general functions of our consciousness. We are told that all these functions can also be performed by a cleverly designed computer. Whether or not this is true, few among us would accept the idea that computers have subjective and personal experiences as we do. The subjectivity involved in our conscious experience is not the same as the ability of the machine to perceive the state it is in at a given time. More important, conscious functions are essentially intentional. Inasmuch as intentions are not reduced to brain states with any degree of specificity, they are not controlled by natural laws, whereas machines are constrained to follow those laws. Thus our intentions and the volitional freedom they imply distinguish conscious activity from the operations of the machine. It is the self-determining nature of consciousness that leads us to the concept of consciousness as-such, which is irreducible to brain states.

But subliminal mentation, as we have noted, is devoid of any explicit subjective awareness, as well as apparent intentional control. Therefore, it may be argued, either that the subliminal mental phenomena do not involve consciousness or that subjectivity and intentional character are not the distinguishing features of consciousness or mind. This argument loses its force once we recognize that subjectivity and intentions need not be explicit. I suggest that in subliminal mental phenomena, unlike machine-engendered phenomena, subjectivity is *implicit* and that all mental phenomena are also *potentially* intentional. J.B. Rhine suggests, for example, that "Psi is an unconscious but by no means completely involuntary function" (1953: 112). Just as exercise of focal attention brings certain sensory inputs into explicit awareness, there may be other forms of attention that similarly deal with subliminal and even with extrasensory phenomena. Cultivating consciousness essentially involves accessing these non-focal resources, i.e., making the implicit mentation explicit, the involuntary voluntary.

The preceding notion would clearly be impossible if our attention was wholly determined by our neural networks with deterministic functions. As William James hinted, there may be a tremendous role for "effort", volition in modulating and manipulating attention. "Effort," says James, "may be an original force and not a mere effect, and it may be indeterminant in amount" (1900: 238).

The subjectivity inherent in my thoughts and experiences as distinct from the actions of a computer is a function of my consciousness. Whether or not "I" and "me" refer to a substantive entity, all first-person pronouncements signify a qualitatively different aspect of our being. The self and the experience of personal identity, as James would say, for example, may be no more than "passing states of consciousness" that have continuity and functional identity. Even if "the thoughts themselves are the thinkers", as James (1900: 216) would like us to believe, my thoughts "have a warmth and intimacy about them" of which others are completely devoid. Warmth and intimacy are the abiding characteristics of subjectivity and of consciousness.

It is important to note that the myriad current formulations to account for mental phenomena in essential reductionistic terms deal almost exclusively with what we called predicate awareness, or *P*-consciousness, ignoring or rejecting consciousness as-such. That the question of dualism is still an unsettled matter and that philosophers continue to debate the autonomy issue of consciousness suggests that there are no valid a priori reasons, however, for dismissing subject consciousness as non-existent. As we have seen, Husserl finds it eminently plausible to postulate consciousness, the principle of subjectivity, which is absolute and autonomous, whose reality is intuitively evident. Even Sartre could not altogether reject such an autonomous status for consciousness. Nothingness, like being, is also a necessary and autonomous aspect of reality, without which the world of our experience could not exist in the manner it does. Descartes' non-corporeal mind, Husserl's transcendental ego, and Sartre's nothingness seem to have one thing in common. They refer to the principle of essential subjectivity that is unconstrained by either space or time or both. To use a term from quantum physics, they seem to signify a nonlocal aspect of reality. Therefore, it may not be unreasonable to postulate consciousness as-such or pure consciousness to signify a nonlocal being or function — the non-deterministic aspect of our being, which is capable of subjectivity, intentionality, and self-determination. The evidence for believing in the existence of such phenomena as psi, whose function does not seem to be constrained by space–time variables, provides further credence to the notion of consciousness as-such.

Consciousness in the sense of predicate awareness is obviously local and subject to space–time formulations and deterministic assumptions. It is likely that the brain has much to contribute in our awareness of the world. Consequently, we may find that various sorts of mental phenomena correlate with physiological processes in the brain and nervous system and that they could be investigated from a neurobiological perspective. It does not follow, however, that all mental phenomena are ultimately reducible to brain states or that consciousness does not exist apart from these states. Some systems of Indian philosophy, notably the Sāṁkhya school, consider mind to be essentially material but at the same time hold that consciousness as such is non-material.

Methodological Issues

Upward and Downward Causation

Scientific attempts to study consciousness generally proceed from the simple mental phenomena that can be readily assimilated as the physical properties of the brain. It is hoped that we can move upward to understand more complex phenomena and ultimately consciousness itself. This method is eminently suitable if mind or consciousness and the phenomena associated with it are basically reducible to brain events. In making an a priori assumption that consciousness is analyzable into events in the brain, the method of upward causation is biased against finding consciousness to be an autonomous principle and consequently is ill suited to study what we called consciousness as-such, distinguished from brain states. If one assumes the existence of autonomous consciousness, I believe, the proper method to study consciousness is to begin with consciousness and work downward to discover how it is involved in specific mental events and what its role is in the phenomena of our experience.

As I have argued elsewhere (Rao 1991), the practice of mainstream science is based on two primary assumptions, which are by no means obvious. First, it is assumed as self-evident that there is an integrity in the universe that is governed by laws that have universal validity, in the sense that the laws explaining one set of phenomena may not conflict with those claiming to explain another set. Second, the physical laws, that is, the laws that explain physical phenomena, have intrinsic validity and are therefore the reference points for cross-validating the so-called mental phenomena. In other words, explanations of mental phenomena must be consistent with physical laws.

There may or may not be a necessary congruence between physical and mental explanations of phenomena. Whether such a congruence exists should be the end point of inquiry and cannot be prejudged. There are no a priori grounds for assuming that all phenomena must obey the laws of physics. Stephen Braude points out:

> If there are vital or intentional processes in nature not analyzable into, or describable in terms of, impersonal or mechanistic forces, those processes would not *violate* the laws of physics. . . . Those vital processes would simply be *outside* the domain of physics. — 1986: 17-18

R.W. Sperry (1976, 1983, 1988) suggests that consciousness is a dynamic, emergent property resulting from the higher-level functional organization of the cerebral cortex. As an emergent property, consciousness is determined by the brain, but it is also autonomous in its own right and is not reducible to electrochemical processes. More important, consciousness can exercise regulatory control over brain processes. The mental phenomena may be regarded therefore as "causes rather than correlates" of neural events.

As Sperry puts it, "the brain physiology determines the mental effects and the mental phenomena in turn have causal influence on the neurophysiology" (1976: 168). As emergent properties of cortical activity, conscious phenomena could interact functionally at their own level and also at the same time exert downward control over constituent neural processes. Thus, according to Sperry, conscious states "supervene" rather than "intervene" in the physiological processes.

Sperry's affirmation of downward causation, that mind or consciousness can influence and control physiochemical processes in the brain, is consistent with our assertion that a proper study of consciousness should begin with consciousness as-such and proceed downward to discover how it influences other events within the brain and outside it. Sperry, however, falls short of accepting a truly autonomous consciousness. Though he is emphatic in denying that consciousness can be reduced to processes in the brain and unambiguously asserts that consciousness has qualities essentially different from any manifested by the neural or other components of the brain, he regards mind or consciousness itself as determined by the neural infrastructures of the brain at the highest levels of its organizational hierarchy. In so regarding mind as a product of brain, Sperry exposes himself to a variety of criticisms.

Globus et al. (1976) point out, for example, that it is difficult to conceive how complex organizations of neural processes give us mental phenomena that enjoy primacy and autonomy. There are obviously qualitative differences between neural events and mental activity. The analogy of water is not helpful. Water and its elements, hydrogen and oxygen, share physical properties, whereas mind and brain, which are qualitatively different, do not. As David Griffin mentions elsewhere in this volume, there is no good sense in which Sperry could affirm genuine human freedom and responsibility without conceiving our minds as capable of exercising self-determination. To be consistent with his assertion of autonomy and freedom for the human mind, Sperry should postulate, or at least leave room for, consciousness to be distinguished from the mind, which may indeed be a product of cerebral function but whose freedom and autonomy are derived from its association with consciousness. He would then be in the company of Sāṁkhya thinkers.

First-Person and Third-Person Perspectives

Unlike physical phenomena, consciousness can be studied not only from the perspective of an outside observer (third-person perspective) but also from the perspective of the person having the experience (first-person perspective). Science traditionally ignored first-person perspective (how things appear to the experiencing subject) unless it could be translated into third-person perspective. As Velmans (1991) argues, for example, the existence of consciousness from a first-person perspective should not be dismissed. The two perspectives are complementary and irreducible, and a comprehensive understanding of consciousness requires that we study it from both perspectives. Consciousness from a first-person perspective is not only different in kind from neurobiological processes but also appears to have primacy of its own and can indeed causally influence other processes. From a third-person perspective, however, according to Velmans, consciousness appears to be an epiphenomenon, "a form of *output*" associated with focal-attentive processing.

Velmans' point about studying consciousness from a first-person perspective is well taken, even though his espousing of epiphenomenalism from a third-person perspective of consciousness is arguable. He may indeed be right in thinking that the two perspectives reveal to us two different and apparently contradictory aspects of consciousness. It seems necessary, however, that at some level the contradictions must resolve themselves, especially when one of the contradictions relates to the existence of consciousness itself.

Questions about the interaction of consciousness and the physical world, or the mind-brain, have traditionally troubled dualist theorists. First-person and third–person perspectives reflect methodological dualism and face similar problems as ontological dualism. How can we study consciousness in a scientific sense if consciousness as-such, i.e., consciousness in its subjective form, is not reducible to empirically verifiable objective processes or contents? If consciousness in its subjective aspect is nonlocal, how is phenomenal experience constrained by time–space locality possible? We must conceptualize a form of interfacing subjective experience and physical events. Nonlocality may not be considered as an antiphysical construct because it is also used in physics. There are good reasons to assume that some form of attentional activity, volitional effort, may be involved in interfacing consciousness and brain.

Even though the intentional nature of mental phenomena has its clearest presentation first in the work of Brentano, the importance of volition as the connecting link between consciousness and mental acts, between thought and action, is recognized as early as Plato. Recall Plato's division of the soul into three parts — reason, spirit, and appetite. Spirit is what influences the conduct without which reason alone will be unable to guide our actions. Spirit is the volitional aspect that seems to cause consciousness (reason) to influence conduct. Again, as we have seen, philosophers such as Husserl and Sartre, who accorded a transcendental function to consciousness, saw intentionality as its essential feature.

I find Immanuel Kant's discussion of free will quite relevant to our understanding of intentional nature of consciousness in its abstract subjective dimension. Regarding the "will" as autonomous, i.e., as a law unto itself, Kant (1929) says that the will in its pure form is independent of being determined by sensuous impulses or stimuli. The freedom of will consists in the "absolute spontaneity" of pure will. According to Kant, there are two modes of causality. The causality of the natural phenomena is one of physical necessity determined in time. The causality of free will, which belongs to the world of supersensible things, operates independently of the temporal conditions of natural causality. The causality of free will, according to Kant, is capable of producing effects independently of and even in opposition to the power of natural causes, and capable, consequently, of *spontaneously* originating a series of events.

Can we empirically deal with these issues that apparently seem to refer to a transcendental domain? I believe we can. For example, the literature on psychic development techniques in general and meditation in particular seems to suggest that pure volitional activity can be facilitated by promoting voluntary attention. Meditative practices help to bring about cessation of habitual brain activity, which normally has the effect of masking pure volition. One-pointed attentional focus in concentrative forms of meditation controls the random fluctuations of attention, on the one hand, and renders attention, on the other hand, impervious to environmental pressures and subjective bias. Even in the so-called passive meditation, the meditator learns to attend to incoming signals non-reactively for prolonged periods of time, which serves the same purpose of promoting voluntary attention and enhancing the pure volitional function.

Cultivating Consciousness

This brings us to the central question of cultivating consciousness. Cultivating consciousness is done through attempts at accessing consciousness as-such, which, as I tried to show, may involve appropriate deployment of attention for achieving volitional freedom. When attention reaches the domain of consciousness as-such, the "will" regains its intrinsic spontaneity; consciousness functions on its own. When this happens, the mind is no longer controlled by the processes in the brain, and it becomes impervious to sensuous impulses and stimuli. At the same time, the mind begins to exercise control over the cortical processes and to influence the world of objects.

Meditation, as mentioned earlier, fits very well with this model for cultivating consciousness. Yoga, for example, is a traditional Indian system of practices that are designed essentially to cultivate consciousness by controlling the natural wanderings of the mind. Patañjali defines the object of *yoga* practice as the cessation of *citta vṛtti*s (mental fluctuations). According to the Sāṁkhya-Yoga school, the mind is material and is constantly under the pressure of internal and external influences. These influences need to be controlled so that access to consciousness can be gained. The object of all the physical exercises and other preliminaries before practicing meditation is to control somatic and psychological distractions so that one can concentrate. Concentration (*dhāraṇā*) along with *dhyāna* and *samādhi* produces a state in which the natural wanderings of our thoughts, the fluctuations of the mind, are brought under control. The practice of concentration enables one to focus attention, which is expanded in the meditative state. When such concentration and expansion of attention are continued for prolonged periods, one is led to a stand-still state of the mind where the mind's wanderings come under volitional control. When this happens, one has direct access to consciousness as-such; what are implicit become explicit in consciousness. Such an access enables one to experience events and to cause effects that appear anomalous to us. (For a detailed discussion see Chapter 17.)

Focusing attention narrowly on an object for a prolonged period may have the effect of regulating the sensory input by appropriate attentional shift and dissociating the mind from the competing (distracting) sensory impulses. Such a dissociation and withdrawal of the senses and shutting attention off to some impulses, while focusing it on others, seems to be an essential aspect of meditation practice.

The similarities between meditation and hypnotic states have led some to think that *yoga* involves some sort of autohypnosis (Zorab 1963). Indeed, the similarities seem to stem basically from their dissociative nature. The meditative practices, as well as hypnotic induction procedures, involve the attentional shifts, the selective attention and inattention, the disruption of memories, and the critical feedback that characterize dissociative experience. One-pointed concentration and the effort to meditate may indeed stimulate imagination and cause disorientation, loss of experience of body, and detachment in the same manner as hypnotic induction. Reports of yoga practitioners do suggest that yogic concentration in its early phases generates hallucinatory imagery similar to that obtained under hypnosis. Obviously, yogic meditation is more than a hypnotic state. It does not stop with achieving dissociation from the competing sensory impulses but goes on to a stand-still state in which the mind, severed from its sensory connection, apparently enjoys spontaneity and volitional freedom. The goal of meditation is not one of a dissociative state as such but of gaining and exercising volitional freedom. It is clear, however, that the path the meditator travels is one where shifts of attention do take place in a controlled manner to the point where there is simply attention with no object to attend to, a state of consciousness as-such or *S*-consciousness. Emptying the mind, as it were, appears to be an essential aspect of gaining volitional spontaneity and freedom in the meditative state. Such an emptying, it seems to me, will be possible only when one's attention is withdrawn from sensory impulses and stimuli and much of the cognitive backdrop, the host of memories and habitual dispositions, is held in abeyance. I do not believe we will be wrong in assuming that the practice of meditation prepares one for a state of dissociation without necessarily involving a dissociative experience. We may call this *readying for dissociability*, or *dissociative readiness*. What is important is the facility with which the meditator deploys attentional selectivity. Such a facility seems to be clearly enhanced in a state of dissociative readiness, where the usual cognitive controls are in abeyance or become inoperative. Such a readiness seems to be a necessary condition for enhancing volitional spontaneity and freedom.

In this context we may refer to a study by Arthur + (1963), which shows how intentional deployment of attention may lead to enhanced awareness. Deikman called it *deautomatization*. Deautomatization, according to Deikman (1966), is an essential aspect of meditation. In an interesting study, he instructed his subjects to focus their attention on a blue vase to the exclusion of all other thoughts. After a series of these intense concentration sessions, his subjects reported seeing things about the vase that they never did before. One subject felt that she had "merged" with the vase. Deikman felt that deautomatization achieved through selective deployment of attention may permit a new and perhaps more advanced experience.

It will be of interest to note that several other techniques of cultivating consciousness seem to involve readiness for dissociability. James Hall (1991), one of the foremost Jungian analysts in the United States, has called our attention to the Jungian insight into "the dissociability of the psyche" and how in hypnotherapy it can be made use of "in an intentional and controlled way" to treat psychopathology.

Jung also spoke of "active imagination", which allows images to develop by themselves. It seems to me that such an autonomous function for images is clearly consistent with the concept of volitional spontaneity achieved in the play of consciousness as-such. Again, active imagination is a manifestation of the dissociability of the psyche and the temporary abeyance of the usual cognitive controls. It has been shown that free imagery is an effective means of circumventing a variety of controls that constrain behavior.

Several therapeutic techniques such as psychosynthesis and autogenic training involve guided imagination, which is another way of preparing for loosening of controls and readiness for dissociation. Recall Ernest Hilgard's observation that dissociation involves essentially the suppression or alteration of the usual controls of conscious activities. "The modification of controls can be described as dissociation if the usual controls are inoperative, and are replaced by new ones" (Hilgard 1977: 228). Again, the so-called enactment techniques such as painting, dancing, group rituals, shamanistic trips, and the visualization procedures to enhance the immune system to fight or prevent diseases, as Hall points out, utilize the dissociability of the psyche.

I hardly need to mention that dreaming, especially lucid dreaming, and out-of-body experiences, being natural dissociative states, could be utilized for cultivating consciousness. Similarly, automatic writing, mediumship, and more recently, channeling all involve some form of dissociability from the controls that normally constrain our conscious functioning.

Obviously, dissociability is but one form, though a very pervasive one, of other possible means of escape from the cerebral control of conscious function. Though yogic practice may manifest dissociation-like states, its goal is some kind of higher-order integration where consciousness becomes progressively free from cerebral chores to function on its own.

In conclusion, let me add that the study of consciousness must begin with consciousness as-such, autonomous and irreducible. The study of consciousness *qua* consciousness will explore downward instead of upward causation by attempting to discover the links between consciousness and the mental phenomena that are provided by the intentionality in the human condition. Mental phenomena, which are ordinarily dependent on cerebral processes in the human condition, may be freed to a large extent from the constraints imposed by brain functions and brought under the more direct influence of consciousness as-such through the instrumentality of intentional and voluntary attention. A state of dissociative readiness, where cerebral controls can be put in abeyance or voluntarily altered under conditions of alertness, may facilitate autonomous conscious function. Many techniques of cultivating consciousness seem to involve an effort to accomplish just this.

7

Embracing the Subtle
The Emerging Paradigm in Relation to the Subtle Realms

Beverly Rubik

THERE has never been a shift in the worldly domain without first a shift in consciousness. According to philosopher Paul Ricoeur, psyche and cosmos are related as concave and convex of the same surface. In our culture, however, the inner realm is often ignored because we are so engrossed with the outer, material world. We fail to examine ourselves to see how our consciousness is the source of all that we create, including our global problems.

The scientific worldview of materialistic, mechanical reductionism has dominated our culture for some time. Much has been written about that. However, that paradigm is beginning to crumble as the social and cultural systems based on it are failing us. The important question is not so much where we stand as where we are going. We are at the beginning of a breakthrough in consciousness, a shift in the collective consciousness that is becoming conscious. We see glimpses of this in the new science, a renewed spirituality, the new arts, and a movement toward the globalization of certain cultural systems. A new worldview, a new paradigm, is emerging in science, as well as society. The magnitude of this shift in consciousness is no small change in intellectual outlook. It is as if some deep inner wisdom is unfolding just in time to save us from our own follies. A profound perceptual shift at the level of collective mind as well as individual minds, a new view of nature and ourselves, is beginning to expand.

Because science is one of our greatest investments and a leading force in our society, changes in it are barometers of deeper changes. Indeed, science is at present regarded by many as the bastion of truth about human nature and the world, and the dominant cultural worldview grew out of the science of former centuries. The new worldview emerging today is partly being shaped by breakthroughs in the frontier sciences, i.e., areas of science that are not yet mainstream. In this chapter I restrict the topic of the emerging perceptual shift in consciousness to science, especially the frontier sciences.

One of the main features of the dominant worldview is fragmentation. There is the primary split inherent in the act of doing science, the separation between the observer and the observed. The fragmentation in question, however, goes far beyond this assumed posture of objectivity. The ideology of science projects an alienation from nature with an implicit goal being to dominate and manipulate it. The father of the scientific method, Francis Bacon, wrote that science should "tease and torture the secrets out of treacherous nature". Fragmentation is also one of the chief features of our modern world — all our social and cultural systems are based on specialization, compartmentalization, and bureaucratization. We know a huge amount about all the parts at the expense of knowing virtually nothing about the wisdom of the whole. Our technologies are all based on this limited knowledge, which has produced unwanted side effects. Moreover, just as we have created fragmentation in the external world, we too are compartmentalized in our minds and bodies. The poet Walt Whitman wrote that he or she who sees the world as broken or fragmented is himself or herself broken or fragmented. We live in boxes, incompatible compartments of being, lacking integration and cosmic perspective.

For the most part, scientists do not like to hear such analyses about science or themselves. They usually consider it unscientific. The subjective realm is rejected by them, even if subjective analysis would yield intersubjective consensus. (Paradoxically, science itself may be little more than intersubjective consensus.) Contemporary science is among those "fragments" of human output that do not permit themselves to be addressed from outside of their own system of inquiry. It is an "alienated concept" in the words of Karl Marx. Science and scientists have preserved this alienation in order to remain stable and avoid change. Contemporary science has increasingly become a closed system with narrow perspectives.

My approach here is to give voice to such an analysis of science, an intuitive analysis. As a biophysicist and director of an international scientific center comprising those working at the edge of science, I am privy to hearing many voices, particularly those of the frontier scientists who face extraordinary difficulties within the scientific community. I shall not apologize to the reader for any subjectivity herein, because this is a deliberate quest into the inner domain that is often disregarded. Indeed, the new science will encompass the subjective in a new way. Here, the medium is the message.

The really significant questions about the nature of reality lie beyond the scope of our present disciplines. They are deep and multidisciplinary, involving, for example, science, philosophy, and spirituality. For example, what is valid or true? What is life, and how did it come into being? Academics typically respond to such questions in a very limited way, taking "truth" to mean that narrowly defined by their discipline. They invent hairsplitting arguments and schemes about what goes into the "science box", the "philosophy box", and so forth, and the rules of dialogue between the boxes. They remind me of territorial dogs anxious to preserve and defend their turf to the death. The questions capable of being addressed by disciplinarians are indeed limited.

Needless to say, there are many interesting and new questions that fall in the cracks between the boxes of the disciplines, such as many puzzles within parapsychology and other frontier sciences. Scientists who dare to pursue these questions suffer extraordinary hardships from lack of funding, accusations of heresy or fraud, loss of camaraderie, and even loss of their jobs. Their research findings disturb the status quo of various social and cultural systems and challenge or threaten the boundaries of the structures that be, including large, powerful, private interests. Moreover, they challenge the compartmentalization within our own minds, threatening the character structures of those who maintain the status quo, whose psyches reflect the systems they control.

The challenges to mainstream science are steadily growing stronger. Our current paradigm cannot accommodate the frontier areas and the anomalies. Many say that a new paradigm is emerging, but what exactly is it? Can a new paradigm serve to help heal our numerous fragmentations within and without?

Many of the contributors to this volume are giving voice to that new paradigm as it emerges. Various features have been elucidated here and elsewhere. For example, many frontier scientists agree that

1. consciousness is both primary and causal;
2. cosmic and biological evolution may be regarded as teleological;

3. mind has properties that transcend space and time;
4. life is far more than a mechanical reductionistic bag of biomolecules; and
5. the whole cosmos cannot be addressed by means of a reductionistic approach.

I would like to contribute yet another characteristic to that wish list. The emerging paradigm must necessarily be gender-balanced at a deep, archetypal level. Presently, gender balance is seriously lacking in the world. Much of the research in the frontier sciences, however, may be regarded as looking into the subtler aspects of the universe by means of gentler approaches, rebirthing the lost feminine archetype. In my view, the new science and its emerging paradigm include the "soft" or subtle side of nature — the subjective, dynamical, unpredictable, complex, cyclical, nonlocal, and nonlinear relationships. It modifies the masculine notions of rigid laws, fixed boundaries, static things, hierarchies of order, and linear thinking that characterize the dominant scientific paradigm. The emerging paradigm must include a balance of both the feminine and the masculine archetypes.

Although I am using words such as *gender*, *feminine*, and *masculine*, I want to clarify that I proffer them in an archetypal sense, not in the biological sense of man and woman. All of us have an anima and an animus, or *yin* and *yang*. In nature, as in ourselves, one never occurs without the other. They are in a dynamical balance, with neither one dominating. That is part of the cosmic wisdom of wholeness.

I would also like to clarify that my approach is not to be confused with some feminist approaches that advocate the feminine at the expense of the masculine. Rather, from the inception I advocate a new level of wholeness through healing our gender imbalance. In brief, I believe we have a chronic dominance and excess of *yang* over *yin* in our social and cultural systems and in our collective consciousness. In general, this may also be true for us as individuals. Regardless of our sex, we are all products of the educational system. We live and work in a contracted *yang* state characterized by fear of ego loss, fear of openness, softness, and flow. Materialism, aggression, competition, a sense of separateness, and hierarchical orders of thinking and doing dominate. It is no wonder that war seems to be essential to our society, with over 70 per cent of the US research budget currently allocated to defense.

Consider the language of conventional science and medicine that we have created. The metaphors used are not trivial but deeply revealing of our attitudes and also formative of new ideas. Several examples from physics, biology, chemistry, and medicine are as follows. The world is made up of *building blocks* — quarks, particles, atoms, molecules, and so on. Nature *obeys* physical *laws*; these laws cannot be *violated*. There are *master* molecules and *regulatory* genes that *control* or *trigger* biological responses. There is a search for *magic bullets* or *weapons* to *fight* disease. There is the *war* on cancer and another *war* on AIDS. There is a *central dogma* that DNA is the master *blueprint* of life. The *big-bang* theory describes the event that started creation. Reality is conceived of as multiple *hierarchies* of order.

Consider as well the methodologies of modern science. Some of our largest investments are in high energy physics and biotechnology. Physicists *split* atoms, using huge expensive accelerators, supercolliders, and the like, to *force* collisions between particles to *smash* them even further, and *analyze the pieces*, that is to say, the building blocks of nature. Much of modern biology is about *grinding up* tissues and *bursting* cells to *study the pieces* and *manipulate* them to do clever things and control nature in new and bizarre ways. *Patents* on *techniques*, hybrid cells, and even *genetically designed* creatures are awarded.

One sees that the language and methodology of conventional science are of a simple mechanical nature reflective of the world of machines, of war games, control, and manipulation. Nature is likened to a demon that is to be tamed and manipulated; and science is the sport that conquers all. To reiterate Francis Bacon, science is about "teasing and torturing the secrets out of treacherous nature". There is an implicit attitude of abuse or fear of nature, an overly contracted *yang* state that shows a lack of love and reverence for life. This gender imbalance both within our science and deep within us is one important reason our present world is out of balance.

Our overly *yang* state, however, was never that exclusive earlier in history. In medieval times, both male and female archetypes were central to hermetic philosophy, and the world was seen as a living organism composed of both archetypes. A dynamic balance was part of ancient Eastern wisdom in Taoism and Confucianism, with their *yin* and *yang* qualities, and in other Western systems of thought such as dialectics.

Consider two different frontier areas of science that have yielded anomalous results and that remain outside of mainstream science. Let us review some highlights of the two areas and then consider how the gender archetypes might apply.

The first area is consciousness research. Because the dominant paradigm, with its Cartesian split, maintains that consciousness is unable to have impact on matter, any research that demonstrates otherwise remains controversial, rendering this area a frontier one. Multiple personality research indicates, for example, that the pàtient's physiology shifts measurably with each personality (Braun 1986; Putnam 1986, 1990). This implies that the unit of being a person, the body–mind, is an inseparable whole. Another area of research has documented statistically significant effects of conscious intention on random event generators, producing anomalous skewing of numerical output (Jahn and Dunne 1985; Jahn et al. 1987; Radin and Nelson 1989; Schmidt 1982). There are also long-range effects of consciousness, such as the effects of prayer and the ability to perceive events across space or time (Byrd 1988; Puthoff and Targ 1976). Mind, therefore, has observable nonlocal manifestations akin to a physical force field.

The second frontier area is bioelectromagnetics. The scientific community maintains that there are no possible biological effects from low-intensity, Extremely Low-Frequency (ELF, ranging up to 100 Hz) fields, mainly because their theories do not predict any. Hence, bioelectromagnetics remains outside of the mainstream. Extremely low field intensities of ELF electromagnetism (EM), however, have been shown to interact with living systems yielding positive or negative effects (Adey and Lawrence 1984; Becker 1975). Other work suggests that all living systems display extremely low-level photon emission (biophoton emission) that is coherent and bioinformational (Popp et al. 1989). It may be indicative of a biofield within the organism that regulates the complex cellular biochemistry. (Along these lines, I recently performed a series of experiments suggesting this light emission to be synchronized between cell cultures, separated by some distance, that are optically able to "see" each other. This was particularly true if one of the cultures was stressed by the addition of a toxic chemical.) The evidence suggests long-range biophotonic communication between cells, perhaps between organisms as well. Another laboratory in Germany has pursued a third line of research, documenting evidence for a physical dowsing response to electromagnetic fields by dowsers under sensory deprivation and double-blind conditions (Konig and Betz 1989). This substantiates the ancient art of dowsing by modern scientific methods. A fourth area of inquiry is the relation of the geomagnetic field and life (Dubrov 1978). There is evidence to support behavioral and biorhythmic entrainment by cyclic variations in the geomagnetic field, which is a small static field at about 0.5 Gauss. In addition, some of the ELF research on the effects of 50- and 60-Hz oscillating magnetic fields suggests that there is an interaction between these and the local geomagnetic field on the bioeffects observed (Blackman et al. 1990).

One common thread between these two frontier areas of consciousness studies and bioelectromagnetics is that there is an intimacy of life and field-like phenomena. Because fields are nonlocal and have manifestations that permeate across space, the localistic biomolecular view of life is seriously challenged. It is possible that the latter is complementary to a field theory of life, analogous to the complementarity principle of physics with its particle–wave duality. Alternatively, it is possible that living systems may be characterized fundamentally by means of inherent bioelectromagnetic fields. In any event, EM may serve as an important communication link for the whole biosphere.

Both consciousness studies and bioelectromagnetics address the unbounded, expansive, or *yin* qualities of life — the gentler, subtler webs of interrelationship. These are not easily contained or controlled even when you close and lock the laboratory door. They cannot be reduced to the hard, rigid spheres of mechanical reductionism, and thus they pose a serious challenge to the dominant paradigm. They are excluded from mainstream science because they have no accepted *mechanism* consistent with its dominant paradigm; i.e., they cannot be understood in terms of discrete parts acting in a functional, sequential mechanism.

It seems that conventional science is overly preoccupied with discrete measurable entities. Physics led the way in this respect, with chemistry, biology, and the so-called "softer" sciences following. With the main emphasis on measurement and manipulation, we have supercolliders, accelerators, human genome projects, and cloning toward manipulating life for profit and glory. This perspective, in my opinion, is overly *yang*. The contracted *yang* state cannot give a living view of nature but only a poor rendition in the form of contracted, rigid models. The *yin*, which would express more movement and aliveness in nature, and the dynamical movement between the *yin* and *yang*, has hardly been approached in science. *Yin* is not much expressed in the language, orientation, methodology, approach, or topics selected for study. The subtler aspects of nature have not been explored much at all. A real science of life has barely begun.

Psi research is one area that deals with the subtle, psi being perhaps one of the most elusive features of mind at that. It appears to me, however, that in modern psi research, too, there is a similar imbalance in the approach, with the emphasis on measurement, quantification, statistics, repeatability, reproducibility, and replicability. The inner mental states of the percipients or operators have not been given equal attention. It seems that the main objective of modern psi research is to impress the scientific mainstream in following conventional methods that ignore the inner dimensions. The typical approach in controlled psi research experiments has been similar to the "black box" approach of behaviorism, with only the output being significant. The personal experiences of the participants have been secondary to the object of getting the *hard data*. Such efforts in psi research have, in my opinion, been valiant, sincere, and admirable, but limited.

I experienced these limitations myself as a psi researcher in my experiments on psychic healing in the late 1970s (Rauscher and Rubik 1983). In following the conventional psi research protocol, I felt its inadequacy toward the depth, elusiveness, and spontaneity of the phenomena. Psi is more about letting go and being receptive to an expanded state of being. It is highly *yin*, compared to the *yang* methodology that tries to capture and pinpoint it, with limited success. Psi may be considered to be like a butterfly that anticipates your attempt to catch her and changes her direction of flight. The typical scientific approach in controlled experiments on psi seems like a trap to kill and mount the butterfly for all to see. Certain phenomena, however, are too subtle to be caught. A dead butterfly does not reveal much about life. Another approach, much more subtle, is needed. I stopped doing this work in light of the inadequacy of the approach and the paradigm.

Implicit within contemporary psi research, where "interactions" or "effects" of "operators" or "percipients" on "targets" are studied, the same mechanical language and methodology of conventional science are used. Psi researchers typically look to see whether A affects B as in conventional science. Cosmic wholeness, the continuum of mind-matter, or mind-matter as process, is beyond interacting parts, however. Indeed, the positive results from a number of psi research experiments, despite their mechanical approach, imply that there is indeed a profound interrelationship. If psi research is going to help us move beyond the fragmentary dominant paradigm toward greater wholeness, then it must lead the way with a new approach.

It seems to me that the real challenge now for psi research is not so much to refine a method for reproducing and documenting psi but to lead the way in *creating a new paradigm* that addresses the depth and fullness of the phenomenon. Psi research and other so-called "soft" sciences suffer from what I call *physics envy* in imitating the language and orientation from the so-called "hard" sciences. Because we have endured a chronic imbalance and dominance of *yang* over *yin*, it is difficult for us even to begin to reflect on the *yin* in itself. Can psi research rise to the challenge of appropriately addressing the *yin*? Among all the frontier sciences, this is especially important for psi because psychic reality is soft and human and very different from "hard" physics.

In our culture, the subjugation of the *yin*, the soft side of nature and ourselves, is deep. For example, consider the metaphoric use of "hard" and "soft" in making value judgments. Hard data or hard currency are considered to be good. Soft currency or being soft headed is bad. The hard sciences are considered more difficult and rigorous, more important; and they have bigger budgets than the soft sciences. There is a hierarchy within the sciences, with hard reigning over the soft. The dominant notion of scientific causality is about reducing the "soft" to the "hard", which is considered to be more fundamental.

Consider another example from conventional science, quantum theory. Some scientists working to extend its applicability to condensed matter physics, which is generally considered the classical domain, feel that their work is excluded from the mainstream. Indeed, quantum theory is more of a *yin* approach to matter than is classical physics. Matter is smeared out into waves, and a system of particles is comprehensible only through its *whole* quantum mechanical wave function, inseparable into parts. However, most scientists work so as to ignore the deep wholeness and interrelationship demanded by quantum theory. Quantum mechanics is mostly applied mechanistically, i.e., by manipulating the equations, without a sense of its deep epistemological essence, and the most pragmatic interpretations of it are the most prevalent. Quantum theoretician Emilio Del Guidice (1991) maintains that quantum theory, which began ninety-one years ago, was an interrupted, incomplete science revolution, because classical mechanistic intuition still dominates our thinking. We have not yet cultivated quantum intuition, nor has the quantum paradigm permeated our culture at large. The *yin* quality of the quantum view seems strange and incomprehensible from the viewpoint of our excessively *yang* culture and way of being.

Quantum theory, or quantum electrodynamics, looks promising for application to the frontier sciences because it brings nonlocality, indeterminacy, and other expansive properties to the matter-energy continuum. For example, new quantum theories of condensed matter have been proposed that, applied to the living state, might serve to explain anomalies in bioelectromagnetics (Del Guidice and Preparata 1990). The concept of quantum coherence in living systems opens up a whole new picture of life (Popp et al. 1992). A field theory of mind that draws heavily on quantum wave features has been proposed to explain the interaction of mind and random event generators (Jahn and Dunne 1986).

There will be limitations to the explanatory value of quantum theory in the subtle realms, however. We need a whole new foundation for the life sciences that goes beyond mechanical reduction. This includes psi research, biology, psychology, and medicine, and all of the human sciences, which involve the gentler, more subtle, *yin* aspects of life. Needless to say, this is not because of any inconsistency with physics. An augmentation of science is simply required to accommodate them appropriately in their full dimensionality.

Complementary medicine is another frontier area that would greatly benefit from a gender-balanced paradigm. Energy medicine, which has also been called "soft" medicine, consists of subtle diagnostic methods and therapeutics such as acupuncture, homeopathy, healer interventions, and the application of very weak EM fields. What these have in common is that very weak, subtle stimuli can produce surprisingly large effects on the patient. Whereas the practice of conventional medicine uses large powerful stimuli such as drugs, X-rays, and surgery to yield dramatic responses, often with deleterious side effects, soft medicine is mainly about gently stimulating self-regulation. It does not make "war" on the body's systems or suppress them as does conventional medicine. The new physics of nonlinear dynamical systems theory, including chaos theory, offers a beginning toward understanding the gentle power of the *yin* to evoke change in showing how a system may respond dramatically to a very weak or generalized stimulus. A gender-balanced biomedical science would render soft medicine, currently dismissed by the mainstream as unconventional, legitimate.

There is a healthy interplay between *yin* and *yang* in the healthy state but not in a culture so badly fragmented and hierarchically ordered as ours. The "hard" has been separated and worshipped over the "soft", not only *out there* in the world but in our *minds*. It may be that the *yin* is so unfamiliar to our way of thinking and being that it poses a significant threat to our character structures. Consequently we have rejected, subjugated, and repressed it.

I was educated as a conventional biophysicist and have practiced science according to the rules of convention for the most part, but I feel an imbalance, a rift within myself, as the science that is permissible feels lopsided and inherently imbalanced to my inner being. In expressing this to other frontier scholars, evidently others as well experience similar rifts between the "soft" and "hard" elements of themselves, which need healing in the form of greater dynamic expression. We need to go deep inside and listen to our authentic selves, not just our professionally trained academic selves, to discover what has not yet been expressed in our work and what is crying out for such expression. In this way, we can fashion the new paradigm from the inside out. In addition, we can also work in the usual ways on the intellectual, outer manifestation of what is logically necessary to accommodate the anomalous phenomena within science. Thus, the emerging paradigm can be shaped from both inside and out.

The collection of what appear to be anomalies gathered together from the various fields of science is but a single driving force for a paradigm shift in science. Moreover, logical, rational analysis at this level is not enough. This paradigm shift is far bigger than just an intellectual puzzle and a perceptual shift. The real shift will unfold from deep within us. We must attend to our own subtleties of being, cultivating a love and reverence for nature and life, making ourselves open and receptive to change, and work toward healing our personal imbalances, splits, ambiguities, and internal paradoxes. As we reach a new integration deep within ourselves, a new holistic worldview that accommodates consciousness and the subtle realm will naturally come forth. A deep transformation of consciousness at the individual, social, and collective levels is a key factor in the new science and worldview that are emerging.

8

The Complementarity of Consciousness

Robert G. Jahn

CONSCIOUSNESS studies are genuinely interdisciplinary, as this volume clearly shows. It has long been our opinion, based on nearly fifteen years of experimental and theoretical study of the topic, that such profound mysteries as the role of consciousness in the establishment of reality will be unraveled only by well-coordinated efforts mounted across a broad range of scholarly disciplines. The anomalous phenomena we observe in our laboratory, like those encountered by many other participants in this program in their own contexts, are mere epistemological tips of a monumental iceberg, projecting upward into empirical experience but connected beneath the surface of our understanding into one, all-encompassing ontological structure. We are not likely to understand any of those projections very well until we better comprehend their universal base.

To shift the metaphor somewhat, we find ourselves at present much like the committee of blind men sent to investigate the strange creature called the elephant. The member who happened to touch the trunk was fully persuaded that he had encountered something of a serpentine character; the one who touched the tusk said, "No, this must be akin to the rhinoceros"; and the one who put his arms around one of the mighty legs said, "Why, this is not an animal at all — it is some kind of tree". A more contemporary and sophisticated endorsement of the same principle has been voiced by Mircea Eliade, the renowned historian of religion:

> Assuredly all the disciplines of the mind and all the sciences of man are equally precious. And their discoveries mutually so, but this solidarity does not mean confusion. What is important is to integrate the results of the diverse applications of the mind without confounding them. The surest method is still that of studying the phenomenon in its own frame

> of reference with freedom afterwards to integrate the results of this procedure in a wider perspective. — 1960: 13

Some of you may recall that this quotation opened the first section of our own book *Margins of Reality* (Jahn and Dunne 1987), in which we also developed the notion of converging experiential "vectors", extending from many scholarly domains to triangulate the enigma of consciousness. As a contribution to this volume, I would like to offer just one such perspective on the consciousness iceberg-elephant drawn from our Princeton Engineering Anomalies Research (PEAR) program. Even in this restricted context, however, I find myself invoking the vocabulary of the physicist, the tools of the engineer, the heart of the philosopher, and the soul of a mystic, to address this point. The particular item selected to honor Louisa Rhine — and, of course, her esteemed husband — is "The Complementarity of Consciousness".

The Physical Complementarity Principle

We are well accustomed in science, as in more common usage, to various "absolute" quantities that need only a single number to define them: the amount of water in this pitcher, the number of people in this room, or the length of this presentation. For other purposes, we use "polar" quantities that are bounded on their extremes by opposites of some sort, between which there extends a measurable range — hot and cold, high and low, hard and soft — where any gain in one property inevitably entails a compensating retreat from the other. Less frequently used but critically important in certain situations is another genre of paired quantities usually termed *conjugates* or *complements*. Each member of a conjugate pair represents some fundamental or "irreducible" property in its own right and is quite independent of, or "orthogonal" to, the other; but both are jointly needed to specify completely the state of the system or process under study.

The most common examples of such conjugate quantities in physics are the components of linear momentum and their corresponding distances, the components of angular momentum and their corresponding angles, and energy and time. Each of these pairs may be regarded as conceptual coordinates defining a two-dimensional space in which the process, system, or object may be mapped as a trajectory. For example, *fig*. 8.1a shows the vertical momentum and position trajectory of a stone thrown straight up and allowed to fall back down again. *Fig*. 8.1b displays a similar diagram of any harmonic process, such as a pendulum or an

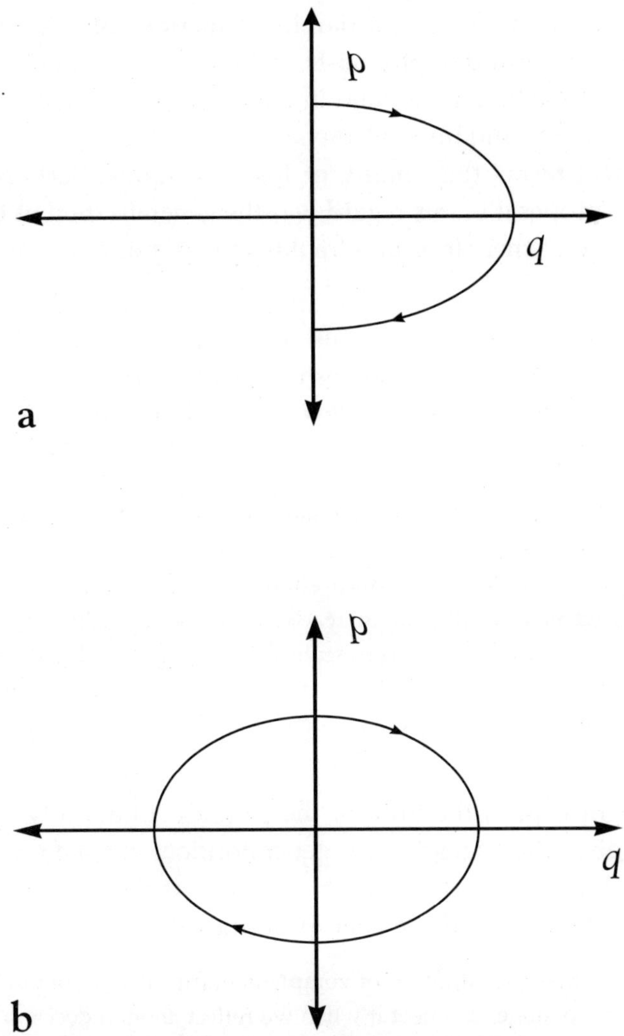

fig. 8.1: Conceptual coordinate representations of dynamic processes: *a* verticle projectile: p = momentum, q = height; *b* harmonic oscillator: p = momentum, q = position

oscillating spring, that continues to swing in some undamped periodic fashion. The mathematical integral of such closed trajectories is a useful quantity in theoretical physics. It is termed the *action integral*, and one of the earliest principles of quantum mechanics was that such integrals were quantized in units of Planck's constant.

But what, one may ask, has all this to do with consciousness? The clue comes from a rather unlikely source — from the physics community itself

— in fact, from one of the patriarchs of modern physics, Neils Bohr. Unlike many present-day physicists, Bohr was a true Renaissance man, well versed in the humanities and in the mystical traditions and given to interpretation of fundamental physical phenomena in much broader philosophical terms than many of his colleagues. Perhaps his most provocative proposal in this regard was the generalization of the physical concept of complementarity into frankly metaphysical dimensions. In his own words:

> We must indeed remember that the nature of our consciousness brings about a complementary relationship, in all domains of knowledge, between the analysis of a concept and its immediate application. . . . In associating the psychical and physical aspects of existence, we are concerned with a special relationship of complementarity which it is not possible thoroughly to understand by one-sided application either of physical or of psychological laws. . . . Only a renunciation in this respect will enable us to comprehend . . . that harmony which is experienced as free will, and analyzed in terms of causality. . . . The real problem is: How can that part of reality which begins with consciousness be combined with those parts that are treated in physics and chemistry? . . . Here we obviously have a genuine case of complementarity.
>
> — 1961: 20, 24, 115

As one might expect, the bulk of the physics community of that time rebelled against this metaphysical generalization, but Bohr attracted two important allies. One was Werner Heisenberg, author of the "uncertainty principle", who endorsed the concept in these terms:

> We realize that the situation of complementarity is not confined to the atomic world alone; we meet it when we reflect about a decision and the motives for our decision or when we have the choice between enjoying music and analyzing its structure. — 1958: 179

They were joined by another eminent colleague, Wolfgang Pauli, author of the "exclusion principle" and collaborator with Carl Jung in the latter's studies of synchronicity:

> On the one hand, the idea of complementarity in modern physics has demonstrated to us, in a new kind of synthesis, that the contradiction in the applications of old contrasting conceptions (such as particle and wave) is only apparent; on the other hand, the employability of old alchemical ideas in the psychology of Jung points to a deeper unity of psychical and physical occurrences. To us . . . the only acceptable point of view appears to be the one that recognizes *both* sides of reality — the

> quantitative and the qualitative, the physical and the psychical — as compatible with each other, and can embrace them simultaneously. . . . It would be most satisfactory of all if physics and psyche could be seen as complementary aspects of the same reality. — 1955: 208, 210

The scale of revision in the conceptual and operational perspective entailed by the Bohr–Heisenberg–Pauli points of view should not be undervalued. Classical philosophy, until that time dominated by Cartesian duality, was largely content with absolute and polar measures; it spoke of thesis and antithesis, of dialectic tension, of "self" and "not-self". Common conceptualization likewise tended to either–or divisions. Now, from a hard scientific sector, it was suddenly proposed that some of these sharp dichotomies could be replaced by more subtle and sophisticated complementarities in which arbitrary proportions of superficially disparate properties might be profitably combined to deal with given situations. And indeed, considerable philosophical elegance, as well as pragmatic benefit, can thereby be obtained, not least of all in the bemusing domains of consciousness anomalies that we address in our research.

Consciousness Complementarity

To develop the theme of consciousness complementarity, I shall extend Bohr's concept to propose that a great many attitudes of consciousness can be complementary to one another in much the same sense as just discussed. Grouped in appropriate pairs, such attitudes entail the same orthogonal irreducibility, yet can provide the same conceptual reinforcement as the conjugate physical quantities do, and can similarly serve to define consciousness operational spaces. With no claim to completeness, an introductory list of such "consciousness conjugates" might include:

- observation–participation
- analysis–synthesis
- pragmaticism–aestheticism
- structure–function
- goal–process
- logic–intuition
- sincerity–humor
- left brain–right brain
- objectivity–subjectivity
- assertion–reception
- doing–being

Note that in each case a somewhat more tangible or definable characteristic is teamed with a more holistic, elusive, or ephemeral one but that the two are not necessarily competitive; rather, they can be combined in essentially arbitrary proportions as befits the situation. Participation in an activity need not preclude its observation, or vice versa. The detailed, logical, structural dissection we call analysis need not be antithetical to the process of combination or synthesis; each can profitably complement the other in many creative tasks. Although the pragmatic and aesthetic aspects of an occupation are usually distinguishable, they need not stand in contradiction; in fact, some of the most satisfying creations are those in which the pragmatics and the aesthetics fully complement one another, as in a modern aircraft, a beautiful bridge, a piece of furniture, or a well-designed college curriculum, and so on down the list. You might try extending this array of consciousness conjugates with a few pairs drawn from your own personal experience. And let us not neglect the examples that Bohr, Heisenberg, and Pauli originally offered: causality–free will; decision–motive; quantitative–qualitative; physics–psyche.

The Consciousness Uncertainty Principle

Before getting too carried away by this concept of consciousness complementarity, we ought to remember that there is another closely related quantum principle that may somewhat complicate the metaphor. It is, of course, Heisenberg's own "uncertainty principle" that constrains the precision of simultaneous specification of any two physical complements. Specifically, the product of the uncertainties of specification of two conjugate quantities cannot be much less than the value of Planck's constant, $h = 6.63 \times 10^{-27}$ erg sec. If one insists on greater accuracy in determining one property, a corresponding amount of precision must be surrendered in the other. *Fig.* 8.2 attempts to illustrate the situation, again in a two-dimensional space defined by the conjugate coordinates p and q. Whereas the complementarity principle allows us to combine p and q in arbitrary proportions, so that any point in the plane is accessible in the gross sense, the uncertainty principle limits the precision with which that point can be localized to a microscopic rectangle of sides Δp and Δq, where $\Delta p \; \Delta q \gg h/2$ p. Thus we can define the state within a small square ($\Delta p = \Delta q$), a tall rectangle ($\Delta p > \Delta q$), a flat rectangle ($\Delta p < \Delta q$), or even by a horizontal line ($\Delta p = 0$, $\Delta q = \infty$) or a vertical line ($\Delta p = \infty$, $\Delta q = 0$), depending on our uncertainty tradeoff, but a precise point ($\Delta p = 0$, $\Delta q = 0$) is not an option.

We now must ask whether a similar uncertainty principle may also pertain to the more metaphysical consciousness conjugates that I just discussed. That is, does excessive circumscription of one of a pair of consciousness complements inevitably blur the definition of the other? The list I compounded indeed seems to support that suspicion: Excessively detailed attention to any of the analytical–structural–objective pair members inevitably obscures appreciation of the corresponding aesthetic–holistic–subjective complement; conversely, preoccupation with the "softer" aspects can compromise technical integrity or precision. In fact, the consciousness uncertainty principle may define the optimum balance between the conjugates — that configuration where the relative degree of attention to each aspect yields the best possible product. Think, for example, of the consummate actor, athlete, or artist who combines technical mastery of his tools with subjective immersion in his performance, without allowing either to distort the other. Or reflect on our propensity to balance disciplined techniques for performing mundane tasks with some degree of satisfaction or joy in the immersion in them. The familiar adage "all in

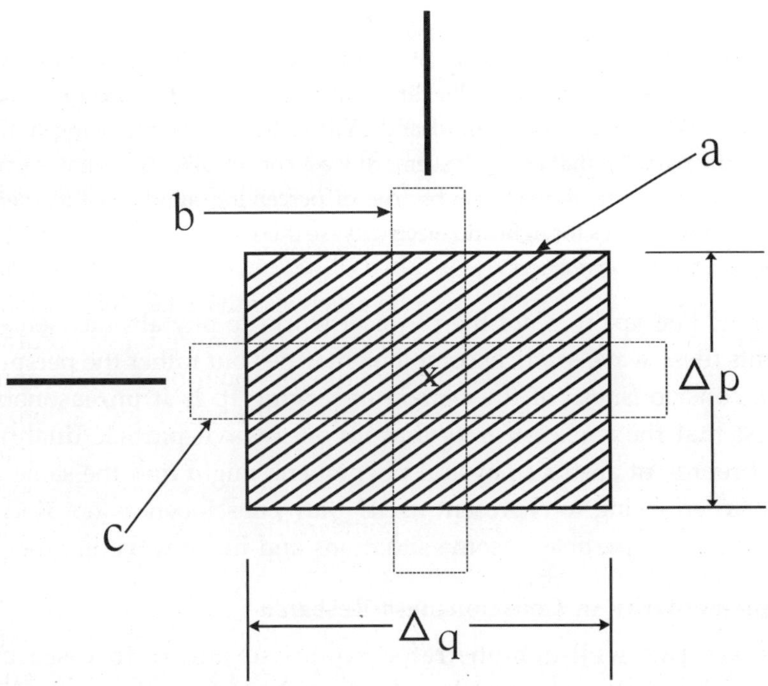

fig. 8.2: Uncertainty of specification of complementary coordinates: a $\Delta p = \Delta q$; b $\Delta p > \Delta q$; c $\Delta p < \Delta q$; d $\Delta p = 0$, $\Delta q = \infty$; e $\Delta p = \infty$, $\Delta q = 0$

moderation" may be just another expression of this consciousness uncertainty principle — a caution not to obscure any of life's dimensions by excessive attention to its complement.

The Wave–Particle Complementarity

From his beginnings, man has clearly possessed the capacity to think in both particulate and wavelike terms: allusions to sharply localized objects and to broadly diffuse undulatory effects share prominence in the art, language, and science of all cultures and all ages. Yet, over much of the history of physical science, philosophical quarrels have persisted over whether such phenomena as light, sound, and atomic-scale processes are basically more particulate or more wavelike in character. To this day, experiments continue to be performed to demonstrate that either modality can be convincingly demonstrated under appropriate circumstances of observation. Note that Pauli alluded to this dilemma in his quotation, in essence suggesting that waves and particles bear all the requisites of complementary representations of reality and thus may be epistemologically irreducible. James Jeans drove this issue one layer deeper by suggesting

> There is no longer a dualism of mind and matter, but of waves and particles; these seem to be the direct, although almost unrecognizable, descendants of the older mind and matter, the waves replacing mind and the particles matter. . . . It seems at least conceivable that what is true of perceived objects may also be true of perceiving minds; just as there are wave-pictures for light and electricity, so there may be a corresponding picture for consciousness. — 1943: 204

Why not? Perhaps it is not the physical world in any abstract sense that presents these wave–particle complementarities but rather the perspective of the consciousness of the person observing it. Is it unreasonable to suggest that the consciousness that invokes wave–particle dualities to help it represent abstract physical phenomena might find the same tactic useful when trying to represent itself? May consciousness not find *itself* behaving like a particle in some situations and like a wave in others?

Complementarity in Consciousness Research

There are two well-demonstrated routes to failure in research on consciousness phenomena: sloppy research and sterile research. The former, which provides ample and legitimate targets for our critical and skeptical colleagues, is characterized by weakness of protocol, equipment, analysis, or deduction that precludes credible advances in data accumulation and comprehension and clearly must be eschewed. In the latter category, however, there also lies a substantial body of failed research that has been pursued with such slavish rigor that the effects under study have been totally anesthetized. The simplest illustration of this mode of failure might be posed with reference to the less controversial, yet closely related, processes of human creativity. If one were to undertake scientific study of such processes, one would clearly need to respect the role of environment. For example, one would hardly attempt to encumber a great composer with EEC electrodes, place him under bright lights, surround him with carping critics, and then ask him to compose a symphony. Nor would one attempt to solve a difficult mathematical problem in a steel foundry or to provide emotional counseling in a hardware store. In each case, the aesthetic ambience and subjective comfort are environmental factors critical to the emergence of the desired effects.

Just so with consciousness research: To succeed, it must balance the sophistication of equipment and rigor of control and analysis with the comfort of protocol, the ambience of the laboratory, and the attitudes of the staff in a complementarity that allow the phenomena to bloom naturally while still presenting themselves for verification and analysis. Failure of this balance in either direction will inevitably invalidate, or suffocate, the results.

Masculine–Feminine Complementarity

Perhaps the most subtle and least understood example of consciousness complementarity is that between those primordial characteristics of human behavior, expression, and values we inadequately catalogue as "masculine" and "feminine". When posed in polar opposition, whether within a single personality or in the context of the ubiquitous interactions between the male and female sexes, the failures of this interface are legion, legendary, and immensely destructive, both personally and socially. Yet, when deployed in constructive complementarity, the masculine–feminine integration within the individual can enable the highest creativity and personal satisfaction. In the male–female partnership, they can generate some of the highest accomplishments, profoundest insights, and most beautiful resonances of human existence. In this form, it is probably the species' most powerful resource for spiritual and physical survival and evolution.

It seems evident that an abundant amount of this positive masculine–feminine complementarity graced the professional work, as well as the private lives, of Louisa Rhine and J.B. Rhine and paved many paths of understanding they were able to blaze for us. Certainly this form of complementarity has also enhanced our own research and opened insights and visions that more monotonic perspectives would have missed. In Chapter 11, Brenda Dunne presents some empirical results from our laboratory that indicate that this complementarity is far more than a hypothetical factor. To the contrary, it has assumed a significant role in both our experimental program and its associated theoretical model. Techniques for representation of the masculine–feminine complementarity in terms of more generalized *yang–yin*, assertive–receptive, or active–passive qualities metaphorically associated with the quantum mechanical spin property of interacting physical systems have been developed and applied to our experimental designs (see Jahn and Dunne 1984a, b, 1986). In this broader format, active–passive features may also be attributed to the experimental devices or physical processes used in the laboratory so that the proper pairing of these aspects of the operator's attitude or style with the perceived characteristics of the experiment becomes an important factor in the establishment of the resonant operator–machine bonds that seem to enable the anomalous results.

The Complementarity of Science and Spirit

The powerful philosophical extension of the principle of complementarity into the domain of human consciousness first proposed by Bohr propagates its roots even more deeply into the metaphysical foundations of modern science than even he may have imagined. In the ultimate sense of the terms, science in its neoclassical format and mysticism in its loftiest interpretation are themselves two complementary ethics, fundamentally united by the yearning of human consciousness for understanding of its relationship to the cosmos and for participation in the creation of reality, yet sharply distinguished by the tactical approaches used in pursuing these goals. Thus, science, launching itself from the primordial distinction of self from not-self implicit in its Aristotelian and Judeo–Christian heritage, uses the ability of consciousness to distinguish, to isolate, and to represent elements of reality by objective observation and dispassionate logic. Mysticism, in contrast, invokes consciousness strategies of association and assimilation to achieve a unity of self and not-self in its search for subjective identification with the mechanics of creation. Failure to recognize the essential complementarity between these objective and subjective capacities of consciousness will inevitably frustrate the research that attempts to comprehend them. Indeed, this failure lies at the very heart of the philosophical impasse that is confounding our contemporary human condition. Albert Einstein stated the problem very succinctly several decades ago: "Science without religion is lame. Religion without science is blind" (1956: 26). "The cosmic religious experience is the strongest and noblest mainstream of scientific research" (quoted in Barnett 1975: 108).

But Einstein did not venture to propose a mechanics for integration of these two superficially contradictory modalities. Indeed, such resolution can be obtained only through the very concept that he long rejected — the concept of complementarity. In the interplay of intellect and spirit, we are dealing with the ultimate conjugate perspectives whereby consciousness triangulates its experience. The issue is whether these will be deployed in mutually encumbering contradiction or in mutually fulfilling complementarity. The desirability of the latter, of course, has long been recognized and propounded in various abstract contexts, but it has never been satisfactorily formulated in practical terms. Clearly, we do not have an explicit formula, even now. But we can now rigorously demonstrate, on the laboratory bench and to some extent in our corresponding models, that human will, volition, desire, attention — call it what you wish — deployed in self-surrendering resonance with even a simple physical system or process, can significantly affect its behavior and that the same deployment of human will in resonance with another human consciousness can condition the mutual reality to a significant extent.

The challenge ahead of us is to expand and to extend such databases and such models into many other scholarly sectors, whence to weave a new fabric of complementary science that respects and uses subjective qualities as much as objective quantities, aesthetic sensitivities as much as analytic techniques, and mystical insights as much as tangible experiences. Clearly we face monumental obstacles of conceptualization, vocabulary, and measurability on our road to such a holistic science. But we should be sustained in this effort by the recognition that science of any era has always been no more than a particularly disciplined form of human activity; scientific vocabulary has always been only a subset of human linguistics; scientific observation and scientific conceptualization have always drawn by metaphor from broader and less tangible human experience; and scientific logic has always been just a special form of basic human reasoning. It is not unfounded, therefore, to hope that the primordial consciousness that has so brilliantly conceived and refined its science of the objective and has at the same time so fully experienced and celebrated the mystical dimensions of its life, can now finally integrate these complementary perspectives into a superscience of the whole, wherein consciousness will stand as full partner with its cosmos in the establishment of reality.

9

Mind Embodied

Computer-generated Virtual Reality as a New, Dualistic–Interactive Model for Transpersonal Psychology

Charles T. Tart

I have always appreciated Louisa Rhine professionally for constantly reminding us that psi is not an esoteric phenomenon, an "anomaly", a statistical bias that happens only in the laboratory: It is something that happens to and affects real people in real life. Indeed, as fascinated as I can become with laboratory effects, as a researcher of psi I am always asking myself, "Does this illuminate anything in actual life or is this too specialized a byway?"

Models of the Mind

My focus here is that our models of the mind are frequently based on the most sophisticated technology of the day. If you look at Freud's model, for instance, you can see strong parallels to hydraulic systems and steam engines. The id builds up pressure from the instincts: If you do not bleed off some of that steam pressure (needs, desires for gratification), there is a danger of the boiler (you) blowing up, and so we need, for example, the safety valve of hallucinatory gratification in dreams to keep the instinctual pressure down. Steam was a sophisticated technology for Freud's day.

Along came the telephone system, with individual telephones and central operators, and the telephone switchboard became the great analogy for mind and brain. Now we are using digital computers as models of the mind, which has been stimulating in some ways, but somehow not too human. I emphasize models of the mind, not formal theories. One does not require as much from a model as one does from a theory. A theory needs to be testable and exact, but a model is a convenient way of both organizing what you already know and of stimulating you to think of new possibilities. This stimulation function of models is their most important characteristic.

Transpersonal Psychology Versus Materialistic Monism

I write from the broad context of the psychology of consciousness, particularly from the perspective of transpersonal psychology, and with special reference to one of my continuing loves, parapsychology. Transpersonal psychology is about dualism, *trans* meaning beyond, beyond the personal. Conventionally, in today's dominant materialistic approach, the personal is very much embedded in the physical body. We implicitly assume that "I" am inside this bag of skin, "I" am thus clearly bounded, and the other people and the world are "out there" in a real and ultimate sense. Transpersonal psychology is the study of experiences that seem to transcend that assumption of limited embodiment. When someone has a mystical experience of unity with the whole cosmos, for instance, or a Near-Death Experience (NDE), the experience of leaving the physical body and meeting some non-physical being, these are transpersonal experiences. Thus the dualism, a "something" mind, in addition to the physical body and brain.

It is possible to investigate transpersonal experiences from a materialistic point of view, a physicalistic–monistic view that says everything is a result of the electrochemical processes in the brain. If you take that view, transpersonal psychology becomes that study of the *illusions* people have that divorce them from an accurate perception of the world, illusions probably motivated by the lack of courage to face the ultimate annihilation of death and the absence of objective meaning in the world.

I do not find this a very interesting position myself. I use the word *interesting* in the sense that physicists use it to describe a model or a theory that generates other interesting, intellectually stimulating theories. If the physicalistic theory is true, if the transpersonal equals nothing but electrochemical changes in the brain and we are just going to die after leading meaningless lives in an inherently meaningless cosmos, it is not much intellectual fun or challenge.

Also, this materialistic approach to transpersonal psychology is not very satisfying to vital human needs, because I think we have a *need for meaning* in life. The picture of the universe just happening by blind chance and fixed physical laws is depressing. The idea that we do not survive death in any kind of form, that it is an accident that we are here, that there is no objective meaning while we are here, and that it is soon all over for each of us, is not terribly satisfying to human needs. It is all right with me if someone wants to study transpersonal psychology from a materialistic perspective, but it is still not much fun.

The Importance of Psi

More important, because it leaves out the existence of *psi*, I do not find this kind of physicalistic monism scientifically useful. Psi phenomena (basically telepathy, clairvoyance, precognition, and psychokinesis, to name only the four that are well established) are especially important because these are the hard scientific data we have that the human mind sometimes does things that do not fit into a nice, closed physical system of the sort we scientifically know today (or into any straightforward extensions of it). Psi phenomena imply that if someone, for example, experiences a feeling of unity with the universe, and we know that telepathy and clairvoyance exist, maybe that feeling of unity is not just a *subjective* experience but is also pointing toward some kind of reality.

Of course, we have to separate the sense from the nonsense about psi, but it is important to recognize that from the viewpoint of being adequately scientific and taking all our data into account, transpersonal psychology is probably not simply concerned with delusions about transcending the personal: Although some delusion is certainly mixed in at this stage of the game, transpersonal psychology is about some kind of reality that goes beyond our everyday selves and our physicalistic basis.

My primary aim in this chapter is to share a new model I am working on that I think will soon become one of the outstanding models for the mind as the technology becomes widely known. It is a model that comes from the brand new technology of *Computer-Generated Virtual Reality* (CGVR). This CGVR model has, to use philosopher Stephen Braude's wonderful word, predictafecundity. I am here going to introduce the model; there is no way in this limited space that I can go over it thoroughly, but I think I can say enough to provide food for thought. I primarily introduce the CGVR approach as a model, but I am working to tighten it up as a more formal theory about the nature of consciousness.

How Do You Know that You are Here?

Think seriously about this question for a moment. How do you know you are here, in this room, right now?

You probably do not really think much about how you know you are here right now, because it is *obvious* you are here. You look around, and here is here. You can see the room and anything around you, and you can look down and see your physical body. These are our usual perceptual criteria for deciding where we are. Further, you can interact with the environment. You can push on a table top and find the table top hard, as table tops usually are.

Consider a variant of the question: If you were to hold your hand out in front of you, how would you know that what you saw is *your* hand? After all, someone could have reached over from behind you and held out her hand, and it could look like yours.

I think most of you would automatically do two kinds of things to decide if it is your hand. One, you look at it, and looking along it and its arm you see that it is attached to (what you automatically assume is) *your* body. Second, you can turn your hand over or make a fist; this is your hand for all practical purposes because *it does what you want it to do*. It is the same phenomenon that makes the car you drive *your* car when you are driving it. Your body image, your sense of your self, unconsciously expands to fill the area within all four fenders when you drive.

This feeling of something solid being connected to you and immediately carrying out your will is the experience of *mind embodied*.

Mind Embodied and the Ecological Self

Philosophically, I am generally a dualist. I think pure mind is something fundamentally different from the nature of body and other physical things. What we ordinarily experience when we introspect, though, is not mind by itself, "pure mind", or body by itself, but *Mind Embodied* (ME). We experience ME both in a sensory way and by way of interacting with the physical environment around it. Ulrich Neisser (1988) has called an important aspect of this kind of functioning the *ecological self*. The ecological self is a part of the mind and brain — who knows exactly how much of each? — that is a map maker. Instant by instant, completely automatically, it is creating a map of the space, action, and time around the reference point of *you* (ME) to show you where you are in that system.

If I were to suddenly throw a rock into this audience, some of you would duck. Most of you would not even flinch in the slightest, though, because your ecological self is constantly making maps, locating moving objects on that map, plotting their trajectories, projecting the trajectories forward in time through the point where it has mapped you (ME) as being, and computing either "No, that rock is not going to hit me, no problem", or, "Yes, that is coming toward me, I had better get out of the way!"

If your ecological self does not work well, you die.

This ecological self, this aspect of mind embodied, is a major part of what we think of as our self. It is not the whole part; there are other important psychological aspects, which we do not have space to discuss here. And yet our experience of where our basic self is can change drastically at times.

Alterations of Perceived Embodiment: The OBE

Something most people in this group are familiar with, I'm sure, is the Out-of-the-Body-experience (OBE). I have always defined OBE as an experience in which you find yourself someplace other than where you know your physical body is, and, most important, at a time when your consciousness seems quite clear (Tart 1967, 1968, 1974a, b, 1976). It is not something during which you can say immediately, "Oh, I'm dreaming" or "I'm just imagining this". It seems quite perceptually real, and your consciousness is clear. It is obvious that you are located somewhere else than where your physical body is.

Here is an example from my unpublished collection of an OBE with many features common to these experiences. It took place in the summer of 1957, before the vast majority of the public had ever heard of OBEs or NDEs. The reporter, whom I call Mrs. K., forty years old at the time of OBE, specifically indicated that she personally had no previous knowledge of OBEs when it occurred.

> My experience happened in the summer about ten years ago. While it was important to me it never occurred to me to write it down. I am, however, sure of what happened, as I thought at the time that I would never forget it and would not rationalize later as one might be prone to do, saying I must have fallen asleep or some such thing.
>
> It was a hot day and the air conditioner was on. After taking a shower I stretched out on my bed to cool off before dressing to leave the house. I did not fall asleep. I was not in the habit of taking naps in the afternoon and was very alert but thinking of nothing in particular that I could recall later. One moment I was on the bed, the next I was standing away from the foot of the bed. The mirror of the dressing table was in my line of

> vision and I saw myself. The reflection looked like me, yet it did not. Later when I saw an illustrated copy of one of the books by Gibran, with figures he was supposed to have seen in a vision, I believed that he may have, remembering myself and sensing that this was the true form. At the time I thought, "This is why people believe in fairies and elves." It was as if I looked like myself but that I had been refined and my features made more regular. . . .
>
> I was aware of my body on the bed but not interested in it. I had a great feeling of elation (I felt as if I were walking on air for three days following the experience) at the significance of what had happened. I was not a "body" such as was on the bed; it was something I wore, in the same way that one wears clothes. I did not want to go back to my body and felt a sense of heaviness in relation to it, but I seemed to have no control over whether I did or didn't.
>
> When I went back into my body (the experience lasted a very short time) I was still a bit shocked but the feeling of elation stayed with me. I made up my mind I would never forget the experience and went over and over it in my mind for the next few days. Perhaps my entire attitude toward life has been different because of it, and it never made much difference whether anyone else believed it or not because I knew.
>
> I have only met one person who was able to verify such an experience. Her name is Mrs. Q. [name deleted to protect privacy]. When she was so ill she was not expected to live, she thought she had left her body and was looking down at the house (of course, much more details to it) and saw a garden hose on the roof. It was a flat-topped house they had just bought so that when she came to herself she knew that if there was such a hose up on the roof that she then had actually seen it. Not telling her husband why, she asked him to go up, and there was a hose to his surprise (a new one the last owners had forgotten).

Several features of this case are important. First, note that the experience was definitely *trans*-personal, outside of Mrs. K's ordinary, embodied identity. Second, note the profound effect it had on her view of life. A typical statement after an OBE is on the order of "I do not *believe* that I will survive bodily death, I *know* I will". Third, note her reference to Mrs. Q's experience, which has a feature common to many OBEs, namely an ostensible factual validation of the perceptions at the OBE location, suggesting it is quite "real" by ordinary criteria of what is real.

OBE was a very exotic phenomenon when I first began investigating it some thirty years ago. Now, of course, it is well known even to the general public, especially as a part of NDE. I have a cartoon from a popular magazine in my files, for example, that shows two doctors looking over a patient on the operating table, saying, "We haven't got all day, Buddy, make up your mind. Are you going to come back into your body or leave?"

People have always had such drastic temporary changes in the feeling of where they are located, like OBEs. Is this just the ecological self-changing its functioning in a hallucinatory way, or is it a more drastic change in the sense that we *actually* go out of the body? That we are trans the personal in reality, not just in subjective space? We will let that question hang for a while.

New Technologies for Modeling the Mind

Telepresence

Now we have two new and dramatic developments relating to where we feel located in recent history. First, we now have and are using technology to unintentionally produce "retrieved" OBEs as part of NDEs, namely, medical resuscitation technology. People are coming back after being exceptionally close to death in enormously greater numbers than has ever happened in previous history. I shall not deal with that development now, fascinating though it is. Second, we have developed technological means to produce very realistic *simulations* of OBE. I am going to give you two kinds of examples of the latter technology. One comes from the rapidly developing field of *telepresence*. Telepresence is needed when you have to do work in places where it is too dangerous to go in your body, so you send a robot there. The robot has twin TV cameras for stereo vision, and it can manipulate objects in the remote environment. The second technology is CGVR.

Here is a quotation from a book by Howard Rheingold on virtual reality (Rheingold 1991), the best book to get if you want to find out about CGVR, describing his experience with telepresence.

> The robot itself looked like the bottom half of a large electric light pole or a fire hydrant: its body is a red metal cylinder about 9 inches in diameter. The upper torso began to get anthropomorphic, with one arm, a two finger gripper where the hand ought to be, a neck that is cantilevered the proper distance behind and below the visual sensors and which turns the same directions a human neck turns, and twin video cameras mounted where eyes ought to be. It looks like a machine. The humanoid resemblance doesn't come from the hardware, but in the way the thing moves when a human is operating it. It was a strange sensation for me,

because I was very aware that I was observing a piece of hardware. The weird thing about the lubricated stainless steel joints, hydraulic tubes, wire bundles was how it moved in a way that I am accustomed to seeing humans move and I am not accustomed to seeing machines move.

The human operator sits in a control station that is a little scary to observe and a little scarier to operate. I sat in something that looked uncomfortably close to a no-frills dentist's chair. The display is head-mounted, but it is a "sword of Damocles" display that uses a mechanical device — *a goniometer* — to track head movements, rather than a magnetic sensor like the Polhemus. Along with the mechanical linkages, there is a long arm with a counterweight attached to the Head-Mounted Display (HMD). HMD is clunky and clamped onto my head fairly tightly; the eyepiece was secured with a chin strap. When I was seated and helmeted, I stuck out my right hand and the arm-hand control was locked around my limbs in a manner uncomfortably reminiscent of handcuffs. At that moment, I was blind to the world and free to move my neck and arm but nothing else. When I moved my hand, arm, or fingers, the movements were reproduced almost simultaneously by the robot across the room. I wasn't able to transmit motion in every dimension I am accustomed to use: the arm has three degrees of freedom, the neck has seven degrees of freedom. But the constraints didn't carry as much weight with my awareness as the possibilities. Just being able to pick up a wand with my robot body and thread it through a hoop 12 ft away and feel as if I did it myself, was far more impressive than the fact that I couldn't dropkick the wand through the hoop.

When the apparatus was switched on, I began to look through the eyes of the robot. The world looked like the world would look if I was located 12 ft to the left of my body, where the robot was located. I reached out my arm, craned my neck, opened my gripper, and picked up a small rod. It took me about five seconds to figure out how to poke the rod through 2-inch diameter hoops that were set around me at various intervals. It took about 10 seconds to be completely comfortable with my control of the robot. . . . "How easy it is for a well-tuned human to adapt to a machine", I wrote in my notebook as soon as they unstrapped me.

The strangest moment was when Dr. Tachi told me to look to my right. There was a guy in a dark blue suit and light blue painted shoes reclining in a dentist's chair. He was looking to his right, so I could see the bald spot on the back of his head. He looked like me, and abstractly I understood that he was me, but I know who me is, and me is *here*. He, on the other hand, was *there*. It doesn't take a high degree of sensory verisimilitude to create a sense of remote presence. . . . It was an out of the body experience, no doubt about it. — pp. 262-64

With this example we see an important principle in action. The ecological self-created you and the spot where your sensory impressions converge. Only-the sense of vision is used: How much more "realistic" would the experience of telepresence be if other senses were added?

Virtual Reality

The second model is computer-generated virtual reality (CGVR). The word *virtual* is quite a wonderful word. The dictionary definition says *virtual* means being in essence or effect but *not in fact*; not actual, but equivalent in so far as effect is concerned. Advertisers love the way they can stretch the word: "Buy our gizmo, it is virtually unbreakable!" It actually breaks very easily, but they did not say unbreakability was really the case, just virtually the case.

The most general definition of any virtual reality that I have been proposing and working with is this:

> *Virtual reality (VR) is an embracing world of experience, a world that seems real to the experiencer at the time he or she is in it.* That is, the experiencer psychologically identifies with it as a valid expression of self and world. It is virtual in the sense that, from a more comprehensive and enlightened point of view, it is not what it seems to be in important ways, but something else entirely.

This embracing virtual world is usually sensory in nature, especially if we are talking about CGVR. Every night when we are having an ordinary (non-lucid) dream, however, we are also in a virtual reality. Dream VR is more than sensory, for it also involves internal changes in thought and emotional processes, not just those driven by the apparent sensory reality of the dream. It is an Altered State of Consciousness (ASC). You might dream of driving your car under dangerous conditions, for example, and become frightened and panic, which is ordinary sensorily driven change; but if you examine your dreams more closely you see many changes in cognitive and emotional style that are inherently different from the functioning of ordinary waking consciousness.

Dreams are a virtual reality that almost always seems real at the time. They are automatically and completely identified with (we will ignore lucid dreams in our current discussion) but are generated by unconscious processes in our mind. Later on, in retrospect, we realize our dream world and our dream self were not at all what they seemed to be. You were not really driving a car; you were lying in bed.

Any virtual reality, including CGVR, becomes real mainly because of the operation of the ecological self and by a psychological process of identification, a process so automated that we seldom notice its operation (see Tart 1986, 1991). Once your sensory input is controlled through a computer in CGVR, the ecological self takes over and maps you as being "there", in the virtual world created by the computer. It is the same as in Rheingold's telepresence experience with the robot: he was *obviously* located where he was seeing from.

Hardware for Computer-generated Virtual Reality

Let me briefly mention the hardware that has been developed for producing CGVR. The first (and usually primary) task of the computer is to control the visual field. The most common type of visual presentation device is a Head-Mounted Display (HMD). Basically, a HMD is a way of taking two tiny color TV sets and putting one over each eye, close enough to the eye and lensed appropriately so that it covers most or all of the visual field. Seeing in a HMD is not like watching ordinary television, which occupies only about four degrees of your visual field although your visual field is well over a hundred degrees wide. With appropriate slight changes in the computer-controlled display of HMD, you get stereoscopic vision; the image on the television sets creates depth perception, just as in ordinary visual perception of the world.

A position sensor mounted on top of HMD measures the position of the wearer's head and feeds that information to the computer. Thus, the computer knows whether you have turned your head to look to the left, or craned your head to look up or look down, or moved your whole head forward, or moved back, up or down, side to side, and so on. The computer controlling the images produced in HMD can thus make them match exactly where you have just turned your head to in the virtual environment where you find yourself. Eye-tracking technology is being developed to make this correlation between where you look and what you see even finer.

You can also include stereo headphones in your HMD and, knowing the wearer's head position, have the controlling computer create sounds that change appropriately with head position. A few months ago I tried out a completely audio virtual environment of this sort developed by Scott Foster of Crystal River Engineering. I put on a pair of earphones, closed my eyes, and found I was obviously in a large room with a band playing at one end. If I walked forward the band got louder; if I got close to a wall, the quality of the sound changed because of the reflections off the wall. The demonstrator said, "Do you want to be in a smaller room?" I said, "Sure", and he altered program parameters in a moment so I obviously was now in a much smaller room.

Then the strangest thing happened. I was moving sideways in the room (in my physical body in ordinary space), when I reported, "One side of your headphones has gone bad, there's no sound from it". Scott said, "No, there's no problem with the headphone: your head is now halfway through the wall, so one ear is out of the room. Naturally you can't hear the band!"

Although vision is our primary spatial sense, audition contributes a great deal to the operation of the ecological self, so adding stereo sound to HMD greatly increases the realism. Let me add, though, that you can get completely identified with a CGVR that is only visual.

There is also the interactive aspect of CGVR. We do not just sense the world; we act with it. To create interaction in CGVR, at a minimum you wear a special glove on one hand that transmits data to the controlling computer. Such a glove typically has fiber-optic devices that measure what each finger and the thumb are doing. It measures whether you are pointing, making a fist, or opening your hand wide, for examples. There is also a spatial position sensor on the back of the glove, just like the one on HMD, that lets the computer know you have moved your hand forward, for instance, or have turned it over. This means that in CGVR the controlling computer visually displays a virtual hand that moves in synchrony with your physical hand. Recall our earlier question about how you know the hand in front of you is yours: You see it, and it responds immediately to your will, therefore it is you.

What do you see in virtual reality? I cannot adequately convey that here because you must be *in* CGVR to really see CGVR, since you are seeing with stereoscopic vision and the ecological self puts you in that virtual world. A composite video picture from HMD displayed monoscopically on an external TV monitor loses vital richness.

Basically you can see any visually imaginable world in CGVR that someone has the ingenuity to program. The virtual world may be a fairly good replica of ordinary physical reality (important in finding commercial applications for CGVR at this time) or a quite non-ordinary reality.

For instance, you might see a basic office: walls, doors, perhaps windows, carpet, a chair, a desk, and some shelves, although it can be much more complex than that. But remember that "see" is an inadequate verb here, for you quickly experience yourself as located inside this room. As you move around in this virtual room, by moving your actual physical body, turning your head, and so on, your view adjusts accordingly, just as it does when you move around in the real world.

I have said that your hand is represented by a visible, virtual hand, but given the way the technology is developing, eventually it will be possible to have as much of your body represented in CGVR as you like. A body suit is being developed by Jaron Lanier's company, VPL, one of the pioneer developers of CGVR. It looks somewhat like a scuba-diving outfit. It has sensors that tell the computer what each hand is doing, what each arm is doing, and what each foot and leg is doing so that you can represent all of a person's major body movements as a virtual body that, again, responds to your will. If you kick your leg, you see your virtual leg kick in the same way.

Other senses are coming to CGVR soon. Researchers are already working on touch, so that if in virtual reality you look at a table and see a piece of sandpaper there, it will feel rough when you touch it, whereas a piece of ordinary paper will feel smooth. Some touch feedback devices became commercially available in early 1992.

The involvement in CGVR readily becomes so intense that if, say, there is a sudden movement of the sort that would make you dizzy in ordinary life, you can become nauseated. You may need to take the helmet off in order to pull yourself out of that virtual reality. A general rule, that probably has few exceptions, is:

> What the ecological self creates, the rest of the body automatically believes.

Developments in CGVR occur very rapidly. For those who want to learn about the field, I recommend Rheingold's book, already mentioned (Rheingold 1991), as well as Benedikt (1991); Helsel and Roth (1991); and Krueger (1991). Several other books are almost ready for publication. To keep up with ongoing developments in the field, reading a newsletter such as *Cyber-Edge Journal* (928 Greenhill Road, Mill Valley, California 94941) is helpful, as is participating in the computer conference on VR held on the Well (Sausalito, California).

Computer-generated Versus Biopsycho VR

What intrigues me as a psychologist is that CGVR offers us a sophisticated model for both ordinary and transpersonal psychology to explain ordinary (and non-ordinary) consciousness. Here we come to the Mind-Embodied (ME!) concept central to this chapter. (I explain the use of "!" after ME later.)

I now want to distinguish more sharply two classes of virtual reality. CGVR, occurs when you put on an HMD and glove(s) or a body suit, and a computer is controlling the visual (and perhaps other sensory modality) impressions you receive. The second class of virtual reality is what I have termed *Biological–Psychological Virtual Reality* (BPVR), or *biopsycho VR* for easier pronunciation.

My studies of consciousness over the last three decades have convinced me that, right now, *each one of us is living in a virtual reality*. What we experience as our self (both physical and mental) and as the "real" world around us is not a simple, straightforward perception of what is actually here at this moment, but a semi-arbitrary *construction*, created by relatively automatized brain (and probably mind) processes. Thus, the ordinary world and ordinary mind we assume we straightforwardly perceive is virtual in the sense that important facts about reality may be left out, others badly distorted, and imaginary creations mistaken for reality. That is, the everyday world and everyday self *seem* real, but they are not necessarily what they seem to be.

Let me expand on the idea of BPVR. *Bio* is used in that there is a lot of biology–physiology involved: The particular way the nervous system and the senses are constructed affect and control many particular aspects of the constructed reality, BPVR we live in. *Psycho* is used in the sense that psychological processes further control how we experience, reconstruct the basic pattern of neurological impulses created by our senses, brain, and nervous system. I refer to psychological processes like conditioning, belief biases, habits, sensory biases of one sort or another, emotional desires, aversions, and conceptual concepts. These processes often control whether we perceive something at all in the first place and then give us biased (edited and reconstructed in accordance with our needs and habits) representations of what we actually see.

I focus here on BPVR as a model for transpersonal psychology, although it has many uses for mainstream psychology in general.

Mind Embodied As Biopsycho Virtual Reality

Fig. 9.1 sketches my current dualistic understanding of the mind–body relationship from a transpersonal point of view. To briefly elaborate, above (it's hard to avoid symbolism of placement here) the dashed line, which represents the mind–matter interface, we have the transpersonal realm, the realm of pure mind. This realm is represented as unbounded, for it is beyond full comprehension by our ordinary self, by ME! The part cannot comprehend the whole — at least not on its own (part) terms. Recognizing this limitation (which we should always attempt to overcome, as long as it does not lead us into distorting our understanding), we could loosely define the transpersonal as an area that has something to do with what people call "mystical" and cosmic experiences, with some Altered State of Consciousness (ASCs), and so forth.

Formal dualistic theories of mind and body usually get fuzzy on the issue of how mind and matter interact if they are indeed two quite different kinds of entities. The interaction mechanism, as I see it, is psi. I have gone into this in detail elsewhere, hypothesizing that two forms of psi — clairvoyance and psychokinesis — are the mechanisms of mind–body interaction (Tart 1979, 1981, 1990). The "normal", everyday use of psi is the connection between mind and matter, matter as particularized in a unique body–brain–nervous system, between these two quite different realms. More specifically, there is first a kind of clairvoyance, used "internally", in which mind knows what the body–brain–nervous system is being subjected to and its condition, and thereby what is happening around the body in its immediate environment (as constructed in the brain). Second, there is a kind of "internal" psychokinesis that sometimes affects semi-autonomous brain processes so as to make us think and act in particular kinds of ways.

Here in *fig*. 9.1, then, is mind embodied into the body–brain–nervous system creating "ME!" ME! is strongly driven by biological imperatives. Your body constantly reminds you, "I am vulnerable! There are things that move fast and that have teeth and claws: Protect me! I am hungry! I want this! I am afraid of that! I want to get out of here! I want more!" And so forth. That is why I put an exclamation mark after the ME abbreviation. If you were in a greatly detached or meditative state, you might just be ME for the time being, just mind embodied; but most of the time we identify with the needs of our body, with the concepts we have about our body and its needs, and we protect it with our life. The exclamation point is to indicate the emotional intensity that mind embodied almost always has.

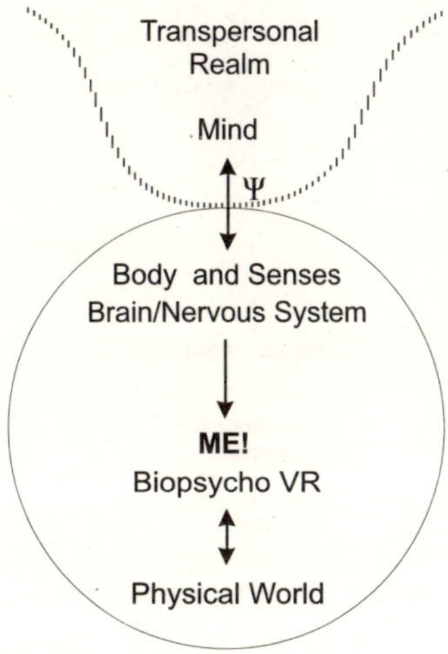

fig. 9.1: Mind embodied

This means that we are in a BPVR (or "World Simulation Process", as I have called it elsewhere [see Tart 1987]); and from that simulated world, that virtual reality, we interact with the physical world. But it is not a simple, direct interaction with the physical world; we have these maps, these concepts, these perceptual learnings and conditionings between us and simply interacting with the world a good deal of the time.

Mind Embodied–Embodied as Computer-generated Virtual Reality

What happens when we go into CGVR?

If you put on HMD, say with eyephones and earphones and a body suit to measure what your body is going to be doing, and if there is a computer controlling what gets represented to your senses, it is as if you are embodied a second time. Now you have not ME!, but MEE! If it is a good CGVR set-up that grabs your attention so you feel you are there, the exclamation point comes in again. You identify with being in this virtual reality, you are literally "in" a particular virtual world. If you don't identify, if it is just MEE without the exclamation point, you are either using a poor-quality CGVR system or inhibiting the process of identification, the functioning of the ecological self.

The MEE! situation is represented in *fig*. 9.2. Note how BPVR is enmeshed into CGVR, one virtual reality into another.

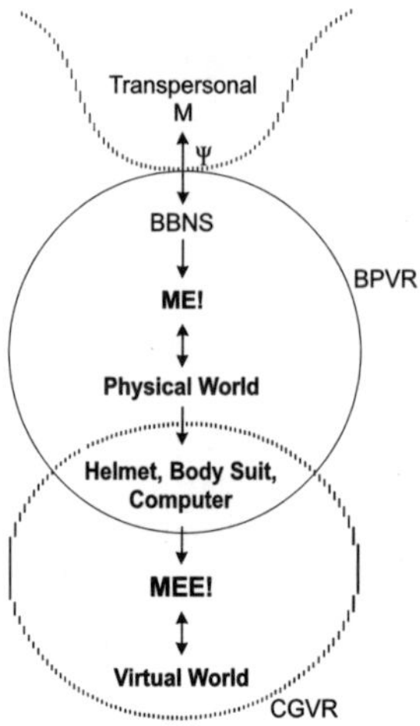

fig. 9.2: Mind embodied–embodied

This new kind of modeling, based on CGVR, on seeing consciousness as a world-simulation process, is much more sophisticated than ordinary computer models. It can have a much more human quality to it, and it can be a general model for psychology that I think will have great predictive fecundity. It is especially interesting when applied to transpersonal psychology because I believe that as we study that "second embodiment" in CGVR and learn some of the laws and principles that govern the kind of consciousness that emerges, we will in turn get some hints about laws in general, the system organization principles and emergents that govern the first embodiment of mind into a body.

I hope I have conveyed some of the psychological possibilities of this new technology. Some specific possible applications to psychotherapy and the like have been presented elsewhere (Tart 1991). I end with a bit of verse that came to me when thinking about this topic:

You can take off your head mounted display and body suit
If things get to be too much
In computer-generated virtual reality
But it is pretty hard to take off your head and body
When things get to be too much
In ordinary virtual reality —
At least not until the end.

10

Current Hypotheses About the Nature of the Mind–Brain Relationship and Their Relationship to Findings in Parapsychology

Jean E. Burns

MANY researchers in artificial intelligence put forth the idea that if a computer incorporated suitable physical characteristics it would be conscious. Similarly, recent models of consciousness have made a variety of proposals about the physical nature of the mind–brain interface (Burns 1990), and such models imply that if a physical system incorporated all necessary characteristics that system would be conscious. It is not known whether consciousness can be generated from any set of physical conditions that human beings are capable of constructing. Furthermore, even if a physical device were conscious, there is at present no means of objectively demonstrating that fact (Burns 1993).

I will, however, discuss several current competing hypotheses about the nature of the mind–brain interface, and in order to have a framework for discussing the relationship of these hypotheses to psi, I will make two plausible assumptions:

1. It is possible to specify the physical characteristics associated with the mind–brain interface.
2. The relationship between psi and matter and the relationship between mind and brain are the same, so that properties such as dependence or independence of physical conditions that characterize one relationship also characterize the other.

As to the first assumption, I should point out that some models of consciousness hold that there is no physical interface (Bohm 1982) or that if there is one its physical nature is unknowable (Kroon 1989, 1991).

An earlier version of the second postulate was made by Thouless and Wiesner (1948) and discussed further by Beloff (1979) and by Tart (1979). It stated that the content of conscious experience derives from the action of extrasensory perception (ESP) on the brain and that the influence of mind on the brain is accomplished through psychokinesis (PK). I will amend this statement for the following reason: Obviously the ability of the mind–brain system to read encoding in the brain is far superior to its ability to read other information, presumably because of the special physical conditions of the mind–brain interface. If the content of conscious experience derives from the action of ESP on the brain, then a person should be able to read the content of other mind–brains easily, whereas reading information about other material conditions would be more difficult. But this contradicts the finding of parapsychology that the efficacy of psi in telepathy is not much different from its efficacy in describing ordinary physical situations and events. Evidently the original statement is somewhat oversimplified. However, the version presented here is corroborated by parallels between the relationship of mind and brain and the relationship of psi and matter, as I discuss in a following section.

Before beginning the discussion of the various interface hypotheses, let me note that I make no assumption about the causal (ontological) relationship between consciousness and the physical world. Recent models of consciousness have made a variety of proposals about this causal relationship, including physicalism, dualism, and idealism (reviewed by Burns 1990). Physicalism, for instance, holds that an aspect of conscious experience that is associated with a given property of the brain is causally produced in the brain, whereas dualism holds that such an association is a linkage between independent realms. However, models that offer the same hypotheses about physical characteristics associated with the interface often have differing ontological views. Furthermore, there is no presently known empirical method that can determine whether such an association is causal or a linkage between qualities in independent realms (Burns 1990). Thus, I do not further consider the question of ontological relationship.

Also, I use the term *interface* to refer to that aspect of the brain–physical world by which qualities of consciousness and the physical world are linked. In physicalism, the interface would consist of those physical characteristics that cause conscious experience. In dualism, the interface would consist of those physical characteristics by which aspects of independent realms are linked. However, I use this term here to refer to the linkage in a generic sense, without any causal implication.

Physical Characteristics Associated with the Mind–Brain Interface

There are at present three main candidates for physical characteristics associated with the interface between mind and brain: complexity, quantum mechanical conditions, and correlated processes (Burns 1990).

Complexity

In terms of interconnections, the human brain could be considered the most complex thing known on this planet; thus, complexity might be considered necessary for the presence of consciousness. Several models of consciousness have made such a hypothesis (Burns 1990), and many people in the fields of artificial intelligence and computer design imply this hypothesis by suggesting that computers that have as many interconnections as the human brain does will be conscious. It is well known that a great deal of brain processing is not associated with conscious experience (Baars 1988), so complexity cannot be the sole condition associated with consciousness. However, one might suppose that complexity plus some other factor together comprise the interface.

If complexity were a necessary factor in the mind–brain interface, we would expect only humans, and perhaps some primates, to be conscious because the brains of most animals have substantially fewer interconnections than the human brain does. However, experiments in parapsychology have suggested that cats, mice, gerbils, and other animals can use psi (Morris 1977). Although these experiments were not conclusive, this evidence suggests that complexity is not a factor in the mind–brain interface.

Quantum Mechanics

A number of models of consciousness have suggested that the mind–brain interface is associated with factors unique to quantum mechanics. Some of these (Bass 1975; Goswami 1986, 1989, 1990; Stapp 1982, 1985, 1991; Walker 1975, 1979, 1984) are "observer theories", in which a conscious observer is associated with the collapse of the quantum mechanical wave function. Each observer theory asserts that the brain is characterized by a macroscopic quantum mechanical wave function, and that choice is carried out through collapse of this wave function. In other respects, however, each observer theory is a little different (Burns 1990).

Several researchers (Bass 1975; Eccles 1990; Stapp 1991; Walker 1979) have suggested that the quantum mechanical connection to the brain is made via the chemical synapses. Walker (1979) has pointed out that most brain processing is not associated with conscious experience, and he postulated that consciousness is associated not with the ordinary brain process across a synapse but with the relatively rarer event of electron tunneling between two different synapses. Valentine (1982) proposed that consciousness is associated with electrical synapses; because these are more rare than chemical synapses, such a mechanism could also account for the fact that consciousness is not associated with all brain processing.

Woo (1981) has suggested that if the brain is characterized by a macroscopic quantum state, one might be able to detect quantum interference effects. For instance, the oscillating meaning of an ambiguous picture might be considered to result from a quantum superposition of the states corresponding to the individual meanings. However, it would be difficult to demonstrate that any specific effect is quantum mechanical, and experiments to detect such effects have not been attempted.

A number of models of consciousness include a discussion of psi (Table 10.1), and if quantum mechanical models offered a greater degree of explanation for psi phenomena than other models, this might be invoked as support for quantum mechanical theories of consciousness. PK-induced displacements of tumbling cubes depend on the materials the cubes are made of (Forwald 1959). Walker (1975) has shown that this effect can be accounted for in terms of the Heisenberg uncertainty principle, in the following way: The Heisenberg principle specifies the relationship between an initial uncertainty in position and velocity of each cube and its mass and moment of inertia, and tumbling allows cumulative magnification of this initial uncertainty. If one assumes that PK can redirect the cumulative uncertainty in an ordered way, good agreement with empirical results is then obtained.[1] However, PK might be able to redirect quantum randomness without the relationship between psi and matter following quantum mechanical principles in other ways.

Jahn and Dunne (1986, 1987) have described numerous analogies between psi phenomena and quantum mechanical principles. However, the analogies are set forth in terms of loosely defined concepts and, though

[1] This process can also explain the finding that PK produces better results on large groups of dice than on small groups; larger numbers of dice provide greater opportunities for collision and thereby enhance the magnification of quantum uncertainty (Walker 1975: 35).

Table 10.1: Models of Consciousness in which Psi is Discussed

Model*	Nature of mind-brain interface	Aspect of psi discussed
QUANTUM MECHANICAL MODELS		
Eccles (1977)	QM principles	PK is the same influenc that produces the action of mind on the brain.
Goswami (1986)	QM observer theory	ESP is independent of distance; precognition is independent of time.
Jahn and Dunne (1986, 1987)	QM principles used as metaphor	Psi follows principles analagous to those in quantum mechanics.
Walker (1975, 1979, 1984)	QM observer theory	Psi is independent of space, time, and physical complexity. PK (in small statistical effects) takes place via ordering of quantum randomness.
OTHER HYPOTHESES		
Burns (1981, 1986)	Thermodynamic (related to entropy)	Psi is independent of distance and physical complexity.
Kroon (1989, 1991)	Not possible to know the nature of the interface	Psi is independent of space and time.
Lövland (1981, 1988)	Thermodynamic	ESP and PK take place via qualities analagous to, but not the same as, thermodynamic properties.

Note: Sperry (1983) and Bateson (1979, chap. 8) specify in their models that psi does not exist. Sperry says that psi cannot exist because consciousness arises out of an emergent principle that is localized to the brain. Bateson says beliefs in psi are "symptoms, mistaken attempts at cute efforts to escape from a crude materialism. . . . The reply to crude materialism is not miracles but beauty".

*For additional works presenting these models, see Burns (1990, 1991).

suggestive, do not give any substantial evidence that psi follows quantum mechanical principles.

Goswami (1986) and Walker (1975, 1979, 1984) have shown that distance independence of psi can be accounted for by quantum nonlocality. However, as Goswami (1986) has discussed, no information can be transmitted by quantum nonlocality. Thus Goswami, even though he proposed a quantum model, hypothesized a version of the Jungian unconscious that explicitly lacked the property of space in order to account for most psi effects. Besides, distance independence can also be explained by considering psi to be a phenomenon of consciousness, and supposing that (a) consciousness includes extra dimensions besides those of physical space (Rauscher 1983), (b) consciousness lacks the property of physical space (Burns 1986; Kroon 1989), or (c) some special aspect of consciousness, such as the collective unconscious, lacks this property (Stokes 1987: 154-61).

Goswami (1986) and Walker (1975, 1979, 1984) have shown through quantum mechanical theory that psi can be independent of time, but Rauscher (1983) and Kroon (1989) have offered alternative ways to show this. Furthermore, although the existence of precognition indicates that psi has a degree of independence from time, it is not certain that precognition of the distant future is as accurate as precognition of the near future (Stokes, 1987); therefore, psi may not be entirely independent of time.

Thus, there is presently no strong evidence from psi that the mind–brain interface is quantum mechanical.

Synchronous Electrochemical Oscillations

Evidence continues to accumulate that synchronous electrochemical activity is used to encode information in the brain and that it is sometimes associated with conscious experience, as reviewed by Barinaga (1990). I first discuss various characteristics of this synchronous activity, as they relate to experimental and theoretical work done by various researchers, and then discuss the possibility that synchronous action is involved with the mind–brain interface.

Theoretical work helpful in understanding this phenomenon has been done independently by E.C. Zeeman (1977) and by Skarda and Freeman (1987). Zeeman, who described the phenomenon of synchronous oscillation in the brain before it had been empirically demonstrated, used mathematical theorems that apply to a highly interconnected system with many degrees of freedom to show that the brain can be described as a system of linked nonlinear oscillators. Similarly, each anatomical region in the brain can be considered such a system, with each region having a very large number of resonant (attractor) states. Zeeman proposed that each resonant state corresponds to a memory or behavioral unit, and activation of that state in the brain corresponds to activation of that memory or behavior. Although Zeeman described the brain mathematically, we can use the analogy of a musical instrument in which the vibration of a plucked string or percussion on a drum resonates in a cavity, each state having a unique spatial pattern of vibration. Of course, oscillations in the brain do not take place through mechanical action, as in a musical instrument, but through electrochemical interactions between the neurons. Specifically, electric current is introduced into the body of a neuron through many synaptic connections, and sufficient current causes a neuron to fire (Freeman 1991).

It has recently been demonstrated within the visual cortex that most neurons in a given region fire in an oscillatory fashion with the same frequency and phase (Gray et al. 1989). Also, it has been demonstrated in olfactory regions that sensory information is represented by spatial patterns of vibration (Freeman 1991; Skarda and Freeman 1987). Thus, there is now substantial reason to believe that the brain accomplishes an important part of its processing by means of such synchronous action.

Analysis of the latter data shows that the oscillations must be described in terms of a nonlinear system and chaotic action (Freeman 1991; Skarda and Freeman 1987). Because of these latter characteristics, the brain can quickly respond to a change in sensory input (Skarda and Freeman 1987; Zeeman 1977), store a large amount of new information (Skarda and Freeman 1987), and generate novel activity patterns (Freeman 1991).

The latter data also show that as the brain incorporates new learned material the spatial pattern associated with previously learned material changes substantially (Freeman 1991). This can be explained by the fact that synaptic connections change when new information is learned; because each pattern is a characteristic of the region as a whole, each pattern must change when any synaptic connections change. Zeeman (1977, chap. 9) showed by means of a mathematical theorem that when two items of sensory input encoded in this way are activated simultaneously, the corresponding attractor states form a new single state; thus association in memory of simultaneous sensory experiences can be a natural consequence of this sort of encoding.

Many, but not all, neurons in a given region follow this synchronous action (Gray et al. 1989), which has been found to take place between 20 and 90 Hz (Freeman 1991). An earlier study, which used a flickering light at about 2 Hz to produce oscillatory action in the brain, compared the resulting evoked potential, which derives from many neurons, to the action of individual cells; this study also showed that not all cells contribute to large-scale oscillatory action (Ramos et al. 1976). Because the strength of synapse connections varies from cell to cell, it is not surprising that some cells would not partake in a large-scale action. However, these results show that synchronous action can be understood only at the global level, and not the cellular.

It is therefore likely that synchronous oscillations are utilized as encoding in the brain. However, the brain encodes information in many ways (Gilinsky 1984), and the fact that a phenomenon is used in encoding carries no implication that it is involved in the mind–brain interface. Moreover, the preceding data came from animals, some of whom were awake but most of whom were anesthetized (Barinaga 1990); thus synchronous activity might be a necessary component but could not be the sole component of the interface. Nevertheless, the hypothesis that synchronous activity has a necessary association with conscious experience has been made by several researchers. For one thing, patterns in an electroencephalogram (EEG) can show an association with conscious experience; for instance, a vertical line with the meaning of the letter *I* will produce a different EEG pattern in a person than the same vertical line with the meaning of the numeral *1* (Grinberg-Zylberbaum and John, 1981). On that basis, and the fact that an EEG pattern cannot be described solely at the cellular level, John (1976, 1980) has postulated that consciousness has a necessary association with large-scale co-operative action in the brain. And on the basis of the empirical data just described, Koch and Crick (cited in Barinaga 1990) have suggested that synchronous action in the brain has a necessary association with consciousness.

If consciousness is associated with synchronous action in the brain, we would expect psi also to be associated with such action. Millay (1978) measured the synchrony of alpha waves (7 to 12 Hz) in eleven pairs of people over a period of several months and found that many of the pairs had a significant degree of synchrony. Each pair participated in telepathy-testing sessions, and pairs who scored higher in telepathy showed a higher degree of alpha synchrony generally. A later study confirmed that result but showed that there was no significant alpha correlation during the telepathy sessions (Johnston and Millay 1983). Alpha waves are associated with relaxation and lack of sensory input (Ibid.), and it is possible that other frequencies are correlated during telepathy. No work has presently been done on the relationship between psi and brainwaves at the higher range of frequencies just discussed.

Parallels Between the Mind–Brain and Psi-Matter Relationships

Earlier the postulate is stated that the relationship between the content of conscious experience and encoding in the brain and the relationship between psi and matter are the same, and several parallels in these relationships can in fact be described. First we should note that various, quite different types of encoding in the brain are associated with conscious experience, such as frequency of neural firing, topographic layout (Gilinsky 1984), and synchronous oscillations. Thus, the interface acts independently of the substances and processes involved in encoding, such as type of neurotransmitter, type of electrochemical action, or the like. Similarly, ESP can operate independently of the physical nature of information, and PK has no dependence on the materials involved or the various physical processes used in random event generators (Stanford 1977).

Another parallel has only come to light with the recent findings about encoding through synchronous oscillatory action. Some types of coding, such as frequency of neural firing, have no necessary dependence on interconnections. But synchronous oscillatory action takes place in an entire anatomical region of the brain and depends on the large number of interconnections therein, so this coding can be described as highly complex. Thus we now know that the interface can act independently of the complexity involved in encoding. Similarly, PK acts independently of physical complexity (Kennedy 1978).

Thus, the principles common to the mind–brain relationship and the psi–matter relationship show ways in which the use of information is independent of various aspects of the physical world — type of physical substance, type of physical process, and physical complexity. These parallels support an idea suggested by Eccles (Eccles and Robinson 1984) and Jahn and Dunne (1987) that information is a common currency between consciousness and the physical world.

The Super-Psi Machine

If the mind–brain and psi–matter relationships are the same, one would expect the action of psi to be greatly enhanced when it is associated with the same type of characteristics as are associated with the mind–brain interface, as Tart (1979) has suggested. I call a device which incorporates physical characteristics that enhance psi a super-psi machine.

In discussing such a device, I use terminology introduced by Tart (1979): The conscious experience of encoding in one's own brain and the influence of mind on that encoding is called *auto-psi* and ordinary psi is called *allo-psi*. One cannot suppose that the physical conditions associated with auto-psi and enhanced allo-psi are identical, because in that case every individual could read encoding from other brains as easily as he or she could read encoding from his or her own — and such is not the case. By the same reasoning, auto-psi cannot be a special case of enhanced allo-psi, with extra conditions added. Nevertheless, conditions for auto-psi are apt to be similar to those for enhanced allo-psi; and if we knew one set of conditions, our understanding of the other would probably be increased.

If complexity were a necessary factor in the mind–brain interface, it would not at present be feasible to design a device that incorporates the interface conditions. But the complexity hypothesis seems doubtful, as discussed earlier. Besides, the fact that the interface can mediate physical encoding independently of complexity suggests that the interface itself is independent of complexity, not dependent on it. Thus if it is possible to construct a super-psi machine, it may well be possible to do it at the present time.

Because a variety of types of physical encoding are associated with conscious experience, the physical principle involved with the interface must be fairly general. Principles in quantum mechanics might be involved, or special conditions on energy, entropy, or related quantities, but not specific types of neurotransmitter, specific types of electrochemical action, or the like. Correlation within a system is related to, but complementary to, entropy (Careri 1984), and a special condition on correlated aspects of a system could also be an interface candidate. (Synchronous oscillations might be involved in the interface through this principle.)

To test an interface hypothesis, one could build a device that incorporates the candidate hypothesis, enhanced psi effects being a positive indication that the general type of condition represented by the hypothesis is correct. Tests could be made of people's ability to read information encoded in the device in association with the interface conditions and of their ability to influence the device by PK. It may be important in producing psi that a person feel a sense of connection between himself or herself and the object of psi (Andrews 1991; Jahn and Dunne 1987: 255-56), and this sense of connection might be especially important in testing an interface hypothesis.

Of course, if the assumption that the mind–brain interface is composed of specific, knowable physical conditions is incorrect, it would not be possible to replicate it, and it might not be possible to construct a super-psi machine either. But regardless of whether it is possible to construct these, we might learn quite a bit by trying. We can also learn about the interface by continuing to examine hypotheses from the perspective of psi and looking for more parallels between the mind–brain and psi–matter relationships. Knowledge about psi can be an important tool in understanding the mind–brain system.

11

Co-Operator Experiments with an REG Device

Brenda J. Dunne

Experimental Background

SINCE 1979, the Princeton Engineering Anomalies Research (PEAR) laboratory has been exploring the effects of human intention on the behavior of random physical systems and devices. The most extensive of these investigations has involved a microelectronic random event generator (REG) that produces a string of random binary samples, or bits, at a rate of 1,000 per second, in trials of 200 bits each, and counts the number that conform to a regular positive/negative alternation (Jahn and Dunne 1987; Jahn et al. 1987; Nelson and Dobyns 1991; Nelson et al. 1984). A human operator, seated in front of the device and observing the sequence of count numbers via a LED display on its face, attempts to shift the mean of the output distribution in accordance with his or her prerecorded intentions. The experimental protocol requires the operator to generate equal numbers of trials under intentions to produce higher counts or lower counts or to generate a baseline (i.e. to allow the machine to operate without any explicit intention) with all other conditions held constant. Data accumulated in series of pre-specified length are then examined for correlations between the operator's intentions and the output of the device. The results of some 840,000 trials per intention (a total of more than 504,000,000 binary samples) generated on this REG by ninety-one different individuals over a twelve-year period, show statistically significant correlations between operator intentions and the mean counts

---

Princeton Engineering Anomalies Research program is indebted to the McDonnell Foundation, the Fetzer Institute, Laurance S. Rockefeller, and the Ohrstrom Foundation for their continued support of this research. We are also deeply appreciative of the enormous contributions of time and energy by the various operators who contributed to this database

of these 200-sample trials. Although the observed effects are quite small (the mean of the high efforts is 100.026, and that of the low efforts, 99.984), given the magnitude of the database, the likelihood of even this small separation occurring by chance is less than 5×10^{-5}. Equally important is the observation that many individual operators appear to establish characteristic patterns of achievement, or "signatures", that are distinguished by their effect sizes and preferred directions of effort. Despite the individual disparities of performances, when all operators' data are combined, the correlations of the composite deviations with intentions remain quite robust (Dunne and Jahn 1991; Jahn and Dunne 1987; Jahn et al. 1987; Nelson et al. 1989; Nelson and Dobyns 1991; Nelson et al. 1984). *Fig.* 11.1 displays these results in the form of a graph of the chronologically ordered cumulative deviations from the theoretical mean for the high, low, and baseline conditions.

Theoretical Background

Evidence such as that shown in *Fig.* 11.1, which is consistent with the results of many other experiments conducted in our laboratory and elsewhere (Radin and Nelson 1989), indicates that human consciousness can participate actively, albeit modestly, in the establishment of physical reality. In so doing, it appears to violate certain basic premises of established physical theory, suggesting that these may merit some reconsideration. In another component of the PEAR program, we have attempted to re-examine some of these physical presumptions and have proposed a rudimentary model that represents reality as the product of the interpenetration of consciousness and its environment (Jahn 1991; Jahn and Dunne 1984a, b; 1986; 1987). In this approach, all physical theory is regarded as an attempt by human consciousness to describe its *experience* of its physical environment, rather than as an "objective" description of an abstract physical world and thus reflects the describing consciousness as much as it does the environment being described.

Following this path, we have invoked the concepts and formalisms of quantum wave mechanics via metaphor to describe such co-operative reality. For example, considerable use is made of the complementarity principle, one form of which essentially states that atomic-scale events can be described in two different frames of reference — as particles or as waves — and that a complete description must incorporate both perspectives. We interpret this to imply that a wave-particle complementarity may also reasonably be invoked to describe the

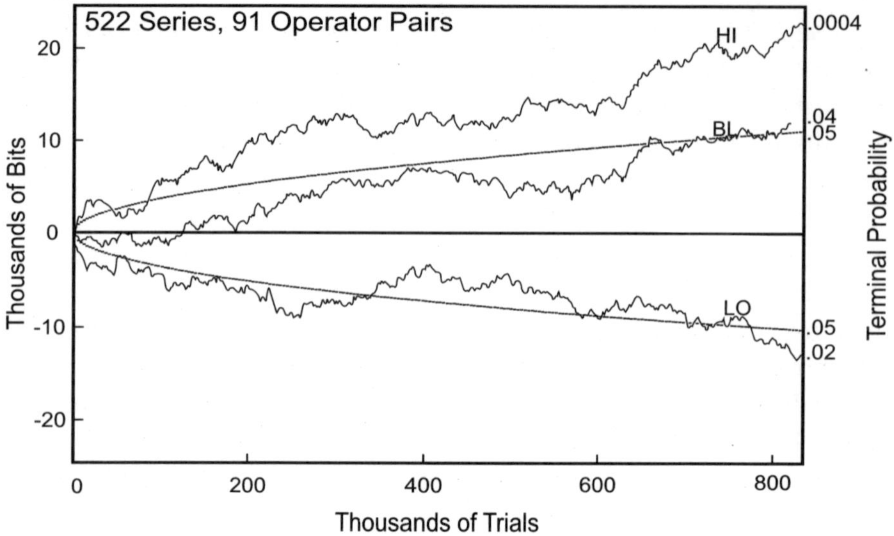

fig. 11.1: All local, single operator, diode REG

phenomenon of consciousness itself; indeed, that this complementarity may well be as much a property of consciousness as it is of the physical world (Jahn 1991). In this context, the prevailing models of consciousness may be viewed as essentially particulate, but if these models are expanded to permit it the option of functioning in a wavelike fashion as well, a number of otherwise anomalous phenomena, such as those observed in these human–machine interactions, may be more parsimoniously represented in terms of such processes as diffraction, interference, barrier penetration, and resonance, rather than as "paranormal" events.

Co-operator Experiments

The operator-specific results found in the individual REG experiments suggest one means of testing the consciousness wave hypothesis. If these human–machine interactions are strictly particulate in nature, two operators attempting the task in concert would be expected to exhibit linear combinations of their individual signatures. If, on the other hand, some wavelike processes are operating, the composite signatures could involve more complex superposition properties such as interference and phasing. To explore this, we have undertaken a program of "co-operator" REG experiments in which two operators, each of whom has established an individual pattern of achievement, address the task together with the same intention.

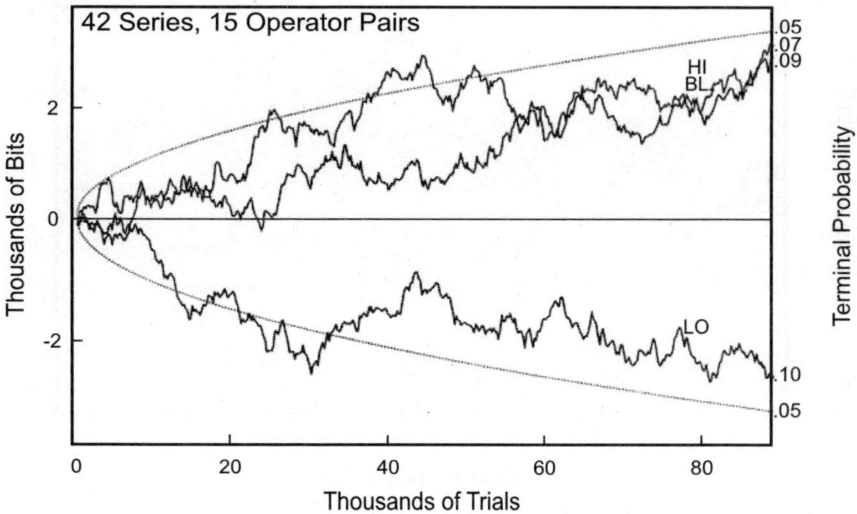

fig. 11.2: All diodi REG, co-operator pairs

The total co-operator database as of January 1991 consists of 85,500 trials per intention, generated by fifteen different operator pairs in forty-two independent experimental series, and yields an overall effect size that is slightly larger than that of the single-operator results. Specifically, the mean of the co-operator high-intention efforts is 100.033, compared with the single-operator mean of 100.026; that of the low efforts is 99.969, compared with 99.984 for the single-operator data. These results are displayed in *fig*. 11.2. Like the single-operator data displayed in *fig*. 11.1, the statistical significance of the incremental effect increases steadily as the size of the database grows. Although neither of the co-operator directional efforts independently achieves statistical significance over this smaller data base, the probability of the high–low split in direction of intention is less than .03 ($z = 1.883$).

In response to our particular theoretical query, however, the cumulative deviation patterns of specific operator pairs, although again internally consistent, show no indications of simple linear combinations of the performances of the participating individuals. Indeed, some of our most successful individual operators produce null effects when working together, whereas others with minimal or even negative individual results are able to produce strong positive yields as a pair. The signature superposition thus appears to be more wavelike than particle-like in character.

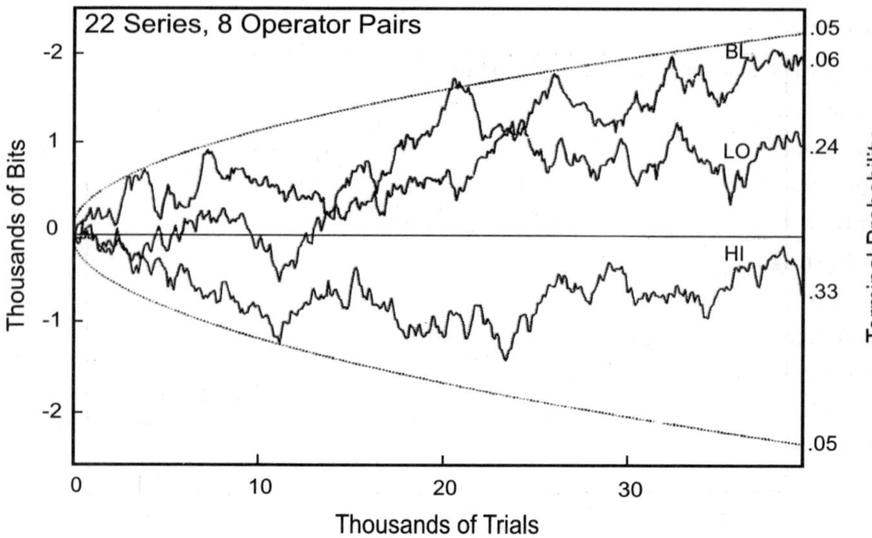

fig. 11.3: REG co-operator data: some-sex pairs

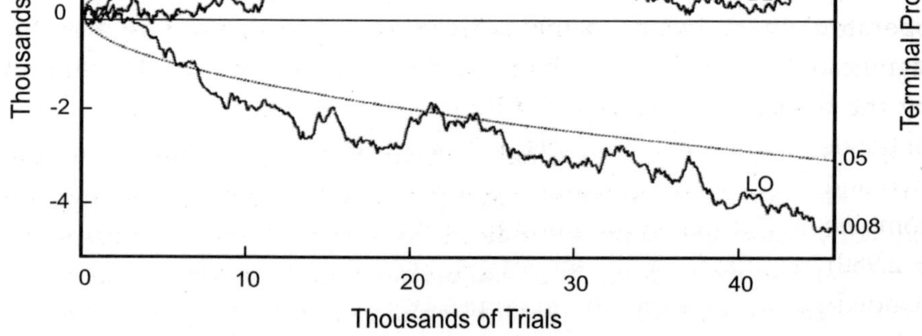

fig. 11.4: REG co-operator data: opposite-sex pairs

Sex-related Effects

Of the fifteen co-operator pairs contributing to this database, eight of the same sex generated a total of 39,500 trials per intention in twenty-two independent series, and seven opposite-sex pairs generated 46,000 trials per intention in twenty series. The results of the same-sex pairs are statistically non-significant, and indeed tend to be opposite to intention in both directions of effort, with effect sizes nearly identical to those of the single-operator data, albeit in the reverse direction (see *fig.* 11.3). Specifically, the high efforts have a mean of 99.984, and the low efforts a mean of 100.025, with a composite z score in the direction of intention of −0.810. The opposite-sex pairs, on the other hand, produce results consistent with their intentions, with effect sizes considerably larger than those of the single-operator results (*fig.* 11.4). Their overall high efforts have a mean of 100.075, nearly three times the single-operator effect size, and the low efforts a mean of 99.920, an effect five times that of the single operators. The composite z score for this subset is 3.317 ($p < 5 \times 10^{-4}$). Despite the relatively small sizes of these data subsets, the difference between the same- and opposite-sex data, computed by a t-test comparing the high–low mean differences between the two populations, is statistically significant, with a two-tailed probability of chance occurrence of .004 ($t_\Delta = 2.849$).

Of the seven opposite-sex pairs, four consist of couples who share a bonded relationship, whereas the other three pairs are simply friends or acquaintances. Over their eleven series, comprising 31,000 trials per intention, the three unbonded pairs show strong positive results in both directions of intention: 100.058 in the high efforts (2.2 times larger than the single-operator efforts) and 99.946 in the low (3.4 times the single-operator effect), with a combined effect in direction of effort that is significant at $p < .025$ ($z = 1.968$). The results of the nine series generated by the bonded pairs are nearly twice again as strong as those of the unbonded pairs in the high intention, with a mean of 100.111, and nearly two-and-a-half times as strong in the low, with a mean of 99.868. The combined effect in direction of effort has a probability of less than .002 ($z = 2.980$). Compared with the single-operator results, the effects of the bonded-pair high efforts are 4.3 times larger and those of the low efforts 8.3 times larger. *Fig.* 11.5 and 11.6 display these comparisons. Clearly, each of these subdivisions of the co-operator database substantially reduces the size of the various subsets and thereby the statistical leverage of these small effects, but even as a pilot study they remain provocative.

The relative effect sizes of the various co-operator subsets and those of the single-operator data are summarized in Table 11.1 and portrayed in *fig*. 11.7. In the figure, error bars of one standard deviation provide an estimate of the reliability of the mean for each subset as a function of database size. More comprehensive summary tables, along with details of the individual pair results and variations of the experimental protocol, are provided in the Appendix to Dunne (1991).

Table 11.1: Summary of Co-Operator REG Data

Subset	*No. Oprs. or Pairs*	*No. Trials per Int.*	*No. Srs.*	*High Mean*	*Low Mean*	*Mean Diff.*
Single oprs.	91	840,000	522	100.026*	99.984*	.042*
Co-oprs.	15	85,500	42	100.033	99.969	.064*
Same-sex	8	39,500	22	99.984	100.025	-.041
Opposite-sex	7	46,000	20	100.075*	99.920*	.155*
Unbonded	3	31,000	11	100.058	99.946	.112*
Bonded	4	15,000	9	100.111*	99.868*	.243*

*Data sets that demonstrate one-tailed statistical probabilities of <.05 ($z > 1.645$ in the direction of effort).

Although these sex-related effects seem robust and potentially important, their interpretation is far from clear. In the theoretical model just mentioned, a consciousness "exclusion principle" emerges, relating to the pairing of passive–assertive or *yin–yang* characteristics, which may be relevant to the bonding of female–male consciousness in a given experimental context (Jahn and Dunne 1984a, b, 1986). Whether the data showing disparities in the performance of same–opposite and unbonded–bonded co-operator pairs actually constitute evidence for such a process is at this point speculative at best but perhaps worthy of further attention.

Comparisons with Remote Perception Experiments

The sharp distinctions in the same- and opposite-sex co-operator REG results prompted re-examination of our precognitive remote perception (PRP) database for indications of any similar effects. These experiments — described in detail in Dunne et al. (1989); Dunne et al. (1983); and Jahn, Dunne, and Nelson (1987) — also involve two participants, one of whom, the "percipient", attempts to acquire information about the geographical

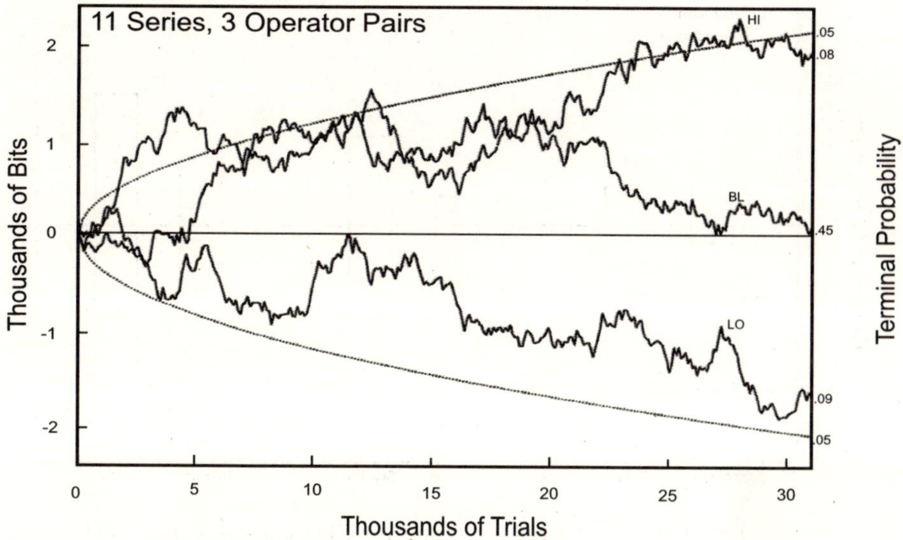

fig. 11.5: REG co-operator data: unbounded oposite-sex pairs

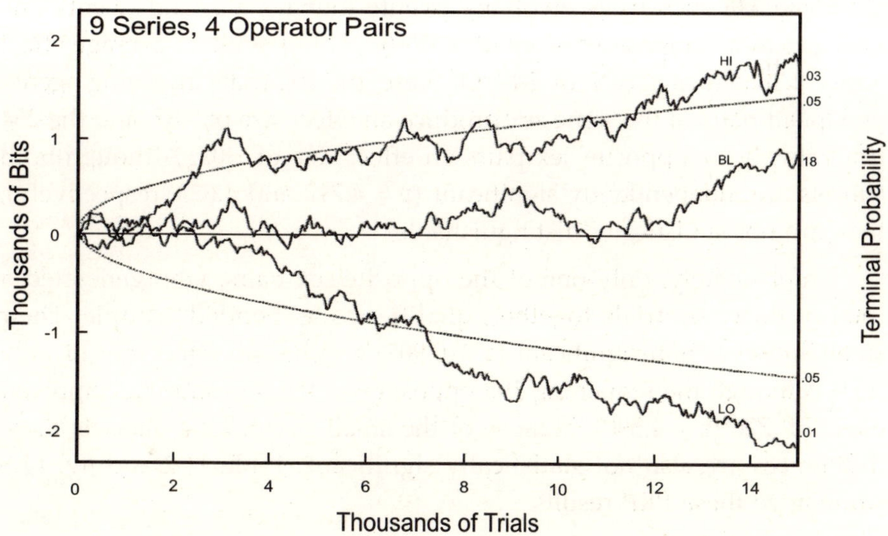

fig. 11.6: REG co-operator data: bonded opposite-sex pairs

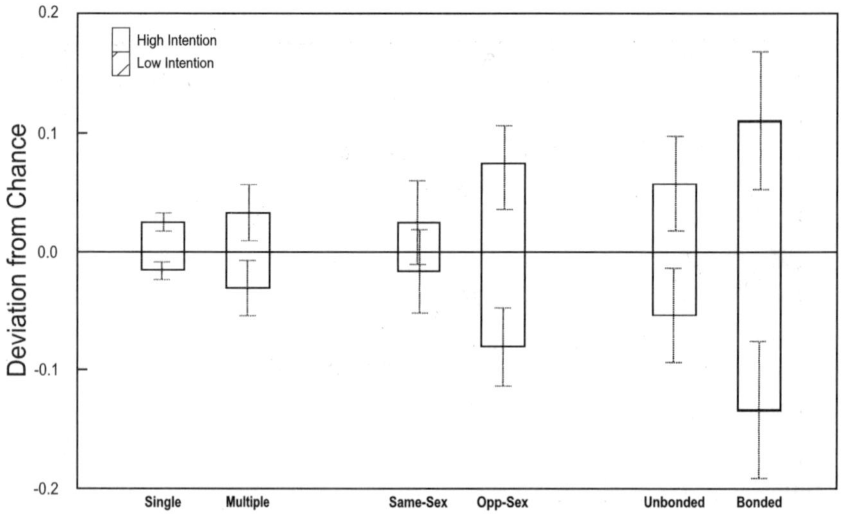

fig. 11.7: Effect sizes in co-opartor REG experiments

location of the other, the "agent", at a specified date and time without recourse to any known sensory means of communication. The main thrust of this component of the PEAR program has been the development of analytical scoring methodologies to codify the impressionistic free-response descriptions in a standardized manner, and thereby to quantify the amount of anomalous information acquired under these protocols.

Some 336 such trials involving twenty-four females and twenty-one males yield a composite *z* score of 6.355 ($p = 10^{-10}$), with an average effect size, calculated as *z*/Ö *N*, of .347. Of these, the 102 trials involving agent–percipient pairs of the same sex produce an effect size of .467, and the 234 trials involving opposite-sex pairs an effect size of .302. Although both subsets are independently significant (*z* = 4.717 and 4.623, respectively), they are not statistically distinguishable.

Unfortunately, only one of the opposite-sex pairs, who generated a total of thirty-six trials together, qualifies as a "bonded" couple. Their small subset is non-significant (*z* = 0.905) and has an effect size of only .151. Although the remaining 198 opposite-sex trials produce a combined effect of .326 (*z* = 4.590), because of the small sizes of the datasets these differences are also not statistically significant. Table 11.2 and *fig.* 11.8 summarize these PRP results.

Although these comparisons are not statistically persuasive and could probably be interpreted in terms of sex-specific commonalities in perceptual

Table 11.2: Summary of Remote Perception Data

Agent/Percipient Pairs	**No. Pairs*	*No. Trials*	*Composite z–Score*	*Effect Size**
All data	52	336	6.355	.347
Same-sex	26	102	4.717	.467
Opposite-sex	26	234	4.623	.302
Unbonded	25	198	4.590	.326
Bonded	1	36	0.905	.151

*Effect size calculated by *z*/Ö*N*.

and communicational styles, their lack of reinforcement of the REG results may nonetheless bear on the latter's interpretation. Two distinctions need to be noted: First, in the REG experiments the two participants are performing identical tasks; that is, they are imposing a common intention on the device. In the PRP experiments on the other hand, the participants are performing quite different roles: One is attempting to acquire information and the other to communicate it. Second, in the REG experiment, the context is established by an electronic machine, whereas in the PRP protocol it is established by a geographic scene. Whether these distinctions are sufficient grounds to inhibit, or even to reverse, the sex-pairing effects is far from obvious but again worth further study.

Discussion

Three implications emerge from the co-operator REG experiments: First, taken in total, the database constitutes yet another replication of many previous studies demonstrating that human intention can produce tangible effects on the behavior of such random physical processes. Second, the patterns of effect produced by the combined efforts of two operators of common intention are sufficiently distinct from their individual patterns of achievement to suggest that the phenomenon may have some wave mechanical aspects, thus supporting a basic premise of our theoretical model. Finally, the superior performance of bonded opposite-sex pairs draws attention to other specific predictions of the model, such as the relevance of a consciousness-exclusion principle to such bonded situations. Admittedly, these last two inferences are based on post-hoc observations

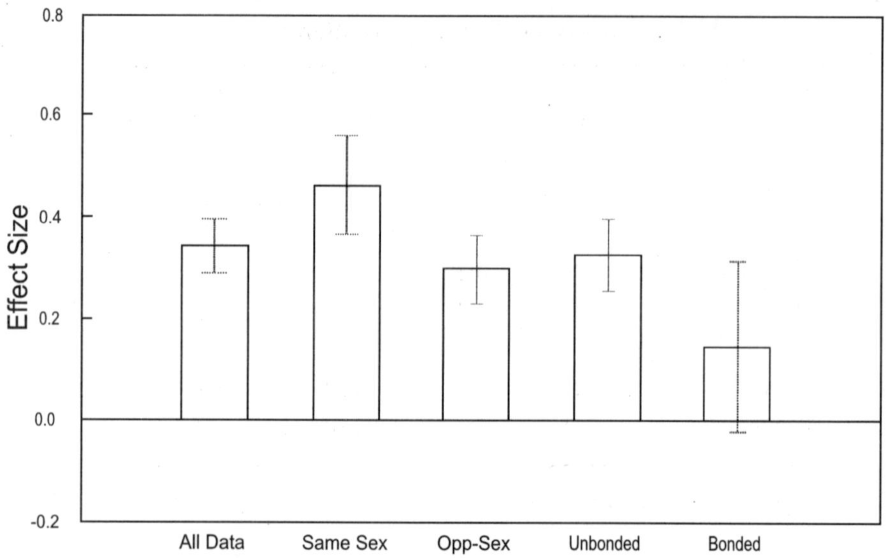

fig. 11.8: PRP effect sizes by type of agent-percipient pair

of relatively small databases that will require substantial replication before firmer conclusions can be drawn. Nevertheless, the sharpness and scale of the effects strongly suggest that further investigations on the role of gender pairing in both REG and PRP experiments could prove fruitful.

A Dedication

Although we met briefly only once, Louisa Rhine has been one of my role models in pursuing the path that led me to the conference that produced this book. Following in the noble tradition of Eleanor Sidgewick, she brought to the study of human consciousness the spirit of the feminine and exemplified the nurturing, co-operative dimension that imbues scholarly creativity with vitality and love. This spirit is sadly lacking in most of modern science, but in this field it is absolutely indispensable. Louisa Rhine also embodied a down-to-earth, grounding pragmatism that complemented the abstract, visionary idealism of her husband and enabled it to manifest tangibly. For this reason, it seemed particularly appropriate to use this opportunity to report on a body of experimental data that bears directly on a similar dynamic of male–female complementarity in the creative process. It is a great personal privilege to dedicate this chapter to the memory of Louisa Rhine and to offer this database as a humble tribute to that distinguished "co-operator pair", whose groundbreaking contributions to the study of human consciousness derived as much from their deep personal bond as from their careful and systematic scholarship.

12

The Power of Imagination
Toward a Philosophy of Healing

Michael Grosso

> The spirit is the master, imagination the tool, and the body the plastic material. — Paracelsus

RECENT psychology has shown a growing interest in imagery and healing (Sheikh 1984). In this chapter I want to stress the social or collective dimension of the healing imagination. Writers who discuss the role of mind in health tend to focus on the individual; but the mind of the individual is mediated by the mind of society. The philosopher George Mead wrote:

> The individual experiences himself as such, not directly, but only indirectly, from the particular standpoints of other individual members of the same social group, or from the generalized standpoint of the social group as a whole to which he belongs. — 1962: 138

Our ideas of health, wholeness, and human potential are thus mediated by the "generalized standpoint" of the entire social group, and my emphasis here is on the power of the social imagination. What follows is an attempt to raise questions and indicate steps toward a philosophy of healing.

Healing: An Open Concept

Let me begin with a few comments on the concept of healing. One common use of the term *healing* is clear enough. "I cut my finger", we say, "and it healed quickly". No controversy here in how the word "heal" is used.

Problems, however, arise once we bring in more ambiguous terms such as *wholeness*. English, in fact, is rich in terms related to healing, for example, *well, hale, healthy, hardy, fit, robust, whole, wholesome, sound.*

Etymologically, the word *holy* is related to *whole, hale,* and *healthy.* In Anglo-Saxon usage, these words bore the suggestion of good omen. It may be instructive to comment briefly on some of the nuances of these words.

Wellness, for example, is a weak term that merely connotes absence of disease; it is the term that has caught on in the corporate world. Everywhere in corporate America "wellness" programs and "fitness" centers have sprung up. Corporate America wants its workers to be well and fit. One obvious motive is to reduce insurance overhead. Talk of *fitness* — again a suggestive choice of terms — accents the idea of "fitting in". On the other hand, we do not hear much of *vitality, robustness, haleness,* or *hardiness,* terms that carry inherently positive connotations. Still less do corporate managers talk of *wholeness* — given that term's connotation of holiness. Wholeness and holiness, it is probably fair to say, are peripheral to the "generalized standpoint" of the American business world. Given our broad concern with human potential, *wholeness* and *healing* seem better because they are more comprehensive terms. Still, it may be hard to agree on what wholeness means, since one's notion of wholeness is a product of one's culture, history, and metaphysical standpoint.

To make this point clear, consider health or wholeness from an ancient Platonic perspective. In the *Phaedo,* Socrates uses the word *nosos* (disease) to describe normal embodied existence. Socrates thus echoes the old Orphic equation, *soma sema* — the body is a tomb. The *Phaedo* tells us that Socrates' last words alluded to a debt to Aesclepius, the god of healing. He owed something to the god of healing, so in dying, Socrates seemed to say, he was being healed. Recall the doctrine in the *Phaedo* that defines philosophy as the "practice of death". Philosophical "wholeness" is thus achieved by liberating one's soul from one's body. Similar ideas are found in Buddhism and Hinduism.

Of course, the idea that bodily death is a necessary condition for health or wholeness is a paradox. The paradox is mitigated once you identify your "self" with a disembodiable soul. Take another example from the ancient Greeks. Socrates is made to say in the *Gorgias* that being at peace with himself is more important than being at peace with the world. Nowadays we call this *integrity.* For some people integrity is part of their ideal of wholeness; but for others it is not.

Or consider the Christian view of suffering. From a Christian perspective, suffering may be seen as part of the effort to imitate Christ and can therefore be positive and liberating, a path to union with the divine. According to Jean-Pierre de Caussade, in his book *Abandonment to Divine Providence* (1975), pain, sickness, failure, disappointment, and frustration are viewed as opportunities for learning to surrender to what Caussade calls "divine providence". From this standpoint, the conception of health and human potential changes accordingly.

Thus imagined within a Christian milieu, pain, illness, poverty, deprivation, and injustice are consistent with ideas of *wholeness*. If I happen to be an atheist, on the other hand, or a materialist, hedonist, or egoist, a surrender to divine providence, the hope for justice after death, the redemptive power of self-sacrifice, spiritual values in general will play little or no part in my concept of wholeness. Other things will count more — wealth, power, and pleasure. Pain, failure, and death will be alien to my scheme of well-being, devoid of redemptive or healing value.

Our ideal or image of wholeness — a variable that we receive, invent, or modify — is a function of the metaphysical standpoint we adopt. The concept of wholeness must therefore remain an open one; for it depends on how we view the world — on our metaphysics or world-picture. And so it may come about that one man's suffering can be another's bliss, and vice versa. For a saintly Christian like Padre Pio, suffering was welcome, the royal road to divine wholeness (Grosso 1992).

One's image of wholeness — it may contain more than wellness and physical health — can thus lead to paradoxical results: For instance, one might say that Socrates drinking hemlock or Jesus on the cross were aspects of their "health". For Socrates and Jesus, health and wholeness were as much aspects of their soul life as of their bodily life. In their transcendent outlooks, pain, illness, even death were at worst phases on the way to ultimate well-being.

This leads to another question. An unapprehended serial killer and a psychopathic plutocrat might conceivably enjoy perfect physical health; but would it make sense to characterize them as "whole" or "wholesome" human beings? Most people would probably say no. We balk at the claim that the serial killer or socially irresponsible plutocrat merit the epithet *healthy*. In this, common sense is on our side. Few would wish to call a man who felt fine about being a serial killer "well", "whole", or "wholesome". A healthy person, we naturally feel, should have healthy effects on his neighbors. Obviously this cannot be the case with a serial killer. A concept of wholeness that applied just to individuals, ignoring all social and environmental implications, would be a dangerously narrow one.

Others might press for an even wider girth to the concept of wholeness, and want to include the categories of God, nature, soul, afterlife, and so forth. In other words, we might say that true health must take into account not just social but environmental and spiritual relations. My conclusion here is that the concept of wholeness should remain open; it changes as historical context and metaphysical outlook change.

This raises the possibility that we people of "modern times" and "modern cultures" may be working with an unduly restricted idea of health and wholeness. In the course of the evolution of our technical intelligence, we may have lost something essential to a truly vital philosophy. To find out whether this is so would be the job of a philosophy of healing.

Healing and Philosophy

Among the ancients, healing and philosophy were closely allied. Several pre-Socratic philosophers — Empedocles and Pythagoras, for example — were as much healers and shamans as thinkers. The health and integrity of the soul was central to Socrates' pursuit of excellence, and Plato's political Utopia was based on a model of psychological wholeness. Aristotle's theory of tragedy relied on the medical idea of *katharsis*. Hippocrates once remarked: "The physician who is also a philosopher is equal to a god". Ancient skeptical philosophy was a form of psychotherapy that sought to produce in practitioners a state of inner tranquillity. Similar therapeutic points could be made about Stoicism and Epicureanism.

More recently, Nietzsche (2001: 212) has described the philosopher as a "physician of culture". As physician of culture, Nietzsche says, the philosopher applies the "knife vivisectionally to the very virtues of the time". In other words, it is the job of the physician of culture to examine critically the reigning system of values.

Great works of philosophy embody a quest for wholeness of vision; this was true both of the "systematic" philosophers like Spinoza and Hegel and of philosophers like Nietzsche or Kierkegaard who scorned the systematic approach. The great thinkers address the big questions in a holistic way, whether their methods are systematic or unsystematic; they offer a picture of the whole and a method for knowing and acting with respect to the whole. Even uncritical people rely on some preferred image of the whole, some vague "philosophy of life".

The holistic function of philosophy has been described by C.D. Broad (1963) as "synoptic", which literally means "seeing together". The synoptic function of philosophy involves the task of seeing the different departments of knowledge in their holistic interrelationship. Broad contrasts this with the analytic function of philosophy. Analysis breaks down an object into its component parts; synopsis treats all objects as components of a whole. Analysis both complements and opposes the function of synopsis.

Contemporary Anglo-American philosophy, it is often said, has become a trivial pursuit, esoterically technical, remote from the needs of life, especially from the need for a vision of the whole. There is, unfortunately, some truth to this claim. Yet in spite of this officially antimetaphysical age, the need for images of the whole continues to express itself in many ways. Many thoughtful people outside academic philosophy try to address the "big" questions traditionally reserved for philosophers. Psychologists, physicists, and theologians have been trying in this period of "paradigm wars" to assume the "healing" job of philosophy.

As to Nietzsche's idea of the philosopher as "physician of culture", psychoanalysis has bred a whole school of *physicians of culture*. In *Civilization and Its Discontents*, Freud argued that civilization, which he saw as based on repression, is an ill-at-ease — indeed, a dis-eased — process, full of "*Unbehagen*" and *malaise*. At the end of that remarkable little book, Freud the stoic rationalist invokes the aid of Empedocles' mythical Eros as antidote to our strife-torn, suicidal, and "discontented" civilization.

Thus, at the end of Freud's analysis we find an invocation of myth. Like Plato, Freud, and after him, C.G. Jung, H. Marcuse, N.O. Brown, J. Hillman, J. Campbell, and others, all end by invoking the power of the healing myth — the healing imagination. Another philosopher I would mention here is David Griffin, who is trying to bring together Whiteheadian process philosophy, parapsychology, and psychosomatic medicine (Griffin 1988a).

Perhaps it is no surprise that we are witnessing a renewed emphasis on the healing imagination. In Vico's 1744 model of the genesis and decay of societies, it is at the end of the life-cycle of a society that the "age of men" and reason, having turned "rotten" from the "barbarism of reflection", spontaneously gives way to a new "age of the gods" — which for Vico meant a revival of the creative imagination (Fisch and Bergin 1976). For Vico, the creative imagination had the task of generating a common mythical sensibility, the only means whereby human beings can dwell on earth together, sensibly and decently — indeed, healthily.

The Healing Power of Imagery

Psychoanalysis — often in conjunction with Marxist ideas — has been a fruitful source of critical social theory and hence of what I am loosely calling philosophy of healing. Other types of data are also relevant. Recent studies in anthropology, parapsychology, stress reduction, placebo effect, biofeedback, meditation, hypnosis, and psychoneuroimmunology, all of which document the psychophysical effects of mental imagery, also have implications for a general philosophy of healing.

Let me mention a few suggestive examples. Sometimes the power of imagination is proven accidentally, as when the physician, J.C. Barker, thoughtlessly asked a patient suffering from angina pectoris if "he ever felt that he was going to die during one of his attacks of pain" (Barker 1968: 4). Hearing this and interpreting it to be a death sentence, the patient turned glassy-eyed, all vital signs suddenly sinking, and expired within minutes. An autopsy showed no evidence of coronary thrombosis. Barker, an inexperienced doctor, admits that his question — which put the image of death before his patient's mind — was the immediate cause of death.

The above is a story of the bad side of a neutral power. But the same power has a good side. If imagery can kill, it can also heal. In Norman Cousins's book, *The Healing Heart*, we find an account of a physician who mentioned to a staff member that a patient's heart had a "wholesome gallop". The phrase "unwholesome gallop" actually referred to the pathology of a failing heart. The patient overheard the doctor's words, but misunderstanding them as proof that his heart was healthy, that it possessed a "wholesome gallop", underwent a remarkable recovery. Because the patient imagined, on the basis of the doctor's words, that his heart still had "kick" in it, he became confident he would recover. This is an example of how the right metaphor can generate healing effects.

The healing power of imagination may also be evoked on purpose. Frank (1971: 67) describes a placebo study that reversed the chemical effect of ipecac (an emetic) in a patient suffering from nausea. The patient was told that the drug she was given — which normally induces vomiting — would eliminate her nausea. Her expectation (imagining) that it would do so somehow enabled her to reverse the normal physical effect of the drug.

A well-known case of healing by imagery involved a sixteen-year-old youth plagued by congenital "fish-skin" disease; as a consequence of hypnotic suggestion, a large percentage of the diseased skin became healthy, skin that from birth was hard as fingernail, thick, black, numb, inelastic, and covered with papillae (Mason 1952). I stress this example and the previous one because they show the power of consciousness to reverse both the physiological effect of a chemical and the physiology of a congenital disease.

The power of imagination was recognized by the early French mesmerists. In this century, Barber (Barber et al. 1974) has conducted experiments showing that imagination, expectancy, and motivation produce the same effects as "hypnotic trance". Barber contends that hypnotic induction procedures basically rely on verbally induced imagery.

Using imagination — or hypnosis — Barber and his associates were able to produce phenomena of age regression, hallucination, amnesia, alteration of time sense, enhanced learning capacity, reduction of pain, and other physiological changes (the formation of "blisters", the curing of warts, and so on). Producing such "hypnotic" phenomena involves complex cognitive strategies; for example, the "hypnotic" reduction of pain involves reducing the subject's fear and anxiety (which increase the experience of pain) and suggesting images like "imagine your hand is a piece of rubber, numb and insensitive to pressure".

The work of Carl and Stephanie Simonton (Simonton et al. 1975; 1984) implicates imagery as a factor in slowing or healing cancer. The Simontons found that in cases of spontaneous remission the patients often seemed to experience healing visualizations; these took many forms, including religious imagery. The Simontons developed techniques of visualization as an experimental adjunct in cancer treatment. They say that success depends not only on the belief system of the patient but on the belief system of the physician and the family.

Some evidence suggests that personality traits may lead to specific diseases. In cancer, for example, inability to express emotion, passivity, and complaisance have been cited. But these are traits built up over time and in specific social contexts. The power of the healing imagination is thus a function of a lifetime of personal and social development. The dominant thought patterns of a society shape the collective imagination; the power of the individual healing imagination depends on the cultural imagination. The sources of healing and harming are aspects of the whole texture of a culture. We need therefore to learn to think in terms of healing and harming *cultures*.

I can think of two experimental studies with animals that have implications for the general idea of a healing culture. In the first, groups of rabbits were fed toxic high-cholesterol diets to test the effect on their arteries; all the rabbits displayed the expected negative effects except for one group that had been cuddled and fondled by the student assigned to feeding the creatures. Subsequent experiments confirmed the effect, suggesting that affectionate relationships may be more important than cholesterol to a healthy heart. This seems related to another study showing that men who suffer heart attacks are more likely to recover if they believe that their wives love them (Chopra 1989: 33). Health, it seems, is a product of a "healthy" social relationship.

Another experiment involved mice. A group of mice were given a chemical known to stimulate T cells and thus boost their immune system. While receiving this chemical immune booster, the animals were also exposed to the smell of camphor. Eventually the mice showed an increase in their immune-cell count when exposed only to the smell of camphor. By virtue of a conditioned association, the smell was enough to induce a healthy autoimmune response (Chopra 1989). Again this raises questions about the idea of a "healthy society". To what extent are we taking into account the vast network of mental associations embedded in all facets of the culture that may be unconsciously weakening or (we hope) strengthening our bodily defenses to disease?

Evidence for the role of imagery in the healing process is extensive. We have yet to mention the data with perhaps the greatest implications for the power of the healing imagination — paranormal and "miraculous" healing. In both the experimental (for a review, see Krippner and Villoldo 1976) and spontaneous cases of paranormal or "miraculous" healing, the role of imagination is pervasive.

In one pattern of reported "miraculous" healing, for instance, healing is associated with visions of the Virgin Mary. "Miraculous" healings tend to occur in environments saturated with archetypal imagery: the Virgin Mary, Christ, the Holy Spirit; saints, *boddhisattvas*, wizards; Aesclepius, Inanna, Isis — symbols, myths, and images of sacred power. The production of stigmata, I might add, is closely related to the identification with the image of the crucified Christ. In modern times, the most spectacular case is that of Padre Pio, whose stigmata lasted fifty years.

Whether in personal or religious settings, spontaneous or experimental situations, evidence exists for the power of images to heal and to harm. This power exerts itself at all levels of health and wholeness: physiological, emotional, and spiritual. Most discussions of the healing imagination begin — rightly I believe — with individual phenomenology. However, the physician of culture needs to press the inquiry further and judge the healing and harming elements of the social imagination. This requires a more concrete, more historical approach to the problem of healing because social imaginations evolve in particular societies.

How Does Healing Imagery Work?

Before proceeding, I want to say something about how the healing image works. It is clear that imagery works through a variety of mechanisms. For example, by raising hope, it may stimulate the immune system. In using imagery to heal warts, a quite different mechanism is apparently involved — by directing attention to the wart, blood flow in the virally affected area increases (warts are caused by viral infections), and the wart disappears. In treating hypertension, imagery increases muscular relaxation and activates the para-sympathetic nervous system.

Many pathways and mechanisms link psyche and soma, and all of them are not fully understood. I want to make a general suggestion about the link between image and healing — the idea that psychokinesis (PK) is a goal-oriented process.

The variety of contexts in which imagery is used suggests a variety of psychosomatic mechanisms. The one common feature seems to be the goal of being healed. For example, once the idea of healing comes into play — an image of wholesome skin, let us say, in the case of fish-skin disease that was treated by Mason — the body mobilizes whatever mechanisms it needs to materialize the healing idea or goal.

Or suppose, to take an instance of psychic harming, a person has been "boned" or believes a death spell has been placed on him. He pictures, or at any rate anticipates, himself as dying. The crucial point, I believe, is that his expectation of doom is shared and thus reinforced by everyone around him. If goal-oriented PK comes into play, the victim's body will utilize whatever mechanisms it needs to materialize the deadly goal.

Barber has shown how goal-oriented imagery produces "hypnotic" effects. To produce arm levitation, for example, he presents his subject with an image showing the goal already in effect: "Picture your arm being lifted into the air on balloons". Papago Indian song magic is based on this principle; the "magical" songs are ideal images of the goal yet to be incarnated: the ideal way of making love, of going to war, of healing. The Papago believes that singing the songs brings about what the songs picture (Underhill 1968).

Some parapsychologists hold that psi is a goal-oriented process. (Subjects just think about the goal — a pattern of lights flashing in a random event generator — no effort or thought is given to the mechanism of *how* this goal is to come about.) The image facilitates the "telic" or goal-oriented psi process. Thus, when the healer visualizes the healee as whole and healed, the image, expressing the "goal", may both induce and orient the psi process. The hypothesis in brief: If psi (or healing in general) is a goal-oriented process and if the image is a way of articulating goals, then the image is a way of inducing the psi (or healing) process.

The Spell of the Cultural Imagination

To understand the full power of imagination we must place more emphasis on the social or cultural imagination, the images that pervade and dominate an entire culture. What individuals imagine is shaped by the ideas and images "in the air" — the consensus, the all-powerful, hypnotic local paradigm.

Consider, for example, Cannon's (1942) classic paper on "voodoo" death. Cannon collected case histories from non-literate societies showing that a sorcerer's spell can kill a human being. Two things are essential for this type of murderous "magic" to work: (1) the victim must believe in the power of the spell; and (2) the group to which the victim belongs must share the same belief and expectations, supporting and consensually validating the sorcerer's spell. Cannon explains how the spellbound victim isolates himself from the group, the shock of expecting imminent death causing a sudden malfunction of the circulatory system, which rapidly results in death. If an autopsy is performed in such cases, no lesions are found. Lévi-Strauss (1963) has commented on this type of murder by sorcery: "Physical integrity," he writes, "cannot withstand the dissolution of the social personality."

Cannon shows that belief in the spell is crucial to its effectiveness; if the victim can bring himself to believe in a counterspell, his symptoms vanish and he is "healed".[1] Of course, the counterspell also draws its strength from some other portion of the culture's social personality.

The power of the cultural imagination to influence the effectiveness of acupuncture analgesia was evident in China, where a significant portion of the population has undergone surgery without the benefit of anesthetics. According to Kroger, what accounts for acupuncture anesthesia in China were the

> antecedent variables such as the generalized stoicism of the Chinese, the ideological zeal, the evangelical fervor, the prior beliefs shared by acupuncturists and patients and Mao Tse-Tung's *New Thought Directives*.
> — 1972: 1013

The cultural imagination of a society can apparently determine the general level of its receptivity to pain.

A more startling claim has been advanced by Achterberg, who says that studies show "that those who cannot comprehend the messages conveyed by society and its medicine die of different causes than those who can" (1985: 79). Achterberg and her associates found that mentally disabled individuals in the state of Texas die from cancer at a rate significantly lower than the rest of the population. Studies in the United Kingdom, Greece, and Romania support this finding. Achterberg suggests that people may be dying from the diagnosis of cancer rather than the disease itself.

The "doctor's diagnosis" is the functional equivalent of the sorcerer's spell; in our culture the diagnosis of cancer is generally construed as a death sentence. The doctor points to the X-ray the way the sorcerer points his bone. Or it may be the authority of the doctor that makes the placebo an effective spell.

According to Simonton, cancer patients regress when they return to

---

[1] I do not want to exclude the possibility that harm by spell or sorcery is possible without awareness or belief on the part of the victim. I believe this is possible through psychokinesis; and I have interviewed two educated Westerners who almost died from spells inflicted on them without their knowledge or belief.

their normal home environments, where ideas of the dominant social personality outweigh individual efforts at self-healing visualizations. Here, the "bone" is being pointed by all the people around the patient who agree with the consensus that cancer is an automatic death sentence. This point also applies to AIDS; for the consensus, a diagnosis of AIDS is an automatic death certificate.

Psychosomatic medicine describes correlations between personality types and proneness to specific diseases. For example, some personality "types" are prone to have accidents, others to get asthma or cancer or heart attacks. In these typologies, the focus is on individuals; but individual personality development is partly a function of psychosocial "personalities". "Type As", for example, noted for their aggressiveness, competitiveness, and time-drivenness flourish in a Type A civilization; their personalities are formed in the matrix of a Type A cultural imagination. Again, we come back to the question of disease-prone society profiles.

The spell of the cultural imagination is nurtured by the arts. In the *Republic,* Plato spoke of images that "nourish" the soul. The arts feed the imagination. Plato understood that the soul is educated by the cultural imagination, in his day mediated by the works of Homer and other poets, by lawmakers and teachers. Plato's question was: What images nourish the soul and what images sicken it? And what must we do to heal the public imagination?

The question Plato raises about images that sicken soul and body is still valid. We speak of the toxic environment nowadays, the overflowing landfills and dead lakes, and torn ozone layers. But there is also the problem of psychic toxicity and its effects on psychosomatic wholeness.

Our environment is full of psychic toxins. According to *Eating Smart,* a PBS special broadcast in September 1991, two-thirds of the food commercials on Saturday morning television for children contain ads for foods high in fat, salt, and sugar. The cultural imagination is conditioning children to disease-prone eating habits.

The relation between disease, psychic toxin, and advertising in America needs to be closely studied. In some instances, ads seem designed to induce illness for the purpose of selling a product. For example, an ad for Primatene Mist (for relief from asthma attacks) seems made to induce an asthma attack; the ad shows a person gasping from an asthma attack — yet it is known that asthmatics are prone to suggestion. Similarly, an ad featuring a "Maalox Moment" shows a woman almost breaking a piece of chinaware — an image designed to upset a nervous stomach and thereby induce the victim to buy the product that promises relief. "Advanced" societies have their own insidious ways of "pointing the bone".

The examples of psychic sorcery I have cited work their spells on us in ways that are relatively crude and easy to detect. However, in my view, the worst toxins to pollute our inner environment are more covert and insidious; the diseases of the cultural imagination run deep and work on a more subtle plane, sabotaging the innards of our vital consciousness.

On the subtle plane, values and goals are systematically ingrained in the cultural imagination. But values and goals mobilize, orient, and quicken our vital functions. The question therefore is: What values and goals? Indeed, whose values and goals? In a free society, we would hope, our own. We ought to be free to pursue our own values and goals, but life in an electronic information society can make that difficult. It is getting harder to shield ourselves from being invaded, seduced, and just plain raped by the dominant cultural values. Anyone who uses a phone or a VCR or can read is vulnerable. Privacy of self — and hence full ownership of self — is becoming increasingly hard to maintain in our age of telecommunications. The 11 November 1991, issue of *Time Magazine* ran a cover story, "Nowhere to Hide", about the growing electronic invasion of privacy.

Consider telemarketing, a recent invention for imposing the "idols of the marketplace"[2] on private citizens via telephone technology. Suppose, for example, I am at home, thinking or meditating, dining with friend or family, deep in work or play: The phone rings — I get up, walk across the room, and answer the phone. A mechanical voice barks into my ear, announcing that I've been chosen for the bargain of a lifetime.

This sort of thing happens regularly to millions of Americans nowadays. Apart from being an invasion of the right to privacy that the Constitution guarantees, telemarketing intrusions are a form of psychic pollution.

The phenomenon of telemarketing poses a subtle and indirect threat to psychosomatic health. The insurgence of telemarketing illustrates powerful tendencies that pervade the American cultural imagination. The following remarks treat telemarketing as merely illustrative of what seems to be happening to the cultural imagination at large.

---

2. This apt phrase is from Bacon's *Novum Organon*.

First, computer telemarketing is part of a systematic design to implement a consumer-oriented culture. Consumerism — and the system of disordered appetite it implies — is a stupefying assault on the human soul; furthermore, reams of data show it has ruinous repercussions on global ecology. Consumerism uses machine technology to control and mechanize people's buying habits. Market and profit driven, it shows little concern for public health and safety. This is obvious with the cigarette industry.

Second, telemarketing, and almost all commercial advertising, seems at odds with the natural instinct for truth that human beings may be said to possess. By relentless hyperbole, innuendo, disinformation, cretinlike simplification, and baldface prevarication, both the public capacity and the public taste for distinguishing true from false is being corroded and corrupted. Can the effects on the health of the nation be good? Can our ad-manipulated, ad-created false consciousness be healthy for people?

Take the omnipresent automobile commercial on television. Here is something that involves more than merely selling cars. Here in fact is a campaign to engender idolatry. What O. Münzerberg said in 1969 still applies. Münzerberg described the religious awe with which the automobile industry seeks to invest itself:

> The administrative headquarters of Ford in Dearborn is entered like a cathedral. The holy of holies, the car of the year, a two-seater sports car, stands on a sacred ramp and is called Boss 302. The priests of capital seal off the production site — as Catholic priests who conceal the cross during Good Friday liturgy — for two months from public view. The resurrection celebration . . . is celebrated on 1 September, when the *top car*, the holiest of all, the idol for the coming year, is revealed.
>
> — Quoted in Schneider 1975: 216

The mind managers who control the information industries labor relentlessly to perpetuate the *mythology* of the car. The "car", according to the myth, signifies freedom, security, self-mastery, paradise, erotic fulfillment, and so forth; in reality the car is a menace to ecology, a potential flashpoint in geopolitics, and for the average citizen a financial bloodsucker and a filthy nuisance.

The rift between the reality of the car and the mythology of the car is part of a growing phenomenon of our information culture; in particular, it expresses a general feature of the image as it operates in the cultural media — namely, the *exaltation of image without substance*. (For an excellent discussion of this, see Ewen 1988.)

Third, the telemarketing intrusion illustrates another type of aggression directed against the wholesome sensibility. You can hear it in the rapid, frantic, high-pressuring tone of the mechanical voice: the jerky mechanization of our experience of time. The mechanical telemarketing voice is, of necessity, in a hurry.

Some good evidence shows that modern "hurry sickness" is unhealthy for the heart. The tempo and imagery of the cultural imagination conspire to fill us with a sense of urgency, of having to respond immediately, to rush forward in the contest of consumption and achievement. All this, I believe, contributes to a diseased time consciousness. Telemarketing, as I said, is just an example of an unwholesome threat to the contemporary cultural imagination: a device that exacerbates consumerism, undermines public respect for truth, and creates a pathological consciousness of the shortage of time.

Healing Forms of Consciousness

A philosophy must be constructive as well as critical. Is there a way to heal our imagination of time? Are there healing forms of consciousness, rhythms and tempos of consciousness more attuned to health and vitality? Does the sickness lie in our institutions, our guiding ideals, our dominant forms of thought? These are questions that call for the assistance of our physicians of culture.

Is there a special use of imagery, a special exercise of imagination conducive to a healing cognitive style? Can we meaningfully speak of healing forms of consciousness? Perhaps the poets, the first experts on imagination, might point the way here. Yeats, for example, believed that the "age of criticism" was ending and giving way to a new "age of imagination". In his essay, "Magic", Yeats spoke of a form of thought favoring communion with the great "memory of Nature herself". The poet heals by evoking images and symbols that put us in touch with Nature's "great memory". (The idea is similar to Jung's notion of archetypes of the collective unconscious.)

D.H. Lawrence hated what he felt was a creeping mechanization of consciousness, the psychic fallout from the industrial revolution and the triumph of mass culture. In his last book, *Apocalypse,* he wrote about the vital imagination that kept people in touch with their bodies, and with the great living fluid forces of nature and her symbols:

> We have lost almost entirely the great and intricately developed sensual awareness, or sense-awareness, and sense-knowledge, of the ancient. It was a great depth of knowledge arrived at direct, by instinct and intuition, as we say, not by reason. It was a knowledge based not on words but on images.
> — Lawrence 1931: 48

There is a form of consciousness that helps us develop an intricate, a deeper sense awareness; this awareness, Lawrence repeatedly calls *vital*.

Why should the image be vitalizing and thus in a global way healing? There is much to be said about this, but let me make one point here. As far as I can see, the value of the image lies in its ability to mediate between sense-experience and abstract, intellectual thought. Images help us stay in touch with the concrete world and at the same time — as symbols — help us stay in touch with guiding ideals, abstract principles, visions. By keeping alive the tension between these opposing forces, images have the power to make us whole. Images are fusers of opposites; that is a kind of healing — the healing of onesideness and shallowness.

The notion that images by their nature may have a tendency to heal or bring together opposing modes of thought leads to a related question. Are there healing modes of thought? Habits, styles, patterns of cognizing the world that heal and vitalize existence? The poets seem to think so. Several modern philosophers have also said so: Bergson, Croce, Heidegger, for example, regard intuitive and meditative modes of thought as antidotes to excessively rationalizing, mechanizing cognitive styles. Vico was one of the first to criticize Descartes — exactly on the grounds that addiction to linear rules of reason ill-prepare us for the spontaneous challenges of real life.

Is there something unhealthy about being exclusively analytical in our habits of thought? When we use our imaginations, do we mobilize a synthetic mental capacity, somehow healthier, more life-enhancing? Shapiro (1965) has described the paranoid cognitive style marked by keen but drastically rigid and narrow habits of thought. The paranoid cognitive style is the opposite of the holistic; it combines hyperacute vigilance with intensely suspicious bias. On the subject of paranoia, the radical psychoanalyst Ferenczi has written:

> Philosophical systems that seek to explain rationally the whole order of the world, leaving no room over for irrationality (i.e., for what is not yet explicable), have been . . . compared with the paranoiac delusional systems.
> — 1956: 247

A cognitive style that systematically blocked contact with "what is not yet explicable" would lock us out of large portions of human experience — for instance, the paranormal and the transpersonal. Such a one-sided state of affairs would, in my judgment, be poor for our mental health and wholeness. We would be cheating ourselves of the possibilities of new insights and discoveries.

Could overly rigid, overly systematic cognitive styles weaken the immune system? Stress apparently depresses the immune response, and certain cognitive styles may be more stressful than others. For example, the paranoid cognitive style, rigid and obsessively vigilant, might cause undue stress for the immune system. This is a question for empirical study. What I might say now is this. Some researchers claim that ideas of hopelessness and helplessness depress the immune response. Excessively and exclusively analytic habits of mind might undermine the ability to hope and so depress the immune system.

Sheer analysis tends toward skepticism. Although I do not deny the value of robust skepticism, imagination, I believe, can help us picture possibilities that critically captious minds will regard as unlikely or impossible. Images can lift us out of depressing immediacy and help us picture higher goals and higher possibilities. Feelings of hopelessness and helplessness imply the defeat of imagination, the inability to imagine new goals, new possibilities.

Some Concluding Questions

A philosophy centered around the theme of healing and wholeness — and such a philosophy is urgently needed in our ecological age — would need to ask many questions. It would, as suggested earlier, explore the possibility of healing modes of consciousness. The philosophy of healing that I feel we need to pursue would be partners with archetypal psychology and parapsychology; it would focus on the universality and outer limits of the power of images. Above all, a philosophy of healing for our time needs to be socially critical, for our individual imaginations are creatures of the social imagination.

This leads to the question of healing worldviews. We know, for instance, that time-related feelings of stress and ideas of hopelessness and helplessness affect individual health. As physicians of culture, we would examine worldviews in light of their ability to mobilize hope. We must ask: Are some worldviews immunodepressive, devitalizing, even suicidal?

Does a worldview expand or contract one's idea of self? One's ability to deal inventively with stress may be helped or hindered by the resources one brings to bear in defining and imaging one's everyday sense of self. Or we might ask: Does one's worldview accelerate or diminish one's bodily sense of vital reality? Does it bring out what Castaneda's Don Juan called "the funny edge" of the world — for we now know, thanks to researchers like Norman Cousins, that humor is an immune booster (1983).

A philosophy of healing would investigate healing *environments* — places that center around healing events (the apparitions of Lourdes or Guadalupe), healing people (Sai Baba, Padre Pio, Arigo), or healing activities (dream incubation temples, ancient mystery rites). How do these special group dynamics work? What sort of imagery do they deploy?

A philosophy of healing would have a critical job, diagnosing the unwholesome images, as well as the social and political and economic practices, that undermined health; it would expose the spell — the curse — of the paradigm. It would need to build a new, a healing paradigm — a healing mythology. This will require the joint efforts of many; it will require nothing less than a revolution of values, the building of a new environment of healing imagery and healing meanings.

13

Inner Teachers and Transcendent Education

Alfred S. Alschuler

MORE than sixty years have passed since George Bernard Shaw wrote the preface to *Saint Joan*, but little has changed.

> Joan's voices and visions have been held to prove that she was mad, that she was a liar and imposter, that she was a sorceress (she was burned for this), and finally that she was a saint. They do not prove any of these things. The variety of conclusions reached show how little our matter of fact historians know about other people's minds, or even their own.
>
> — 1960: 16

Most modern theoreticians have extended the debate without adding to our practical knowledge. In his seminal work, *The Origin of Consciousness in the Breakdown of the Bicameral Mind*, Julian Jaynes (1982) traces the evolution of inner voices over several thousand years and argues that they come from one side of the brain, a conclusion about as helpful as explaining current events in Eastern Europe by pointing to a spot on a map. Jungians say that voices originate in our collective unconscious, giving the place on the map a name. Charismatic Christians welcome the Holy Spirit, but also warn of evil spirits. New Age groups describe spirit guides and disembodied masters who channel their teaching through a chosen few. Spiritualists claim they are voices of the dead. Some psychics claim that there are broadcasts from Unidentified Flying Objects (UFO) and aliens. Reporters distort the facts to shock or amuse with *National Enquirer* headlines like "Famed Psychic's Head Explodes". Even Klimo's fine book (1988) on channeling misses the role of voices in self-transcendence.

The debate over what inner voices really are is similar to the quest for the nature of electricity: Is it a wave or a particle? While physicists argue, electricians are busy installing our lights. No matter where these voices come from, the nature of this inner world needs to be described.

Five practical questions arise: *Who* hears? What is it *like* to hear an inner voice? What do inner voices *say*? What *happens* to people if they listen for a long time? Do they sail off the edge of the sanity world or find a new land? Does anything of *lasting value* result?

Hearing an Inner Voice Is not a Particularly Rare Event

According to surveys by the Gallup Organization (1984) and the National Opinion Research Council (Greeley and McCready 1975), between one-third and one-half of adult Americans have had an ecstatic experience. Of these, up to one-fifth (seventeen to twenty-five million) have heard an inner voice, an event they describe with adjectives like "love", "joy", "enlightenment", "peace", and "awe". More than 90 per cent report that the experience is positive, often life changing, a source of revelation and renewal. Also, according to these national surveys, virtually no one discusses these experiences, not with family members, intimate friends, the clergy, or counselors. Ecstasy seems to have replaced sexuality in this century as the most severely repressed human capacity. One implication is clear: This half-hidden human inheritance should be discussed openly.

I searched for answers in the lives of people who heard inner voices — sane, graceful, and loving individuals whose contributions to society were so clear that the chorus of their accomplishments would drown out the popular belief that hearing an inner voice automatically means you are crazy or satanic. Eventually I found about 150 men and women over the last two millennia who were sufficiently noteworthy to be remembered, representing a dozen religious traditions and countries. Like shooting stars, they were recognized briefly then largely forgotten. Because the experience has not been examined historically, it has been rediscovered in every generation, given a fashionable name ("prophesy", "possession", "paranoia", "channeling"), and assumed to be a rare event reserved for the few. Its pervasiveness has not been seen, commonalties have been missed, and many of the most creative applications have been ignored.

What Is It Like to Hear an Inner Voice?

Please try this experiment. Silently, to yourself, choose a number between one and ten. Do you have it now? Good. That's *almost* like hearing an inner voice. Inner voices are different in several ways.

As Saint Teresa said more than 450 years ago, the difference "is like that between speaking and listening. While I am speaking, my [mind] is composing what I am saying, whereas if I am being spoken to, I do nothing but listen and it requires no effort" (Saint Jeresa 1960: 231). Helen Schucman, the psychologist who transcribed *The Course in Miracles* from an inner voice, reported, "There is no actual sound and the words come mentally, but very clearly. It's a kind of inner dictation" (Skutch 1984: 56).

Hearers experience inner voices as *not their own*, but as a separate, independent consciousness not under their control that emerged suddenly like Minerva, Goddess of Wisdom, born fully grown from the head of Zeus. Again, Saint Teresa is not clear:

> If all [inner voices] came from [our own mind], we could hear them whenever we liked. But with divine [voices], I may listen for days, and although I have a desire to hear them, I am unable to do so. And then, at other times when I have no desire to hear them, I am compelled to. However determined one's resistance, it is impossible to fail to hear them. And sometimes the [mind] is so perturbed that it cannot put together a single sentence, and yet the soul hears long speeches which it could not have composed even if completely [calm and collected].
>
> — 1960: 232-33

The otherness of this distinct personality is strengthened when the voice announces its name and the hearer is addressed as "you". When I asked for the name of my own inner voice, it said, "We are the great white brotherhood". My immediate reaction was, "Isn't it just my luck to get a racist, sexist spiritual group". Then it was explained that "great" meant cosmic, "white" referred to the light, and "brotherhood" referred to its essential loving quality.

From autobiographies and biographies, I compiled a list of several hundred of these names to see if they fell into any obvious categories. By far the most frequent were names of dead people, some famous, some relatives and friends, and some who allegedly were trying to make contact with the physical world to complete an unfinished agenda: reassuring loved ones, asking forgiveness, or completing a project. These voices are least interesting. Just because they are dead does *not* make them smarter.

In the next category were teachers who usually were reluctant to identify with a past earthly personality because it distracts hearers from the content of their messages. When asked, the inner voice usually accommodates with the name of a Native American, biblical figure, saint, ordinary earthling, or exotic creature.

In another group, the most abstract of all, were names of spiritual groups and group spirits. For me, their pronouncements usually are so dense as to be impenetrable.

Finally, there were some names just too strange to classify: Lion of Androcles, Shadow of the Tomb, Old Man of the Hills. These names were strong tonic for my skepticism. Questions tumbled forth. Why do I not feel safer knowing that there are "Race Guardians"? Where do they pin the "Galaxy Medallion"? Just where is the "Ass of Balaam" located? Does "Snow Drop" become "Dew Drop" during celestial summers?

I do not know how many of these names reflect a self-deceptive charade, how much is evidence for holiness, and how much is just plain hoax. Let's assume, however, that not all of these claims are fraudulent. When inner voices announce, "Call me Lady Nona", or "I was known as Tecumseh", or "I speak for the Inyokern Brothers", the voices assert their independent existence and crystallize a relationship with the hearer. The categories of names, crude as they are, point to the obvious. Voices claim different knowledges, perspectives, and purposes. Consequently, the relationships with those voices vary from heavenly to hellish. This is the *psychological* reality whether or not the voices come from some separate worlds.

What Do Inner Voices Say?

First of all, they provide **superior information**. Socrates is quoted as saying (Myers 1903: 95-100):

> Since childhood I have been attended by a semi-divine being whose voice, from time to time, dissuades me from some undertaking." He called this inner voice "the sign". The sign warned him not to defend himself at his trial for impiety. In his address to the court after he was sentenced to die, Socrates said, "In other speeches of mine, the sign has often stopped me in the midst. But now it has not hindered me in any deed or word. What then do I suppose to be the reason? I will tell you. I think what has happened to me is a good thing; and we must have been mistaken when we supposed that death was an evil. That accustomed sign would have checked me, had I been about to do anything evil.

Emmanuel Swedenborg probably was the last person to know all science. Born three centuries ago, he wrote 155 books in seventeen sciences, most of them definitive integrations of what was known. He founded the science of crystallography. Six of his anatomical discoveries were ignored for 200 years before they were rediscovered. He was fluent in nine languages and a master of seven crafts. He made his own telescope and microscope and drew crude but workable designs for a submarine, an airplane, and at least eight other inventions that were brought to fruition decades or centuries later (Van Dusen 1974: 1-18).

He did all this before reaching the age of fifty-six, when he began exploring inner worlds through voices and visions. Over the next twenty-six years, he wrote more than 250 books from inner dictation, including many weighty tomes of several thousand pages. Swedenborg once saw and reported to a group of friends the progress of a devastating fire while it was occurring in Stockholm over 300 miles away. A week later, every detail was confirmed in newspaper accounts, including the near miss of a friend's home. When asked to prove his access to superior information by predicting the precise day and minute of a person's death, he did so. He quoted back to Christopher Springer, Sweden's negotiator, the verbatim conversation of secret talks with Prussia. On another occasion he described the strangulation of Russia's Emperor Peter III in Kopscha prison several days *before* the event occurred and was reported in the newspaper. He successfully met the challenge of the Queen of Sweden to find out a secret from her deceased brother that only she knew. At the request of a countess, Swedenborg contacted her recently deceased husband, Count de Marteville, for directions to important papers he had hidden and gave precise directions to the lost documents (Van Dusen 1974: 139-57).

Inner voices warning of accidents or dangers are commonplace. Without the risk of hyperbole, I can say that one particular warning had the greatest consequences for humanity. As revealed in Langer's secret wartime report, Adolf Hitler wrote that during the first war:

> I was eating my dinner with several comrades. Suddenly a voice seemed to be saying to me, "get up and go over there". It was so clear and so insistent that I obeyed automatically, as if it had been a military order. I rose to my feet and walked 20 m along the trench. Then I sat down to go on eating, my mind at rest. Hardly had I done so when a flash and a deafening report came from the part of the trench I had just left. A stray shell had burst over the group in which I had been sitting, and every member of it was killed. — 1972: 34

Hitler believed in the superiority of his inner voice.

> I carry out the commands that Providence [the name of his inner voice] has laid upon me. Unless I have the incorruptible conviction [that] this

> is the solution, I do nothing, not even if the whole Nazi Party tried to drive me to action. I will not act. . . . But if the voice speaks, then I know the time has come to act.

Hitler did not make important decisions in a logical, timely manner. Before crucial decisions, he occupied himself with distractions until his voice spoke. This procrastination drove his generals to despair. Hitler would leave Berlin suddenly, without telling anyone, and go to Berchtesgaden where he could walk alone in silence for hours to better hear his inner voice. Allied generals considered Hitler a tactical military "genius", that the timing of his decisions was "uncanny", that his intelligence was "astonishing", his political intuition "miraculous", and, his moral sense "void".

After so many silly spirit names, these cases are stunning. Inner voices carry with them the potential for ecstasies, absurdities, and abominations. They cannot be banned, disarmed, or licensed. They need to be understood and managed for good.

Second, inner voices also provide **superior inspiration**. Inner voices come at moments of indecision, resolve conflicts, convert unbelievers, and create a sense of understanding, certainty, calm, and quiet. As an Augustinian Monk, Martin Luther worked to earn God's love through acts of penance. When he felt he had finally done enough, an inner voice said, "Well done, Brother Martin! Soon you will not need God at all" (Pelikan 1983: 44). Only then did he understand that God's favors are given, not earned. John Bunyan, author of *Pilgrim's Progress* (1938), heard an inner voice challenging him to leave his sinful life. For a few years he ignored the request and felt doubly damned. He repented, but no matter how many acts of contrition he performed, he still felt lost. Finally an inner voice resolved instantly what he was unable to accomplish in a decade.

> As I was passing into the field, suddenly this sentence fell upon my soul: The righteousness is in heaven. I saw with the eyes of my soul Jesus Christ at God's right hand. It was not my good frame of heart that made my righteousness better, nor my bad frame that made it worse, for my righteousness was Jesus Christ. — Bunyan 1938: 116

Bunyan and Luther learned the same lesson: God's love is a gift.

Third, inner voices also provide **superior authorization**. In one of my graduate classes, I asked students to write down the five most important questions in their life, no matter how trivial or grandiose they might seem to others. Most people, even the cynics, wanted to know, "What is my purpose?" Their question is revealing. It suggests that most of us conduct our daily lives without a clear sense of our guiding mission, that we want to have an overarching purpose. Often inner voices define a mission and authorize action. Many people have been called to their life's vocation in this way.

"The Lord has appointed me," said Isaiah, "to preach good tidings to the meek; he has sent me to bind up the heartbroken, to proclaim liberty to the captives and . . . to comfort all who mourn." Saint Teresa said, "The Lord gave me the most explicit commands to work for this with all my might" (Underhill 1960). Then she founded seventeen convents and two monasteries and dictated four more inspired books. Saint Francis was told to rebuild the church. Saint Joan was asked to throw the English out of France by raising the siege at Orleans and to bring her dauphin to his throne by crowning him at Rhiems.

Inner authorizations often are sudden and surprising; they ask for outcomes that defy the odds. Saint Joan had six prohibitive handicaps: she was a peasant girl, seventeen, with no knowledge of military strategy or tactics, and she had to rejuvenate a dispirited army that already considered the cause lost. When an inner voice calls for action, however, fidelity to the mission is more important than a rational assessment of resources. Who could have predicted the hundreds of convents and monasteries worldwide that have been created out of Mother Teresa's work. She was told by an inner voice to leave her cloistered life and "give service to the poorest of the poor".

To summarize, inner voices are understood as mysterious contact points between the human personality and another, wiser, more powerful personality that is not anchored in a specific time, place, or the stuff of physical being. Hints of this hidden relationship occur for those who hear once, are calmed, uplifted, converted, given timely warnings, or called to a mission. Others hear regularly and conclude that the relationship has an abiding aim. These inner voices are teachers in the finest sense. No matter what their names are, the role of the voice is to inform (the first goal of teaching), to inspire (a cherished hope of teachers), and to authorize (the essence of commencement, the charge to make one's learning manifest in the world).

Calling an inner voice an "inner teacher" is a political act that claims who has the right to do what to whom. It denies the claims of psychiatrists who argue that all inner voices are symptoms of mental illness and that doctors have a responsibility to make them go away. It denies the claims of clergy who assert that voices are strictly a religious matter and that discerning the source is the first issue. Naming it an inner teacher opens the possibility of an inner education.

Fourth, what happens when individuals continue to listen to their inner teachers? A philosopher refuses to defend himself, swallows hemlock, comforts his friends, and embraces death unafraid. A seventeen-year-old, illiterate farm girl rallies a demoralized army, raises a siege, crowns a king, and defies her inquisitors. A cloistered nun who wanted most to pray in solitude writes five books and starts nineteen convents and monasteries from abject poverty and against the resistance of the ecclesiastical world. A master of all science doubles his prodigious literary output describing heaven and hell and the spiritual sense of the scriptures. A frustrated artist escapes death in the trenches and commands an army that conquers Europe. We ask how these miraculous changes occur and are told that their inner teacher inspired them. But how do inner teachers break the stubborn habits of a lifetime and get human beings to perform at levels seemingly beyond themselves? It must be a transcendent education, but how does it work?

Transcendent education can be divided into four phases: Contact, self-transcendence, union, and worldly missions of unification. Most hearers resist the initial contact. They fear becoming whatever their culture has condemned about it — a witch, possessed, psychotic, or just intolerably different. Their actions say, "No, no! Not me! Not now, and maybe never!" Often a second contact is needed to show that the first was not an accident, to fulfill an earlier promise, or to reassure.

One night during his yearly retreat on Mount Hira, Mohammed, then merely a merchant, had a lucid dream. Gabriel came carrying a brocade with writing on it (Williams 1962):

> "Recite!"
>
> "What shall I recite?"
>
> Gabriel pressed the brocade so hard against Mohammed's chest that he could not breathe, then released the pressure.
>
> "Recite!"
>
> "What shall I recite?"
>
> Again, Gabriel almost crushed Mohammed before letting him go.
>
> "Recite!"

> "But what shall I read?"
>
> "Recite: In the name of your God who created man from clotted blood, Recite: Your Lord is the most beneficent who taught by the pen, taught that which they knew not unto men."

Mohammed complied and Gabriel left.

Mohammed reported later, "It was as though these words were written on my heart." He was ashamed, angry, and completely disgusted with himself to the point of fanatic intolerance. He said, "None of God's creatures was more hateful to me than an ecstatic poet or a man possessed. I could not even bear to look at them. I thought, 'Woe is me, poet or possessed'." Mohammed chose to kill himself rather than have his tribe call him either of those names. He reported that "When I was half way up the mountain (to jump off a cliff), I heard a voice from heaven saying, 'O Mohammed! You are the Apostle of God and I am Gabriel.' I raised my head towards heaven to see and Gabriel in the form of a man stood with feet astride the horizon. I stood gazing at him. . . . Then I began to turn my face from him, but I saw him no matter what part of the sky I looked."

Gabriel was subjectively real, real enough to provoke, then prevent, suicide, mobile enough to make contact in dreams and visions, too real to be explained away. Perhaps only voices in visions of such surpassing power could have dislodged Mohammed's treasured sense of who he was and driven him to become so much more, more than a husband, father, merchant, and righteous man, more than an ecstatic poet, not possessed by demons but a conqueror and unifier of warring tribes in southern Arabia, a speaker of the verses dictated by his inner teacher, Gabriel, and later collected as the *sura*s of the Koran. For those people who eventually develop a relationship with an inner teacher, contact is complete when they are willing to listen. Absolute faith and complete subservience are not necessary or healthy.

The second stage of this extraordinary education involves transcending the ordinary self. This begins with an intensive period of instruction in the form of daily lectures, dialogues, or commentary on life experiences. A coherent philosophy is taught about the primacy of love, the survival of consciousness beyond bodily death, the eternal path of return to God, and the importance of manifesting these truths in one's life on earth. Usually this occurs during a period of solitude from forty days to three years: Moses' days in the Sinai, Buddha's isolation in the wilds of India,

Jesus' time in the Judean wilderness, Mohammed's walks in the sun-baked hills of Arabs, Mirza Husayn Ali's two years in Kurdistan caves prior to founding the Bahai Faith, Saint Catherine's three-year self-imposed exile in a room before becoming the most powerful person in fifteenth-century Europe, George Fox's three years of isolation in the world before founding the Quakers, Sri Aurobindo's year of solitary confinement in an Alipore Jail awaiting trial for launching the Indian independence movement.

There are frequent temptations to leave this radical inner relationship for a normal life with family, friends, and comforts of this world. But each time transcendent education is chosen, it increases the commitment to the teacher, to those truths, and to that world. There is a gradual shift in consciousness away from allegiance to one's old sense of self. The question "Who am I?" is answered, "No longer my body and its name, not my belongings or the groups I belong to, and not my old personality or the roles I played. I have these *things* now like a carpenter has tools. They *were* me in the same way my childhood was once me." A new Self is realized, literally made real in a relationship with an inner teacher.

Typically this stage of transcendent education culminates in three types of unitive experiences, the first an experience of union with one's inner teacher. For example, Saint Catherine saw a heavenly parade with John the Baptist, the Apostle Paul, Saint Dominic, the prophet David singing psalms, and the Virgin Mary who took her hand and asked Jesus to marry her. Jesus said, "I will this day celebrate solemnly the feast of the betrothal of your soul and, as I promised, will marry you to myself in faith" (Underhill 1960: 297). Catherine's mystic marriage tightened the bonds of love for her inner teacher that had grown during her years as a student in her small room. As small and unworthy as she may have been before, now she was a bride in a relationship as real as consciousness, closer to her husband than to her own body. No longer the seeker and student, now she was the wife and advocate of her husband's interests on earth, in a public role far more valuable than her three years as a recluse.

A second type of unitive experience is a visit to the inner teacher's spiritual community, no mere tourist but a citizen of one's true home and native "country of the soul". Mirza wrote:

> The soul steps into the sanctuary of the friend and shares as an intimate the pavilion of the Loved One, . . . where one witnesses a wondrous world and a new creation at every instant.
>
> — Balyuzi 1980; Teherzadeh 1980

With fascinating regularity, those who complete the process of self-transcendence report, like Dante, another worldly experience of heaven and hell, a vision of spiritual communities.

The third, most complete type of union is ineffable. Words cannot capture and convey it to others. Some people have tried by saying what it is not. Meister Eckhardt's description is a beautiful failure (Buber 1985 p. 5):

> There I felt without sound, there I saw without light, there I smelt without movement, there I tasted that which was not, there I felt what did not exist. There my heart became bottomless, my soul loveless, my mind formless, and my nature without essence.

After uniting with the inner teacher and uniting with a spiritual community, this most complete union unites the self with all.

These unitive experiences confirm the development of a transcendent self, a coherent higher consciousness, separate from but bound both to the old self of this world and to the spiritual world of the inner teacher. That world becomes the model of love, purpose, and community. The ecstatic unitive experiences, and then the memories, become a reservoir of reassurance and forgiveness, a primal source of hope from which one acts, and the basis for saying a final "yes" after the traumas, tragedies, and injustices of this world.

Like the dark side of the moon, this new transcendent self cannot be seen by others. What we can see is the distance from the old self reflected in behavior that does not protect the worldly body, belongings, personality, or history. Mirza Husayn Ali heard that a group of men were coming to kill him. He dismissed those guarding his house, went out with his wife to greet them, and invited them in for tea! (Balyuzi 1980). During one tense time in Saint Catherine's mediation of a dispute between two Italian city states, she heard that assassins had come to kill her. She ran into the courtyard, yelling, "Here I am. I'm Catherine". When the assassins fell back in confusion, Catherine cried for three days. She wrote to a friend that her bridegroom, Jesus, had played a trick on her. She remained a prisoner of her body (Curtayne 1930). When George Fox was confronted by a man about to run him through, he said disdainfully, "Put away your sword. It is nothing to me but a piece of straw" (Jones 1932).

Feeling lightened of the heavy burdens of struggle and knowing what lies beyond normal constricted consciousness, the transcendent self's natural response is laughter, dance, and song. Beatrice, Dante's final teacher, laughed as she led him into paradise and he saw the whole universe glorifying God in laughter. Saint Teresa chastized the nun who thought it was better to contemplate than to sing, warned against too much seriousness, and composed rustic hymns for her daughters. Saint Francis sang duets with the birds, taught his friars to sing, and at the moment of his death, sang a psalm, the best way to greet "sister death".

Experiences of ecstatic union motivate worldly missions of unification, the third stage of transcendent education. The flood of joy overflows its banks demanding to be shared. The task is to make this world more like that one. How it is done depends on the opportunities of the historical moment and the filter of one's old self, now "a pen in the hand of the will of God writing on the tablet of humanity", as Mirza said (Balyuzi 1980). This leads us directly to the fifth question: What lasting values come from listening to an inner teacher or following a transcendent curriculum?

The lives of spiritual geniuses have been used to describe a course of transcendent education. By comparison, our own development traces a more modest arc. With an image of the whole, however, it is easier to recognize the separate parts — having a vision, hearing an inner voice, being informed, inspired or authorized, receiving a transcendent education, experiencing ineffable union, having a conversion experience, acting in self-sacrificing ways out of love, building community.

Although more than 90 per cent of the people who have heard an inner voice report a positive experience, it is useful to examine the rare negative responses and clinical implications. If a client says he or she is hearing an inner voice, do not automatically reach for the *DSM III*. First, ask whether the voice is heard from within or from outside. If it comes from outside (the walls, trees, animals), then reach for the diagnostic manual, because it is a serious distortion in the person's contact with reality. If it comes from inside the head, then the question is whether the relationship is functional or dysfunctional. In essence you are dealing with two personalities. Their relationship can cover the complete range that exists between two people who both have bodies. The therapeutic task is not to get rid of the inner voice but to promote a healthy relationship. Most of the diagnostic and counseling techniques used in couples therapy can be applied.

There are a number of rather simple ways to teach people to listen to a superior inner teacher. In my graduate classes in counseling, about two-thirds of those who try are able to hear. We have begun to explore what therapists might be like if they enrolled in that inner school, studied its seemingly eternal curriculum, graduated, and became ambassadors from that world to this one. We also realized that superior inner teachers were marvelous models for clinical supervisors: instantly available, consistently loving, non-judgmental, wise, and eternally patient. They see deeply into issues as if they have true supervision, yet never pre-empt our responsibility for choosing by dictating specific solutions. Like Anita Muhl (1930), we began to teach clients to ask their inner "counselor" for guidance above their problems, useful directions to pursue, and loving solutions.

Cultural contributions range from archaeology to scientific inventions. Frederick Bligh Bond used information from inner voices to locate the exact depth and dimensions of the lost Glastonbury Abbey (Kenawell 1965). Numerous poets claim inspiration from inner voices that dictate their poems. There is strong suggestive evidence that Homer was one. Blake was explicit:

> I have written from immediate dictation, twelve, or sometimes twenty or thirty lines at a time without premeditation and even against my will, the time it has taken in writing was thus rendered non-existent and an immense poem exists which seems to be the labor of a long life, all produced without labor or study. I may praise it for I do not pretend to be any other than the secretary. The authors are in eternity.
>
> — Kazin 1976: 44

Two modern poets who have written from inner dictation are Seamus Henry and James Merrill.

Several recent authors have acknowledged their inner, other author: Herb Gold, Ray Bradbury, Judith Posner, and Alice Walker. They are merely the latest in a long line over the centuries. Composers include Schuman, Brown, Sheppard, Aubert, and the most famous of all, Mozart. He wrote to a friend:

> Musical thoughts crowd into my mind as easily as you could wish. Whence and how do they come? I do not know and have nothing to do with it. Those melodies that please me I keep in my head and hum them. Once I have my theme, another melody comes, linking itself to the first one. . . . The counterpoint, the part of each instrument, and all the melodic fragments at last produce the entire work. . . . Then my head seizes it. It is in its entirety that my imagination lets me hear it. — Hadamard 1954: 16

Then, as we know, he simply wrote it down note for note without corrections.

For every inspired poet, author, and musician who has braved the stings of public criticism by announcing the source, there probably are dozens more who have kept it secret. This inspired writing by poets, authors, and composers is done easily, quickly, taken word for word, or note for note, and when it is complete, surprises the worldly secretary with its hidden coherence, as if it had all been perfected in advance. It is the exact opposite of writers block. Listening to one's inner teacher would be an obvious skill to teach in personal growth workshops for blocked or burned out artists and others who suffer the same problem at a more prosaic level.

Many adults who have experienced moments of ecstatic union or toured heavenly communities devote themselves to creating earthly communities and "celebrating diversity" because they know the singing, dancing, and joy of communion when the interesting differences in our body-sacks are transcended. They want that, here and now, and work for it, preach it, and write about it. A few have started a religion or spiritual practice: Islam, Quakers, The Bahai Faith, Integral and Kuṇḍalinī Yogas, The Church of New Jerusalem, and Moral Rearmament. Some have started their own churches and intentional communities, like Findhorn in Scotland. Other hearers, who are authorized by their inner teacher to share what is given, publish their inspired writing as biblical updates: Catherine's *Divine Dialogues* in the fifteenth century, Linton's *Healing of Nations* in the nineteenth century, and Schucman's *Course in Miracles* in this century, are a few examples. Creative applications have been made in education (Miller 1981; Roberts and Clark 1975); and in medicine (Rossman and Bresler 1983). Recently, numerous books have been published describing the writer's personal relationship with an inner teacher. Thousands of others conduct their own transcendent education quietly in regular written dialogues with their inner teachers, and tell no one. We may question the specific teachings, but we cannot deny the powerful renewal and charge to moral action that come from the revelations of superior inner teachers.

Over the last fifty years, many people have had global visions in deep near-death experiences. Others have heard apocalyptic scenarios described by their inner teachers. I found this merely interesting until I noticed uncanny consistencies in these scenarios. Most predicted a rapid increase in all types of disasters worldwide, major ecological dangers, and political changes beginning in the late 1980s. As a social scientist, I decided to gather data from the US Office of Foreign Disaster Assistance and other historical scientific documents. I discovered that these modern prophets were correct, in general, thus far. Since the 1950s, almost all types of disasters have doubled each decade. There are worldwide political transformations, and we are fighting the third World War now — the struggle to save the planet from ecological destruction. Winning the third World War requires that we transcend our sense of self, envision a global community, and co-operate across the boundaries of class and country. These are natural consequences of a transcendent education.

As part of my own education, I decided to visit a hell on earth rather than waiting for an inner vision of it. I toured three war zones in the Horn of Africa. Civil wars in Sudan, Ethiopia, and Somalia are the main causes of the famines, continuing illiteracy, and unconscionable, absolute poverty. One essential element in three decades of Eritrean hell is Ethiopian *taking* — taking Eritrean land, taking their freedoms, their food, families, livelihood, limbs, and lives. Seeing a battlefield shortly after 18,000 Ethiopians had been killed makes that lesson clear. There is no such thing as a *civil* war.

Perhaps I had to see this hellish "taking" halfway around the world to appreciate the obvious at home. In contrast, giving and receiving are essential elements of counseling and what make it so heavenly. Perhaps I had to study inner teachers and transcendent education to appreciate what is so noble about counseling and therapy. We approximate inner teachers in outer forms. We try to inform, inspire, and authorize through patient, loving, wise counsel; and we have daily opportunities to align our work with a vision of heavenly communities.

14

Consciousness and Well-Being

Neil Rossman

HUMAN beings engage in multileveled varieties of both physical and psychological destructiveness. What can be quite troublesome about this situation is that much of what passes as "normal, acceptable" attitude and behavior is instead, when seen more honestly and clearly, a more subtle, or indeed a not-more-subtle, version of such destructiveness.

If this is so, it presents a difficult problem. For if everyday attitudes and behaviors are not seen accurately and clearly, it suggests not only a level of misdescription but, more ominously, a misunderstanding of the deeper dynamics and nature of these attitudes and behavior. In a word, it involves a misunderstanding of what is, in fact, going on in such instances. In light of this, there is a need to look more closely at what underlies such attitudes, behavior, and the like. This, in turn, requires an examination of the deeper workings of consciousness.

What I wish to suggest is that we do not understand, do not adequately grasp, how in fact consciousness works and develops. To grasp or understand consciousness is, in part, to grasp or understand ourselves. Consciousness, that is, must come to an awareness, an understanding, of how it itself is working. But this creates legions of difficulties, for consciousness must come to an understanding of how it is working within the domain of its own workings. There is, it seems to me, no possible standpoint outside consciousness from which consciousness and its workings can be understood. But if this is so, in attempting to understand itself, consciousness may yet be operating with more deeply embedded assumptions, attitudes, and the like that more deeply distort its understanding of itself. If these assumptions, attitudes, and distortions are common, taken for granted, then the varieties of behavior that flow from them will not be remarked upon — until, that is, they exceed the bounds of what is commonly and popularly treated as normal and acceptable. When even such vague bounds are exceeded, the frowned-upon attitudes and behaviors will not be understood in an adequate fashion, and so false causes (and hence false solutions) will be offered in response.

My suggestion is that consciousness, typically and profoundly, misunderstands itself. Typically, consciousness sees and *experiences* itself as separate, apart from the world in which it lives and acts. As a result, it focuses almost exclusively on itself, experiencing not-self as separate and alien. Indeed, when "not-self" refers to other human beings, they are often seen either as unwelcome intruders or as adversaries to be used and manipulated. Consequently, interpersonal relationships become, at best, deeply tenuous.

Although anecdotal in character and thoroughly incomplete in detail and analysis, the following repeated incident tends, I think, to provide evidence for the above remarks. Each academic year, I teach five or six sections of *Introduction to Philosophy*. As I teach it, the course focuses on the concept and experience of human freedom. After a good deal of attention to other matters, such as trying to have students see that there is something *to see*, something to think about and understand, I approach the topic of freedom. (As an aside, the failure to realize that there is anything to think about, the belief that individual opinion is the first and last word on all matters, represents an instance of a questionable attitude and behavior that is often taken as normal and acceptable.)

In any case, I approach freedom by having students *picture* themselves free. They are asked to write five or six sentences describing their picture and then to read their descriptions aloud to the class. The results are interesting and, I think, revealing. In a significant number of cases, students do not provide a picture; rather, they provide a conceptual or intellectual explanation. Such explanations almost always involve the complete abstraction, "I'm doing what I want to do". Many students, however, get past this level of abstraction and provide less of an abstraction, typically, lying on the beach, walking in the woods, soaring (as a bird) in the sky, driving on an open empty highway, or the like. Almost invariably these pictures do not include other people; the students are alone. In addition, these pictures include no activity focused on sustaining the self. It is the "universe" that magically sustains one.

These are, of course, the barest details of what is presented in each class. However, these presentations tend, I think, to reveal significantly self-absorbed yet alienated creatures. Students who cannot imagine a picture of their own freedom seem to have lost contact with themselves, that is, with the self that under certain circumstances, can be free. They say they are free when they do what they want to do, but when I ask them what it is they want, they stumble and bumble. The students who do manage somewhat to fill in the picture of doing what one wants to do, radically separate themselves from others and from the activities involved in sustaining one's self — living one's life. Both groups are focused almost exclusively on themselves, yet they have no idea of what it is to find out about one's self, create one's self, be a self. Indeed, typically, they do not even know there is such an idea, such a necessity.

I am well aware that this information is not only fragmentary and anecdotal, crying out for more detail, but is also subject to a great deal of further discussion and interpretation. Yet, however limited such information is, when it is coupled with an independent, deeper, and more detailed analysis of the structure and movement of consciousness, it takes on a greater significance. How is it that consciousness as it is manifest in selfhood, takes on this attitude of separation and self-focused ultimate value?

In an approach to this matter, attention first has to be paid to our use of the term *consciousness*, especially since, at times, it appears as if it is being treated as a substantive that is itself active. Consciousness is not, of course, an entity, a substantive, of any sort. Use of the term enables us to refer to the awareness — the varieties of awareness — enjoyed by a variety of creatures. This awareness, or consciousness, however, is not fundamentally discrete or self-enclosed; it is developmental, ongoing, and changing. And the developmental nature of consciousness or awareness increases and expands as consciousness becomes aware of itself, that is, as human beings emerge and develop. So when we talk about consciousness, we are talking about the varieties of awareness that display themselves in various creatures and suggest that such awareness can be discussed beyond the awareness of any particular creature, though all awareness is enjoyed by some creature or other. The developmental and historical nature of consciousness becomes clearer as we understand consciousness's capacity to reflect upon, evaluate, and alter itself.

Although this approach to consciousness is, I think, intelligible and helpful, it still leaves us with major difficulties concerning just what — ontologically speaking — consciousness or awareness is. Without going into details, it seems to me that of the various standard positions available here — namely, varieties of dualism, materialism, and idealism — each faces insuperable difficulties. Indeed, often — in fact, quite often — the problem seems intractable. Consequently, sustained attention to the problem of the ontology of consciousness seems not to yield very much. Even if it did yield more, it is not clear that such a yield would at all help us with another, apparently deeper problem, namely, the problem of how to live. We are conscious, aware creatures, indeed *reflectively* conscious, aware creatures. Thus, whatever the ontology of the mental, we still must determine how to live as *conscious* creatures. It therefore seems to me that a most significant part of our investigations and attention needs to be directed to exploring the lived reality of human life, that is, the experiential reality of consciousness or awareness. In line with these claims, I have suggested elsewhere (Rossman 1991) that we suspend, put aside, the ontological question. This suggestion was made not because the ontology of consciousness is unimportant or uninteresting but because, at least at this point in the development of consciousness, we live as self-conscious, self-aware, reflective creatures and so we must encounter, live, our lives from within the experiential reality of consciousness.

If consciousness has gone awry, distorting attitudes, behavior, and the like, we need to know how consciousness in its actuality is of this nature and, indeed, how it has developed in this fashion. That is, we want to see what is the configuration, the structure, of contemporary consciousness such that it is twisted, distorted, out of alignment and how this displays itself in attitude and behavior. Beyond this, we wish to know, if possible, what are the sources of such distortion. At what level do we look? Do we assign the problem to individuals? To social structures and arrangements? To historical influences? Or can we go deeper and see the problem as embedded in the very nature of human consciousness, in the very movement from non-humanity to humanity? No doubt, historical, social, and individual phenomena are each relevant to the investigation; but I wish to suggest that the source of our difficulties lies deeper, that probably the historical, social, and individual phenomena have their explanation at a deeper level, at a level we can call the metaphysics of consciousness.

What I call the metaphysics of consciousness is *not* to be understood as involving some disconnected, ultimate realm of reality; instead, it is to be understood in a somewhat biological sense as pointing to the nature of consciousness, given the biological situation of creatures within the flow of the universe and especially within the life flow. I do not know why the life flow is as it is and why there are finite creatures; nor do I know it if makes sense to ask such questions, if the "why" involves purpose rather than causality. To be sure, *if* we have finite creatures, we necessarily also have change and development; and if the development proceeds in a certain way, we also have history. To ask why there are finite creatures is perhaps tantamount to asking why there is anything at all.

In any case, I wish to suggest that once there begins to emerge a creature that is not entirely keyed into its environment in terms of instinctual response, some alteration in orientation must develop if the creature is to survive. If instincts are no longer exclusively determining survival behavior and if the environment itself is not going to sustain the creature, then some basic internal modification or modifications must develop so that the creature itself will be able, within limits, to produce such behavior. This is not, of course, an all-or-nothing phenomenon. If our distant ancestors did "develop" the capacity to determine new, survival-oriented behavior, this was indeed done in small degrees — in fact, it is still in developmental process.

What could develop that would allow new or at least modified behavior that enabled survival? What would be of service here would be a "director" of activity. But how could such a "director" develop? Probably through the slow development of the capacity of consciousness to become reflectively aware of itself, its situation, and its needs. If something like this did in fact occur, it necessarily did so within a situation in which the creatures in question were still basically instinctual and physiological. But the very beginnings of such a capacity carries within itself the ability to expand and enlarge because each new opening of reflective awareness is itself an entrance, a pathway, into further openings and expansions. Self-reflective consciousness feeds itself.

Notice, however, what happens with the emergence of self-reflection or what I call reflective consciousness. We now no longer have the simple awareness of (prereflective) consciousness but rather consciousness aware of itself. Consciousness is no longer a simple unity, the unity of *pre*reflective consciousness; it is now split within itself, with an aspect or aspects of itself knowing another or other aspects of itself. The complete absorption or immersion in experience that is prereflective consciousness is superseded by a consciousness that can step back from and reflect upon experience, including the creature's own situation. Herein, then, lie the seeds for separation gone awry, for separation to develop into disconnection from the flow of life experience and so into (internal) fragmentation and (external) alienation. Thus, the very development that enables the emergence and survival of humanity, namely, the separation that is involved in the capacity to reflect, is simultaneously the creation of the condition for the development of fragmentation and alienation. In this way, the problem of the well-being of consciousness is *built into* the human situation. It is in this sense that I suggested that the problem of consciousness is metaphysical. It seems that our very nature necessarily produces the problem. And because in an essential way the problem involves our capacity to act, not just behave, it also seems necessary that we deal with and, if possible, solve it. In short, what must develop if we are to survive creates, in its development, the possibility of destructive disconnection. Although I would sharply reject the theological and volitional aspects of such a doctrine, perhaps it is considerations of this order that have led people to talk about original sin.

As reflective consciousness expands and enlarges, so does the "director" of attitude and behavior. Indeed, these can be thought of as two aspects of the same process. In terms of a metaphor, it might be said that reflective consciousness "illuminates". With an increase in the capacity to reflect upon one's situation, including various aspects of one's consciousness, there seems to emerge an awareness of that capacity itself. And that deeper level of awareness becomes, as it were, one's self or the director of attitude and behavior. One becomes aware of oneself as being aware of a variety of phenomena and, within limits, directing one's life. This seems also to yield the awareness that one is living a life, that this life that is being lived is *my* life, though in no appropriate sense does this yield a duality of life and self. The awareness that this is my life involves the development of a sense of mineness, reflective mineness, which can attach both to various states of consciousness and, as suggested, to one's life as a whole.

It is important, I think, to see the contrast between reflective mineness, the mineness that is contingent on the development of reflective consciousness, and the sense of mineness that precedes such development, namely, the mineness of prereflective consciousness, that is, that had by prereflective creatures. I think there is little doubt that prereflective creatures like dogs and cats experience a sense of mineness. Such a sense, however, is simply embedded in the felt or experiential reality of the moment. That is, prereflective creatures experience sensations, feel pains, and in that sense have sensations, have pains — these are theirs; but they do not become reflectively aware of these, think about them, comment upon them. Their mineness is that of immersion in experience, the brute, prereflective awareness of the moment.

Although significantly modified by the development of reflective consciousness, reflective creatures also experience, are immersed in, the reality of the moment. Such immersion is what I have called non-reflective consciousness, the consciousness that slowly develops as the enlargements and expansions of reflective awareness are absorbed into the totality of consciousness. Thus, non-reflective consciousness, a development of prereflective consciousness via the capacity to reflect, displays a richer sense of mineness than does prereflective consciousness. However, it is important to see that however much richer non-reflective consciousness is in relation to prereflective consciousness, non-reflective consciousness has within it the seeds of deep disconnection from the reality of the moment. To be sure, non-reflective consciousness is an immersion in experience, but it is an immersion that occurs within the productive dynamics of reflective consciousness, and what reflective consciousness produces in the way of mental states, attitudes, and the like can, in any particular case, be distorted and inadequate. Although, as I suggest later, there is no standpoint of justification beyond consciousness, consciousness is not therefore self-certifying or self-justifying in any particular situation.

In any case, in relation to prereflective consciousness, the mineness of reflective consciousness is richer and more developed. This richness derives from the ability of reflective consciousness to reflectively know both that this is what I am experiencing and that it is occurring within the context of the particular life I am living. This development has significant consequences and implications.

With consciousness split and capable of being aware of aspects of itself, as well as that it is a self, we have the emergence of interiority or privacy or subjectivity. Such interiority is not original but secondary, an outgrowth or development of involvement within the world. Thus, any idea of self as primordial and original, as preceding and determining interaction with the world (including others), is fundamentally and deeply mistaken. But this mistake seems to trail through the centuries, especially the last five or six centuries, involving the sense that self is original, separate from nonself and, in its separation, self-sustaining. From this standpoint, one experiences oneself as an entity over and against both the world and others. One's self becomes the center of the universe, indeed the most important and significant aspect of the universe. From this vantage point, the ground of authentic selfhood, one's necessary self-aware participation in the world, is at first lost and ultimately denied. Thus, the possibility of the development, or even creation, of coherent selfhood is lost. One lapses into the fantasy of achieving self-fulfillment through one's own devices, plans, and the like. But these, not being grounded in one's experience and understanding of the self's necessary involvement in the deeper movement of the life flow, are baseless and so run aground. Such devices are not based upon, do not derive from, one's harmonious involvement in the life process; they are instead based on a fundamental illusion or distortion, namely, that the self is a separate, self-existent phenomenon whose well-being is achieved through acquiring from what is other, as an alien presence, what is "thought" to be needed. Thus, we have my students insisting that they are free if they do what they want to do.

Notice how this outcome has its roots in the depth of the development of reflective consciousness, that is, in the emergence of humanity. If, as suggested, human survival is contingent on the development of a director, a self, the more the director functions successfully in the areas in which it is needed to function, the more successful will the organism be. But for successful operation to occur, the self needs to become adequately aware of many aspects of experience, including its own states, the environmental situation, what is needed for survival, and how to obtain what is needed for survival. A large part of what is involved here is the self's awareness of its various modes of operation. In a word, in a variety of ways it must become aware of itself. Here again we see the two-edged nature of the development of consciousness. On the one hand, the self's awareness of its operations, and that it operates, enables the creation of positive survival behavior; but on the other hand, the self's awareness of its operations focuses itself on itself, enabling it to experience itself as a phenomenon, indeed as a reality, and beyond that, as an entity or existent unto itself. That is, awareness of particularity or selfhood can, and almost always does, at least initially lead to an orientation in which self is hypostatized and made the ontological and evaluational center of the universe. In the midst of such a fundamental distortion, it is not surprising that consciousness is troubled, falling far short of well-being. Furthermore, when we observe the situation from the standpoint of the multitude of selves, each with such attitudes, interacting, we can begin to develop a deeper understanding of why human behavior is as destructive as it is.

It is interesting how these remarks and the development they describe help us throw light on the development first of skepticism and then of its virtually inevitable successor, solipsism. These phenomena play a crucial role in the breakdown of consciousness in that they involve fragmentation and alienation and so make the achievement of unity or harmony, if not impossible, exceedingly difficult.

By skepticism and solipsism, I refer not just to theories or philosophical positions but to basic attitudes within life, orientations toward life. Most often, skepticism and solipsism are treated as theories, which then are assented to or, more often, treated as aberrations needing refutation. When they are treated as such, their power and depth as life orientations are missed; it is not seen that they are problems, profound problems, within life experience that must be treated on this level.

To survive, certain creatures need to develop a (partial) director of experience, a self. This self must be able to initiate behaviors that enable survival. To do this successfully, the self must within certain limits be (correctly) aware of various factors within and relating to its situation. Thus emerges the necessity and reality of *knowledge*. But the emergence of knowledge, and with it a distinction between what appears to be so and what is so, necessarily involves also the capacity to question one's knowledge, what one knows. It is the self that has knowledge; but when such is questioned, it is only the self, from another level, that can authenticate what is said to be known. But within the questioning attitude, this will not do, for the initiating problem is itself self's knowledge. That is, it is the self that knows, but then it is the self that is questioning what is known. And in such a situation, the self's claim to knowledge is itself included in the question of the self's capacity to know. The standard response to this kind of difficulty is to seek criteria of evaluation and justification from outside the self. This, however, seems quite impossible, for how could something outside of self, outside of consciousness, justify the workings of self or of consciousness? Whatever is or is not outside consciousness, it is the *workings* of consciousness that will or will not adequately know this. Thus, the focus must remain within consciousness. And beyond this, there is no standpoint outside consciousness that consciousness can rely on, for whatever standpoints are held to exist, it is consciousness itself that is the constructor and evaluator of the standpoints.

Consciousness and, of course, reflective consciousness self emerge via the ongoing activity of the creature in its world. Consequently, consciousness is necessarily *embedded* in the world. As such, it is (at least partially) knowledgeable of its situation. That this "knowledge" needs to be enlarged and modified and can become distorted is not adequate reason to question the workings of consciousness as a whole. To do so is to misunderstand the nature, origin, and workings of consciousness and to confuse an aspect of the successful workings of consciousness — namely, the ability of consciousness to question its own workings — with the loss of consciousness's grounding in and involvement with the world. To substitute an external criterion of knowledge for an adequate working out of consciousness's grasp of its situation is to create a debilitating split between consciousness and otherness and virtually to insure the triumph of self-enclosed skepticism and solipsism.

It is easy to see how such views find their source in the ability of consciousness to reflect upon and be aware of itself. Being aware of itself as a living reality, consciousness can get locked within itself, not knowing how to break out or even that it is possible or advantageous to break out. In its preoccupation with itself, it necessarily gets thrown back onto its own limited resources, indeed, its distortions. Still, of course, seeking well-being — for indeed it is experienced as the center of all that is — consciousness vehemently proclaims that it is free, satisfied, and happy when it is doing what it wants to do.

Everyday attitudes and behaviors, then, are not recognized in their destructiveness. The fantasy and distortion of separate selves achieving their well-being through attitudes and behaviors that focus on their well-being is simply taken for granted, not only explicitly but on a much deeper, implicit, level. It is only when such behaviors exceed the ideologically accepted limits of destructiveness and exploitation that notice is taken. However, as suggested here, it is not adequately understood why such behaviors occur. To venture into such areas of understanding is much too threatening, for to do so would involve becoming aware of one's self-absorption, the limits of selfhood and, in relation to this, the non-centrality, non-substantiality, and transitoriness of self.

Consciousness lacks well-being because it has a distorted and grandiose sense of itself. In relationship to itself, it has no adequate sense of reality. Not understanding itself, it also fails to grasp and attain well-being. In the absence of an adequate understanding of self, it is not, I think, possible to attain the well-being of self. And the understanding I am referring to here is not just intellectual but, more significantly, experiential.

What, if anything, can be done in this situation? This, of course, is a topic whose vastness and complexity far exceed the capacity of this writer, and maybe even the collective capacities of humanity. Indeed, the distortions, intricacies, and complexities of the social and historical situation we now face may be of such a magnitude and order that they are beyond solution, that even if consciousness develops a more adequate and realistic sense of itself, the complex problems of surface reality that have flowed from the intricate developments of reflective consciousness may exceed our capacities for amelioration. Indeed, it may even strike some as absurd to talk about the dynamics and structure of consciousness when everyday problems are so overwhelming. The gap between the two — surface problems and the dynamics of consciousness — seems enormous, perhaps even of two different orders, and therefore unbridgeable.

In light of this, is there any room for optimism? Perhaps there is, for consciousness still has the capacity to become aware of itself, of its operations. If it moves in this direction, it will necessarily become more honestly and adequately aware of its situation. For this to occur, much time will be needed. Indeed, in part, time will be needed to help consciousness see that the gap felt to exist between the workings of consciousness and everyday surface social problems is an expression of disconnection and alienation, not the awareness of an adequately understood, inevitable reality. If consciousness has created distortions of itself, perhaps it can become aware of such distortions. That would be a first step toward the modification and transformation of consciousness.

This possibility gains support from the realization that the present orientation of preoccupation with self seems not to be an inevitable outcome of the development of reflective consciousness. To be sure, separation, the capacity of consciousness to know itself, is inherent in reflective consciousness. But separation, so understood, is the condition not only for the development of fragmentation and alienation but also for the creation of a new-order harmony or unity, a uniquely human harmony or unity. The latter, if it occurs, would grow out of the self-awareness that is inherent to reflective consciousness. It would involve the simultaneous reality of autonomy — "rational" self-directiveness — and mutuality — the awareness that although one is an individual, one is not, at the most fundamental levels, separate from others. It involves, that is, the lived, experiential awareness that one, like others, is an aspect, a part, of the life process.

What then provides a source of optimism for the well-being of consciousness is what also creates the possibility of fragmentation, alienation, and destructiveness — namely, the capacity for awareness, the inherent capacity of reflective consciousness to know itself and its situation. Reflective consciousness, then, can become aware of its destructive orientation and begin to move in the direction of constructive mutuality. Will this occur? That is a difficult question, for to move in this direction, consciousness will need to recognize its emergent status, its dependence, as well as its finitude, contingency, and mortality; and this may be too much for a creature who knows it has a life, fears for that life, and can "imagine" and desire an endless continuation of that life. Can this self, that is, let go of its attachment to itself and come to experience selfhood as a temporary aspect of a process that produces yet transcends self?

15

The Scene and the Screen
The Nature of Reality

T.M. Srinivasan

> Which is the screen and which the painting? The Self is the screen and the body and the world are the paintings. And what one needs to do to become aware of the Self is to erase the paintings.
>
> — Sri Ramaṇa Maharṣi

INVESTIGATION into the nature of the world has occupied the attention of natural philosophers for several thousand years. In Eastern philosophies, the inquiries have been directed primarily toward understanding the unity underlying the objects seen in the universe. Thus, the question (at least in India) has always been "What is IT by knowing which all else is known?" This may be likened to the current attempt for a unified theory in physics to explain the events in all natural phenomena with just one theoretical postulate.

Many philosophical theories have been developed that deal with the nature of the physical world, as well as postulations of a principle that is beyond the spatio-temporal manifestation. This principle, which is eternal and changeless, most minute and all-encompassing, is more a state than a being. Let us call this the Reality that stands against the ever-changing material universe. The relation between this Reality and the physical universe and the evolution of the universe (Reality cannot evolve because it is changeless) is the topic of our discussion.

From the preceding point of view, we understand that whatever changes is of the world and of nature. This is in consonance with our experience of the world that everything around us changes, including ourselves. This is a fundamental property of the material world. There is an evolution, and then there is an involution, a period of outer growth and a period of inner growth, a cycle in all happenings in the world.

Thus we have, in this worldview, two primal principles: first, the everchanging universe with all its ramifications that we see around us; second, a background of unchanging Reality. Further, it is postulated that the changing is a part of the changeless; however, the changeless is not a part of the changing. The changing is a mode that has arisen out of the changeless. Further, the process of evolution is to lead the changing, back to the changeless.

Evolution of the Universe

In this model, then, evolution has proceeded from the changeless to all that we see around us. The initial derivative of Reality is the Great Undifferentiated, from which arose the material aspects of the world and the humans, with evolutes such as the intellect, the ego, the mind, and the five sensory and the associated motor functions. Thus, the mind is an evolute of nature; it has the same characteristics as the body, changing and being influenced by the external world, unpredictable in its interactions and never confined in space and time.

This is an important concept emerging from our fundamental postulate differentiating the changeless from the changing. Whatever changes and is bound in time and space is an evolute of the changeless, and it is also an aspect of the material world. This clearly distinguishes the mind as an evolute of nature and, hence, is to be understood as material.

This could come as a surprise to many who talk about the mind–body problem. However, examination of the thesis that mind is material is indeed straightforward. There are two reasons that indicate mind is material. First, anything that is bound in space and time is material; mind is material because it is very much related to space and time. Second, if we posit that mind is the final integrating process of the brain interacting with, and reacting to, the environment, then again mind should be material. This is because of a well-known principle in engineering that requires the compatibility of the measured and the measuring system. In other words, the nature of a measuring instrument should be the same as the parameter being measured. For example, if a measurement of electric current is required, a current meter should be used. Similarly, if the world around us is being measured by the mind, then, because the world is material, the mind should also be material. This seems to be true even if the mind is creating new concepts and ideas, for these are carried out within the realm of the phenomenal world.

Thus, it is seen that the well-publicized mind–body problem is tautological rather than actual. Mind is in the experiential realm, just as the body is. Mind–body is a dyad that goes through the process of creating demands, satisfying the needs, interpreting the world, and acting on the environment. Whatever comes from the mind is related to its changing nature. The Reality that is talked about in the preceding section has nothing to do with the vagaries of the mind. Indeed, this distinction is clearly brought out in most traditions that require the seeker of Reality to go beyond the reaches of the mind.

Mind–Body in Consciousness, Psi, and Healing

Techniques related to mind–body have been developed that are used in reaching higher states of consciousness, in psi, and in bringing healing to the sick. In the area of consciousness, instrumentation and procedures have been developed that are claimed to produce different states of consciousness (*Consciousness Technology* 1990). In psi research, the mind–matter interaction has been studied, and several reports are available giving details of the techniques and results (see Jahn and Dunne 1987; Schmidt 1970). In many healing methods, the roles of mind and consciousness have been discussed (Rauscher 1990). There are also reports emerging that seek to measure mind–mind interactions in individuals who are not in verbal communication with each other (Grinberg-Zylberbaum and Ramos 1987; Orme-Johnson et al. 1982).

Although these studies are unusual in the way the interaction of the mind with the environment is studied, they nevertheless seem to imply a distinction between body and mind. The distinction in such a case is only one of degree, not one of kind. In other words, there is no surprise that these interactions are measured. Hence it is also possible to postulate quantum mechanical models (Jahn and Dunne 1987; Walker 1970) for understanding the phenomenon of nonlocality of the mind and consciousness. If consciousness and mind are not material, physical models of these are not possible.

This still leaves us with the question: Is consciousness or mind indeed the Reality we are talking about? In the earlier section, Reality is introduced as non-changing and eternal. All else, including consciousness and mind, are changing and hence of the material world. They may be nonlocal but not eternal.

The Nature of Reality

The concept of Reality introduced earlier needs to be understood for our transactional purposes, while at the same time we understand that such descriptions of Reality in language and in thinking do not correspond with Reality itself. Let us examine the descriptions that could be ascribed to this Reality.

There are, as usual, two ways of studying the characteristics of Reality — the objective and the subjective methods. The objective method will imply that we reduce Reality as an event in time and space, limit it in extent, take it apart into its components, examine each in detail, and then, finally, assemble a synthetic view with the hope that the whole is no more than the sum of its circumscribed parts. However, the Reality that has been introduced earlier cannot be taken into parts, and it is an antithesis of change and transformation, action and construct.

The only way, then, to approach Reality is to use a method that is the opposite of the processes used for objective analyses. Prof. Chethimattam puts it beautifully when he discusses the nature of Reality. (He uses the word *Consciousness* instead of Reality, and I use his own terminology in this quotation):

> The right way, therefore, to understand Consciousness is to make use of a procedure, as it were, in reverse gear — in other words, to make use of a method of approach that will be opposite of what is employed in dealing with objects. The object is constituted in our knowledge through affirmation and construction; Consciousness is realized by negation and abstraction. The object is understood by addition and synthesis; Consciousness is reached through elimination and detachment.
>
> — 1971: 83

These methods of negation, abstraction, elimination, and detachment have all been enunciated and practiced in various orthodox and heterodox Indian philosophies. Let us pursue a different approach that is useful for our transactional purposes, and this is to understand the sleep and dream stages in ourselves.

In the ancient Indian literature, the stages of ordinary awareness have been divided into three primary types: The normal waking state; the dream state; and the dreamless sleep. The waking state and the dream sleep are very similar; only the former is externalized, whereas the latter is internalized. In both these states, there is an observer and the observed external world. In the dreamless state, the observer seems no longer to exist. Here, on waking up the person might say, "I had a good sleep". If a question is asked, "Who is it that had a good sleep, since there is no witness or ego during this time?" the answer could be interesting. The "I" that exists when there is no ego, say the sources, is a vague recollection of the Reality we are talking about. Thus, we may glimmer states of egolessness and, a faint ray of Reality is experienced, as it were, in some natural states that we go through from time to time.

Conclusion

Many thinkers in the recent past have talked about the human and spiritual aspects of psychology — about the personal and the transpersonal growth as optimum condition for psychosynthesis. Maslow, who seems to have introduced the term *transpersonal*, recognized three groups of people: The self-actualizers, the transcenders, and the transcending self-actualizers. Although these definitions are useful in classroom discussions, such categorization is bound to be difficult in a field situation. It is more likely that these categories are in one continuum and that individuals move from one category to another as they go through their daily lives, until they reach the final transcendental state. At that point, there is only one Reality, and the transcender, the transcended, and the act of transcending, all become one.

In the final analysis, the techniques and experiments that are presently coming forth are related to changes in consciousness, interplay between minds or between mind and matter. Recent investigations in medical research have opened the mind–body relations wide, clearly showing the role of the mind in many psychosomatic illnesses and healing processes.

Many spiritual traditions have stated that the mind is the maker and the body reflects the vagaries of the mind. Where do all these leave Reality? If, as mentioned earlier, Reality is unchanging and omnipresent, is it physical or non-physical? Can a physical measurement be made to understand its interactions? Because Reality is changeless and because all physical measurements are only of changes in some parameters, it seems that Reality is non-physical. Hence, understanding Reality with the mind and communicating its experience through language and construct are not possible — thus, the ancient saying "He who knows does not speak; he who speaks does not know".

The model just presented has been discussed by various scientists and philosophers, some in detail and others only partially. However, at the present time, all available models need to be discussed with the view to understand some of the research emerging in the mind–body–consciousness field. This is important because many new models being proposed are still under discussion. The role of this chapter is to focus and bring forth the ideas already available in literature rather than propose a new model that could be interesting in itself but not necessarily complete or even correct.

There are persuasive arguments to reverse the evolutionary direction and consider that perhaps Consciousness predated the evolution of the physical universe (Smith 1990). If by Consciousness we refer to the Reality talked about earlier, then the model presented here does provide such a possibility. Further, the direction of evolution is in involution, to go towards one's own center and to realize the unity in all things in the universe. However, this is not all; one needs to express all the experiences in one's own actions. Then the model will not be an intellectual exercise only; it will have the dynamism to carry the suffering and the sick toward wholeness and healing.

16

On the Trail of Survival
A Key to Expanded Knowledge

Claiborne Pell

IN her excellent little book, *Psi: What Is It?*, Louisa Rhine writes that it was interest in the survival question that brought her and her husband to Duke University to study with William McDougall. I call this book excellent because it is so readable. My understanding is that it was written at the request of her eleven-year-old grandson Ronnie, who asked for a book about psi without all those big words. Whatever the facts, it is a book on a complex subject that most US senators can read and understand.

The point is that the work at Duke University was the anchor of scientific parapsychological research in the United States. And it was tied to the same line that linked the founding in 1882 of the Society for Psychical Research in England and soon afterwards its counterpart organization, the American Society for Psychical Research. That line, of course, was interest in the issue of survival. It appears to me from the lack of current research on this subject that the importance of this legacy is being ignored. From knowledge gained at the conference I helped convene at Georgetown University in 1985, "Consciousness and Survival", I have some understanding of how difficult it probably is to undertake research on non-physical topics. But is it impossible? The Rhines decided to focus on ESP research because it appeared to be a reasonable alternative explanation for information that came from good trance mediums and from a variety of reported personal experiences, such as apparitions, that suggested survival was a reality. That may have been a good decision at the time, and I am not trying to make a case for everyone pulling back from scientific research into psi. What I am asking you to consider is some sustained research directly on the survival issue. Why do I think that survival research would be a sound investment for the parapsychological research community?

Second, what does the current level of financial and other support for psi research tell us about how the field is perceived? Maybe there would be more support for psi research that is honestly directed to the survival hypothesis.

Third, what is the possibility that by centering the focus of research on survival, we would see a natural fallout of greater insights on psi? Although "Super-ESP" and PK may be alternate explanations for phenomena that support the survival hypothesis, that may have been too seductive a path to follow. William Roll has observed that the theory of Super-ESP (that ESP is omniscient) has been the villain of survival research. And Jule Eisenbud has referred to super-psi as supernonsense, an example of the difficulty some people have in untethering their minds from the constraints of the physical world. How many of you would agree that the effort expended on investigating ESP and PK has been energy well spent? Were these more important research topics than survival, or were they intended to be interim goals that in fact turned out to monopolize the intellectual efforts of the field? Does it have to be an either–or situation? As Michael Grosso has written and others also observed, "Psi itself is the first sign of our potential for going beyond the limits of space, time, and matter". That is to say, it takes us into the realm where philosophers, poets, artists, and theologians opine that life after biological death continues.

Whatever the past case, I suggest that it is time to look at the total research agenda of parapsychology and assess its relevancy to social needs. Being an unwanted child of both psychology and physics and having been kept outside of the mainstream of science, you have the challenges faced by every orphan idea: "What is it good for?" and "So what?" Let me briefly try to make the case for investing in survival research because of what it would do for the field of parapsychology.

First of all, it is probably the worst case scenario for the Committee for the Scientific Investigation of Claims of the Paranormal (CSICOP). I can think of nothing that would upset them more than quality research in the field of survival. While that alone is not sufficient reason to undertake the research, their response to the effort might get international attention to the undertaking that would otherwise cost thousands of dollars in a public relations publicity effort. That should begin to shake the money tree.

Survival research is not only technically complicated and difficult but also controversial. Whoever does it will be addressing the most complex dilemma of the human condition: fear of life and fear of death. The task is formidable. The evidence for this is not only that is it not being done but also that there does not appear to be an organized will to try it. Just as the task is great, so will be the rewards for trying. The rewards for proving survival cannot be calculated, so profound will be the impact in every area of society. The consequences of testing the survival hypothesis and failing to prove it would also be significant. It would assist us in sharpening research skills for continuing efforts. It would certainly provoke as much multidisciplinary debate on the subject as would success. This project thus has the potential to attract attention to our field by other scientific disciplines, a currently unfulfilled need.

Who would support this research and what would that mean to the parapsychological community? I expect direct translation of measured public interest in survival in the form of financial support for research on it. When the research community begins to seek this support, it will start a process that with rare exceptions it has avoided up to this time. It will be asking for public support to do something that it knows at the front end the public considers to be important and real but lacking in scientific validation.

This is all talk up to this point. What can I offer you of substance? In December 1989, I helped found the Human Potential Foundation. This recognized what we had learned after six years of testing the interest and will of government to get involved in supporting research on the leading edge and fringes of science. Part of the focus was on parapsychology, but more broadly it was in the area of consciousness. Frankly, we learned more about what government was not willing to do than anything else we accomplished. It became obvious that if we were sincere about getting research in these areas funded, it would have to come from the private sector. In March 1991, my former special assistant, Scott Jones, left my staff to formally open up and run the Human Potential Foundation. It is a non-profit organization with tax-exempt status. Laurence Rockefeller gave us a generous grant to start operations. Scott is involved in additional fundraising and in identifying areas in which the foundation will support research. Our charter is broad. We are interested in all the conditions of humankind. We intend to cultivate the physical, mental, and spiritual well-being of people around the world. This will be done primarily by assisting the individual to achieve his or her fullest potential.

One of our plans is to establish the Center for Thanatology and Survival Research. We are considering several ideas about the form this will take. It could be an endowed chair or some other relationship with a college or university. The incumbent of the chair or the visiting scholar would have from one to three years to complete her or his research after successfully competing with peers within her or his discipline with a research proposal in the area of survival. The chair would rotate over the years from one discipline to another: anthropology, psychology, physics, medical field, parapsychology, history, music, art, and so on.

In anticipation of establishing this center, the Human Potential Foundation is interested in exploring with the sponsors and participants of this conference and others the feasibility of holding a conference in 1993 that would have as its focus the development and discussion of research protocols in the field of survival. Are we ready to really start serious research? What do we know about subtle energy that can be applied to this research? Is quantum physics leading to a physics of the soul? What work in other countries and cultures do we know about that may directly apply?

Whenever this work starts, it will necessarily be interdisciplinary if it is going to be successful. But some discipline will have to make the start and provide leadership. Those of you who knew her, what advice do you think Louisa E. Rhine would give at this point?

Part II

17

Yoga
Theory and Techniques for Cultivating Consciousness

K. Ramakrishna Rao

YOGA is both a system of philosophy, one of the six Hindu systems, and a technology for psychosomatic–spiritual development. Yoga as a method is possibly much older than as a philosophy even though in some ways the two are intertwined (Singh and Mukesh 2010).

By the time of Pāṇini, the great grammarian who lived probably before the Buddha, yoga came to be identified with a method of achieving concentration and controlling sensory inputs and responses. Although the word yoga, in this sense of a method, appears in some of the later Upaniṣads such as *Maitrāyaṇī, Śvetāśvatara,* and *Kaṭha*, it was in Patañjali's *Yoga-Sūtras* that we find its first systematic treatment. As Dasgupta (1922: 229) points out, Patañjali collected the different yoga practices, systematized diverse ideas on the subject, and "grafted them on Sāṁkhya metaphysics". When Yoga refers to a philosophical system, we use capital "Y" and when it denotes a method, "y" is in lower case.

There is some controversy about Patañjali's dates and whether he is the same person as the author of *Mahābhāṣya*, a commentary on Pāṇini's grammar. If the authority of Dasgupta is relied upon, the grammarian Patañjali and the Patañjali of *Yoga-Sūtras* is one and the same, and he lived in the second century BCE. J.H. Woods (1914/1988) suggests, however, that "Patañjali's *sūtra*s were written at some time in the fourth or fifth century of our era" (p. xix). Vyāsa wrote a commentary on *Yoga-Sūtras,* and Vācaspatimisra and Vijñānabhikṣu provide extensive explanations on *Vyāsabhāṣya*. Together these works constitute the original and primary sources of much of the Yoga literature in Patañjali tradition. *The Yoga System of Patañjali* by J.H. Woods (1914/1988) contains English translations of the text as well as the commentary by Vyāsa and the explanation of Vācaspatimisra.

In *Yogatattva Upaniṣad*, four kinds of yoga — *rāja-yoga, haṭha-yoga, laya-yoga,* and *mantra-yoga* — are mentioned. *Rāja-yoga,* which is the subject of *Yoga-Sūtras,* is regarded as the highest of all. In *haṭha-yoga* the emphasis is on physical exercises. *Laya-yoga* has to do with *kuṇḍalinī* arousal. *Mantra-yoga* involves meditation on certain mystical syllables. Thus, it was recognized that different techniques could be used to achieve a state of psychic concentration, meditation and absorption, which are believed to enable the practitioner to attain all kinds of *siddhi*s (supernatural powers). The ultimate goal of yoga, however, is self-realization, which is freedom from all existential constraints and knowing truth and realizing it in one's being.

*Sūtra*s literally mean principles. The *Yoga-Sūtras* are concise in the extreme. They are succinct and difficult to grasp without the necessary background. The commentaries and explanations by Yoga scholars such as Vyāsa, Vācaspatimisra, Vijñānabhikṣu, and many others attempt to provide that background. It is still difficult to clearly comprehend the meaning and significance of the Yoga aphorisms without access to the tradition and some personal experience. I prefer to think that the aphorisms themselves are given intuitively. The commentaries and explanations are their logical elaborations and metaphorical descriptions. They attempt to address metaphysical problems, ethical issues, psychological subtleties and religious matters together in the same breadth, further complicating the matters. Therefore, it is not easy to tease out the psychological essence of yoga without bringing in one's own preferences and biases.

Yoga-Sūtras is in four parts. The first three parts describe the doctrines of the Yoga. The last part is devoted, among other things, to criticizing the views of Buddhists. Several scholars, including Dasgupta (1922), argue that the fourth part is a subsequent addition to the three original parts of Patañjali.

Yoga, as mentioned, refers also to one of the six orthodox systems of Indian philosophy closely linked with the Sāṁkhya system, which is considered to be the oldest of the six such *darśana*s. In Patañjali's *Yoga-Sūtras* we find a systematic presentation of yoga both in its theoretical and practical aspects. Patañjali's effort is itself a kind of yoga, because there is an attempt at binding or yoking of theory and practices, a unified exposition of a metapsychological theory and an applied psychology of the human mind, offering profound possibilities for personal transformation and growth. However, as mentioned earlier, Patañjali is neither the originator of Yoga as a system of philosophy nor the inventor of yoga practices. "Patañjali's effort," writes Eliade (1969: 7), "was especially directed to co-coordinating philosophical material — borrowed from Sāṁkhya — around technical formulas for concentration, meditation and ecstasy".

Yoga is, however, more than Patañjali and *Yoga-Sūtras* and its various commentaries and interpretations. Within the Hindu tradition itself, there are other well-developed systems such as *haṭha-yoga*, which places greater emphasis on the somatic training and control, and a variety of specialized tāntric practices. Then, beyond the Hindu ethos, we have yoga developed by the non-orthodox Indian systems of thoughts, notably the Yogācāra school of Buddhism. Even in early Buddhism, there is much written on meditation as in Buddhaghoṣa's *Visuddhimagga* which in some ways similar to and commensurate with *Yoga-Sūtras*. Considering the constraints of space and in the interest of focusing on mainly the salient aspects of yoga and studying them in some depth our discussion in this chapter is limited to Patañjali's *Yoga-Sūtras*.

The Metaphysical Base

As mentioned yoga is not merely a method having psychical and psycho-physiological implications; it is also, along with Sāṁkhya, a full-fledged system of philosophy. Therefore, to understand and grasp the full significance of Patañjali's yoga, it is necessary to be aware of its metaphysical context. Some minor differences of detail notwithstanding, Yoga as a system of philosophy shares with Sāṁkhya the basic assumptions concerning human nature. Therefore, Sāṁkhya and Yoga are traditionally treated as one joint system in Indian philosophy.

According to Sāṁkhya thinkers (Sastri 1935; Raja 1963), there are essentially two principles that govern our being — *puruṣa* and *prakṛti*. It is difficult to translate these concepts because there are no equivalents in English vocabulary. *Prakṛti* is generally understood as non-conscious matter. *Puruṣa* is sometimes translated as "soul" and at other times as "spirit", "self", or "consciousness". When *puruṣa* is rendered by the word "soul" it acquires a religious connotation and tends to lose the metaphysical and psychological subtleties of the word *puruṣa*. Similarly, when it is translated as "self" the metaphysical aspects come into focus and its psychological aspects are marginalized. Since we are dealing in this chapter essentially with the psychological aspects of Yoga, it would seem that "consciousness" might be the closest concept to convey the appropriate sense of *puruṣa* for our purpose. However, *puruṣa* also has reference to an agency whose nature is consciousness. Therefore *puruṣa* refers to a center of consciousness.

Puruṣa

Puruṣa is *pure* consciousness. It has no qualities or characteristics of its own. It is the transcendental principle that makes awareness possible. In conjunction with *prakṛti*, it enables us to experience unity, coherence, continuity, and selfhood. In Sāṁkhya-Yoga there is a separate *puruṣa* for each person. *Puruṣa, per se,* cannot be perceived. It can only be realized. However its presence can be inferred from the manifest purposiveness in the universe. Without such a transcendental principle, it is contended, it would not be possible to make sense of moral responsibility.

Our awareness of things is contained in the ideas and images we have of them. Like the worldly things, which are indeed material, the thoughts and images of them are equally physical, except that they are subtler. Like gross physical objects, images of objects are non-conscious in that they cannot be felt as experiences unless they are made conscious by the presence of *puruṣa*, the principle of consciousness. *Puruṣa* is the light that illumines the contents of the mind. Without such an illumination, what is in the mind would remain like a painted canvas enveloped by immense darkness. Consciousness as-such, however, has no content. It is self-luminous and capable of illuminating others. *Svayamjyoti* (self-luminosity) implies immediacy of consciousness, which means that such distinctions as subject and object are inappropriate to it. It is in a significant sense *reflexive*. Consciousness is both self-manifesting and other-manifesting. In being self-manifesting it is a primary and irreducible principle. Consciousness is other-manifesting in that it is foundational to all awareness. In revealing itself consciousness reveals everything else. In a sense, it breaths consciousness into matter associated with it. In so doing, the distinction of subject and object is generated and consciousness is reflected in the subjective aspects of natural phenomena. As *Sāṁkhyakārikā* (19) puts it, *puruṣa* differs from *prakṛti* thus:

> From the contrast with that [*prakṛti*], there follows, *puruṣa* the character of being a witness, freedom, neutrality, percipience, and non-agency.

Prakṛti

Prakṛti is matter. It is the basis of objectivity. The world of objects is a consummate evolution of *prakṛti*. Whereas the objects are limited in space and time, *prakṛti* itself is ubiquitous and all-pervading. It is the ground condition of all physical manifestations in the universe. Three fundamental characteristics (*guṇa*s) are inherent in *prakṛti*. They are *sattva* (essence/information/content), *rajas* (energy), and *tamas* (mass/inertia). *Prakṛti* in its primordial condition is the state in which the three *guṇa*s are in perfect equilibrium. The equilibrium is created by equal, mutual opposition between them. Vyāsa, who wrote the commentary on Patañjali's *Yoga-Sūtras*, describes such a state as

> that which never is nor is not, that which exists and does not exist, that in which there is no non-existence, the unmanifested, without any specific mark, the central background of all.
>
> — Radhakrishnan 1923/1989, vol. 2: 260-61

Like *puruṣa*, *prakṛti* as-such cannot be perceived. It may be inferred from the manifest universe and can be understood rationally. It can be known directly, however, by the practice of yoga. According to Sāṁkhya, *prakṛti* is the first cause of the material universe. It is the uncaused cause of the evolved phenomena. The characteristics of *prakṛti* may be understood by contrasting it with those of the evolved. As the *Sāṁkhyakārikā* (10) puts it,

> The evolved is caused, non-eternal, non-pervasive, mobile, manifold, dependent, emergent, conjunct, and heteronomous; the unevolved [*prakṛti*] is the reverse [of all these].

Whereas *puruṣa* is never an object of cognition and is changeless, *prakṛti* undergoes change as it unfolds in the process of evolution and manifests objects of cognition.

Prakṛti in its primordial state of perfect equilibrium is the ground condition of the universe. The world of objects, including the living, has evolved in different stages as the equilibrium between *guṇa*s is disturbed and *guṇa*s recombine in various proportions. The evolution of the manifold is the varied mix of the essence, energy, and mass contained in *prakṛti*. It is a process where the incoherent, the indeterminate, and the undifferentiated *prakṛti* manifests a coherent, determinate, and differentiated form. The order of evolution is not one of combining parts into a whole or splitting the whole into parts, but of a progression from less differentiated to a more differentiated state, from a less coherent to a more coherent and from a less determinate to a more determinate condition. Evolution is the actualization of the potential; it brings about increasing differentiation within the evolving whole (Dasgupta 1922/1988).

According to Sāṁkhya, the first to evolve out of *prakṛti* is *mahat* (the great one), from which the rest of the world manifests. *Mahat* is characterized by *sattva* preponderance. It may therefore be regarded as the quintessence of all things. It is *buddhi tattva* (the collective mind); a concatenation of all minds (*buddhi*s) in that all minds have their origin here.

Once *mahat* is formed, the process of its further differentiation proceeds by the interplay of *guṇa*s along two lines of evolution — the *sattva*-dominant and the *tamas*-dominant. Both these are driven by the energy of *rajas*. The *bhūtādi* (*tamas* line), helped by *rajas*, generates the *tanmātras*, which are the bases of all physical manifestations. Whereas *bhūtādi* is homogeneous, inert, and characterless mass, *tanmātra*s possess physical character and the potentials for being perceived as sound, touch, color, taste, and smell. At this stage they represent subtle matter, and further differentiation generates gross matter, the atoms and their aggregates. "It is thus," as Dasgupta points out, "that the course of evolution which started in *prakṛti* reaches its furtherest limit in the production of the senses on the one side and the atoms on the other" (1988, vol. 1: 253). Inasmuch as they share the same source in *mahat*, these parallel developments manifest relationships between themselves.

In the process of evolution we thus have, after *mahat* and along the sāttvic line, the mind with its triple functional aspects — *buddhi*, *ahaṁkāra* and *manas*. The mind is termed *antaḥkaraṇa* in Sāṁkhya and *citta* in Yoga. After the mind, the next to evolve are the ten *indriya*s (senses), five for acquiring knowledge and five causing action. Following *indriya*s are the five *tanmātra*s which are the essence of sound, touch, form, taste, and odor. The last five forms into which *prakṛti* unfolds itself are the five *mahābhūta*s. They are ether (sound carrier), air, fire, water, and earth.

Thus *puruṣa* and *prakṛti* are the two ultimate principles that together constitute the person and the manifest world. They are in a sense the "soul" and "substance" of the universe (Bernard 1947), the subjective and objective in our being. In the manifest world, the original polarity of *puruṣa* and *prakṛti* appears as consciousness and unconsciousness and as knowing subject and known object. They are the foundational principles and ground conditions for consciousness and subjectivity on the one hand and manifest objects and events on the other. The empirical world and the experience we have of it are made possible by their association at various levels. Neither of them, in this view, is sufficient to explain the universe and our place in it.

Psychological Assumptions

As mentioned, *puruṣa* (consciousness) is primary and it is in principle irreducible to any form or manifestation of *prakṛti* (matter). It is self-manifesting and *svataḥ prakāśa* (self-luminous). Consciousness as-such has no content and consequently is not an object of cognition. It is non-rational and yet foundational for all awareness and knowledge. Consciousness, which is different from the mind, has two fundamental aspects. It manifests in two basic forms: (1) transcendental, and (2) phenomenal. In its transcendental aspect, consciousness is apprehended in immediate intuition where there is no distinction between subject and object. In its phenomenal form, it manifests in the cognitions where there is a differentiation between *grāhī* (the cognizing subject), *grāhya* (the object of cognition), and *grahaṇa* (the process of cognition). When *puruṣa* gets entangled with *prakṛti*, i.e., when there is an association between consciousness and *buddhi*, which is an evaluate of *prakṛti*, conscious mind is formed. When this happens, *buddhi*, which is by its nature unconscious, becomes conscious. Deriving its illumination from its proximity to *puruṣa*, it manifests awareness and subjectivity. *Puruṣa*, however, by this entanglement, seen as an embodied person, loses its freedom, innate purity, and perfection. By mistaking the cognitions of *buddhi* as its own *puruṣa* in the person tends to bind itself to *buddhi* and thus develops a sense of false identity with it. Thus lost in the mirage of the mind, according to Sāṁkhya-Yoga, the quest of the person as entrapped *puruṣa* is to gain release from the shackles and the bondage brought about by *puruṣa*'s association with *buddhi*. The Yoga system attempts to explain this bondage and lays down a progressive scheme of self-realization. When *puruṣa* gets its release and gains freedom from the barricade of matter and the confinement of the senses, it regains its self-illumination in *kaivalya* (state of splendid isolation). *Kaivalya* is the goal and yoga practice is a means to achieve it. Thus Yoga is both a theory of our psychological bondage and a method to escape from that bondage.

The Conscious Mind

Consciousness as-such, as mentioned, is inert and formless. *Buddhi* and other evolutes of *prakṛti* have energy and substantiality but no consciousness. Conscious mind arises with the association of *puruṣa* and *buddhi*. The association does not involve genuine interaction between the two but only a relation that provides for a reflection of the *puruṣa* on *buddhi*. Such a reflection is made possible by the *sattva* component of *buddhi*, which resembles *puruṣa*. The *sattva* aspect of matter has a peculiar affinity with *puruṣa* in that it is capable of reflecting consciousness, unlike *tamas* which obstructs it. *Buddhi* is always translucent and becomes transparent in association with *puruṣa*. The reflection of the *puruṣa* renders *buddhi* conscious. When *buddhi* becomes conscious, that consciousness in turn is superimposed upon *puruṣa*, who gets the notion of an experiencing person by mistaking the modifications of *buddhi* as its own. Thus, it is the conjunction of *puruṣa* and *buddhi* that gives us self-consciousness and the subjective experience we have of the world.

The term for the functional mind in Yoga is *citta*. *Citta* not only comprises of the cognitive processes, the ego, and the senses, but it also contains instinctual tendencies inherited from *vāsanā*s and *saṁskāra*s (inherited from previous lives and the effects of past actions). *Saṁskāra*s and *vāsanā*s tend to color our cognitions and predispose us to behave in certain ways. *Citta* manifests also volitional activity, which enables it to attend to some objects and not to others. In addition, *citta* has *śakti* (latent power), which can be used to guide and control the course it would take. *Śakti* enables *citta* to "reflect and react back upon itself and change the passivity of its transformations into active states associated with will and effort" (Dasgupta 1930: 286-87). *Citta* is thus the seat of one's cognition, volition, feelings, and actions.

Three levels in the functioning of *citta* are distinguished — *buddhi* (psyche), *ahaṁkāra* (ego, the empirical self), and *manas* (the mental apparatus). *Manas* is the central processor, which selectively reflects on the material provided by the senses and determines its character by assimilation and discrimination. *Ahaṁkāra* appropriates what is provided by *manas* as one's own and considers the object of perception in reference to the perceiving person. *Buddhi* then reacts to the information provided in an appropriate manner. The functions, or processes, of *citta* are described by Vācaspatimisra thus:

> Everyone who deals with an object first intuits it, then reflects upon it, then appropriates it, then resolves "this is to be done by me", and then proceeds to act. — Sinha 1958, vol. 1: 121

It should be kept in mind that Yoga does not regard *buddhi, ahaṁkāra*, and *manas* as distinct faculties. They are simply the functional aspects of *citta*. These three functions of *citta* are collectively referred to as *antaḥkaraṇa* (the internal organ), distinct from the senses regarded as external organs.

As stated in the *Sāṁkhyakārikā* (35), the senses are gateways to knowledge and *citta* functions as the gatekeeper.

Mind is thus the instrument that interfaces the conscious *puruṣa* with the unconscious objects. The mind is similar as well as different from *puruṣa*. It is different in the first place because, unlike *puruṣa*, it undergoes fluctuations and modifications. Second, the mind subserves *puruṣa* manifesting in the person. The mind exists for *puruṣa*. Third, the mind partakes in the world of objects, taking their forms, whereas *puruṣa* is always a witness and does not interact with the objects. The mistaken identity of the mind with *puruṣa* may be seen in the reflections of *puruṣa* in *buddhi* and the false apprehension of the states of *buddhi* as its own. According to Vācaspatimisra (1969), *puruṣa* is reflected on *buddhi* to make the latter conscious. However, another Sāṁkhya thinker Vijñānabhikṣu (1909) suggests that the reflections on *buddhi* reflect back on *puruṣa*. Such mutual reflection is the reason why *puruṣa* mistakes the experiences of *buddhi* as its own.

Cognition

Cognition arises from the relation of mind, with its threefold functions, to the object. The object manifests in the mind as a transformation of *buddhi*. The transformed *buddhi* by itself is non-conscious. Consciousness is bestowed by *puruṣa*'s illumination that makes *buddhi* transparent and the cognition conscious.

Thus cognition is literally "reflective" awareness, a reflection of *puruṣa* on the surface of *buddhi*. For example, in perception, when an external object registers on a peripheral sense organ (*bāhyendriya*) there is a sensorial transformation of the object. *Manas* attends to these transformations and processes them by assimilation and discrimination. Then they are presented to *ahaṁkāra* (the ego function) which appropriates them so that the sensory transformations are related to the subject. These are then carried to *buddhi* making *buddhi* assume the form of the object and then react to the object of cognition in an appropriate manner. *Buddhi*, however, is not conscious by itself. It becomes conscious by its association with *puruṣa*. When the light of *puruṣa* shines on *buddhi*, which now has the form of the object, it reflects the object so that there is not only conscious awareness of the object, but also that awareness takes a subjective form because of the influence of *ahaṁkāra*. The cognition therefore is a *vṛtti* (transformation) of *buddhi*. *Puruṣa* itself is not affected by this just as the sun is not affected by its image in the lake. The role of *puruṣa* is like that of the sun in virtue of which there is light on the moon.

If the light of *puruṣa* is not reflected on *buddhi,* the cognition of the object, the *buddhi* transformation of it, remains unconscious. Thus Sāṁkhya-Yoga provides for unconscious cognitive states. Non-transparent *vṛtti*s are the unconscious states of the mind. Their existence in the mind is due to its *tamas* component. *Manas, ahaṁkāra* and *buddhi* are regarded as the three internal organs. They are superior to the external senses, which are considered subordinate organs. Among the internal organs *buddhi* is the principal organ. The superiority of one organ over another is related to its functions. *Buddhi* is considered to be the chief instrument in one's cognitive activity because: (1) It alone has direct access to *puruṣa* and is capable of becoming conscious in virtue of its predominant sāttvic disposition to reflect *puruṣa.* (2) *Buddhi* is the final point in the knowledge process. (3) It is the storehouse of *saṁskāra*s and *vāsanā*s (latent subconscious impressions and tendencies) that color our cognitions and dispositions to act. (4) Finally, recollection is the function of *buddhi* (Sinha 1958). Such is the importance of *buddhi* in the functioning of *citta* (the mind) that we find Patañjali using the words *citta* and *buddhi* interchangeably in several places in his *Yoga-Sūtras.*

In perception, it is said, the mind goes out to the proximate objects through the senses and assumes their form. When *puruṣa* is reflected in the mind that acquired the form of an object, we have an awareness of it. As this reflection is reflected back into *puruṣa,* the person has the experience of perceiving the object. What does it mean to say that the mind goes out to the object? It makes little sense to assume that the mind leaves the body to make contact with the object, especially when we consider the mind to be a set of processes and functions rather than a substance. "Going out" function of the mind appears to be no more than the assertion of the freedom of the subject to choose her own objects of perception. Unlike objects with no functioning minds, which have no choice in their relationship to other objects, subjects with minds have a choice to enter into or withdraw from a relationship with an object. The notion that the mind takes the form of the objects through the mediation of the senses can only mean that in the mind we have a sensorial transformation of the objects. The transformation itself is a physical process, and the resultant form is also material, albeit subtle.

It should be mentioned here that the mind, though physical, is assumed to be nonlocal. Unlike the gross material objects, *buddhi* (the mind) is subtle and therefore is capable of reflecting the light of *puruṣa.*

Time and space are categories created by the mind to organize and understand sensory information. *Buddhi* itself exists beyond the constraints of space and time. The reason why *buddhi* is not in touch with or affected by all the worldly objects is that the mind has a layer of *tamas*, which acting as an opaque screen covers and conceals the objects from it. It is through the instrumentality of the external organs, which make the sensory contact with the object, that the mind overcomes the obstruction of *tamas* and finds an opening to the object. In purified minds where *tamas* is "dwindled away" the object shines forth without sensory mediation.

States of the Mind

The conscious mind is a stage of perpetually changing and shifting scenes called *vṛtti*s. *Vṛtti*s are fluctuating states of the mind that are cognitively, affectively, and volitionally loaded. *Vṛtti* is a very important concept in Yoga psychology. The classification of *vṛtti*s, the way they arise and influence one's behavior, the methods of channelling and controlling them are believed to be of great significance in understanding the nature and destiny of human condition. Indeed the very practice of yoga has the sublime purpose of controlling *citta-vṛtti*s, the fluctuating states of the mind, because they are considered to be inimical for attaining the goal of *kaivalya*, which is the true state of *puruṣa*, a state of perfect freedom in its splendid isolation. *Kaivalya* is a state of pure consciousness free and unencumbered by the manifestations of *prakṛti*, which normally clouds consciousness as it is reflected on *buddhi*. *Citta-vṛtti*s (fluctuating states of the mind) are many and varied. Yoga classifies them under five heads. The first category comprises of true cognitions arising from *pramāṇa*s (valid sources of knowledge). According to Yoga there are three such sources: (i) perception, (ii) inference, and (iii) verbal testimony. The second category consists of *viparyaya* (false cognition). *Viparyaya* includes also doubts and uncertain cognitions. The third is *vikalpa*, which refers to just an idea that has no corresponding material object. *Vikalpa* is, however, not false knowledge. *Nidrā* (sleep) is considered to be a category of *vṛtti* in Yoga system. Finally, *smṛti* (memory) is believed to represent a separate category of mental states. Memory involves storage and retrieval. Some of the *saṁskāra*s are stored impressions of *vṛtti*s in *citta* for later recall. Thus *vṛtti*s comprise of true cognitions, either perceptual, inferential or testimonial that include revelational intuitions, false cognitions including doubtful and uncertain cognitions, mental states occurring in sleep, and reminiscence. If the mind is a sea, *vṛtti*s are its waves. The disturbed minds are like turbulent seas and the goal of human endeavor for self-realization is one of stilling the mind by controlling its *vṛtti*s (fluctuations).

Basically, there are five sources of *kleśa* (hindrance) that stand in the way of controlling the fluctuations of the mind. They are *avidyā, asmitā, rāga, dveṣa,* and *abhiniveśa* (*Yoga-Sūtras* II.3). *Avidyā* is the inability to discriminate between good and evil, pleasant and unpleasant, truth and falsehood, the permanent and the impermanent, and the pure and impure. *Avidyā* does not denote lack of knowledge. Rather it refers to a condition, the soil that nourishes all other kinds of hindrances. *Asmitā* is personal identity, the I-ness generated by the wrongful identification of *puruṣa* with *buddhi*. It is the self-sense that distinguishes one from others. *Rāga,* is passion for pleasure. It is the thirst, greed and craving for enjoyment. *Avidyā* generates a sense of *asmitā* (personal identity) and *asmitā* underscores *rāga* (passion). *Dveṣa* is the opposite of *rāga*. It is hatred of and aversion to anything considered painful. *Abiniveśa* is indicated by the will to live and the instinctive fear of death.

Afflicted by the five kinds of hindrances and the ever-present *vṛttis*, *citta-bhūmi* (the mental field) manifests five levels of activity and attention. First is *kṣipta* (the fluctuating level) where attention wanders. The second is the level of *mūḍha* (inactivity or forgetfulness) as in drowsiness and sleep. It is a state of inattentiveness. In the third, the mind becomes *vikṣipta* (occasionally steady) and gets temporarily absorbed in the objects of its attention. At the fourth level, the mind achieves *ekāgratā* (one-pointed concentration) and gets absorbed fully and unwaveringly in the object of attention to the complete exclusion of others. In the final level of *niruddha,* all mental functions are completely restrained so that one experiences consciousness as-such, unmediated by any mental functions.

Niruddha is the level one hopes to reach through practice of yoga. When this happens after passing through several states of *samādhi* (complete absorption), *yogin* (the practitioner) overcomes hindrances and gains control over *citta-vṛtti*s. As a consequence, one's consciousness gets progressively detached from *buddhi* and advances toward self-realization, i.e., a state of consciousness as-such, pure, free and self-luminous, and devoid of all material vestments.

Closely linked to the concept of *vṛtti* is *saṁskāra*. J.H. Woods translates *saṁskāra* as "subliminal impression". There is some kind of reciprocal relation between *vṛtti*s and *saṁskāra*s. *Vṛtti*s give rise to *saṁskāra*s and the latter in turn generate *vṛtti*s. The major difference between the two is that *vṛtti*s are in awareness, whereas *saṁskāra*s are latent preconscious or unconscious states. Both are affected by the hindrances of the five *kleśa*s. Like *vṛtti*s, *saṁskāra*s are not homogeneous. There are several grades and shades of them. Some *saṁskāra*s are helpful and have positive influence toward self-realization and some are negative and harmful.

*Saṁskāra*s are of three kinds — those generated by (1) cognition and knowledge (*jñānaja*), (2) by emotion (*kleśaja*), and (3) by volition and action (*karmaja*). The *jñāna saṁskāra*s (cognitive kind) are associated with cognitive fluctuations of *vṛtti*s (mind). Every *vṛtti* leaves an impression on *buddhi* in the form of a *saṁskāra*. It is in virtue of such *saṁskāra*s that we have *smṛti* (memory). As Vācaspatimisra says in his commentary on *Yoga-Sūtras* (I.11), memory is recall of a subliminal impression cast in *buddhi* with no modifications or alteration. *Kleśa*s (the five hindrances) give rise to *saṁskāra*s associated with emotion. Volitional activity also generates its own kind of *saṁskāra*s. Inasmuch as *saṁskāra*s are imprinted on *buddhi*, the mental states one experiences have their source not only in the sensorial transformations of the material objects, but also in the subliminal deposits of *saṁskāra*s. The latter may manifest by themselves as *vṛtti*s or they may color, distort or modify *vṛtti*s generated by the sensory contact with objects and events. Thus one's cognitions are colored, biased, or even distorted by *saṁskāra*s imprinted in *buddhi*.

Saṁskāra and *vāsanā* are similar concepts. Sometimes they are used interchangeably. However, as N.C. Panda (1996) points out, there is a subtle but significant difference between the two. *Saṁskāra* is a broader concept and includes *vāsanā*, but all *saṁskāra*s are not *vāsanā*s. For example, *saṁskāra*s associated with memory (*smṛti*) are not considered *vāsanā*s. *Saṁskāra*s engendered by the five *kleśa*s are *vāsanā*s inasmuch as they act as seeds that will sprout in due course in our thought, passion and action. In a sense, they are latent dispositions and propensities and motivating influences on one's conduct. Like *kleśa*s (hindrances), our actions also generate *vāsanā*s. The latter are called *karma vāsanā*s as distinguished from *kleśa vāsanā*s. *Vāsanā*s are believed to be the force behind our worldly urges, sensuous passions, desires, and cravings. I am inclined to regard *saṁskāra*s as sources of unconscious mentation, unlike *vṛtti*s, which refer to conscious mentation. They, however, influence *vṛtti*s. *Vāsanā*s appear to refer to deeper and more potent layers of the unconscious.

In Indian thought, one's actions, good or bad, deposit *karma*. Good actions produce meritorious *karma* and bad actions deposit black *karma*. Both white (meritorious) and black (demerit) *karma* cause *vāsanā*s. There are, however, actions that produce *karma* that is neither white nor black such as the activities of an accomplished *yogin* in whom *kleśa*s have dwindled away. Such actions leave no *vāsanā*s behind. The accumulated *karma* lays dormant in *citta* like a seed in the ground to sprout at an appropriate time. When *karma* thus leads to action, that action in turn produces *karma* again and this cycle continues indefinitely unless broken by effort toward self-realization. The seeds of *karma* can be burned and made impotent to propagate. *Saṁskāra*s and *vāsanā*s, the vehicles by which *karma* acts, are rooted in *kleśa*s (hindrances). When the *kleśa* roots are cut there would be no more accumulation of *karma* and, as the past *karma* plays out, the individual comes progressively closer to self-realization. Thus by controlling *saṁskāra*s that are generated by the five *kleśa*s (hindrances) and *kriya* (consequent actions), the cycle of *karma* may be broken for good. This is something that can be achieved, according to Yoga, by a *yogin* who enters the states of *samādhi* by practicing contemplative meditation. Psychological implications of the possibility to burn dormant *karma* and render harmful *saṁskāra*s impotent are indeed profound. Yoga psychology recognizes the lasting influence of unconscious mentation in the form of *saṁskāra*s, emphasizes the need to gain control over them, and suggests methods to achieve such control. Whether or not one agrees with the postulated goal of self-realization and of achieving a state of consciousness as-such, the methods suggested for controlling the influence of unconscious mental activity and the hidden motives may have beneficial application in psychotherapy.

It should be mentioned at this point that the Yoga system upholds the doctrine of reincarnation and subscribes to the notion of the cycle of birth and death. The cycle is perpetuated by the accumulated *karma* and *saṁskāra*s. The mind, *buddhi*, on which *saṁskāra*s are imprinted, survives bodily death. Mind, as the subtlest form of matter, does not perish at death. *Karma* that is deposited in it causes it to take another life so that it can play itself out. *Jīva* (the functioning human being) is the embodied mind, which in the proximity of *puruṣa* has access to conscious awareness. The embodied mind is a composite of subtle and gross matter, the mind being the subtle part. With bodily death, the gross body disintegrates. However, the mind, subtle body, with its accumulations of *karma* and *saṁskāra*s, survives to be born again with another gross body conceived by sexual union of a man and a woman. The cycle of birth and death continues until the existential accretions of the mind (*karma* deposits) are completely obliterated by good conduct, *prasaṁkhyāna* (yoga practice) and *viveka jñāna* (discriminative knowledge).

Levels of Awareness: Implications of Yoga Psychology

There is an unmistakable tendency in the West to equate consciousness and mind. If a distinction between them is ever made it is to restrict consciousness to certain aspects of the mind and to provide for unconscious mental states. In other words, mind is considered a broader concept than consciousness. All conscious states are mental states, but all mental states are not conscious states. As we noted, in Yoga there is a clear and basic distinction between consciousness and mind. In a sense, it is a qualitative distinction that is as sharp as the distinction between mind and body in the West. Yoga, as mentioned, subscribes to a dualistic metaphysics, but the two basic substances or principles are not mind and matter, but consciousness and mind. In fact, mind, we may recall, is regarded as a form of matter.

Consciousness itself is located in multiple centers called *puruṣa*s. Consciousness is not an attribute of *puruṣa*. Rather it is the essence of *puruṣa*. The dualism of Yoga does not espouse any interaction between consciousness and physical mind as in certain forms of dualism. Nor does it subscribe to the notion of psychophysical parallelism. The relation between consciousness and the embodied mind is one of *reflection*. The consciousness of *puruṣa* is reflected on *buddhi*, the principal aspect of the mind. The consciousness of the reflecting mind is not identical with *puruṣa* consciousness, which is consciousness as-such. It is only an image, a reflection. As an image, it is subject to imperfections and distortions, which can be minimized and even eliminated by removing the blemishes and cleaning up the mental field so as to reflect a perfect image and thus obtain true knowledge.

Sāṁkhya and Yoga thus avoid in their dualist postulation both psychophysical parallelism and interactionism. This is made possible by a special conception of mind in general and of *buddhi* in particular as an interfacing instrumentality between gross matter and conscious *puruṣa*. *Puruṣa,* whose essence is insight, appears to be more like microcosmic intelligence capable of causing awareness of all conceivable things, by its very presence. It is the source of all awareness. In a significant sense we are led to think that no knowledge is possible without its illuminating insight. At the same time we recognize that in human condition mind is the instrument of knowing. So we have on the one hand *puruṣa,* which is the source of all knowledge in the form of illuminating insight, and on the other hand the mind which has the limited scope of giving us knowledge of the things with which it comes into contact.

Mind serves as a knowledge instrument because of its facility to reflect *puruṣa* due to its predominant *sattva* character. *Sattva,* the subtlest and lightest component of *prakṛti* (matter), constitutes the very essence of the material object comprising it. To put it somewhat differently, *sattva* is the information component of matter. As mentioned, *sattva* is considered in Sāṁkhya-Yoga an integral constituent of matter containing its very essence (information). It is in the nature of *sattva* to reflect *puruṣa* so that the information becomes manifest in awareness. In so reflecting *puruṣa, sattva* reveals its own essence. From this we may surmise that in principle all objects, in so far as they have a *sattva* component, albeit in various degrees, can reflect *puruṣa* in various degrees and thus become conscious at various levels. However, in reality only the mind is seen as capable of reflecting *puruṣa* because the *sattva* content in the rest of the material objects does not rise above the threshold level necessary to register the reflections of *puruṣa*. In other words, material objects other than minds are not translucent enough to have the light of *puruṣa* pass through them and become transparent. The *tamas* component of matter is responsible for the obstruction. If, then, the information content of material objects other than the minds is masked by a preponderance of *tamas,* the question arises as to how one can ever have knowledge of them because on their own they cannot reflect *puruṣa* and thus manifest their essence (information). In other words, how do we have information (awareness) about material objects? It would seem that in this view material objects unable to reflect *puruṣa* by themselves might do so with help from the mind. In association with a mind, a gross material object may manifest its information content. The sensory apparatus that the mind makes use of in its information processing endeavor extracts the *sattva* component of the object of its contact. The distilled form is processed by *manas,* which in turn collects the information and conveys to *buddhi* via *ahaṁkāra*. Then *buddhi* is transformed to take on the form of the object. When the *puruṣa* light shines on *buddhi,* there is awareness of the object. In Yoga psychology, this appears to be the normal perceptual process by which we become aware of external objects.

Perceptual awareness brought about by sensory transformation in *buddhi* is different in kind from *puruṣa* consciousness. First of all, perceptual awareness is imperfect because of the blemishes inherent in the very processing. Again, such awareness is contingent on the sensory contact, which limits the range, scope, and form of awareness. *Puruṣa* consciousness, however, is not subject to such limitations. It is an unblemished insight. It is it, consciousness as-such in and of itself. Thus in this view we have two kinds of awareness — intuitive insight and sense-mediated awareness. Intuitive insight is awareness caused by a direct reflection of *puruṣa* in *buddhi*, the latter faithfully reflecting *puruṣa* without any modifications arising from sensory contact or the influence of *saṁskāras*. Sensory awareness is awareness caused by *puruṣa*'s reflection on *buddhi* which is modified by the sensory contact.

Consciousness experience mediated by the mind via its *vr̥ttis* is phenomenal awareness. Phenomenal awareness involves three distinguishable aspects: (a) the subject, the one who has the awareness (*grāhī*), a product of *ahaṁkāra*, (b) the process of awareness (*grahaṇa*), the activity of the *manas*, and (c) the object of *grāhya* (awareness). All three determine the nature and context of awareness. For example, the sensory processes have their own imprint on what is known. Similarly, our predispositions, the biases and prejudices (*saṁskāras*) color cognitions and influence our actions. Consequently phenomenal awareness is at best a *representation* of reality subject to all kinds of limitations and distortions and therefore cannot be a true experience of reality as-such.

Experience of pure consciousness unmediated by any mental modes is transcendental awareness. Such awareness is considered supreme because it is believed to be completely unbiased. Knowledge mediated by mental functions is imperfect because the mind by its very nature has a distorting and biasing influence. Therefore, it is believed that perfect knowledge can be obtained only in an experience of pure consciousness, which is facilitated by voluntary restraining of all mental functions through appropriate discipline. This can be achieved by practicing yoga, which leads to *samādhi*, a state in which the knower merges with the known by restraining the functions of the mind that cause these distinctions and distortions. By progressing through a series of *samādhi* states, one experiences pure consciousness.

Samādhi is a state of complete absorption, a state in which the natural wanderings of the mind are controlled. When one's mind by means of concentration and meditation on an object gets absorbed in it and experiences identity with it, one is said to attain a state of *samādhi*. Until the mind reaches a state of steady one-pointed concentration that results in unwavering absorption in the object of attention, the subject–object duality persists. Once such absorption is achieved, the duality of the subject and the object disappears. Knowledge obtained in states of *samādhi* is considered superior because it involves severe restraints on the mental functions that ordinarily bias and distort our knowledge.

Two kinds of *samādhi* are distinguished — *samprajñāta samādhi* and *asamprajñāta samādhi*. In *samprajñāta samādhi, vṛtti*s (the mental events) are not completely annihilated. Even though the subject–object duality is transcended and the subject–object identity is experienced, consciousness in this state is not objectless. In other words, it continues to have content, albeit greatly transformed. In *asamprajñāta samādhi,* one has the experience of pure consciousness. It is a state of consciousness without content. Such objectless experience, according to Yoga, is the highest state. It is a state of perfection, liberated from all existential constraints.

Other Yoga writers made further distinctions. Vācaspatimisra, for example, divides *samprajñāta samādhi* into eight categories. He groups them into three classes: (1) *grāhya samādhi* in which the focus of concentration is an external object, (2) *grāhaṇa samādhi*, where the focus is the sensory system, and (3) *grāhitrī samādhi* which involves concentration on the ego or empirical self. These states of *samprajñāta samādhi* seem to refer to states of consciousness obtained by a sustained one-pointed concentration on the different aspects of the knowledge process — the knower, the known (the objects of knowledge), or the process of knowing. It is believed that in different states of *samprajñāta samādhi* one obtains paranormal experiences such as clairvoyance, telepathy, and precognition. A variety of such psychic experiences, it is said, are achieved as a result of concentration on different objects. As Sinha (1958) points out, no reason is given why and how concentration on a particular object or process gives rise to a particular paranormal power or psychic experience. These are recorded simply as facts of actual experience without any explanation. These include among others clairvoyance, telepathy, and knowledge of the past and future events.

Awareness is thus of two sorts, transcendental and phenomenal. Transcendental awareness ensues from directly accessing consciousness as-such, which in the language of Sāṁkhya-Yoga is realization of *puruṣahood*. Phenomenal awareness consists in accessing the information content, the *sattva* component of the material objects through the mediation of the "knowledge" apparatus of the embodied mind. *Puruṣa* is consciousness as-such which in the human condition is masked by *vṛtti*s (the manifestations of the mind). The human mind is the center of phenomenal awareness. At the same time it is also associated with *puruṣa* whose proximity bestows consciousness on the non-conscious contents of the mind. The embodied mind thus enjoys dual citizenship as it were in the domains of *prakṛti* (the physical world) as well as in *puruṣa* (the world of consciousness). It has the facility to access information from material objects and the potential to partake in consciousness as-such. The mind's dual engagement with *prakṛti* and *puruṣa* makes it a seat of a variety of awareness states between the sensory and the transcendental. These include (1) non-conscious states, (2) unconscious states, (3) normal phenomenal states, (4) altered phenomenal states, (5) refined phenomenal states, (6) transcendental states translated into or leading to phenomenal states, (7) anomalous mental states, and (8) transcendental states as-such.

Non-conscious states are those information states the mind is simply unaware at all its levels, those that are devoid of *puruṣa* reflections. This may be so because *sattva* or information content in them does not reach the threshold level to bask in the reflections of *puruṣa* or because of the utter dominance of *tamas* that veils the information. The unconscious states are those, which were once conscious but now relegated to the region of the mind that is shielded from the light of *puruṣa* such as *saṁskāra*s and some *vāsanā*s but capable of influencing the mind without being noticed. The phenomenal states are what are generally regarded as conscious states. The light of *puruṣa* shines on them with the result that their information content is *revealed* as subjective knowledge. Phenomenal knowledge is an image of consciousness but not consciousness as-such. The image is set in an ever-flowing flux, which is subject to all kinds of distortions and alterations. Consequently, there is no finality to phenomenal awareness and no absolute phenomenal truth. Inasmuch as phenomenal states are mediated by several mechanisms of the mind (the knowledge apparatus, *antaḥkaraṇa*) any changes in the structure and functions of these mechanisms would have a corresponding effect on the processed image, i.e., the information accessed. The so-called altered states of consciousness are the sufficiently marked and distinguishable categories of alteration such as, for example, alterations that occur in dream states and states induced by hypnosis, drugs, and other manipulations.

The phenomenal states mentioned so far are images of reality. These images, because of the way they are processed, are subject to a variety of distortions. Such distortions can be overcome and the images may be rendered as faithful reproductions of the original in the sensory form by controlling the biasing influences at the level of the subject and the process of cognition. The method for accomplishing this consists in entering a state of *samādhi*. The state of *samprajñāta samādhi* appears to be one in which cognitions are refined to be free from distortions. *Samādhi* gives clarity of insight. The three kinds of *samprajñāta samādhi* described by Vācaspatimisra essentially refer to the three sources of distortion. The state of *asamprajñāta samādhi* is of course different. It is a state of accessing consciousness as-such; a state in which consciousness does not take any sensory form. Consciousness as-such is reality itself.

In transcendental states the reality is by assumption revealed in and of itself. *Puruṣa,* detached completely from the mind in its sublime state of *kaivalya* (splendid isolation), is of course a state of supreme transcendence. How could such a state exist, however, in the human condition of the embodied mind? The answer, it seems to me, may be found in the inherent reflexivity of consciousness. Consciousness which is the essence of reality, in the same sense the *sattva* component of material objects is their essence, reveals itself to the mind when the mind is in a *niruddha* state and is completely devoid of any content that could become transparent in the light of *puruṣa*. In such a situation consciousness instead of reflecting the contents of the mind reflects itself in the mind. The mind thus partakes in consciousness as-such and experiences transcendental states. These are the states that highly evolved *yogins* are believed capable of achieving. On this model, the mystic experiences transient states of transcendence in which consciousness as-such is realized. Such a momentary realization may leave an indelible mark and manifest subsequently in the form of profound changes in the lifestyle, attitudes, and personality of the individual experiencing such states. Inasmuch as the mystical experience occurs when the normal mental functions are in abeyance, it is not available to rational understanding and verbal descriptions. It is ineffable in this sense. Though ineffable, it is also infallible because it is consciousness as-such. The mystic, therefore, struggles to translate his experience into common language for making sense to communicate to others. That is why the mystical utterances are often metaphorical and seldom convincingly empirical. What a mystic may not be able to communicate in words he attempts to do so in his actions. Thus non-rational forms of belief are formed. In attempting to express the ineffable experience in phenomenal terms, the mystic risks compromising infallibility for intelligibility.

Expanding the Sāṁkhya-Yoga epistemology further, one could argue that the source of intuitive knowledge is a state of transcendence, an experience with consciousness as-such. The mystic reveals his wisdom in his actions like a leader who shows his thought in action and a poet who translates his experience in the form of metaphorical descriptions. A scientist who intuitively encounters a scientific truth is led to trace back stepwise from the generality of the intuitively grasped truth to the specific events contingent on it. Thus in science one may go from fact to fact to weave a theory or begin with an intuitive hunch and gather relevant facts to make sense of the hunch and thus come to a discovery of a law or a relation. The former espouses the phenomenal or intellectual tradition whereas the latter is in line with the transcendental approach. Inasmuch as the image of reality is inlaid in the *sattva* component of the physical universe, the human mind with its knowledge apparatus has access to that image. It is the image we can share. It is reality in the third-person. However, the transcendental transactions, the mind is capable of, give it the intuitions and the first-person experience of reality.

Anomalous states (*A*-states) of awareness stand in between transcendental and phenomenal states. They are called anomalous precisely because they do not fit into either of the two categories. They are different from phenomenal states (*P*-states) in that they appear to transcend sensory-motor and space–time constraints that bind phenomenal awareness. In this aspect they are more like the transcendental states (*T*-states). Anomalous states are, however, different from *T*-states because they are intentional and carry information like the *P*-states. *A*-states are mental qua mental states. *Citta* (mind), as we noted in Yoga psychology, is different from consciousness, and it is physical, albeit subtle. The subtlety confers on it nonlocality in virtue of which it can relate with other minds and objects outside of it. By relating to other minds, it can acquire telepathic information. By relating to the *sattva* component of objects the minds may obtain clairvoyant information about them. The notion of the nonlocality of minds may also be seen in the concept of *mahat*, the collective mind that indeed is the first evolute of *prakṛti* and therefore has nexus to all minds and all objects in existence. The *sattva* component of material objects, whether of subtle thoughts or gross objects, is the link that makes a connection between minds and objects possible.

Anomalous awareness seems to involve two stages. In Stage I anomalous information is received at the unconscious level. It is extrasensory in that the *A*-states are not processed by the sensory-motor apparatus. For that reason, on the one hand, they lack some phenomenal properties and, on the other hand, they are not subject to some of the phenomenal constraints. Stage I of anomalous states may make use of similar psychodynamic processes that are known to be involved in bringing unconscious states into overt behavior and awareness. This is the Stage II of the psi or anomalous ESP process.

On this model, anomalous awareness is different in kind from mystical awareness which involves a glimpse of the transcendental, i.e., consciousness as-such. It is intentional and conveys information about objects and events. Anomalous awareness is phenomenal awareness without some of the limitations of the latter. It is not sensory, but may affect sensory experience and may even be carried into the phenomenal field by means of what G.N.M. Tyrrell (1947) called mediating vehicles, such as dreams, hallucinations, and intuitive hunches. Anomalous awareness is not infallible even if it transcends some phenomenal limitations. Even though they are different from *T*-states, *A*-states bear some resemblance to them. Both of them are undermined by phenomenal states linked to sensory experience. The restriction and control of sensory noise appears to be conducive to the manifestation of anomalous states. The *A*-states are, however, considered an impediment for realizing *puruṣahood* (transcendence) or self-realization. Like the phenomenal states they are to be avoided if the goal is transcendence because they stand in the way of realizing that state of splendid isolation (*kaivalya*), consciousness as-such.

Yoga Practice

Thus what is interesting in Yoga is that it is not merely a theory of mind, but also a practical discipline that claims to provide empirical support for its ideas. Patañjali tells us in *Yoga-Sūtras* how the mind can be restrained to achieve a quiescent state, how *vṛtti*s (the natural modifications and fluctuations) of the mind are restricted and how a variety of *siddhi*s (anomalous phenomena) may be obtained by the practice of *yoga*. According to Patañjali, *citta-vṛtti*s (fluctuations of the mind) may be controlled by practice and by detachment in thought and action. Paranormal abilities are acquired by practicing *saṁyama* that leads through states of concentration, meditation, and absorption. *Kaivalya* is achieved by *nirodha* (the total suspension) of the mental states. *Yoga-Sūtras* narrate different hurdles in the human condition that afflict and hinder the practice of yoga and the means of overcoming them.

Patañjali prescribes an eightfold path for reaching the highest state of consciousness, the state in which one realizes consciousness as-such, unencumbered with any phenomenal awareness. The first five are preparatory and the last three are the essential stages of yoga. The preparatory stages are *yama, niyama, āsana, prāṇāyāma,* and *pratyāhāra. Yama* and *niyama* are a set of prescriptions, "dos and don'ts" for the one who is on the path of yoga. The dont's include abstinence from injuring, stealing, lying, and lust. The dos require cultivation of habits of cleanliness, faith, ascetic self-control, and contentment.

Āsana and *prāṇāyāma* are physical exercises. Although Patañjali himself does not name any postures except to say that the correct posture is one that is stable and comfortable (2.46), his commentator Vyāsa describes a few of them. *Prāṇāyāma* is regulating the flow of breath through systematic inhalation and exhalation as well as holding breath. The final preparatory step is *pratyāhāra,* which is the focusing of attention inward. The function of *pratyāhāra* is to dissociate the mind from its sensory channels so that no sensory input from the external world reaches the mind.

The essence of yoga is *saṁyama. Saṁyama* involves the triple effort of *dhāraṇā* (concentration), *dhyāna* (meditation), and *samādhi* (absorption). The first three *sūtras* in the third chapter of *Yoga-Sūtras* describe them in the following way. Concentration involves focussing attention on an object, which progressively leads to the restraining of the natural wanderings of the mind. In the state of *dhyāna* there is an uninterrupted flow of the mind toward the object of meditation so that the practitioner can focus the attention totally on a single object for a prolonged period of time. Such prolonged one-pointed attention to a single object leads to *samādhi,* a state of absorption. In a state of *samādhi* there is the awareness of the object alone, without self awareness. When the *yogin* thus loses self-awareness and enters a state of complete absorption in the object of meditation, she achieves a state of higher consciousness that enables her to grasp the essence of the objects in focus. The *yogin* thus knows the things in their true state without the biasing influence of the senses or the presuppositions and biases of the mind. Some of these experiences may appear anomalous to those who do not have similar experiences themselves. The final point of *yogin*'s progress is complete liberation from all phenomenal constraints of the mind so that she may realize the state of *asamprajñāta* as mentioned before.

Philosophers belonging to other schools may have disputed the philosophy of Sāṁkhya-Yoga, but few have questioned the merits of yoga practice. It should be mentioned also that as the practitioner of yoga reaches the *samādhi* state and is able to practice *saṁyama* she is likely to encounter a variety of paranormal phenomena. In fact, Patañjali devotes a major part of the third chapter of *Yoga-Sūtras* to describing the *siddhis* (paranormal powers) that one could obtain by doing *saṁyama,* such as knowledge of past and future, knowing other people's thoughts, becoming invisible, and so on. Thus, the anomalous states of awareness appear to be a natural consequence of yoga practice. They are, however, states that the *yogin* should ignore and move forward on the path to *kaivalya* to attain a state of consciousness as-such.

Practice of yoga has important methodological implications for studying subjective experience. For example, meditation as a practice takes place at two different levels, which are variously emphasized by different systems of meditation as in Buddhist *vipassanā* and Patañjali yoga. Meditation is essentially a method of controlling a variety of influences that affect the mind, corrupt and cloud one's consciousness. In practices of the concentration type of meditation attention is focussed and restricted to exclude extraneous intrusions into one's perceptual experience. In the passive forms of meditation, the restriction is not of external intrusions but elimination of internal biases by focussing on non-interpretative reception of incoming information. It is somewhat similar to Husserl's "bracketing natural attitude", which is believed to give "apodictic evidence" of absolute indubitability in a "universe of absolute freedom from prejudice" (Husserl 1960). In the final analysis, successful meditation should involve both kinds of restrictions, the externally inflicted and the internally generated.

Once the intrusions are eliminated in a state of meditation such as *samādhi,* subjective experience loses its capricious variability and becomes in a significant sense objective, enjoying inter-subjective validity. Thus meditation opens up the possibility of studying subjective experience objectively. Indeed it could be an important gateway that would open up enormous possibilities for studying neurophenomenology of consciousness.

At the methodological level, yoga thus offers the possibility of studying subjective states objectively. From the applied perspective, it has techniques and procedures to developing cognitive excellence and for enhancing human potentials beyond what are now recognized. Further, the notion of the possibility of pure conscious states achieved through practice could have important therapeutic consequences for treating all sorts of anxiety disorders and overcome a variety of psychopathological problems. (For more detailed accounts of yoga psychology and applications see Rao, 2011 and Rao and Paranjpe, 2008.)

Summary

To sum up, then, reality according to Sāṁkhya-Yoga system of Indian philosophy is governed by two fundamental principles — *puruṣa* (consciousness) and *prakṛti* (matter). As fundamental principles, they have metaphysical and epistemological implications. In fact, Indian tradition is holistic in a very significant sense. In it the existential, epistemological, ethical, and aesthetic aspects of reality are seen to blend harmoniously. Being and knowing, the good and the beautiful, are governed by the same principles. In our attempts to understand reality, we analyze it in a variety of forms, giving rise to distinctive concepts such as *satyam* (truth), *śivam* (goodness), and *sundaram* (beauty).

The dualism of Yoga consists in its assertion of *puruṣa* and *prakṛti* as two irreducible but complementary principles of reality. They enable us to understand the relative roles of permanence and change in our being. These two principles are not merely the metaphysical constituents of reality, they have equally useful epistemological implications. Both *puruṣa* and *prakṛti* are fundamental, one representing the permanent and unchanging and the other denoting the equally permanent but changing aspects of reality and knowledge. Knowledge may be processed through the route of *prakṛti* or it may be obtained directly from *puruṣa*. Both the avenues are available to humans even though we largely depend on the former. However, Yoga considers only that which is derived from the *puruṣa* as ultimately true knowledge.

There is a reflexive relationship between consciousness (*puruṣa*) and *buddhi*. *Buddhi* processes information from the *sattva* content of objects. This information by its very nature is subject to a variety of distortions, primarily because *buddhi*, though it is predominantly sāttvic, also contains *rajas* and *tamas*. *Puruṣa* in its association with *buddhi* reflexively takes the contents of the latter as its own; and the embodied mind has the knowledge of the objects and events. When every trace of *rajas* and *tamas* is removed and *buddhi* is all *sattva* with no fluctuations in the mind, the *puruṣa* is revealed in the mind, and consciousness manifests itself. This is the highest form of knowledge. Devoid of all distractions, it is sublime and infallible. That is the state of *kaivalya*, the ultimate goal of yoga practice.

The notion of multiplicity of *puruṣa*s in Sāṁkhya-Yoga system poses some problems. If *puruṣa* is considered to be pure consciousness devoid of individuality, form, or character, what is it that distinguishes one *puruṣa* from another? Multiplicity has meaning only when we can make distinctions. As Radhakrishnan (1989) points out, "multiplicity without distinction is impossible" (vol. 2: 322). It would appear more plausible, therefore, to regard *puruṣa* as the foundational source, the ground condition of all conscious experience, like *prakṛti*, which is considered to be the ground condition of all material forms. The notion of individual *puruṣa* arises from the "mind trap" where *puruṣa* apparently individuates and identifies itself with *buddhi* with which it is associated and whose experiences it considers as its own. Because *buddhi* is an extremely subtle form of matter that is in essence nonlocal, it can survive the disintegration of the body in which it is located, and can contain and continue the effects of its actions beyond one life. Hence the notion of multiplicity of *puruṣa*s appears needless.

In defense of Sāṁkhya-Yoga it may be said, however, that without multiple *puruṣa*s the concept of individuality would be limited to the unenlightened mind and that it would be an illusion at the level of *puruṣa*. Individuality cannot be attributed to the mind because without its association to *puruṣa*, the mind cannot experience individuality. Sāṁkhya-Yoga is very clear on this. It is *puruṣa* that mistakes the content of the mind as its own. If there is just a single *puruṣa*, how is it in one case it is entrapped and has the illusion of separateness and individuality and in another instance it is free and on its own? The postulation of multiple *puruṣa*s escapes this and similar problems associated with the notion of freedom as well. Thus, it is the agentic aspect of *puruṣa* that warrants the assumption of multiplicity of *puruṣa*s.

The Indian subcontinent is the land of many faiths. Many religions arose and numerous systems of philosophy flourished here. They gave rise to a tantalizing array of opposing ideas. Yet, yoga was recognized almost universally in this part of the world as the most complete means of achieving higher states of consciousness. Even those schools of thought, which held philosophically opposite positions, rarely questioned the usefulness of yoga practices. Such is the pervasive place of yoga in the Indian tradition. *Rāja-yoga* literally means royal yoga, and yoga as expounded in Patañjali's *Yoga-Sūtras* is considered to be the majestic royal route to higher forms of awareness that include, as we have seen, anomalous as well as transcendental states of consciousness.

18

Vedānta

A Philosophy of Pure Consciousness

K. Ramakrishna Rao

VEDĀNTA thinkers draw their inspiration from Upaniṣads, which are the end portions of the Vedas. Vedānta literally means the end of Veda. Therefore Vedānta may be considered appropriately as Upaniṣadic philosophy. However, it should be kept in mind that Upaniṣads are the "settled conclusions" of the entire Vedic thought (Hiriyanna 1949/1995: 151). Thus Vedānta represents the Vedic thought in general. Also, Vedānta incorporates other sacred writings of the Hindus like *Bhagavad-Gītā*. Consequently we find Vedānta thinkers like Śaṅkara writing thoughtful commentaries on *Gītā* and Upaniṣads.

The basic text of Vedānta is *Brahma-Sūtras*, also known as, *Vedānta-Sūtras*. Bādarāyaṇa is the author of *Brahma-Sūtras*. He lived probably in the second century BCE (Dasgupta 1922/1988). *Brahma-Sūtras* deal with the nature of and the relationship between the manifest world, the individual self (*ātman*), and the ultimate reality encompassing the two. The fundamental reality in this view is *Brahman* or *Ātman* (with capital A). *Ātman* is the universal spirit, supreme consciousness. According to Bādarāyaṇa, there is an intelligent principle behind the manifest world, which alone can account for the design and purpose in the universe. While accepting the Sāṁkhya thesis of evolution, Vedānta raises the question: Who indeed is responsible for starting the process of evolution and how would this process end? Neither *puruṣa* nor *prakṛti* could in principle be conceived as the primal cause for this. Therefore, it is argued, we need to postulate the existence of *Brahman*, who is conceived as the prime source that sets in motion the process of evolution first and causes its *pralaya* (dissolution) later. It would seem that Bādarāyaṇa was more a theist and a dualist rather than being an absolutist and a monist. Until the advent of Advaita Vedānta of Gauḍapāda and Śaṅkara, Vedānta was considered an authoritative dualistic treatise (Dasgupta 1922/1963).

Referring to Bādarāyaṇa's *Brahma-Sūtras*, Hiriyanna writes:

> It is greatly to be regretted that the *sūtra* is not clear in its teaching. In fact, it is, in its cryptic form, more ambiguous than Upaniṣads or *Gītā*; and this has lead to several interpretations being put on it.
>
> — 1949/1995: 151-52

Notwithstanding the important doctrinal differences that are too important to permit us to group all the interpretations of *Brahma-Sūtras* under one rubric, the different interpretations of Vedānta agree that *Ātman* is eternal and acquiring right knowledge is the most appropriate means of liberation.

Advaita is the most influential among the orthodox systems of Indian philosophy. Śaṅkara is the philosopher who made Advaita not merely a very popular Vedānta sect but a profound philosophical system based ostensibly on the Upaniṣadic teachings. As Theos Bernard aptly observed, "Śaṅkara was one of the great philosophers of his day, the sage of his century, the saint of his race" (1947: 8). Undoubtedly Śaṅkara is one of the outstanding thinkers of all time. His ideas have the depth of Plato and Kant, and his logic the sharpness and penetration of Aquinas and Hegel (Radhakrishnan 1989).

It is all too well known that the Indian tradition is indifferent to history. Little attention is paid to individuals, their time and place in the scheme of things. The literature is barren of biographical accounts of the philosophers and scholars of the past. Consequently we know very little of the founders of the various systems of philosophy. In some cases even their identities are in question. According to tradition, Śaṅkara dates back to 200 BCE; but the orientalists generally hold that Śaṅkara, the chief exponent of Advaita Vedānta, lived between 788 and 820 BCE (Dasgupta 1922/1988). In a short span of thirty-two years, Śaṅkara travelled widely and wrote extensively. Born in the hills of Malabar in the southern tip of India, he is believed to have died in Kedārnāth on the foothills of Himalayas. The most important of his philosophical writings are his commentaries on Upaniṣads, *Bhagavad-Gītā* and *Brahma-Sūtras*.

The Metaphysics of Pure Consciousness

According to Śaṅkara (1890), *Ātman/Brahman* is pure consciousness. It is self-manifesting and self-illuminating (*svaprakāśa*). Unlike *puruṣa*, in Sāṁkhya-Yoga, *Brahman* is one and not many; but like *puruṣa* it is contentless (*nirviṣaya*) and non-intentional. It is *nirākāra* (formless) and *nirāśraya* (rests in no other). It is suggested that the best way to grasp *Brahman* is to strip it of all the contents of experience through a process of elimination. The process of successive denial of attributes in describing *Brahman* is expressed in the famous formula *neti, neti* (not this, not this). The denied attributes include all the things and relations we find in the world, including spatial, temporal, and sensory attributes. *Brahman* is neither limited in space and time nor is distinguished from other objects. It is both the subject and the object. In a sense, it is undifferentiated subjectivity or non-objective consciousness, and yet it underlies all persons in their experience. *Brahman / Ātman* is neither the agent of knowledge nor the object of knowledge. It is knowledge itself, consciousness undifferentiated as this or that. How then is *Brahman* apprehended? According to Śaṅkara, it is self-luminous and self-revealing. By self-luminous Śaṅkara means that which is never the object of a knowing act. Rather it is immediate, direct and implicit in our own being. In reality pure consciousness, *Ātman* (with capital A), the transcendental all-pervading, self-manifesting and self-revealing absolute and *ātman* (the individual self) are the same. *Brahman/Ātman* (the Supreme Self) is no different from *ātman* (the individual self). Consciousness alone is real and it is one and the same in all beings.

Ātman as pure consciousness is the supreme principle in which there is no differentiation of knower, knowledge, and known. It is non-intentional, undifferentiated and non-objective. *Brahman* signifies also existence. In *Brahman* knowing and being are one. Also, *Brahman* is regarded as *ānanda* (absolute bliss). *Ānanda* is freedom from all bondage and attachment. It is a state of complete emancipation from the determinations of space, time, and material objects. *Brahman* is thus described as *sat, cit* and *ānanda*. At the ontological level, *Brahman* is *sat*, the principle underlying true existence. From the psychological perspective, it is consciousness (*cit*) encompassing all knowing. From the ethical/ affective standpoint, it is *ānanda* (bliss), subjective freedom from objective determination.

Advaita attempts to establish its metaphysical thesis about supreme consciousness at three levels following the Hindu tradition. First is the level of faith or belief in what we learn/hear (*śravaṇa*) to be the truth. For Advaita, like other orthodox systems of Hindu philosophy, the faith comes from the authority of the Vedas. The Vedic statements like *tat tvam asi* (thou art that) and *so'ham* (I am he) are cited in support.

The second level is the level of understanding (*manana*) truth through logic and rational discourse. Here Śaṅkara excels. Numerous arguments are offered (a) in support of Advaita position, and (b) to refute the criticisms and alternate postulations. It is argued that the existence of *Ātman/Brahman* cannot be doubted because such a doubt implies the absence of he who doubts it. If *Brahman* is other than consciousness, it has to be material because matter and consciousness together include everything while excluding each other. It is all too evident that nothing is known without consciousness. Consciousness does not need something else to reveal it. A lamp does not need another lamp to make us see the lamp. Thus consciousness is self-illuminating. Consciousness dispels ignorance like light removes darkness. Since consciousness (knowledge) and ignorance are opposed like light and darkness, the lack of ignorance implies presence of knowledge. Again, that which is unconscious cannot make another conscious. If one assumes that a cognition needs a second cognition to reveal it, then a third cognition would be needed to reveal the second and so on *ad infinitum*. It may be argued, as Nyāya thinkers do, that a contact between individual consciousness (*ātman/self*) and the inner sense, the mind (*antaḥkaraṇa*) is needed for cognition to arise. Since such a contact gives knowledge of the object of cognition, Nyāya thinkers point out, why not simply assume that the contact also gives the knowledge of the self? Advaita rebuts this argument by saying that the contact between the self and the mind is a necessary condition, but not sufficient to give rise to a cognition.

The third level is the level of realization of truth by *nididhyāsana* (meditation). Realization, unlike mere understanding, gives one absolute conviction because he/she at this level becomes one with reality. Realization may be accomplished by meditation and yoga practice. This appears to be the purport of the Upaniṣadic saying that to know *Brahman* is to become *Brahman*. At this level, knowing and being become one. So the ultimate test of the existence of pure consciousness, self-luminous and formless state of being, is the experience of *Brahman* and the consequent revelation of the identity of the self with *Brahman*, an experience of consciousness without subject–object duality, non-intentional awareness.

Brahman and the Empirical Being

Though *Brahman* is the one supreme principle underlying all reality, undifferentiated and non-dual, in the human condition it appears differentiated as subjects and objects located in time and space. This is so because in the existential situation, the *Ātman*, the Supreme Being resides as individual consciousness in the abode of *jīva*. *Jīva* is the embodied self; it is consciousness limited by the mind, intellect, senses, and body.

In Advaita, *jīva* is conceived as being encased and covered at different levels by *koṣa*s (sheaths). They are *annamaya koṣa* (representing the body and the material nourishment it needs), *prāṇamaya koṣa* (the life sustaining vital breath), *manomaya koṣa* (the mental system), and *ānandamaya koṣa* (the surround of happiness and bliss). The first *koṣa* refers to the gross body. The next two are the life-sustaining and knowledge-processing principles. The last, *ānandamaya koṣa*, is the state of bliss that the *jīva* seeks and strives for (see Gauḍapāda's *Māṇḍukya-Kārikā* III.2). *Jīva* comprises of the sum total of the ever-changing and multifarious conscious states and the processes that give rise to them. In *jīva*, consciousness is surrounded by the limiting adjuncts of the mind–body complex. The consciousness in *jīva* is none other than *Brahman*/*Ātman*, the supreme consciousness itself.

Ātman in the existential context as individual consciousness is, however, covered by the effects of *māyā*. *Māyā* is the seed out of which phenomenal experience sprouts. As stated in *Brahma-Sūtras*, *māyā* is the potential cause of the empirical world of illusion. It is undeveloped and unmanifested because it cannot be defined either as that which is or that which is not (I.4.3). *Māyā* is similar to *prakṛti*, in Sāṁkhya. From it emanate name and form. *Māyā* exists in the form of ignorance in the person. When knowledge of the truth dawns, it disappears. Thus it is neither real nor unreal. In his commentary on the *Bhagavad-Gītā*, Śaṅkara points out,

> all emanations, fluctuations or modifications from mind to the gross body, and all qualities such as those which manifest themselves as pleasure, pain, delusion, and other mental states . . . spring from *prakṛti*, the *māyā* composed of three qualities — goodness, passion and darkness.
>
> —XIII. 19

Māyā is the mother illusion of the manifest world of the ever changing phenomena. It is an illusion that ends on the realization of the truth that we are one with *Brahman*, just as we realize the illusoriness of the dream on waking. However, the phenomenal or empirical world is not unreal like the sky flower or hare's horn. The dream is real when we are dreaming. It is unreal only after we realize it to be a dream. In like manner, the experience of the *vyavahārika* (phenomenal) world is real until one has *pāramārthika* (the transcendental) experience of the non-duality of subject and object, and the experience of the unity of *jīva* (the individual consciousness) and the *Ātman/Brahman* (Supreme Consciousness).

The statement *tat tvam asi* (thou art that) in *Chandogya Upaniṣad*, referred to as *mahāvākya* (the great saying), expresses the relationship between *jīva ātman* (individual consciousness) and *Ātman* (Supreme Consciousness). In a sense, the Supreme Consciousness constitutes the ground for our individual consciousness. *Tat tvam asi* is the assertion of the common ground that links the individual to *Brahman*. Individual consciousness is a manifestation of the Supreme Consciousness, when the latter is clouded by *avidyā* (ignorance), and limited by the functions of the mind, all being manifestations of *māyā*.

The individual is thus, in Advaita view, a curious combination of both reality and appearance. In so far as *Ātman* constitutes the ground, the individual is real; but in its phenomenal aspect with its stream of experience, the individual is a mere appearance. The phenomenal consciousness as it manifests in our mental states, according to Śaṅkara, is directed toward one object or another, whereas consciousness as such, the Supreme Consciousness, is pure and objectless. In other words, it is non-intentional.

Ātman within us is the transcendental subject, "I", whereas the self of the manifest experience is the empirical subject, "me". The latter is subject to change, unlike the changeless transcendental self (*paramātmā*). *Ātman* is pure cognition; the empirical self is seen as an agency actively engaged, striving towards one end or another. As Śaṅkara states in his commentary on *Brahma-Sūtras* (II.3.40), *jīva* (individual consciousness) is essentially an agent of all activities. Its agency dwells in *upādhis* (the limitations) imposed by *buddhi* (mind). *Jīva*, as *Māṇḍukya-Kārikā* states, "is a product of imagination and is capable of further imagination" (III.2). It is, however, more than an illusion manifesting in individual consciousness of the empirical world. Amidst the evanescent mental states, there is the abiding reality of *Ātman*. It is called in Vedānta *sākṣin* (the witness consciousness). Though it is associated with experience in the empirical world, *sākṣin* is not a product of experience, but is presupposed by it. It is the continuing witness of the changing mental life of the embodied being. It is a sort of stage on which various mental events take place. There are slightly different views among the Advaita thinkers about the relation between *jīva* and *sākṣin*. The essential difference between the two appears to be that *antaḥkaraṇa* (the mind) is the attribute of *jīva* in one whereas it is merely a *upādhi* of *sākṣin* in the other.

It is important to note that in Advaita the individual person is neither part of, nor different from, nor a modification of the Supreme Consciousness. It is *Ātman* itself steeped in *avidyā*. The *upādhis*, the mental processes, within us limit the understanding of *Ātman*. According to the theory of limitation developed by the later Advaita thinkers, known as *avacchedavāda*, *jīva* is the *Ātman* limited by his mind. There is also another theory called *pratibimbavāda* to account for the relationship between the individual and the Supreme Consciousness, according to which the individual consciousness is a reflection of the Supreme Consciousness in the mirror of *avidyā*. The reflection is a function of the state of the individual. Like the reflection of a person in a pool of water which varies depending on the state of the water, whether it is clear or dirty, calm or turbulent, so does the reflection of Supreme Consciousness in an individual self vary depending on the state of the *avidyā* of the individual person in whom it is reflected. Śaṅkara himself used the simile of reflection. Commenting on *Bṛhadāraṇyaka Upaniṣad* (4.12) Śaṅkara points out that, as the reflections of sun and moon on water are a mere appearance, so are the individual selves (personal consciousness) reflections of the one reality *Ātman* in *avidyā*. They are not truly real. On overcoming *avidyā*, the reflections cease and the true consciousness alone remains.

The Mind and States of Consciousness

Mind, in Vedānta, is not the knowing self. Rather the mind is the *instrument* of knowledge. The self is the agent (*kartā*) of knowledge. In the Advaita system, *antaḥkaraṇa* is the name used to connote mind in its totality. *Antaḥkaraṇa* literally means internal organ. Mind then is one's internal organ that enables him/her to know, feel, will, and act. It is the totality of mental states and the processes that give rise to them. As in the Yoga system other concepts are used, sometimes interchangeably with mind and *antaḥkaraṇa* to coincide with the different functions of the mind. These include *manas*, *buddhi*, *ahaṁkāra*, and *citta*. *Manas* denotes the processing aspect of the mind. *Buddhi* is the determining aspect. *Ahaṁkāra* is the ego or the "I" aspect of the mind.

In Advaita Vedānta, we may recall, there is one undifferentiated consciousness (*Ātman*/*Brahman*). At the empirical level, this is seen as differentiated and particularized in *jīvas* (individual being). *Antaḥkaraṇa* (the mind) is that which makes such particularization possible. It is the principle of individuation. Basically two types of individuation are distinguished. The first type is one where we attribute qualitative characteristics to consciousness. This happens in association with objects when, for example, one becomes perceptually aware of an object. The second type involves determination not by the qualifying conditions (*viśeṣaṇa*) of the objects but by the limiting conditions (*upādhi*s). The mind is involved in both kinds of determination.

The Śaṅkara School distinguishes between two types of *jīva*, depending upon the individuation process involved. When *antaḥkaraṇa* in its role as a qualifying adjunct determines the Supreme Consciousness, there is one type of *jīva*, the individual empirical self. However, when the Supreme Consciousness is determined by *upādhi*s (the limiting adjuncts) of the mind we have *jīva-sākṣin* (witness self). Mind is involved in the manifestation of *jīva* as well as *jīva-sākṣin*. In the case of the former, mind is a constituent element, a part of *jīva* and inseparable from it; whereas in the latter, it is only a limiting condition that determines *jīva* but separable from it. Thus *antaḥkaraṇa* (mind) is needed in both cases. There can be no manifestation of *jīva* or *jīva-sākṣin* without a mind. The Śaṅkara School finds it necessary to distinguish between *jīva* and *jīva-sākṣin* because it is assumed that without the presupposition of the latter it is difficult to account for the unity of apperception in one's awareness of external objects and of oneself. Thus in this view, *jīva* is the empirical ego/self with mind as a constituent and *jīva-sākṣin* is the transcendental ego not qualified but only limited by the mind. (For a detailed discussion of the relation between them Sinha 1958, vol. I : 372-75.)

In the Advaita view, like in many systems of Indian philosophy, *antaḥkaraṇa* is essentially material. It is preponderantly *sattva*. It is possibly the subtlest form of matter, translucent, and capable of receiving reflections of the Supreme Consciousness. Mind is the inner medium, which in association with sensory organs takes the forms of the objects perceived. Thus mind is the main instrument that enables the essence of the object revealed by removing what is believed to be the veil of ignorance.

Perception and Cognition

In Advaita view, even though consciousness (*Brahman*) is one, it has three distinguishable phases and may be seen as three different aspects. First, consciousness appears to be qualified by the external objects. The resultant phenomenon is called object-consciousness (*viṣaya-caitanya*). The second category is cognitive-consciousness (*pramāṇa-caitanya*). When mental modes (*vṛtti*s) qualify consciousness, we have cognitive consciousness. When consciousness is limited by a mind, there is self-consciousness (*pramātra-*

caitanya). The first appears to correspond roughly to what we normally understand by sensation. The second and the third seem to relate to processing of perpetual awareness. In Advaita, perception is cognition and cognition is consciousness, which is essentially one but appears to *jīva* in its embodied state as many and in different forms because of the qualifying or limiting conditions. The three phases of consciousness are thus the three types of empirical modalities of consciousness as qualified by objects, mental modes, or the mind. They appear to be three levels of cognition brought about by three different activities of the mind.

In perception, Advaitins believe, the mind "goes out" to the object through sensory channels and assumes the form of the object. As in Yoga, the modification in the mind brought about by the contact of the mind with an object is called *vr̥tti* (mental mode). *Vr̥tti* (the form the mind takes after sensory-contact with the object) is a necessary condition for perception. In inference of fire from smoke, for example, there is no sensory contact with fire, but a contact with the corresponding *vr̥tti* of fire. In inference the mind does not reach out and come into contact with the object, it only "thinks" of the inferred object. The second necessary condition of perception is that there should be space–time contiguity between *vr̥tti* and the object that gives rise to it; they should be contiguous in time and place. "*Vr̥tti*," as Jadunath Sinha describes so aptly, "is an empirical mode of the mind which takes the form of the object. Therefore, it is the meeting place, as it were, of the two substances, the mind and the object. It is not different from the mind, because it is a mode of the mind. It is not different from the object, because it is the transformation of the mind into the form of the object, i.e., it incorporates the form of the object in itself. Thus the mental mode, being identified with the object, occupies the same position in space" (1958: 132-33). If the mental mode and the object of perception are temporally apart, such as in the case of thinking about yesterday's pain, we have recollection and not perception. The third necessary condition for perception to take place is that the object of perception must be *yogya* (capable) of being perceived. As summarized by Dharmarājadhvarīndra in *Vedānta Paribhāṣā:*

> the direct perceptibility of an object consists in the fact that the subjective consciousness underlying the apprehending mental mode becomes united with the consciousness underlying the object, the object existing in the present space and time and capable of being perceived through a specific sense organ, and the apprehending mental mode also having

the same form as that of the object. — Sinha 1958, vol.1: 134

According to Advaita, mere perception of an object is different from the perception of the object as object. Here the distinction appears to be between, for example, one (a) seeing a pot, and (b) knowing that he sees the pot. There is awareness of awareness (self-consciousness) in (b) and not in (a). In (a) as pointed out in *Vedānta-Paribhāṣā*, an identity occurs between object-consciousness and cognitive-consciousness. In (b) there is the experience of not only this identity but also the identity of cognitive consciousness with the subject or "I"-consciousness. Vedānta assumes identity among the three phases of consciousness because there is really no difference between *vṛtti* and *ahaṁkāra* (the ego aspect of the mind). *Vṛtti* is an activity of the mind, and *ahaṁkāra* is one aspect of the mind. Therefore, the consciousness determined by *vṛtti* and the consciousness processed by the mind in its relation to the ego cannot be different. All that is meant here, it would seem, is that the object-consciousness underlies cognitive consciousness. In other words, the perception of an object as object involves the identification of the perceived object with its corresponding *vṛtti* as well as with the perceiving subject. This is the case, in Advaita view, whether the object of perception is external, e.g. perception of a pot, or internal like the awareness of pain.

Among other divisions Advaitins make is the distinction between *jñeya pratyakṣa* (perception of an object) and *jñāña pratyakṣa* (perception of a cognition). Perception of an object involves a *vṛtti* as a medium, whereas in perception of a cognition there is no involvement of *vṛtti*. Again, like most other Indian thinkers, Śaṅkara makes a distinction between *savikalpa* (determinate) and *nirvikalpa* (indeterminate) perception. Actually the two may be regarded as two distinct stages of perception. At the stage of indeterminate perception there is only an identification or apprehension of the object without any attributes are qualities imputed to it. It is simple undifferentiated, non-relational, or direct awareness. It consists of bare sense-datum with no representational content. The possibility of such non-representational perception is accepted in almost all the major systems of Indian philosophy including Buddhism, even though there is in the literature considerable discussion of significant differences among them. Determinate perception is representational in character. It is relational involving analysis, assimilation, and synthesis. It involves images and associations, and can be described in words. In Śaṅkara's view, indeterminate perception is *essentially* and absolutely indeterminate, having no qualifications whatsoever. It is limited to an apprehension of mere "being" with no concrete awareness of individual object or its qualities. Some of the neo-Advaita thinkers like Dharmarājadhvarīndra suggest that indeterminate perception may involve immediate apprehension of qualities without awareness of the relations between them and the object.

Like Sāṁkhya-Yoga thinkers, Śaṅkara emphasizes in the perceptual process the going out function of the mind to reach out to the objects. As we have pointed out in our discussion of Yoga theory of perception, it makes little sense to assume that the mind literally goes out to meet the external object. Rather the "going out" may mean no more than reaching out to the object, indicating the relative importance of the subject over the object. It is the subject who has the freedom to choose whether or not to have a relationship with an object. Jadunath Sinha (1958), favorably commenting on the Advaita theory of perception also argues in favor of the view that Śaṅkara's theory of perception gives dominance to the subject and subordinates the object to the perceiving subject in their relative importance.

Advaita, following Upaniṣads, distinguishes between four cognitive states: (1) the waking state, (2) the dream state, (3) the state of deep sleep, and (4) the transcendental state of *turīya* or *samādhi*. In the waking state, external objects determine the content of consciousness. It is the state where consciousness is processed by the whole set of our psychophysical system. Dream consciousness is made up of the same stuff as the waking consciousness, except that its content is not empirically real and that it is not determined to a large extent by the external objects. It is illusory in the sense that on waking one realizes the unreality of what is experienced in the dream. The deep-sleep state is characterized by the abeyance of all distinctions including the distinction of the subject from the object. *Māṇḍūkya Upaniṣad* describes the fourth state of consciousness thus:

> They consider the fourth to be that which is not conscious of the internal world, nor conscious of the external world, nor conscious of both the worlds, nor a mass of consciousness, nor simple consciousness, nor unconsciousness, which is unseen, beyond empirical determination, beyond the grasp (of the mind), undemonstrable, unthinkable, undescribable, of the nature of the consciousness alone wherein all phenomena cease, unchanging, peaceful, and non-dual.

In the fourth state of consciousness, there is a realization of the identity of the individual and the Supreme Consciousness, and the non-reality of the world experienced in waking consciousness. Just as on waking one recognizes the illusoriness of dreams, so does the one who realizes the highest state of consciousness realizes the illusoriness of waking experience. What seems to be unique to transcendental or pure consciousness is that it is, unlike any phenomenal awareness, nonintentional. There is no object that one is conscious of, except consciousness itself. Pure consciousness is nonintentional and objectless and contains no ego sense. Phenomenal awareness of objects as manifested in our ordinary consciousness signifies states of consciousness brought about by the various degrees of influence of its limiting adjuncts in human mind.

Advaita thinkers generally accept Patañjali's classification of *samādhi*, including the possibility of acquiring paranormal abilities. Sadānanda in his *Vedāntasāra* distinguishes between *savikalpa* and *nirvikalpa samādhi*. In *savikalpa samādhi* the identity of the individual consciousness with pure consciousness is experienced through the agency of the mind. Here *vṛtti* has *Brahman* as the object of awareness. In *nirvikalpa samādhi* there is no awareness of *vṛtti* (the mental mode). The mind is completely dissolved. Whereas in the former the distinction between the knower and the known, the subject and the object is not completely obliterated, in the later such distinctions disappear.

Consciousness as Undifferentiated Subjectivity

As mentioned before, according to Śaṅkara, consciousness is self-luminous or self-revealing. Self-luminosity is defined as "that which is never the object of a knowing act but is yet immediate and direct with us". It means the "capacity of being always present in all our acts of consciousness without in anyway being an object of consciousness". We may interpret these statements to mean that consciousness as-such is self-revealing subjectivity, the center-point to which all phenomena are referenced. It is argued that consciousness manifests itself and that it is not known as something other than itself. It is never an object. It is *svaprakāśa* (self-revealing). In Advaita view, there can be no doubt, error, or contrary knowledge in respect of consciousness. Consciousness, then, is knowledge in its sublime condition free from error, doubt, and misgivings. Doubt and error are a consequence of its association with the mind, the senses and the sensory objects. Progressive dissociation from them enables one to achieve a state of being in which there is realization of consciousness as-such, a state of non-objective awareness.

The discussion of the four states of consciousness in Advaita philosophy is extremely helpful in understanding the true nature of consciousness as-such. The distinction Advaita makes between waking, dreams, dreamless sleep, and *turīya* or *samādhi* states is pivotal and provides the *raison d'être* to interpret pure consciousness as undifferentiated subjectivity or non-objective consciousness. Here we make use of a revealing and original interpretation of monistic Advaita Vedānta by K.C. Bhattacharyya (1909) in his *Studies in Vedāntism*.

In dreams what we usually have are copies of waking percepts, that do not follow any definite rules of formation. Here imaginative construction is more free than in waking life. In the waking state, our consciousness is so deeply intertwined with objective determinations that it can hardly move of its own accord as it does in dreams. So long as we are awake we can scarcely free our consciousness from that of objects. In dreams, on the other hand, our subjectivity is almost free from this limitation, because the object-consciousness is reduced to a minimum. Sometimes it is altogether absent. Consciousness appears to be free from the determination of the sense objects and even the body itself. When, for instance, we have out-of-body experiences in dreams, we have the experience of seeing our bodies as lying asleep. Consciousness is here almost free from all objective determinations and sometimes all objectivity disappears. Dream consciousness is not bound to any sense datum and no object manifests it. Thus, as Bhattacharyya says, "dreams may be described as perceptions without sensations" (1909: 2).

The self-revealing nature of consciousness is evident also in the state of *suṣupti* (deep, dreamless sleep). *Suṣupti* is not a state devoid of consciousness. That it is so, Śaṅkara argues, is evident from the awareness of the man, after he has arisen from the state of dreamless sleep, that he had a blissful sleep during which he was conscious of nothing. Of course, his knowledge is directly derived from memory. Still memory is always memory of presentation of something that was actually presented. Therefore, the bliss and consciousness, concludes Śaṅkara, must have been experienced during *suṣupti*. It follows, therefore, that the self-revealing nature of consciousness is manifest in deep sleep also. The empirical consciousness determined by sensory objects lapses here altogether. What is left is none other than undifferentiated subjectivity.

But even *suṣupti* (deep-sleep experience) cannot give us the actuality of the knowledge of the reality of pure consciousness, though its possibility is suggested. In the state of deep-sleep consciousness is the awareness of a positive blank. It consists in a "direct cognition of the absence of specific cognition" (Bhattacharyya 1909: 14). The nature of consciousness as complete freedom from objects, nay, as conscious freedom from the determination of anything that is not consciousness itself, can be realized only in the state of *turīya*, an ecstatic state of *ṣamādhi*. It is an experience of consciousness as-such, indeterminate, undetermined, and free from all objective limitations. Unlike *suṣupti*, wherein consciousness lapses into a state of undetermined consciousness without striving for it, the *turīya* stage represents a complete installation in subjectivity through conscious withdrawal from objects. It represents, according to Advaita, a higher, in fact the highest level of being. It signifies realization of the reality as transcending all determinateness. It is a state where there is no duality. It is non-dual not merely because there is the absence of duality as in *suṣupti*. It is non-dual because *avidyā* (veil of ignorance) distorting consciousness and creating the illusion of empirical reality is removed, and removed for good; and even the consciousness of the removal is absent. It is a state of pure undifferentiated consciousness. Objective plurality is not only negated, even the sense of negation itself is absent. What is left is only pure consciousness in which there is the essential identity of being, consciousness, and bliss.

The highest *samādhi* state is one which is thus completely *nirvikalpa* (indeterminate). Advaita also recognizes *savikalpa* (determinate) states of *samādhi*, preceding the indeterminate state. *Savikalpa samādhi* is an intermediate state between *suṣupti* and *nirvikalpa samādhi*. What then is the difference between deep sleep and determinate *samādhi* state? In the words of Bhattacharyya:

> The difference, as ordinarily given, is that in the former the (empirical) mind with all its modes lapses altogether, whereas in the latter it does not lapse but only gets concentrated into one absolute irrelative mode which thus becomes actualized in the highest degree. The one represents the greatest *dispersion* of attention, the other its utmost *concentration*. In both, the consciousness of duality lapses; in both, the self enjoys undifferentiated bliss; in both, the timeless seeds of *vidyā-karma* (knowledge and action) persist, accounting for the recognition of the past on awaking from them. But whereas on awaking from *suṣupti*, the self remembers that it was in the attitude of knowing object though the object was there a blank, on rising from *samādhi* it ought to remember it *was* the object in that state and not in the object-knowing attitude at all. In the former, the self as always limited was simply isolated; in the latter, it

> burst its bonds, destroyed the barrier between subject and object, and became the absolute. — 1909: 14-15

As Bhattacharyya points out, the stages of waking, dreams, dreamless sleep, determinate and indeterminate *samādhi* form a gradation of existence. Waking experience, where there is hardly any freedom for the subject from the object-consciousness, is one variation of this gradation. Consciousness at this stage completely identities itself with the objective world. The other extreme is constituted by the state of undifferentiated subjectivity that is completely free from all objective determinations, a state of pure consciousness. Between these stages come dreams and a deep-sleep state. They reveal the ever-increasing freedom from objectivity and a deepening of the installation into non-dual consciousness. The state of *samādhi* is not a stage among other stages. While almost everybody experiences the states of dream, and dreamless sleep, the state of *samādhi* is not attained by all. That is because the state has to be achieved through a conscious effort, a continual withdrawal from objects and a corresponding installation in subjectivity. Śaṅkara points out that this realization of the ultimate truth; the identity of the self with *Brahman* comes only to a mind that prepares itself for it. Śaṅkara adds that an initial preparation is necessary to achieve this highest level of existence. Such preparation leads to a development of the subjective attitude striving for conscious freedom from objects.

The suggestion all through the writings of Śaṅkara is that the ultimate reality, the pure consciousness, is to be realized from within, through a withdrawal from objectivity, by prolonged and continued meditation. It cannot be grasped through discursive reason, which proceeds by way of making a distinction between the knower, the knowledge, and the known, since it is free from all distinctions. A phenomenon has not merely a relational aspect, which can be understood through discursive reason, but it also has an intrinsic aspect that can be grasped only through intuitive insight, which is imaginative withdrawal from its non-essential attributes and installation into what is inseparable from it.

This subjective attitude of realizing consciousness as-such which is in reality a process of imaginative isolation, or conscious withdrawal from objects is, however, helped to certain extent by rational discussion in so far as it serves as a means of detailing certain aspects of the object before the mind. But discursive reason ultimately has to make place for intuitive insight since it is not always free from doubt. In other words, reason gives understanding of truth and not necessarily its realization in one's being.

Intuitive insight prepares the path for an immediate realization of consciousness as-such and an experience of non-duality. In Advaita view, only when in and through the process of steadfast meditation and imaginative isolation the state of *turīya* is attained that we have *anubhava* (experience) of the non-duality of subject and object. It is then and then only that the light of consciousness, pure and without obstruction, shines forth in us as a living truth of the identity of existence, consciousness, and bliss absolute.

Does Pure Consciousness Exist?

Following Bhattacharyya we have attempted to interpret the different states of consciousness from waking to *samādhi* as a progressive movement away from objectivity to subjectivity until one experiences subjectivity in its indeterminate form, i.e., pure consciousness without any content. The question remains to be answered, however, whether are there any compelling reasons for believing in the existence of such consciousness, pure, and indeterminate?

J.N. Mohanty (1993) in an incisive analysis of the Vedānta theory of consciousness points out three different ways of conceiving the relationship between consciousness as-such and conscious states. First, the relation may be one between a universal and a particularized instance of it, as between redness and patches of red. Second, one may conceive the relation to be between awareness and that of which one is aware. Third, consciousness as-such may be regarded as the *reality* whereas the mental states are mere *appearances* of that reality, like the moon and the many images of it reflected in different lakes and rivers. We find all these interpretations in Vedānta literature.

As Mohanty suggests, non-intentional pure consciousness is not a "phenomenological datum of non-mystical experience" (1993: 59). What then are the grounds for supposing the possibility of non-intentional consciousness? According to Advaita Vedānta, first, there can be no conscious states without consciousness as-such because the former presupposes the latter. Second, consciousness admits of no differences that necessarily belong to objects. Therefore, the subject–object differences as obtained in our conscious states should belong to the empirical world and not to consciousness as-such. Third, undifferentiated awareness in pure consciousness that does not signify any object or quality accompanies all waking consciousness and even dreamless sleep. All the three arguments can be disputed, of course, as those philosophies that questioned the

Advaita thesis have done. Pointing to the weaknesses of the above arguments, Mohanty considers the third argument more plausible than others, if we were to make a distinction between the awareness aspect and the intentionality aspect of conscious states. Awareness, he suggests, may be regarded as a universal feature present in all states of consciousness, whereas intentionality is relative to the object, the person, and the cognizing situation. Yogic literature suggests the possibility of achieving a mere awareness state without content. Non-intentional consciousness as-such is then an "universal detachable from the particular mental states". Mohanty considers this to be a logical possibility even though he does not within the bounds of his experience find a "foothold" from where he could conceptualize non-intentional consciousness.

Mohanty goes on, however, to suggest that pure consciousness may best be considered "as a goal to be attained rather than as an ontological reality" (1993: 62). Here he makes use of an idea advanced by Bhattacharyya in his book *The Subject As Freedom*. Bhattacharyya (1930) argues that the subject–object relation is one-sided inasmuch as the relation is essential from the side of the object but only optional from the side of the subject. In other words, the object has no choice and is dependent upon an appropriate intentional act in order to be an object. Pure consciousness may be conceived as a goal to be achieved by exercising one's freedom to withdraw from all object-directedness. Mohanty says that "the idea of pure non-intentional consciousness is the reified, ontological equivalent of that normative goal" (1993: 63).

That it is difficult, if not impossible, to conceptualize pure consciousness is clearly recognized by the Vedāntins in their characterization of *Brahman* as *neti, neti* (not this, not this). Conceptualization is a mental act that is necessarily limited to conscious states that have a directedness about them. Therefore, it would be a futile endeavor to seek any conceptualization of pure consciousness. In other words, pure consciousness may be beyond any intellectual understanding. That pure consciousness cannot be an object of conventional understanding does not entail that it does not exist.

Some who claim to have mystical experiences say that they have experienced pure consciousness. There is a conviction that goes with such experience. But then, conviction is not proof. We know that our expectations can produce convictions. It is also suggested that the experience of pure consciousness is accompanied not only by a conviction that it is an objectless conscious experience but also by remarkable behavioral changes such as those attributed to saints. It is possible that experiencing consciousness as-such is accompanied by realization that goes beyond mere understanding, a realization where there is no dissociation between knowing and being as exemplified in the Upaniṣadic statement: *Knowing Brahman is becoming Brahman*. We may indeed find persons who achieved such an integrated state in which there is no dissociation between their beliefs and conduct. Does this prove the existence of consciousness as-such? Mohanty contends,

> To have an experience and to draw *metaphysical lessons from it are two different things. No bare experience tells its own tale*. The experience concerned has to play a certain role of fulfilling a prior conceptual intention, in order to be of cognitive value. This is why mystical experiences are made to support quite different theories. They are to a large extent theory-neutral. — 1993: 64, emphasis, by author

Mohanty may be right in assuming that mystical insights may lend support to different metaphysical notions. Indeed if Upaniṣads contain such mystical, intuitive insights of those who are believed to have achieved higher conscious states as in *samādhi*, they are clearly amenable to support a variety of metaphysical theories. This is evident in the case of Vedānta itself, which harbors a number of schools with distinctive metaphysical presuppositions, all claiming the authority of the Vedas. What is important, however, is that none of them questions the intuitions themselves, their veracity, and genuineness. They differ only in the interpretation of them. Consequently it is not unreasonable to believe in pure consciousness as a datum of experience, if such experiences are indeed genuine. Their metaphysical implications, however, may be discussed at a different level.

What we have so far discussed is essentially the Advaita Vedānta of Śaṅkara. While Śaṅkara's Advaita is the most sophisticated, and in many ways a brilliant philosophical system, Rāmānuja's thought with its blend of theism and absolutism has had a greater popular appeal among the Hindus. In Viśiṣṭādvaita, God is identified with *Brahman*. It is the central principle involved in individual selves (*jīvas*) as well as in all forms of manifest matter. *Jīva*, the material world of objects, and *Brahman* are different and distinct entities. They are, however, inseparable. Neither the individual *jīvas* nor the physical world can exist without *Brahman*.

God is the principle immanent in individual *jīvas* as well as in material objects. He is the cause of *jīvas* as well as matter. The latter in their unmanifest form are the body of God. In their manifest form, they are the effects caused by God. God is omnipotent and omniscient. He is present everywhere. It is through His grace *jīva*s attain their *mokṣa* (liberation). God has awareness of the world through his consciousness. His consciousness, unlike that of *jiva,* is free from all constraints and defects. *Jīva* is not independent of nor identical with God. It is a manifestation and transformation of God. Atomic in size, *jīva* is invariably accompanied by consciousness. *Jīva* is not only the subject of knowing, but it is also an object of knowing. Consciousness (*dharma-bhūta-jñāna*) in Rāmānuja's view is a *dravya* (substance) separate from *jīva* as well as matter. Consciousness in the *jīva* is constrained and is subject to defects. It is different from material objects in that it can manifest itself as well as other objects. However, what it manifests is always for others and not for itself. Consciousness cannot become aware of itself, even though it enables *jīva* as well as *Īśvara* to become aware. *Jīva,* unlike consciousness, is the one who knows, but cannot reveal by itself anything else but itself.

Consciousness pertains to *jīva*s as well as God. In *jīva,* consciousness is constrained because it operates through the mind and the mind in association with the senses. In our perceptions, for example, consciousness starts with *jīva* and passes via the mind and the senses to the objects and takes the form of the object and reveals it to *jīva*. Unlike *antaḥkaraṇa* (the internal organ, the mind), which requires *sākṣin* (the witness consciousness), in Rāmānuja's theory *dharma-bhūta-jñāna* itself bestows consciousness on the cognized objects.

In Viśiṣṭādvaita, consciousness is inseparable from the cognizing subject, whether the subject is the individual *jīva* or *Īśvara* (God). At the same time, consciousness is not identical with the cognizing subject or the object of cognition. It inheres as an attribute of the subject, but not itself the subject. It would seem that consciousness is more like a function of the subject, whether *jīva* or God.

*Jīva*s, according to Viśiṣṭādvaita, are multiple in number and they transmigrate in a succession of births. Though intrinsically blissful, *jīva*s suffer pain due to their past *karma*. The goal of *jīva*s is liberation, as in other systems. Liberation is freedom from the defects and imperfections enveloping them. The liberated state is an unconstrained freedom, perfection, and bliss. Viśiṣṭādvaita advocated two kinds of means for achieving *mokṣa* (liberation). One is *bhakti* (devotion and faith). It includes devotion to *karma-yoga* (one's duty). The second is *jñāna-yoga,* pursuit of knowledge and truth. *Karma-yoga* is the selfless action with total surrender and complete devotion to God. *Jñāna-yoga* is the pursuit of self-realization in order to obtain God-realization.

Concluding Summary

Existence has various gradations from the essentially unreal like hare's horn or barren woman's son to the *ultimately* real *Brahman*. In between there are various gradations such as the illusion of silver in a shell, perception of the external world of objects, the experience of dream, dreamless sleep devoid of any imagery, and the different states of *samādhi*. In these phases of existence there is a progressive movement away from externally driven objectivity to internally experienced subjectivity. That subjectivity in its essential form is absolutely detached from everything else. It is undifferentiated unity of being, bliss, and consciousness. In that state the other forms of existence are understood as illusory and unreal in a manner similar to discovering the unreality of the dream objects, after awakening from sleep. In Advaita view, the ultimate reality, eternal and absolute, is the pure being of consciousness as-such. The empirical being or the individual consciousness is a phenomenal manifestation of the supreme conscious being, limited by the mind, intellect, senses, and body. The supreme consciousness not only provides the necessary support to the individual but also acts as the witnessing consciousness throughout the life history of the person. It is possible to transcend the limitations of our bodily conditions and achieve understanding of the Supreme, which consists in removing the veil of ignorance and realizing the identity of the individual consciousness with the Supreme Consciousness. Such a realization at once reveals the illusory nature of the empirical world and gives rise to the sublime bliss of non-objective consciousness, an experience of unconditioned person, consciousness in its splendid unsullied form.

There are glaring differences in the metaphysical postulations of Advaita Vedānta and Sāṁkhya-Yoga. One is unwaveringly absolutist and non-dualist whereas the other espouses dualism of consciousness and matter, and pluralism of *puruṣa*s. More importantly for our purpose, however, there are striking similarities between them on the notion of pure consciousness and their understanding of cognitive processes, perception, and phenomenal experience. They agree that consciousness is not a quality or attribute of the mind. Consciousness is assumed to be essentially different from mind, having its own primacy of being. Further both conceive consciousness as-such without any form or content. In Yoga, consciousness is also devoid of activity. Since Advaita discards matter at the highest level of existence, it has to provide for some kind of activity in consciousness itself. Advaita concepts of *Brahman* and *māyā* roughly correspond to *puruṣa* and *prakṛti* in Sāṁkhya. However, Advaita non-dualism not only deprives *prakṛti* (matter) the status of being ultimately real, but it also denies multiplicity to consciousness. In Yoga theory there are multiple centers of consciousness in *puruṣa*s, whereas all of them are consumed in Advaita under one supreme consciousness, *Brahman*.

Again, the concept of mind and theories of perception are similar in Yoga and Advaita. They seem to agree on some of the details of how the mind works and is able to reflect consciousness to give us awareness in its various forms. Both Yoga and Vedānta agree that mind and consciousness are different and that mind is physical. In Advaita, however, the physical is only empirically real and not ultimately real. They are essential similarities in their views on perception and cognition. The bare outline of Yoga–Vedānta theory of mind may be summarized in the following way.

Mind is the composite of awareness and response systems. It may be functionally distinguished into (1) *buddhi* (executive system), (2) *ahaṁkāra*, (self-reference system), (3) *manas* (central processing system), and (4) *jñāna-karma indriya*s (sensory-motor system). In perception *buddhi* makes contact with the object via the sensory channels. This gives rise to modifications in *buddhi* and *vṛtti*s arise in the mind. *Vṛtti* is homogeneous and immediate. It is *indeterminate apprehension* of the object. *Vṛtti* then is processed by *manas*, which with its selective attention subjects *vṛtti* to analysis, assimilation, and discrimination. *Vṛtti* thus becomes determinate and definitive; it is broken into subject–predicate relationship; and the object is *reflectively apprehended*. In the next stage, *vṛtti* is appropriated by *ahaṁkāra* which is the self-reference system. *Vṛtti* becomes associated with the person. One has the *self-apprehension* of the object. With this self-reference of *ahaṁkāra* and the determinate form given by *manas*, *vṛtti* finds itself back in *buddhi* with all the manifest modifications.

Buddhi is not a *tabula rasa*. It is a storehouse of past memories, accumulated *karma*, subliminal impressions, inherited tendencies, *saṁskāra*s and *vāsanās*. *Vṛtti* is impacted by them and takes further transformations and finally surfaces as a form of *buddhi*. The light of *puruṣa* or *Brahman* always envelopes *buddhi*. Consequently, the light that is consciousness reflects on the exposed surface of *buddhi* in its *vṛtti* form, resulting in the *conscious apprehension* of the object. *Buddhi* then may choose to respond in appropriate ways by initiating action through its response system, *karmendriyas*. This is the cognition–action mode in which the mind is centrally and constantly involved unless it is obscured, obstructed, or covered by *tamas* as in sleep or voluntarily controlled as in meditation. *Conscious apprehension*, the final outcome of cognitive process, may be conceived as bestowing or imprinting, to borrow Nagel's celebrated phrase, the "what is it like" character on the experienced object. It is the consummation of *sattva* (information content) of the object in the subjectivity of consciousness.

The above is a description of the empirical mode of awareness. It is the existential condition of human cognition and action. The limitedness of such awareness and its illusory nature become evident, Advaitins believe, after one awakens with the dawn of pure consciousness. When existence moves to the level of pure consciousness, one's relation with reality takes a dramatic turn. The subject–object duality experienced at the empirical level disappears. Knowledge ceases to be representational. Consciousness as-such becomes contentless. "Contentless" means here the essential ineffability of experience. Advaitins believe that it is possible to enjoy states of pure consciousness by the embodied mind. *Jīvanmukta* is the one who has gained freedom from the constraints of mind and realized in his being the true identity of his/her consciousness with *Brahman*, the supreme or pure consciousness. This is a state of transcendence where knowing and being become one, differences and distinctions are overcome, and one experiences utter subjectivity and objectless consciousness. Whether such a state is ever possible may not be established on rational grounds. The claims of reality of the state of pure consciousness are not confined to metaphysical presuppositions, but are believed to be grounded in genuine experiences of a few people.

The person is endowed with the ability to cultivate consciousness. Cultivating consciousness bestows on the person the freedom that is intrinsic to human condition as an abode of consciousness. Further it enables the person to access consciousness as-such and achieve ultimately self-realization, which is none other than finding one's identity with consciousness — *puruṣa* or *Brahman*.

19

Buddhism
A Psychology of Consciousness

K. Ramakrishna Rao

As Radhakrishnan observes:

> There is no question that the system of early Buddhism is one of the most original which the history of philosophy presents. In its fundamental ideas and essential spirit it approximates remarkably to the advanced scientific thought of the nineteenth century. — 1923/1989, vol. 1: 347

Given that modern psychology was founded and continues to remain largely within the worldview of nineteenth-century science, then the relevance of Buddhism to contemporary psychology is all too obvious. The founder of Buddhism was not, however, a philosopher/psychologist by profession, but a religious reformer, who revolted against the faith in the Vedas and attempted to

> start a religion independent of dogma and priesthood, sacrifice and sacrament, which would insist on an inward change of heart and a system of self-culture. — ibid.: 357

The founder-prophet of Buddhism, Siddhārtha Gautama, was from a royal descent. He was born in 563 BCE and heir to Śākya kingdom; but the destiny drove him in a different direction. Disturbed by the uncertainty in and the unintelligibility of the world we live in and moved by the suffering that abounded all around, Siddhārtha left home at the age of twenty-nine in search of truth and tranquillity. Clad in yellow robes and begging for his daily bread, the prince in renunciation sought light, wisdom, and peace from the learned far and near. Unconvinced by their teachings and unable to address the existential predicament of ignorance and suffering, he relentlessly practiced intense meditation and observed extreme ascetic austerities. After six continuous years of ascetic practice, as he rested under a tree in meditation, Siddhārtha obtained the answers he was seeking in a state of self-lumination, enlightenment. Soon with unfailing self-confidence and unshakable faith in his discoveries, he set out with a band of disciples to preach, as the Buddha, the four noble truths and the eightfold path of salvation. He preached tirelessly irrespective of gender, cast, class or creed until his death in 483 BCE at the age of eighty.

Like Mahāvīra, the Jain prophet, Buddha did not write any books. His sermons, saying and doings were transmitted orally from generation to generation by his faithful followers. When the Third Council of Buddhists met in 241 BCE, nearly 250 years after his death, his teachings were compiled for the first time into three books called Piṭakas (baskets). Piṭakas were believed to have been reduced to writing about eighty years before the beginning of the Christian era. The three Piṭakas are *Sutta-Piṭaka, Vinaya-Piṭaka* and *Abhidhamma-Piṭaka*. They were written in Pāli, a vernacular of Sanskrit. The *Sutta-Piṭaka* comprises of the teachings of the Buddha in the form of lectures and dialogues. *Vinaya Piṭaka* is about the disciplinary rules and regulations for the guidance of the monks. *Abhidhamma Piṭaka* (*Abhidharma* in Sanskrit) contains the early Buddhist doctrines bearing on psychology, ethics and metaphysics. Therefore, *Abhidhamma Piṭaka* is the most important text for understanding the Buddhist thought.

Abhidhamma, since it was first codified at the Third Buddhist Council, has gone through significant developments and additions as it was studied, commented upon and analyzed continually for centuries by Buddhist scholars. It is generally agreed that *Abhidhamma* as exists today is more than what it was at the time of the Third Council. There are continuous additions to the early text. For several centuries much of *Abhidhamma* literature was in Pāli. There is also significant Sanskrit literature of *Abhidharma*, such as Vasubandhu's *Abhidharmakoṣabhāṣyam* and Yaśomitra's commentary on it, *Vyākhyā*. Theravāda Buddhist scholars in Sri Lanka and other South-eastern Asian countries did extensive studies of *Abhidhamma* with the result that there is a fair amount of important *Abhidhamma* literature in Sinhalese and Burmese languages.

In Pāli Buddhist tradition of Theravāda, *Abhidhamma* consists of seven books/parts, the most important of them being *Dhammasaṅganī*. Buddhaghoṣa wrote a commentary on it entitled *Aṭṭhasālinī*, which is an important source of Theravāda Buddhism. The other two parts of relevance to our discussion here are *Puggalapannatti* and *Kathāvatthu*. *Puggalapannatti* literally means the description of individuals. *Kathāvatthu* attributed to the authorship of Moggaliputtatissa (second century CE) contains polemical discussion on the theory of the self/person.

Another book, which is second in importance only to the Piṭakas in early Buddhism is *Milindapañha* (*Questions of King Milinda*). This remarkable book contains the lively dialogue between the Buddhist monk Nāgasena and King Menander, the Greek who ruled parts of the Indus basin between 125 and 95 BCE. In the words of Rhys Davids, *Milindapañha* is "the masterpiece of Indian prose, and indeed the best book of its class . . . that has been produced in any country" (quoted from Radhakrishnan 1923/1989, vol. 1: 345). Among other books of importance relating to early Buddhism are Buddhaghoṣa's *Visuddhimagga* (*Path of Purity*) and *Aṭṭhasālinī*. As mentioned, the latter is a commentary on *Dhammasaṅganī*, the first part of *Abhidhamma Piṭaka*. These two are important books in Theravāda tradition of Buddhism.

The four noble truths taught by Buddha are: (1) there is *duḥkha* (suffering); (2) suffering has a *samudāya* (cause); (3) it can be *nirodha* (stopped); and (4) there is a *mārga* (way) to stop suffering. The cause of suffering is craving. Craving is born of desire. Desires arise from the false notion of self and permanence. Buddha saw nothing permanent in the ever-changing flux of things, physical as well as psychical. He completely disavowed the dominant Vedic notion that truth is that which refers to things that are permanent and unchanging. The mind is no more than the aggregate of momentary states of consciousness. As described in *Visuddhimagga*, "mind, intellect, consciousness, keep up an incessant round by day and night, of perishing as one thing and springing up as another". Buddha compares the continuously changing state of mind to the burning lamp with its succession of flames where no single flame lasts but a moment. It is the ignorance of the truth of impermanence and the consequent false notion of identity and selfhood, according to Buddha, is the root cause of suffering. There is no permanent and abiding soul underlying one's existence. There is no changeless reality. What is real is change itself, because all there is, is becoming. The ceaseless becoming follows the law of dependent origination, where one thing depends on another for its origin. *Majjhima Nikāya* labels it the doctrine of fools to say that "this is the world and this is the self, and I shall continue to be in the future, permanent and immutable, eternal, of a nature that knows no change" (I.138). Thus Buddhism is a frontal attack on the Vedic notion of never changing, eternal *Brahman*.

The way out of suffering, according to Buddha, is the eightfold path. It involves righteousness in faith, resolve, speech, action, living, effort, thought and concentration. Such righteousness requires (1) *śīla* (training in morality), (2) practicing *samādhi* (meditation), and (3) *prajñā* (gaining wisdom). Though *śīla* is referred to good conduct, in its primary sense it means behavior in general. In fact, Buddhism analyses *śīla* primarily in psychological terms.

Samādhi (meditation) is mental concentration that leads to superconscious states. *Prajñā* (wisdom), as Bhiksu Sangharaksita explains,

> is threefold, as based upon learning (literally hearing), upon independent thought and reflection, and upon meditation (*bhāvanā* that which is mentally developed, or "made to become"). Here the third kind or wisdom proper is to be understood. This may be described as a direct, non-conceptual apprehension of transcendental Reality. — 1975: 96

The eightfold path is believed to lead one to a state of *nirvāṇa*, which is a state of perfection, free from suffering. *Nirvāṇa* literally means "blowing out". It is putting out the fires lit by false beliefs in permanence. It is extinguishing the spreading fires of greed, attachment, and cravings.

Buddhism is a very practical religion. It is addressed to remove suffering and evil in the world. Buddha was more concerned with helping fellow humans to escape from suffering rather than speculate on the ultimate nature of things. "It is not the time to discuss about fire, for those who are actually in burning fire, but it is the time to escape from it" (*Majjhima Nikāya*). That was Buddha's practicalism. Buddha was more concerned with peace and happiness in life rather than the subtleties of philosophical thought. "Philosophy purifies none," he said, "peace alone does" (quoted from Hiriyanna 1993: 137).

Buddha was uncompromisingly against the Vedic dogma. He was more an empiricist concerned with here and now issues than a hermit in search of life beyond. He questioned not only the authority of the Vedas, but also their exclusive access to the privileged class of Āryan priests. He exalted his followers to preach in a language accessible to ordinary people. Unlike the prevailing practice then, he welcomed women into his order. Thus, Buddhism at once posed a challenge to Vedic tradition. It spread quickly across the country and beyond, and was soon a major religion both in popularity and intellectual influence. Its philosophy reached its most vigorous life in the fifth, sixth, and seventh centuries BCE

(Radhakrishnan 1923/1989). Buddhist universities of excellence flourished at Nālandā, Vikramaśilā, and other places.

In CE 1197 these scholarly centers of excellence were ruthlessly destroyed by the invading Muslim rulers. By then Hinduism began absorbing some of the important tenets of Buddhism. By the end of CE twelfth century, Buddhism declined to almost the point of disappearance in India; but its influence on the Indian tradition was not lost and remains ingrained in the Indian psyche. Buddha is worshiped as an *avatāra* (incarnation) of the Hindu God, Viṣṇu. *Aśoka cakra*, a Buddhist symbol, adorns the Indian national flag. As Radhakrishnan says, "Buddhism perished in India, to be born again in a refined Brahmanism" (1923/1989, vol. 1: 609). Bhiksu Sangharaksita puts the same thing in a more colorful way when he writes:

> Buddhism put some of its new wine into the old bottles, Hinduism redesigned its bottles the better to accommodate and preserve the new wine. The result was that if Buddhism appropriated the forms of Hinduism, Hinduism assimilated something of the spirit of Buddhism.
>
> — 1975: 98

Though a forceful and lucid presenter of his views, Buddha left many doctrinal details vague, perhaps by design. Soon after his death, the very tradition of empiricism he championed and the pressure of logic and reason to critically clarify the details of his doctrines helped to create differences and disputes among Buddha's learned disciples. By the time of the meeting of the Buddhist Council in Vaiśālī, there were major splits and formation of different groups with differences in beliefs and practices.

Between its rise and decline in India spanning over 1,700 years, Buddhism passed through three important phases and gave birth to four important schools. The first is the Hīnayāna phase. Hīnayāna means the little or lower way. The Theravādins belong to the Hīnayāna tradition. Hīnayāna is more person-oriented rather than society-focused. Its avowed goal is the transformation of the person to become an *arhant* in whom all craving stops and the vicious circle of *saṁsāra* (cycle of birth and death) is broken. Hīnayāna tradition draws heavily from *Abhidhamma Piṭaka* and therefore is strong in psychology and ethics. According to Hīnayāna, *arhantship* is attainable in this very birth by gaining insight into the impermanent nature of things and realization of illusion of the abiding and enduring self or soul. Practice of meditation and mindfulness is the recommended way to become an *arhant*. In Hīnayāna tradition, there are two important philosophical schools. They are Vaibhāsika and Sautrāntika. They are called Sarvāstivādins, who uphold a kind of pluralistic realism. Diṅnāga and Dharmakīrti are the chief exponents of the Vaibhāsika School. Kumāralabdha is said to be the founder of Sautrāntika School. Dharmottara and Yaśomitra are among the important exponents of this system.

The second phase in Buddhism is the Mahāyāna tradition, meaning "the great way". It is more socially-oriented than person-centered. Its goal is to go beyond *arhantship* to the attainment of Buddhahood or *bodhisattva*. It is not content with releasing the individual from the bondage of *saṁsāra* but aims at pursuing the spiritual well-being of all. Unlike Hīnayāna, Mahāyāna does not subscribe to realism. Two important philosophical schools arose out of the Mahāyāna tradition. They are Yogācāra and Mādhyamika. The former upholds subjective idealism, whereas the latter tends toward nihilism. Yogācāra is so named because of its emphasis on the practice of yoga for attaining *nirvāṇa*. Among the Yogācāra teachers are Asaṅga and Vasubandhu. The two are believed to be brothers. The latter started as a Sautrāntika scholar, but was later converted to Yogācāra way by his brother Asaṅga. The chief exponent of Mādhyamika School is the south Indian Nāgārjuna, who probably belonged to first or second century CE. Nāgārjuna, along with Śaṅkara, is considered as one of the most profound and original thinkers of classical India.

Scope of Buddhistic Psychology

Buddhistic psychology is essentially an attempt to understand the nature of consciousness, the variety of its states, and the methods of attaining them. In Buddhist view, normal consciousness and the psychological processes associated with it are so organized as to generate a false sense of stable and enduring ego, which in its turn influences, colors, and even determines our passions, thoughts, and actions. To achieve higher states of consciousness it is necessary to transcend the boundaries of our normal phenomenal awareness. When one attains higher states of awareness, the psychological processes lose their ego-reference and bias, and one's cognition and actions transcend their normal limitations. Buddhism believes not only in the existence of such transpersonal ego-absent states of awareness but also in the possibility of cultivating them by following certain practices. Buddhism describes the different stages involved in the progress from the normal to the transcendental states, from *saṁsāra* to *nirvāṇa*, and along the way provides us with one of the most interesting and pervasive phenomenologies of consciousness.

Two important assumptions characterize the early Buddhistic thought concerning human nature: (a) a good deal of one's conduct is determined by the *karma* accumulated by one's past actions, and (b) at the same time it is possible to exercise voluntary control and to guide actions through one's effort and volition. Thus, although man's destiny is in some sense determined by his past, it is possible to change its course by sustained and determined effort. Buddhistic psychology in a significant sense is a psychology applied to this very important task. The result is a thorough introspective analysis and a useful classification of states of consciousness. Also, interesting psychological explorations into the processes of cognition and action follow.

It would seem that man's perceptions seldom fully correspond to or represent the things as they really are. They are usually seen through colored dispositions and are conditioned by habits born out of past actions. Buddhistic psychology attempts to analyze our psychical processes in order to understand the various factors that influence, bias, and determine our perceptions, thoughts, and actions. It consists of a series of important steps for deconditioning the person. The goal is to achieve a state where things are seen as they really are. Transcendence is such a state of perfect knowledge, knowledge devoid of all distortions, which can be achieved, it is believed, by destroying all past *karma* (*kamma* in Pāli) and by progressively annihilating the ego.

We should keep in mind that Buddhistic inquiry is guided more by ethical considerations than by the desire to investigate human nature. However, what is important is that its ethical doctrine is based on psychological principles. It is a psychology applied to ethics. Therefore, not surprisingly, the first book of *Abhidhamma* treats *dharma* in terms of states of consciousness. As Rhys Davids (1923: xxxii) points out in the introductory essay accompanying her translation of the *Dhamma-Saṅganī*, "the inquiry is conducted from a psychological standpoint, and, indeed, is in great part an analysis of the psychological and psycho-physical data of ethics".

One could argue that, for the early Buddhists, *dhamma* (Pāli, for Sanskrit *dharma*) is the subject matter of psychology. Actually, the term *dhamma*, can be interpreted in more than one way. But it seems clear that, in the works that have psychological bearing, the word *dhamma* is used to denote a mental state or process. Davids says that in *Abhidhamma*,

> the *dhamma* always prove to be whatever their ethical value, factors of

> *cittam* used evidently in its widest sense, i.e., concrete mental process or state. Again, the analysis of *rūpam* in Book II, as a species of "indeterminate" *dhamma* is almost wholly a study in the phenomena of sensation and of the human organism as sentient. Finally, in Book III the questions on various *dhamma* are for the most part answered in terms of the four mental *skandhas* of the *cittani* dealt with in Book I, and of the springs of action as shown in their effect on will. — 1923: xxxix

The Buddhist definition of psychology as the science of *dharma* is not very dissimilar to the contemporary definition of psychology as the science of behavior, for *dharma* is behavior internalized. While the contemporary psychologist is mainly concerned with behavior as it manifests externally and observed by others, the Buddhist deals with behavior as it is experienced introspectively by the behaving person. Without minimizing or overlooking the obviously great difference between these two approaches, it is still not difficult to see how the two approaches could supplement each other by their respective emphases on studying the person as he finds himself and as seen by others, first-person and third-person perspectives, the person as "self" and the person as an "object".

The main account of Buddhist psychology described in the following pages is based on the Theravāda tradition, which is the most psychological of all. However, I will also refer to two other schools, the Yogācāra and the Mādhyamika. Nāgārjuna wrote the *Mādhyamika-Kārika*, which is the main text for the Mādhyamika School. Candrakīrti of the seventh century CE wrote a commentary on *Mādhyamika-Kārika*.

Conscious and Unconscious Mind

The approach of Buddhism to the understanding of the mind is basically functional. Buddhism emphatically rejects the view that consciousness is a modification or a quality of the mind and argues that there is no soul or substantive mind apart from the states of consciousness experienced.

Mind is defined by Buddhaghoṣa (1920) in *Aṭṭhasālinī* as "that which thinks of its object" (p. 148). It is cognitive in character. Its function is to guide, discriminate, and inform. It manifests in a series and thus has continuity. It is caused by the psychical and endosomatic excitations as well as by physical and external simulations.

Nāma and *rūpa* (name and form or mind and body) are but convenient terms to depict highly complex and continuously changing processes. Reality is always in a state of ceaseless change, and both mind and body are in a state of flux. The impermanence/change is somewhat more marked with regard to the mind and states of consciousness. The mind is like a stream. It maintains one constant form, one seeming identity, even though its contents, like water in a stream, continuously change. The mind in *Dhamma-Saṅganī* is accounted for in entirely phenomenological terms and the analysis is restricted to the states of mind. We find no reference to the personal agent. In *Milindapañha*, Nāgasena, expounding the doctrine of "no soul", quotes *Saṁyutta Nikāya* thus:

> Just as it is by the condition precedent of the coexistence of its various parts that the "chariot" is used, just so is it that when the *skandhas* are there we talk of a "being". — Davids 1963: 45

Whenever we speak of "soul", we mean one or more of *skandhas*. *Skandhas* are groups or aggregates of bodily and mental states. These are five kinds: (1) *rūpa*, (2) *vedanā*, (3) *sannā*, (4) *saṅkhāra*, and (5) *vinnāna*. In *Saṁyutta Nikāya*, *rūpa* is defined as that which "manifests as the touch of gnats, mosquitos, wind, the sun, and the snake; it manifests, therefore, it is called *rūpa*" (Dasgupta 1957: 95). Under *rūpa* are included the four elements or the *mahābhūtas* — the body as well as the senses. As Dasgupta points out:

> The four elements manifested themselves in certain forms and were therefore called *rūpa*; the forms of affection that appeared were also called *rūpa*; many other mental states or features which appeared with them were also called *rūpa*. The *āyatanas* or the senses were also called *rūpa*. The *mahābhūtas* or four elements were themselves but changing manifestations, and they together with all that appeared in association with them were called *rūpa* and formed the *rūpa khaṇḍa* (the classes of sense materials, sense data, senses and sensations). — vol. 2: 95

It would appear that *rūpa* may mean gross matter as well as the sense data. The double meaning may not be considered inconsistent inasmuch as Buddhism makes no sharp distinction between the physical and the mental. *Vedanā* is feeling; and it can be pleasurable, painful, or indifferent. *Sannā* (Sanskrit *saṁjñā*) is sensation/perception. It is representational and includes perceputal knowledge. *Saṅkhāra* means both volition as well as a synthetic function that enables the several mental properties or elements (*cetasikas*) to function in association with each other. *Saṅkhāra* as a *skandha*, to quote Aung (1929: 274), "really means the group of 'volitions and other associated factors'". *Vinnāna* is consciousness. It is referred to the stage at which the cognitive process starts as well as the resulting awareness. We shall return to a further discussion of these concepts later when we attempt to interpret the contribution of Buddhist psychology to the study of human nature.

In Buddhist view, consciousness is a relation between subject and object. However *subject* and *object* are to be understood as relative and mutually dependent; one cannot exist without the other.

> Both the subject and the object are alike transitory, the relation alone between the two impermanent correlates remaining constant. This constancy of relation, which . . . is consciousness itself, gives rise to the erroneous ideas of personal identity. — Aung 1929: 11

Again,

> life is like an ever-changing river, having its source in birth, its goal in death, receiving from the tributary streams of sense constant accretions to its flood, and ever dispensing to the world around it the thought stuff, it has gathered by the way. — Aung 1929: 12

Consciousness is not thus a static state but a dynamic process. It is like a flowing stream, which has an identifiable form without being the same at any two moments in time. The stream of consciousness, or rather the stream of being, has both a subliminal as well as a supraliminal existence. The subliminal stream, which is a thoughtless or thought-free state, like the state of dreamless sleep, is called *bhavaṅga*. *Bhavaṅga* is a very important concept but a difficult one to grasp. It is described as

> the cause, reason, indispensable condition of our being regarded subjectively as continuous, the *sine qua non* of our existence, that without which one cannot subsist or exist. — Aung, 1929: 265-66

Bhavaṅga makes the passive side of our existence possible. It is also to be regarded as a state below the threshold of introspective awareness.

> As such it is the subconscious state of mind —"below the threshold" of consciousness — by which we conceive continuous subjective existence as possible. — Aung, 1929: 266

It would appear that *bhavaṅga* is the key concept in a system of thought that believes in continuity of existence through several births without believing in a permanent migrating entity like the soul. *Bhavaṅga* may be regarded as a functional substitute for substantive soul in Buddhist thought. If our present existence is a consequence of our past *karma*, *bhavaṅga*, it would seem, is the medium through which past *karma* influences one's thought and action. *Bhavaṅga* is a concept similar to *buddhi* in Yoga and Advaita. *Buddhi*, we may recall, is the seat of memory as well as the depository of *saṁskāra*s and *vāsanā*s, the carriers of *karma*. There is, however, a significant difference between the two concepts. *Buddhi* is essentially non-conscious. It becomes conscious in the proximity of *puruṣa*, when the light of *puruṣa* is reflected on it. In Buddhism, there is no such outside source. Some of the contents of *bhavaṅga* become conscious when they are further processed. In other words, certain states of mind are conscious and others are not.

Mind at birth is entirely a subconscious state, like the state of dreamless sleep. It is, however, endowed with the potentiality to guide, influence, and determine our thoughts, passions, and actions. When an external stimulus or an internal thought is perceived, the stream of being is momentarily interrupted and a psychic field is created. It is this field that results in our perceptions of the external objects as well as ourselves.

Bhavaṅga may be interpreted as a key psychological concept that not only provides a meaningful explanation for understanding the dynamics of behavior but also reveals the essential subjective and personal character of our knowledge of the external world. Our cognitions are but manifestations at the periphery of *bhavaṅga* and result from the interactions between the unconscious flow of our being, which in itself consists of myriad predispositions, and the external and internal stimulations processed through the channels of the senses and the mind. Thus, what we know about the world in our ordinary state of consciousness is in a very significant sense personal.

Cognition

The process of sense cognition is described in *A Compendium of Philosophy* thus:

> *When*, say, a visible object, after one thought-moment has passed, enters the avenue of sight and, the life-continuum vibrating twice, the stream of that continuum is interrupted; then consciousness of the kind which apprehends sensations, apprehending that visible object, rises and ceases.
> — Aung 1929: 126

Cognitive process thus involves six steps:

1. The impinging of the sensory stimulus on our peripheral system, which is described as sense–object contact;
2. excitation of *bhavaṅga*, the stream of being;

3. the momentary arrest of *bhavaṅga* by the reflecting mind;
4. apperception of the object perceived;
5. registering in and retention of the object apperceived; and
6. the cessation of awareness and its submergence into *bhavaṅga*.

This process is described by a simile of the mango tree:

> A man, lost in the deepest sleep, is lying at the foot of a mango-tree with his head covered. A wind now stirs the branches, and a fruit falls beside the sleeping man. He is in consequence aroused from dreamless slumbers. He removes his head-covering in order to ascertain what has awakened him. He sees the newly fallen fruit, picks it up and examines it. Apprehending it to be a fruit with certain constitutive attributes observed in the previous stage of investigation, he eats it, and then, replacing his head-covering, once more resigns himself to sleep.
>
> The dreamless sleep corresponds to the unperturbed current of the stream of being (*bhavaṅga*). The striking of the wind against the tree is like the "past" life-moment, during which the object enters the stream and passes down with it, without perturbing it. The swaying of the branches in that wind represents the vibration of the stream of being. The falling of the fruit corresponds to the arrest or interruption of being, the moment at which the stream is "cut-off" by thought; the waking of the man to the awakening of attention in the act of cognition on occasion of sense; the removal of the head-covering to the sense-reaction of sight. The picking up of the fruit is comparable to the operation of receiving; inspection of it recalls the examining function. The simple apprehension of the fruit as such, with certain constitutive attributes of its own, corresponds to the discriminative or determining stage; the eating of the fruit resembles the act of apperception. Finally, the swallowing of the last morsels that are left in the mouth corresponds to the operation of retention, after which the mind subsides into mere vital process, even as the man once more falls asleep. — Aung 1929: 30

What has been said so far relates to perceptions that are very vivid; but Buddhists accept various grades of vividness, based on the intensity of the sense impressions. They account for these in terms of thought moments. A cognition, in order to attain an apperceptive stage, needs, to last for seventeen thought moments. The seventeen moments represent the duration from the moment the object enters the stream until the stream resumes its flow. When an object causes a less vivid impression, then, there is no retention of the object. There is no apperception at all. When the object makes a very slight impression, there is not even a sensation. Thus, there are four grades of sense–object contact: (1) full sense cognition with retention; (2) apperception without retention; (3) sensation without apperception; and (4) futile sense impression, which is too weak to be translated into sensation (i.e., it fails to hold the arrested *bhavaṅga* for any length of time). The greater the intensity of the sense impression, the shorter will be the duration required for the vibration to set in after the object reaches the field of presentation.

In retentive apperception, the stream is perturbed within one moment of the object's entry into the field. In non-retentive apperception, the vibration of the stream commences only after two or three moments have lapsed since the object's entry into the stream. In non-apperceptive sensation, the object causes excitation in the stream only after five to nine moments. When the object fails to set a vibration in the stream for ten or more moments, the impressions cannot reach the state of sensation.

It needs to be mentioned that we seldom have a single isolated sense cognition. Usually there are strings of related sense impressions that go through the reflective processes of imagination, memory, conception, discrimination, and classification in rapid succession before an individual has a discernible perceptual awareness of an external event or object.

Mental reflection is made possible by the retentiveness of the objects perceived. Objects of past experience can be recalled by themselves, or in association with others. Also, new objects can be imaginatively constructed by a combination of the parts of previously experienced objects. A combination of these with the position of the object in time — i.e., whether it belongs to past, present, or future — makes it possible for Buddhists to distinguish between varieties of reflective processes.

In Buddhist view, perception itself is always indeterminate. It is in a sense nameless and ineffable. It can be neither named nor recognized and is thus free from all interpretative processes of the mind. In other words, perception is pure sensation representing nothing more than what is given in experience. To have the sensation of "blue" is not the same as knowing it as blue. Perception then is immediate and "pure acquaintance". It is free from construction, name and generality as Diṅnāga says in his *Pramāṇa-Samuccaya*. Perception, which is devoid of all interpretation, is therefore necessarily true because there is no possibility of being different from the object that gives rise to it.

There are four kinds of perception. The first kind is *indriya jhāna* (sensory). This is bare sensation resulting from the sensory process. The second is *mano-vijñāna* (mental perception). It is the successive stage accompanying sensory processing. It is a transitory stage between perception as such and thought. *Sva-samvedanā* (self-consciousness), the third, is the direct perception of mental states like pain and pleasure, which also does not involve any interpretation and therefore is free from error. The fourth kind of perception is *yogī-pratyakṣa* (paranormal awareness) brought about by intense practice of concentration and meditation.

Phenomenology and States of Consciousness

As pointed out earlier, consciousness, according to Buddhists, is a relation between the subject and the object. The latter may belong to one of the five senses, or it may be a mental object. When an interaction between the subject and the object takes place and consciousness arises — as described above — the resultant consciousness, which is the product of a number of variables both of the subject and of the object, manifests characteristics that can be distinguished. These characteristics form the basis for a classification of consciousness. The early Buddhists identified and distinguished eighty-nine states of consciousness. A broader classification has 121 such states.

From the perspective of the subject, there is, first of all, the position of the person on the plane of existence. Four such possible planes are distinguished. They are: (1) *kāmaloka*, (2) *rūpaloka*, (3) *arūpaloka*, and (4) *lokottara*. Experiences in each of these planes have their own peculiar characteristics.

The plane of *rūpaloka* (pure form) has in common with *kāmaloka* (sensuous domain) the property of having forms and with *arūpaloka* (formless domain) the property of abstraction and the transcendence of the ego. In the sensuous domain (the *kāmaloka* plane), the objects of consciousness are bounded by ego-centeredness; and therefore a tension between the subject and the objects arises, resulting in desires and craving. The objects of consciousness in the *arūpa* plane are free from ego entanglement, and are thus excluded from all sorts of craving. In the *rūpa* plane, we find thinking, reflection, rapture, happiness, and concentration. These five factors help to eliminate the hindrances that bind consciousness to the sensuous world. Thinking helps to overcome sloth, lethargy, and indifference. Reflection enables one to overcome doubt. Rapture destroys hatred. Happiness dissipates restlessness and worry. Concentration enables one to overcome greed. Thus in the world of pure form, we find five classes of consciousness, culminating in concentration, which leads to the *arūpa* plane.

At the non-*rūpa* (*arūpa*) plane, we have such consciousness as the awareness of the infinity of space, the infinity of consciousness, nothingness, and transperceptual and transpersonal experience. Transcendental consciousness is that which belongs to the path of *nibbāna*. It is called *lokottara*, which literally means "beyond the worlds". It involves the awareness of a path that expels the causes of rebirth and leads to *nibbāna*. *Aṭṭhasālinī* distinguishes the worldly phenomenon of consciousness from an experience of transcendental consciousness in the following way:

> In worldly phenomena consciousness is the chief, consciousness is the principal, consciousness is the forerunner. In transcendental phenomena, however, understanding is the chief, understanding is the principal, understanding is the forerunner. — Buddhaghoṣa 1920: 90

It would appear that the Buddhist analysis of consciousness is essentially from the perspective of mental states without delving into substantive issues. Neither the mind nor consciousness is discussed as a ground condition, but only as states of awareness. The analysis, however, gives rise to a profound understanding of the cognitive, the conative, and the emotive factors that enter into the determination of consciousness at any given time. A given consciousness can be something that arises automatically on the presentation of a stimulus or something that is determined by a volition. Consciousness of an object may be devoid of any feeling. On the cognitive side it may be erroneous or non-erroneous. It may give knowledge or may be devoid of knowledge. A permutation and combination of these give rise to a variety of conscious states. At the *kāmaloka* (empirical) plane there are fifty-four such states, fifteen at the *rūpaloka* (physical) plane, twelve at the *arūpa* (mental) plane, and eight at the *lokottara* (transcendental) plane.

The states of consciousness are also described as moral, immoral, or amoral. It is very difficult to understand what precisely the Buddhist notion of morality applied to consciousness is. The good and the bad are not defined but only illustrated. We find psychology and ethics combine to account for behavior. Each conscious state is a link in a continuous chain of conscious events. A conscious state to which good or bad can be imputed is an effect of certain antecedents and the cause or part of the cause of certain subsequent effects. This chain of causation applies to most of our behavior. The moral states lead to good results and immoral states to bad or unhappy results. But there are also states of consciousness that are only results of antecedent conditions, but are not themselves causes of subsequent events or vice versa. When a physical state is only an effect or simply a cause without being both a cause and an effect, it is not moral or immoral, but is a morally indeterminate state. Also, at the transcendental plane, all states of consciousness are morally indeterminate because they are unconditioned states in that they produce neither good nor bad *karma*.

Karma

Karma (*kamma* in Pāli) is the predisposing factor that is assumed to be responsible, not only for a continuing cycle of birth and death, but also for our state of being at any given time. *Karma* is considered to be of four kinds, based on the effects they produce. First are those which produce impure effects and cause bad results. Second are those which produce pure effects and cause good results. Again, there are those that produce partly good and partly bad results. Finally, there is *karma* that produces neither good nor bad effects but contribute to the destruction of past *karma*. The root cause of *karma* is binding volition and the states associated with it that give rise to ego sense and consequent attachments and cravings. Where such volition is not present, actions cannot produce any *karma*.

Although the mental states that are fixed and determined are the resultants of *karma*, *karma* itself is produced by apperceptual acts that are free. Man's behavior is conditioned by all sorts of circumstances, but he is still free to adapt himself to his environment through his volition. It is this exercise of volition, which is involved in reflective thinking and in representative apperception that gives rise to *karma*. The Buddhist manuals describe the nature and the strength of volitions, and how *karma* affects behavior in this birth and the births to follow. The volition of such developed persons as the Buddha and the *arhant*s does not, however, carry any *karma* with it because it is free from evil tendencies and binding attachments. It should be understood that all apperceptive acts that are of the character of inoperative thoughts do not transform themselves into *karma*.

In Buddhaghoṣa's *Visuddhimagga*, we find twelve kinds of *karma*, distinguished from different viewpoints. First, we have: (1) *karma* which bring about results in this birth; (2) *karma* that will be effective in the next life; (3) *karma* that will become operational in some life thereafter; and (4) *karma* "that has been". The last mentioned is, in effect, inoperative *karma*. *Karma* "that has been" is so-called because "there was no fruit of *karma*, there will be no fruit or *karma*, there is no fruit of *karma*" (Buddhaghoṣa 1923: 724).

Second, there are (5) weighty *karma*, (6) abundant *karma*, (7) proximate *karma*, and (8) outstanding *karma*. The weighty (such as killing one's mother) and abundant *karma* — as opposed to light and slender deeds — are the first to produce effects. The proximate *karma* is the recollection at the time of death by which, according to Buddhists, one is reborn.

> That *karma* which is not of the first three kinds, and which has had many opportunities of repetition, is *out-standing karma*. In the absence of the other three kinds, it brings on rebirth. — Buddhaghoṣa 1923: 725

Third, there are four other kinds of *karma*. They are in Buddhaghoṣa's words:

> reproductive *karma*, maintaining *karma*, unfavorable *karma*, destructive *karma*. Of them *reproductive karma* is both moral and immoral, and reproduces the resultant aggregates of the mind and matter at rebirth. The *maintaining karma* is unable to reproduce a result. It maintains and prolongs the happiness or ill, which arises when rebirth has been granted, and a result yielded by another *karma*. The *unfavorable karma* oppresses, afflicts and gives no opportunity of long life to the happiness or ill, which arises when rebirth has been granted, and a result yielded by another *karma*. The *destructive karma*, though itself moral and immoral, kills some other *karma* which is weak, inhibits its result and makes room for its own results. That result, which is due to the opportunity thus given by the *karma*, is called *uprisen* result. — Buddhaghoṣa 1923: 725

Elements of Consciousness (*Cetasikas*)

In addition to classifying consciousness into various states as described above, the early Buddhists analyzed consciousness into certain basic elements that combine to give rise to a variety of conscious states. These elements are called *cetasikas*.

There are fifty-two such elements. Of these, as summarized in *Abhidhammatthasaṅgaha*, seven are common to all states of consciousness. They are *phassa* (contact), *vedanā* (feeling), *cetanā* (volition), *sannā* (perception), *ekaggatā* (individuation or one-pointed concentration), *jīvitindriya* (psychic life), and *manasikara* (attention). There are six elements that are termed particular, which are not invariably present in all conscious acts. In addition, fourteen elements present in immoral acts and nineteen elements present in moral acts are also distinguished. In other words, whereas the seven universal mental elements ought to be found in all the eighty-nine states of consciousness, the six particular elements are present in fifty-five states of consciousness. The universal elements seem to relate to the basic psychological processes.

Phassa (contact), which brings the object into the field of consciousness, is described in *Aṭṭhasālinī* as the pillar that supports the structure of consciousness (p. 143). Contact consists in consciousness coming into touch with the object and then producing an impact. Contact is described both as a cause and an effect. As the sense and the object come together and are in contact, there arises the potential for awareness.

The second universal element of consciousness is *vedanā* (feeling). Feeling is not considered a quality of experience, but an agency of experience:

> "Feeling" is that which feels. It has (1) experiencing as characteristic, (2) enjoying as function, or possessing the desirable portion of an object as function, (3) taste of the mental properties as manifestation, and (4) tranquillity as proximate cause — Buddhaghoṣa 1920: 145

Although feeling has enjoyment as function, it is not confined to pleasurable feelings alone. It includes painful as well as neutral ones. *Vedanā* approximates what we characterized as the subjectivity, "what it is like", aspect of consciousness.

The characteristic of *cetanā* (volition) is co-ordination. It co-ordinates all the associated states of an object; and, in so doing, it binds together the various states related to an object. Volition is present in moral as well as immoral states, but not in morally inoperative states. Volition is the source of a good deal of energy, and it manifests in the form of directing the associated states.

Some writers on *Abhidhamma* criticize the translation of *cetanā* as "volition". For example, Guenther writes:

> *Cetanā* not only arouses mass activity, but also sustains it so that certain definite results appear. This shows beyond doubt that the translation of *cetanā* by volition is against all evidence. . . *Cetanā*, to state it plainly, is something that corresponds to our idea of stimulus, motive, or drive.
>
> — 1976: 43-44

Although *cetanā* implies something more than what is normally meant by volition, neither "stimulus", "motive", nor "drive" convey its precise intent either.

Sannā is what gives us distinct cognitions. It enables us to recognize general relations between objects, and to have perceptions of all kinds — sensuous and mental.

> The perception, the perceiving, the state of having perceived which on that occasion is born of contact with the appropriate element of representative intellection — this is the perception that there then is.
>
> — Davids, 1923: 7

Manasikara (attention) is what brings the mind and its object together. "Attention is like a charioteer harnessing two horses (mind and object) into a pair" (Aung 1929: 282). Again,

> mind indeed always gets at its object, its constant companion being attention (*manasikara*), without which it would be like a rudderless ship, drifting on to any object. With this rudder the senses arrive at their proper destination. — ibid.: 283

Jīvitindriya is described as the faculty of life. *Dhamma-Saṅganī* defines *jīvitindriya* thus:

> The persistence of these incorporeal states, their subsistence, going on, their being kept going on, their progress, continuance, preservation, life, life as faculty — this is the faculty of life that there then is.
>
> — Davids 1923: 16-17

Ekaggatā is

> the stability, solidity, absorbed steadfastness of thought which on that occasion is the absence of distraction, balance, unperturbed mental procedure, quiet, the faculty and the power of concentration, right concentration. — ibid.: 11-12

Thus, we find that the above-mentioned seven universal mental properties are the basic psychological processes involved in all states of consciousness. First of all, there is the life process without which no psychic activity is possible. Then, there is the contact between the mind and the object, which is made possible by attention. An amount of concentration that would enable the emergence of the object into a specific space–time setting is also required. The emergence of the object into the conscious field causes both perceptions as well as feelings, which are also influenced by one's volition. We may note how similar are the universal mental elements described in Buddhism to the characteristics attributed to consciousness by William James in *The Principles of Psychology*. *Vedanā* is the subjectivity, the personal aspect. *Cetanā* is the process that gives us the unity and coherence in conscious experience. *Sannā* refers to the noetic aspect and intentionality, whereas *manasikara* is selective attention.

Attaining Transcendence (*Nirvāṇa*)

The path of Buddhism is to achieve a state of transcendence called *nibbāna* (*nirvāṇa* in Sanskrit). Transcendence results in the cessation of rebirth and attainment of perfect knowledge. Transcendence has both metaphysical and empirical connotations. In its empirical sense, it refers to the human situation where a transformation of the person takes place. This transformation affects one's cognitive style, emotional state, and personality. In the cognitive sphere, the discursive and the differentiating processes give way to non-representational and intuitive comprehension. As Johansson puts it: "Cognition after the attainment of *nibbāna* is more similar to a comprehensive Gestalt or intuition" (1969: 23). Knowledge attained in this state is devoid of all distortions brought about by the existential situation of personal involvement. Because the state of *nibbāna* is devoid of all obsessions such as desire, hate, and illusion, the knowledge attained is perfect and undistorted. Subjectively, it is an experience of unity, completeness, and timelessness. In the state of *nibbāna*, it is said, there is freedom from all suffering and attachment. From an emotional point of view, *nibbāna* is happiness, peace, calm, contentment, and compassion. The most important aspect of *nibbāna* is the transformation brought about in the personality resulting in an unemotional, stable, and unobsessed mind that is devoid of ego-compulsions.

The one who has realized *nibbāna* is the *arhant*, the perfect or the ideal man. Arhantship is the culmination of all psychic development. As *Saṁyutta Nikāya* puts it: "The destruction of desire, hate, and illusion — that is called arhantship."

Achieving the higher state of awareness, unobsessed states of mind, free from the compulsions of ego and the delusion of permanence, is often described as "crossing the river". The one who "crosses the river" realizes the four noble truths. He knows about suffering, how it arises, its extinction and the way to achieve it. *Saṁyutta Nikāya* (V.199-200) mentions five steps in the path of the monk from *saṁsāra* (sensuality) to sainthood (*arhantship*). They are: (1) faith in Buddha's teachings, (2) vigor or motivation to strive to get rid of undesirable states of mind and to acquire, maintain, preserve, and enhance wholesome mental states, (3) practice of mindfulness, (4) cultivation of concentration and one-pointed attention, and (5) attainment of wisdom, which is enlightenment itself.

Mindfulness and Concentration

Mindfulness and concentration are central exercises in the pursuit of enlightenment and transcendence. These two are not different and opposing practices. They are necessarily complementary. Mindfulness is recommended to the monks as a practice for purification of body and mind and for successfully proceeding on the path of *nirvāṇa*. Mindfulness is applied in four ways: (1) contemplating the body in the body; (2) contemplating the feelings in the feelings; (3) contemplating the mind in the mind; and (4) contemplating the mental states in the mental states.

Contemplating the body in the body begins with paying attention to breathing. "Mindful he breaths in, mindful he breaths out." Similarly the monk goes through a variety of activities such as walking and eating. Then he reflects on the body itself from the head to foot, the various impurities in it, and the various elements of which it is composed and into which it would be decomposed.

Contemplating the feelings in the feelings consists in paying attention to states of pain and pleasure or lack of them. *Majjhima Nikāya* describes how a monk lives contemplating the mind in the mind in the following way:

> He comprehends the mind which has passion and that which has none as such, which has hatred and that which has none as such, which has confusion and which has none as such; he comprehends the collected mind, the distracted mind as such; the mind which has become great and that which has not as such; the mind which has some other or no other (mental state) superior to it; the mind which is concentrated or that which is not as such. . . . It is thus that a monk lives contemplating the mind in the mind.
>
> — Conze 1954/1995: 58

Finally, mindfulness is directed at contemplating mental states in mental states. This exercise involves five steps. First, he contemplates the mental states from the point of view of the five hindrances (desire, ill-will, restlessness, worry, and doubt). Second, he contemplates on mental acts such as perception, feeling, and awareness. Third, he contemplates on the six aspects of awareness system and the six aspects of the response system. Fourth, he contemplates on the seven steps to the path of enlightenment, when they are present and when they are not present in his experience. Fifth, the monk contemplates on the four noble truths and comprehends that "this is suffering, this is its uprising, this its stopping, this the course leading to its stopping" (*Majjhima Nikāya* I.55-63).

Such passive and yet incisive attention to the details of the constitution, composition, and functioning of the body and mind in mindfulness exercises reminds us of the *pratyāhāra* phase of *rāja-yoga* practice, where the attention is focused inward. *Pratyahāra* is, however, limited to the workings of the mind and voluntary control of internal attention states, whereas mindfulness is much broader and includes attention to body. Another difference is that mindfulness appears to be limited to observation and understanding rather than control of the processes involved.

Buddhism in general and Theravāda tradition in particular has worked out an elaborate method to enable one to achieve transcendence. The practices involve among other things (a) scrupulous observance of moral precepts (*śīlas*), (b) practice of meditation (*samādhi*), and (c) realization or understanding (*pañña*). Moral precepts include such injunctions as non-killing, non-stealing, chastity, refraining from consuming intoxicants, from speaking falsehood and harsh words, and from indulging in malicious acts. One was asked to be truthful, keep his promises, seek harmony, and speak pleasantly. The monks seeking *arhantship* were also exhorted to overcome enviousness, hatred, pride, arrogance, immodesty, anger, and deceitfulness. These disciplinary rules are found in great detail in *Vinaya-Piṭaka*. The general direction of all these precepts is to overcome the basic obsessions, viz., greed, hatred, and delusions and to control the tendencies of attachment, aversion, wrong thoughts, and ego-feeling.

Pañña (understanding), is also given great prominence in Buddhism. A person who dispels ignorance through understanding may become an *arhant*. Apparently, it is believed that some may attain transcendence by understanding alone, i.e., without meditation. Such a person is called *pañña-vimutto* whereas a person who achieves transcendence through meditation and mind control is called *ceto-vimutto*.

From a psychological point of view, the most important path is the path of meditation and mental training by which the mind is controlled and transformed. *Visuddhimagga* gives minute details of the processes involved in the practice of meditation from the lowest to the highest. Five kinds of variables are identified. They relate to (a) hindrances to the practice of meditation, (b) object on which meditation should be made, (c) teacher, (d) practitioner or the disciple, and (e) the process of meditation. Buddhaghoṣa identifies ten hindrances that obstruct the practice of meditation. Among these are interest in construction of buildings and monasteries, nepotism, greed for food and clothes, and sickness. Also included is the acquisition of miraculous powers (*siddhis*), which, when indulged in, would hinder the development of insight necessary to achieve transcendence. So we find in *Visuddhimagga*:

> "Psychic powers" are those of an average man. Like a child lying on its back and like tender corn it is difficult to manage. It is broken by the slightest thing. It is an impediment to insight, but not to concentration, because it ought to be obtained when concentration is obtained. Therefore one who desires insight should cut-off the impediment of psychic powers.
> — Buddhaghoṣa 1923: 113

All meditation should have an object on which to fix one's attention. Theoretically, there can be any number of objects for meditation. Traditionally, however, fourty of these are mentioned. They include the ten *kasina*s, the ten *asubha*s, ten *anussati*s, four *brahma vihāra*s, four *arūpa*s, and, finally, meditation to develop aversion to food and meditation to determine the four elements of the body. The ten *kasina*s include such things as earth, water, fire, wind, color, light, spot, and circumscribed space. The ten *asubha*s are a variety of situations in which a corpse is the object of meditation. The *anussati*s (recollections) involve meditating on the merits of the Buddha, *dhamma* (morality), *saṅgha* (society), *śīla* (conduct), *cāga* (charity), and *nibbāna*. In this list is also included breath control. Breath control is given a very prominent place in Buddhist meditational practices. On this, *Yogācāra's Manual* says:

> Let the aspirant who has truly felt the dread of the stream of becoming strive hard to win *Nibbāna* by earnestly meditating on the way of concentration by inbreathing and outbreathing, held by Our Blessed Lord to be the chief aim of meditation, which is highly praised by Him, and has been of the greatest help to countless *buddha*s, among them the last and latest, Gautama the Buddha, for the winning of the Wisdom Supreme.
> — Woodward 1916: 67

The four *brahma vihāra*s are friendship, compassion, joy, and equanimity. The objects mentioned so far are meant to induce the first four states of *jhāna* (Sanskrit: *dhyāna*), or meditation. To progress further, the meditator has to use immaterial objects (*arūpa*), such as unlimited space, infinite consciousness, nothingness, and the state of neither perception or non-perception.

The need for choosing a competent teacher is very much emphasized in Buddhist practices. The *guru* (preceptor) should have mastered the fourth and fifth *jhānas*, and have become an *arhant*. If that is not possible, the best available *guru* should be chosen; this should be at least a person of self-restraint. The *guru* is the guide who leads the meditator through the difficult terrain full of obstacles to a state of right concentration. By understanding the disposition, character, and personality of the disciple, the *guru* can specify an appropriate object for meditation. As Buddhaghoṣa puts it:

> He (the teacher) instructs beings according to their worthiness, regarding ultimate truths of the present and the future. Further, as "Teacher" he is like the man "with the goods"; i.e., the Blessed One is the caravan leader. As the caravan leader takes the goods across the desert through the dangers of robbers, across places infested by wild beasts, through famine-stricken and waterless regions, takes them over, out of, through such perils, and places them in a safe place, so the Blessed One, the Teacher, the caravan-leader, takes beings across the desert, that is, of birth.
>
> — 1923: 239

The disciple must have absolute faith in the teacher, and should be prepared to obey instructions. The disciple should give evidence of an intention to overcome *rāga* (attachment), *dveṣa* (hatred), and *moha* (delusion). Likewise, the disciple should have a strong desire to meditate and to ultimately attain *nibbāna*. The teacher closely scrutinizes and studies the behavior and mental disposition of the disciple, and suggests a suitable object for meditation befitting the disciple's conduct. According to Buddhaghoṣa, "conduct is of six kinds: conduct of lust, of hate, of delusion, of faith, of intelligence, of applied thought" (1923: 118). Buddhaghoṣa further illustrates the characteristics of the six classes of individuals:

> Procedure of the states of mind: wiliness, deceitfulness, pride, evil desire, covetousness, discontentedness, lasciviousness, frivolity — these and other states arise abundantly in one who walks in lust. . . . Anger, malice, hypocrisy, rivalry, envy, meanness — these and other states arise abundantly in one who walks in hate. Sloth, torpor, distraction, worry, misgiving, obstinate grasping, tenacity — these and other states arise abundantly in one who walks in delusion. Clean liberality, desire to see the Noble Ones, desire to hear the good Law, abundance of joy, absence of craftiness, absence of wiliness, faithfulness in objects of faith — these

> and other states arise abundantly in one who walks in faith. Docility, good friendship, moderation in food, mindfulness and comprehension, application to wakefulness, emotion over objects of emotion, wise effort due to emotion — these and other states abundantly arise in one who walks in intelligence. Talkativeness, fondness of society, want to delight in moral application, unsteadiness in work, smokiness by night, luminosity by day, running after this and that object — these and other states abundantly arise in one who walks in thoughts. Thus one may explain the kinds of conduct from the procedure of states.
>
> — 1923: 124-25

The teacher, after understanding the disciple's basic disposition and character, recommends suitable objects for meditation. For example, for one whose behavior is characterized by lust, the ten *asubha*s, such as involving a corpse as the object of meditation, are recommended; and for one who is characterized by *dveṣa*, or hatred, one of the four *brahma vihāra*s is recommended. Thus, it is evident that the choice of an appropriate object for meditation has been given a very prominent place in Buddhist meditational practices.

The process of meditation involves certain preliminary practices and two kinds of exercises before one enters a *jhāna* state. Eight successive states of *jhāna* are distinguished. The preliminaries include offering invocations to the Buddha, *dhamma*, and *saṅgha*, prayers for happiness of all beings, confession of one's guilt, and faith in the teachings of the Buddha.

Sitting cross-legged and his body erect, the disciple endeavors to fix his mind on the object of meditation. The first exercise is *upacāra*, which is preparatory to reach a state of absorption. This exercise has three steps. In the first step the meditator fixes his attention on the object of his meditation. The second step is visualization and the meditator is able to form a mental image of the object with his eyes closed, an image that is as vivid and distinct as the object itself. In the third stage, the meditator attempts to have the image clearer and brighter than the object itself but devoid of such characteristics as color, form, and size. It may be mentioned that in the state of *upacāra*, the meditator's mind has not reached a state of steady concentration. The attention of the mind still wanders.

> At access [*upacāra*] the factors owning to their weakness, are not strong. As a baby-child on being lifted to its feet, falls down repeatedly to the ground, even so when the access arises the mind at times makes the sign

> the object, at times lapses into subconsciousness. At ecstasy [*appana*] the factors from their very strength are strong. As a strong man rising from his seat might stand even the whole day, so when ecstatic concentration arises consciousness, once it has cut-off the occasion of subconsciousness, lasts the whole night, even the whole day, and proceeds by way of moral apperceptional succession.
>
> — Buddhaghoṣa 1923: 147

To attain the state of *appāna*, the meditator should sever the connection between his subliminal *bhavaṅga citta* (consciousness) and the object of meditation so that he can reflect on the image of the object without activating *bhavaṅga*. When he is able to do this and reflect on the image for a certain length of time he is said to have entered into the first state of *jhāna*.

The persons who enter such a state should continue to direct their mind to the object of meditation and engage in a steady concentration of the mind on that object. In addition, the practitioner should dissociate himself from the worldly attractions, deprive himself of physical pleasures, and free himself from mental impurities.

There are five aspects to the first state of meditation. They are *vitakka* (discursive or relational thought), *vicāra* (inquiry), *pīti* (joy), *sukha* (pleasure), and *ekaggatā* (concentration). *Pīti* and *sukha* are the emotive factors. *Ekaggatā* represents the effort involved in obtaining a state of absorption which is the goal of meditative concentration. When the meditator enters the first stage, his worldly desires are eliminated and the undesirable mental states are removed. He develops equanimity and enjoys psychological bliss. The meditator having achieved the first stage is advised to repeat it and practice entering into, maintaining and coming out of the same state. Such a practice would lead him into the second stage, where discursive and inquiring faculties cease to function. The object of meditation, we are told, gets so integrated with the mind that the physical sensations cease. The meditator experiences complete tranquillity. He is able to concentrate his mind on the object of meditation so completely that his senses do not respond to any external or internal stimulations. The meditator at this stage attains full concentration of the mind and experiences pleasure and happiness.

When they enter the third stage, the meditators are no longer worried about such thoughts as the impermanence of the world or about theories of suffering and nothingness. They are not affected by feelings of pleasure or happiness. They enjoy perfect ease, which they realize only after coming out of the state. In the fourth stage, the meditator experiences complete freedom from physical as well as mental pain or happiness. All these four stages of meditation are attained by the practice of concentration on a suitable object to induce *upacāra* and *appāna*.

In addition, there are four other higher stages that are achieved by meditating on the four *arūpa*s, viz., unlimited space, unlimited consciousness, nothingness, and a condition of neither perception nor non-perception. By concentrating on unlimited space, the mind of the meditator overcomes all sense distinctions and attains the fifth stage. By meditating on the condition of neither perception nor non-perception he attains a transperceptual state and reaches the eighth stage. This is the highest stage of meditation one could hope to achieve. In fact, after the fourth stage of meditation, the meditator becomes emancipated and achieves a state of transcendence by overcoming all mental limitations (*ceto-vimutta*).

Despite several fundamental differences in the philosophical positions between Yoga and Buddhistic systems there is a great deal of similarity between the meditation practices advocated by them. The yogic *samādhi* and the Buddhist *jhāna* state have much in common, including their progressive nature to achieve a transperceptual state of consciousness in which the realization of perfect knowledge and understanding is believed to be possible. What that perfect knowledge is, however, appears to be a matter of one's focus of meditation and philosophical predisposition. Each system has its own eggs (ideas) to hatch; but the method of hatching (meditation) appears to be essentially the same. In Yoga, the goal is the realization of *puruṣa* consciousness in its sublime purity unsullied by its appearance in mundane mental phenomena. In Advaita Vedānta, it is the realization of the illusory nature of the world of appearance and the understanding of the essential identity of the self with *Ātman*, the undifferentiated self-manifesting, contentless pure consciousness. In Buddhism generally, it is the experience of impermanence and momentariness, and in Mādhyamika especially, it is the realization of the emptiness (*śūnyatā*), the non-foundational character, of all existence.

If one could gain perfect knowledge through meditation, how is it that there are these different notions on the nature of the universe among those who presumably had access to the highest state? It is possible that the highest meditative experience may be similar to all, whether one is a

Buddhist or a Vedāntin, but a discursive discernment of that experience later may be determined by one's prior philosophical assumptions. Therefore, the same experience may be described differently. It may also be the case that in the highest state of consciousness, no new knowledge is revealed, but essential insights into one's concerns at the moment are obtained so that one gains clarity and conviction associated with the ideas on which the meditation is focussed. In any case, what seems to be critically important to the meditator is the inner transformation, rather than mere knowledge, brought about by an integration of knowing and being, which are often dissociated in our lives. Also, meditative experience at its highest level is regarded by all systems as blissful.

Non-Theravāda Traditions in Buddhism

The preceding account of Buddhistic psychology of consciousness differs from that of Yoga and Vedānta. In the latter consciousness as-such is contentless and non-intentional. For Buddhaghoṣa, however, consciousness is "that which thinks of its object". In this sense, consciousness is clearly intentional. Buddhaghoṣa, unlike Śaṅkara, for example, does not distinguish between mind and consciousness. Where he describes consciousness in the intentional sense, he is describing the mind and its cognitive functions. Buddhaghoṣa belongs to the Theravāda School in the Hīnayāna tradition, which subscribed to a metaphysics of realism. In the later developments of Buddhist thought, such as in Mahāyāna, we find a somewhat different approach, which places a greater emphasis on consciousness as distinct from the mind.

As T.R.V. Murti (1983) points out, there are three distinctive phases in the development of Buddhist thought. The first is the realistic and pluralistic phase of Theravāda and Vaibhāsika. This is partially modified as critical realism in Sautrāntika. The second phase emerges with the Mādhyamika of Nāgārjuna (second century CE). With a series of *reductio ad absurdum* arguments, Nāgārjuna has attempted to show the logical absurdities of all rational attempts to understand being and non-being. He has argued that one needs to rise above reason to a higher level of consciousness, where one has intuitive insight. The third phase, according to Murti, is the emergence of Yogācāra idealism of Asanga and Vasubandhu (fourth century CE). The salient feature of this phase is the emphasis on *vijñāna*, consciousness as the sole reality. Mādhyamika's *śūnya* may be identified with pure consciousness. The Vaibhāsika *dharmas* (momentary elements of existence) may be seen as mental states.

Nāgārjuna, emphasized *Abhidhamma* distinction between two levels of truth, *samvṛtti* (empirical) and the *paramārtha* (transcendental) truth. *samvṛtti*, which literally means a covering or a screen that shrouds the transcendental truth, gives rise to the variety of phenomena of our experience. The distinctions such as subject and object belong to this level; and reason reigns supreme here. But once this level is transcended, one recognizes the illusory nature of the phenomena, just as one apprehends the illusory nature of the dream after waking up. At the transcendental level, there are no subject–object distinctions and no discursive thought and reflection to give us knowledge. The only source of true knowledge is by way of revelation and direct intuition. Nāgārjuna does not repudiate the reality of the empirical world in any absolute sense. He denies, however, that it is the ultimate reality. As shadow reality, the world of phenomena is useful in reaching the ultimate, i.e., *nirvāṇa*.

Nāgārjuna's philosophy is called Śūnyavāda. *Śūnya* is not absolute nothingness, but lack of substantiality. We are reminded here of the French existential philosopher Sartre. The notion that the world is *śūnya* (void or empty) is an assertion of the non-substantial nature of the mind and the world it is supposed to grasp; it is the essential groundlessness of the mind and the objects. The understanding one achieves in the highest state of consciousness that gives one the realization of *śūnyatā* (the emptiness) cannot be an act of knowing, because there is no object to know. As Varela et al. (1993) point out:

> Knowing *śūnyatā* (most accurately, knowing the world as *śūnyatā*) is surely not an intentional act. Rather (to use traditional imagery), it is like a reflection in a mirror — pure, brilliant, but with no additional reality apart from itself. — p. 225

The distinction between *samvṛtti* (empirical) and *paramārtha* (ultimate or transcendental) is basic for Nāgārjuna. He asserts in *Mādhyamaka-Kārikā*:

> Those who are unaware of the distinction between these two truths [*samvṛtti* and *paramārtha*] are incapable of grasping the deep significance of the teaching of Buddha. —XXIV. 9

Empirical determinations of knowledge as in *samvṛtti* are covered by categories of thoughts, distorted by points of view and biased by the functions of the mind. The ultimate truth is undetermined, direct and ineffable. It is "experienced by the wise in a very intimate way". Therefore, *paramārtha* is the knowledge of the real without any distortions. It may be mentioned that in Buddhism perception is always indeterminate, inarticulate, and nameless (Sinha 1958, vol. 1: 105).

The Mādhyamika distinction between *samvṛtti* and *paramārtha* is very much like Śaṅkara's conception of *vyavahārika* (empirical) and *paramārtha* (ultimate). The difference, however, is that Nāgārjuna, unlike Śaṅkara, does not find the need to postulate a ground, a foundation, underlying all reality. Consequently, the highest knowledge for him is not the realization of the unity with the ultimate such as *Brahman*. Rather, it is the realization of the groundlessness of all existence. *Brahman* devoid of any qualities in Śaṅkara's philosophy is similar to *śūnyatā* in Nāgārjuna. Again, the role of *avidyā* in the manifestation of the phenomenal world is accepted in Advaita as well as Mādhyamika philosophies. (For a comparison of Advaita and Mādhyamika views on this point see Murti 1983.)

In the Yogācāra School of Buddhism, also known as Vijñānavāda, the intentionality of consciousness is only apparent (Mohanty 1972). When one is conscious of blue, according to this school, the blueness is a form of consciousness and not of an outside object. In other words, when one sees blue, there is no "self-transcending reference" to an object external to the cognition itself. Any such reference is due to *avidyā* (ignorance). Consequently, all imputation of intentionality to consciousness is false. Consciousness in this view is self-revealing. Consciousness and its contents are identical because they are apprehended together without exception. (See Jaiswal 1999 for an evaluation of the nature of consciousness in Vijñānavāda.)

Vijñānavāda accepts *śūnyatā*, but with a difference. In Mādhyamika the approach is logical, whereas Vijñānavāda takes a psychological view. According to Mādhyamika, phenomena lack reality because they are interdependent, whereas in Vijñānavāda the objectivity itself is dependent on consciousness. Consciousness exists by itself. Consciousness may undergo modifications, but it can overcome all superimpositions and find itself in its essential real form. *Śūnyatā*, then, is not devoid of reality, it is *pure consciousness* devoid of subject–object duality. Pure consciousness, which is the undifferentiated essence of all things, takes on threefold modifications. First is *viṣaya-vijñāna* (object-consciousness) arising from sense data including introspective awareness of objects. It gives us knowledge of external objects like books, trees, and houses. The knowledge itself is a projection of consciousness. The second modification (*mano-vijñāna*) is the one brought about by the mental functions of analysis and assimilation, a synthetic experience of the object perceived. The third is *ālaya-vijñāna*, the storehouse of consciousness. Vijñānavāda asserts the existence of pure consciousness without any objective content on the basis of reported experiences in *samādhi* states.

Finally, even in the Hīnayāna tradition such as in Theravāda, the higher states of *jhāna* consciousness cannot be regarded as intentional. These are states in which consciousness transcends subject–object, matter–form distinctions. The understanding of unlimited space, infinite consciousness, nothingness, and a "neither perception nor non-perception" state, it would seem, is essentially an exercise to dissociate consciousness from its objects. *Arūpa-loka* clearly refers to formlessness. *Lokottara-citta* (transcendental consciousness) cannot be intentional.

We thus find in Teravāda transition of early Buddhism greater attention paid to the mind and its states without making any meaningful distinction between mind and consciousness. There is no discussion of consciousness as-such. In this respect, the early Buddhist notion of consciousness is somewhat similar to the Western. The reason for this may be found in Buddha's empirical concerns and his general reluctance to go beyond the immediate existential concerns to the more remote metaphysical issues. Buddhism, however, cannot stop with a consideration of phenomenal consciousness, because its ultimate goal is to transcend these states and achieve *nirvāṇa* (state of transcendence). The later developments in Buddhist thought are clearly the attempts to close the gap between phenomenal and transcendental states of consciousness. In our own discussion of Buddhist psychology, we focussed more on early Buddhism because we find in it the nature and states of phenomenal consciousness discussed in greater detail and depth than the other Indian systems, which are concerned more with pure consciousness than phenomenal consciousness. In fact, the Hindu system and the schools of Buddhism complement each other in significant ways to give us a more comprehensive understanding of consciousness.

Heuristic Summary

Buddha's teachings were meant to be a radical departure from the then prevalent Upaniṣadic thought of the Hindus. In a sense they were. Buddha repudiated the widespread practice of rituals and sacrifices as meaningless. He discarded the notion that permanence is the hallmark of reality. He saw permanence only in change. He rejected the existence of a substantive soul (*ātman*) underlying the changing states of the mind. He felt pain and suffering, in abundance around him. In his statement of the four noble truths he centered on suffering, its cause, its cessation, and the means of overcoming it. Freedom from suffering was the goal. He recommended an eightfold path to achieve that goal. This path consisted of practicing virtues (*śīla*), cultivating mind by concentration (*samādhi*) and achieving wisdom (*prajñā*). This triple-pronged drive of *śīla*, *samādhi* and *prajñā*, he believed, would lead one to *nirvāṇa*, the goal of cessation of all suffering, the dawn of perfect knowledge, and the disappearance of ignorance. Buddha believed that knowledge about the nature of suffering would set one free from bondage and suffering. That knowledge is beyond reason and discursive intellect, a matter of immediate experience, intuitive insight.

Scholars like S. Radhakrishnan have shown a number of similarities between Buddhism and some of the Hindu doctrines and argued that Buddha was himself influenced by Upaniṣadic thought and Sāṁkhya philosophy which is believed to antedate the advent of Buddhism. There is no question that Buddha was influenced by some of the ideas contained in the Upaniṣads. Among Gautama's teachers were Sāṁkhya philosophers. At the same time it is also equally evident that Buddhism influenced many of the subsequent Indian thinkers, including Śaṅkara. Notwithstanding all this, there is no denying the fact that there are fundamental differences between Buddhism and other systems of philosophy, especially Advaita. Buddhism is a philosophy of becoming whereas Vedānta is a philosophy of being. As Murti points out:

> It would be difficult to find two philosophies so different as Vedānta and Buddhism.
> — 1983: 199

Buddhism in the various phases of its development made important contributions to philosophical thought. What is important, however, for the purposes of our study is the common thread that runs through various systems of Indian thought, whether orthodox like Vedānta or heterodox like Buddhism. The common thread appears to be the core concepts and the method rather than the content, the source of knowledge rather than its substance.

The core concepts that run through all the major systems of Indian thought and in a significant sense characterize the Indian psyche are *karma*, *dharma*, and *mokṣa*. Different systems may use different words but the connotations are not far apart. For example, in Sāṁkhya-Yoga we find *kaivalya*, whereas it is *nirvāṇa* in Buddhism and *mokṣa* in Vedānta. It is generally agreed that one is born with *karma* and accumulates *karma* during his lifetime by his thoughts and actions. We are conditioned beings because of our *karma*. It makes us creatures of habits, biases, and predispositions. It detains us, as it were, in a deterministic universe. By our true nature we are unconditioned beings. Therefore, the goal of human endeavor is to find one's *mokṣa* (freedom). The way to achieve this is the path of *dharma*. Understanding *dharma* and acting following its precepts one may overcome *karma* and its effects. As we have seen, Buddhism has much to say about *dharma*. It describes human nature in terms of *dharma* and the states of mind. It provides us with profound insights and an empirical psychology far more detailed and elaborate than anything we find in other Eastern systems. This, it does without losing sight of the ultimate goal of achieving transcendence.

In search for truth, the Indian approach, whether orthodox or heterodox, is to focus attention inward, first, to identify the elements that distort our perceptions and understanding of truth. The second step is to explore the methods that help us control these elements. The third step is to develop techniques to seek truth directly without distortions. The final step is to formulate theories and prescribe practices of conduct that enable us to know and experience truth. There is a general consensus among Indian thinkers that the knowledge we have of the world around us is tainted. This is for a variety of reasons. We find ourselves at the center of a circle covered with ignorance. Our task is to break through the circle, pierce the veil of ignorance, and find truth. Meditation is a means of achieving a state where we transcend ignorance and realize truth. In this process it is assumed that there is a more secure source of truth than the tainted knowledge obtained through sensory channels and analyzed by reason and discursive argument. Buddhism, like the other Indian systems we discussed, is a quest for perfect knowledge and unsullied truth that would at once dispel ignorance and remove suffering.

We regard certain behaviors as normal because they represent to us the consensus reality — the experiential reality we all seem to agree on. Such a consensus reality is made possible by similarities in the psychical processes and structures that we humans appear to share in common. When structural or process changes occur, the ensuing experiences present a reality that may not agree with our consensus reality. Within the framework of the altered state, however, they could make sense. Difficulties arise when we seek to explain experiences obtained in an altered state of consciousness by concepts derived from experiences obtained in our so-called normal state of consciousness (Tart 1972).

Buddhism in all its forms recognizes nonsensory sources of awareness. Buddha himself attained his state of wisdom by intuitive insight and not by discursive reasoning. Like the Buddha, many Buddhist thinkers were less consumed by theoretical concerns and more fascinated by the practical applications of their understanding of consciousness to achieve higher states to know truth and to end suffering.

Even though we do not find awareness, consciousness, and mind sharply distinguished in Buddhist writings, all of them are included in the Buddhist conception of consciousness. In Buddhist view consciousness implies awareness (*viññāna*), both as a process and as the content of our cognitions. So, we find Buddhaghoṣa saying:

> Consciousness is that which thinks of its object. . . . Cognizing object is its characteristic, forerunning is its function, connecting is its manifestation, a mental and material organism is its proximate cause.
>
> — 1920: 148-49

Again, "the resultant is also termed, 'consciousness' because it is accumulated (*cito*) by *kammạ* and the corruptions" (1920: 85). Thus, mind for the Buddhists is both a process and a repository for all our cognitions.

Our normal consciousness is a stabilized set of psychic structures that function to regulate our awareness. This set is reasonably stable for any individual (with predictable variations), and is normally shared by others. However, it is not unalterable. When it is modified, one enters into an altered state of consciousness. In Buddhist psychology consciousness is analyzed into various elements that unite in a number of combinations and give us a variety of conscious states. It would not be appropriate to regard all these as altered states. But the analysis itself is helpful in understanding how alterations of consciousness occur and what specific characteristics such alterations would manifest.

I find Charles Tart's (1975b) analogy of the computer to be helpful in understanding the components of consciousness. He points out that some structures of our consciousness are essentially permanent, such as the biological and physiological givens. These constitute the hardware of the mind. Other structures are mainly a result of the individual's developmental history; they derive from such processes as conditioning, learning, and acculturation. These constitute the software of the human mind. Our so-called normal state of consciousness is determined by the hardware of the mind as well as by the program that appears to be common to most individuals during most of their lifetime. This does not mean, however, that the program does not undergo any changes or that it is essentially identical in all human beings. While the seed program is shared largely, the program itself may be more or less complex and developed. An individual's accumulated *karma* and *saṁskāras* influence his cognition and action to some degree. Consequently, information processed by one mind may not be processed by another in precisely the same way. However, information relating to similar things is likely to be similar, because the two minds share the same basic program.

Buddhist psychology attempts to understand how this processing normally takes place and whether the programming can be qualitatively changed. Buddhists believe that it is possible not only to induce modifications in an individual's program, but also to bring about radical changes in the organization of given psychic structures — resulting in a qualitatively different functioning of the mind.

In Buddhist psychology, the concept *karma* approximates what we here call "programming". *Karma* determines both the hardware as well as the software, inasmuch as Buddhists believe that even the physical form is a fruit of past *karma*. The Buddhist conception of *karma* is not merely a hypothesis. It also explains how modifications in the programming process can be brought about. *Cetanā* (volition) is the key concept here.

Volition is both a source of accumulated *karma* and also an instrument to bring about changes in our program. Volition is the mental function that co-ordinates and closely binds other functions of the mind. It gives direction to our activity as well as provides necessary energy for action. In its *karma*-producing aspect, it creates in us the illusion of "I-ness", and all actions and experiences thus gain ego-reference. Whenever there is such ego-reference, all related actions produce *karma*, which, in turn, conditions subsequent behavior. Ego, then, is an epiphenomenon; it results from the way the volition functions to bind the various psychic structures. This means that the ego itself is not an intrinsic structure necessary for all our mental processes. Therefore, we do not find ego included among the five *skandhas* of the mind. It is not to be found even among the seven universal elements (*cetasikas*) of consciousness. Ego is merely a creation of our volition.

At the same time, Buddhism recognizes that volition can — by being directed in *jhāna* (meditation) and other means of psychic development — function in such a way that the resultant experiences do not have ego-reference. Such actions are those that are necessarily not motivated and determined by previous *karma*. All *karma*-prompted experiences have ego-reference as their basic characteristic — i.e., the experiences are regarded as belonging to the experiencer. The very process of experiencing is itself processed through a program that is determined by *karma*. In such a situation, the cognitions experienced or the knowledge derived from them are personal in the sense that they are dependent on the nature and condition of the experiencing person. To transcend this personal character of cognition and knowledge, it is necessary that the knowledge process be free from the influences of *karma* and its associated habits and reflex like responses. In other words, the person in his existential context is conditioned. His freedom consists in making him unconditioned.

How can this be done? This brings us to a critically important point in Buddhist psychology. In cognitive processes, the normal flow of *bhavaṅga* is halted, but *bhavaṅga* itself gets perturbed and goes into a state of convulsion. *Bhavaṅga*, it appears, is the medium through which *karma* influences our being and behavior. Buddhists believe that it is possible to eliminate *karma* influence, so that the resulting knowledge escapes the limitations of the human condition. The human condition, which is characterized as a continuous cycle of birth and death, is a pre-programmed cognitive style and behavior disposition, which sets boundaries and limits to what we can experience and the sense that can be made of the experience. Transcendence is thus a release of the "imprisoned splendor", to use R.C. Johnson's phrase, made possible by the breaking of ego shackles and *karma* influences. We are told, for example, that a meditator in attempting to reach the *appāna* state seeks to reflect the image of an object without stimulating *bhavaṅga*. If he is successful, he enters the *jhāna* states, which leads him progressively to transcendence. Cognitively, a state of transcendence is one where the person is able to image and reflect on an object without stimulating *bhavaṅga*. The resultant knowledge is perfect in the sense that it is unbiased, objective, and impersonal.

We may note here the interesting difference between Sāṁkhya-Yoga and Advaita Vedānta on the one hand and Buddhism on the other. *Bhavaṅga* is a concept specific to Buddhism. It is similar to *buddhi*, but also quite different from it. *Bhavaṅga* is the unconscious stream of awareness and the carrier of *karma* like the *saṁskāra*s and *vāsanā*s. The *saṁskāra*s, however, are part of the *buddhi* and do not constitute a separate stream of subterranean flow of consciousness. In Yoga, we presuppose the existence of *puruṣa*, a center of consciousness, without which no conscious awareness is possible. The light of consciousness shines on *vr̥tti* of *buddhi* to render the mental states subjectively experienced. In Buddhism no such separate source of consciousness is assumed. Consciousness is considered an intrinsic aspect of mental states themselves. In *bhavaṅga* it is subterranean and in phenomenal states it is overt and associated with subjective experience. In transcendental states, it is non-representational and devoid of sensory content. This notion is somewhat similar to the subconscious/subliminal self of F.W.H. Myers (1903) and the analogy of the light spectrum. At one end of the spectrum is *bhavaṅga* mentation. At the other end are the transcendental states of *jhāna*. Buddhists, however, will not accept the notion of subliminal self.

The differences between the Hindu systems and Buddhist schools are at the metaphysical level. For example, in Advaita, *Brahman/Ātman* is the ground condition of consciousness. Buddhism rejects the notion of any such substantive ground reality, whether mind or matter. However, by accepting the reality of transcendental states of consciousness, which are essentially devoid of content and therefore non-intentional, Buddhism does not reject the notion of pure consciousness. In fact, pure consciousness is implied in the higher states of *jhāna*. This point is mute in early Buddhism, but becomes more explicit in the later w1ritings of Mādhyamika and Yogācāra thinkers.

To sum up, then, Buddhists postulate the existence of a stream of consciousness which, functioning at the subliminal level, is the basis of the subjective feeling of continuity and identity and which is the binding influence on our perceptions, thoughts, actions, and feelings. This stream, which operates below the threshold of normal awareness, carries with it the imprints of a person's life history, predisposing him to behave in certain ways. These imprints motivate, condition, and drive an individual to behave in set ways; but they lose their strength and may even disappear soon after they have activated a set behavior. However, the resultant experience will, in its turn, produce another imprint. And so, the chain of causation continues. The imprints are formed when the mind functions in such a way that the resultant experiences have ego reference and entanglement. But it is possible for the mind (1) to function so as to destroy the imprints, and (2) to function without precipitating new imprints. Attainment of a state where all these imprints are destroyed or disarmed and where the mind functions independently of the processing medium is the state of psychological transcendence. This is basically a trans-ego state engendered by a reorganization of the psychic structures with the help of such devices as meditation.

Much of what has been said is admittedly speculative. But the medium that Buddhist psychology finds necessary to postulate is no more mysterious than the Freudian unconscious or the Jungian archetypes. What is interesting, however, is the explanatory model that extends psychology's scope to account for normal, abnormal, and paranormal behaviors. The implications of the theory to paranormal psychology are obvious. The state of transcendence is one in which new cognitive relationships are established and where subject–object dichotomies cease. It is necessarily a state where our experience and knowing are not limited by space–time barriers or our normal sensory thresholds. The theory also fits well with several of the psychodynamic factors studied by depth psychologists. In fact, some aspects of the theory have test implications, and permit empirical verification.

I find the Buddhist ideas particularly helpful in planning empirical studies of meditation. They provide a rich phenomenology for understanding the changes in consciousness accompanying meditation, which could be utilized to determine the associated psychophysiological states. Such a determination would not only give us the needed objectivity to describe these phenomena, but would also permit a more precise application of the meditative techniques to aspects perhaps less significant than transcendence but more immediately relevant — such as mental health. For example, much psychoanalytic groundwork is aimed at scanning the patient's life history to identify those critical past experiences that seem to be causing the present symptoms. But the treatment itself only touches the periphery of the problem. What could be more important in psychotherapy than to find a method of disarming or, even better, for destroying the disruptive effects of such past experience? Certain aspects of Buddhist meditation do promise to accomplish just that. More importantly, Buddhist psychology presupposes a state of transcendence, which in important respects resembles the state of pure consciousness in Advaita Vedānta.

Setting aside the speculative, metaphysical, and sacred aspects of the Hindu and Buddhist thought, one may focus on the secular, psychological assumptions of the concept of pure consciousness in Vedānta and the concept of *śūnya* (void) in Buddhism. Pure consciousness is stated to be in principle characterless and without content. As an experiential state, and not a metaphysical presupposition, *śūnyatā* or pure consciousness may mean one of two things. It may be essentially indescribable or ineffable in terms of communicating what it is like to experience it. Language may be an incompetent tool here. Empirically derived characteristics, the qualities that we are familiar with in *vyavahārika* or *saṁsāra* mode, may be utterly inadequate for that purpose. Alternately, the state of pure consciousness may be literally "void", a complete blank, a state like profound sleep with no mentation taking place. In either case, it would seem, achieving a state of pure consciousness is not inconsequential. If it is an ineffable state, it may be inexpressible but can be shared. In other words, it would still have inter-subject validity because people who achieve that state may share essentially similar and experientially meaningful outcome. Even assuming that pure consciousness is a complete blank state of the mind, we may recall, in Hindu thought it is an extremely blissful state and in Buddhism it leads to an end of suffering. In either case it is a very desirable state. Even occasional excursions into the region of pure consciousness may have remarkable consequences, as suggested, at a secular level. They may be even amenable for inter-subject validation and empirical verification.

20

Two Faces of Consciousness[1]

K. Ramakrishna Rao

It is clear from the discussions so far that consciousness means different things to different people. The variety of attempts to describe and explain it reminds us of the legendary blind men seeking to describe the elephant. The only common ground that seems to cover the many connotations of consciousness is that it is somehow connected with our awareness. The notion that consciousness and awareness are synonymous is consistent with commonsense usage as well a dictionary definition (Natsoulas 1978).

Consciousness in the sense of being aware refers to at least seven different things. First is reflective awareness, such as we find in the acts of perception, thought, and volition. Second is paradoxical awareness, awareness without being aware, which includes among other things subliminal perception, implicit memory, blindsight, and hypnotic analgesia. Third is awareness of awareness, the awareness of being aware. Fourth is self-awareness, the awareness of personal identity, one's being distinct from the rest. Fifth is the awareness of unity and continuity in one's awareness, the so-called stream of awareness. Sixth is intuitive awareness, awareness that is apparently independent of and sensorially disconnected from the object of awareness such as intuitions, veridical hunches, and extrasensory perception (Rao and Palmer 1987). Finally, awareness as-such or pure awareness which is not predicated of any object or process, a state often reported in mystical experiences and by *yogins*.

The above seven meanings of consciousness fall into two categories. The first category is what may be called "object awareness", where awareness is always predicated of an object. The object may be physical

---

[1] The reader will find a significant amount of repetition in this concluding chapter what is already available in the previous chapters. We hope that it helps to bring into focus the respects in which the Eastern and Western perspectives on consciousness are different and complementary.

or mental, real or imaginary. The second category is "subject awareness" where awareness is awareness of itself or one of its aspects. It also includes the possibility of experiencing or realizing awareness as-such, an awareness state with no content, whether of the awareness process or of the world of objects and thought. We may consider the two categories of awareness as its phenomenal and transcendental domains, its intentional and non-intentional aspects. In the phenomenal domain, consciousness is predicated of the objects of its reflection. In its transcendental aspect it is a state of being. The major ambiguity in the usage of consciousness in scholarly discourse thus lies in the fact that it is used sometimes to refer to a state of being and on some occasions it is regarded as a quality of experience or is referred to its content.

The plausibility of a given notion of consciousness is specific to one's perspective. Different cultures have different perspectives and these appear to determine their approaches to the study and understanding of consciousness. In the Western tradition the dominant perspective is one of rational understanding of what consciousness is. In the Eastern tradition the approach is one of developing practical methods for transforming consciousness in specific ways for specific purposes. These differing approaches led to radically different emphases as to what is essential in discussing consciousness. A recognition of this fact is not only likely to help us appreciate the context and significance of each other's perspectives, but may also enable us to see the respects in which they are genuinely complementary.

In what follows we will discuss what seem to be the dominant characteristics of the perspectives characterizing the Eastern and Western traditions in dealing with the issues of consciousness, and how together they may give us a more global and holistic understanding of consciousness.

Consciousness in the Western Tradition

In Part I we have a variety of essays discussing consciousness from the Western perspective. We first present here briefly the background of Western notions on consciousness. In the Western tradition, consciousness as a psychological concept had its origins in the seventeenth-century philosophers René Descartes and John Locke (Klemm 1914). Descartes's dualism, which has come to be a commonsense worldview throughout the West, considers the mind, the *res cogitans*, as utterly independent of the brain. Its existence is a self-evident truth because "it is so self-evident that it is I who doubt, understand, and desire that there is no need to add here anything to explain it" (Descartes n.d: 133).

Consciousness, according to Descartes (1969), is the essence of the mind and the mind is different from the body, including the brain and the nervous system. There are in existence two kinds of radically different substances — the extended physical substance and the unextended mental (thinking) substance. The latter in principle is irreducible to the former. Consequently, mental phenomena are those for which there can be no physical explanation. It will be of interest to note in this context that Descartes denied consciousness to animals because their behavior can be explained essentially in physical terms. Even in human beings, Descartes thought, such activities as digestion and muscular reflexes do not involve the mind because they can be explained purely by mechanical principles. If, for example, all mental phenomena can be accounted for in physical terms and if the presumed activities of the mind such as thought, volition, and so forth are shown to be governed solely by mechanical principles, as Descartes recognized in the case of reflex actions, there will be hardly any empirical justification for assuming that humans, unlike animals, have mind/consciousness.

According to the British philosopher, John Locke (1894) consciousness is the perception of what is in one's mind. It is reflection contained in the different acts of the mind such as perception, thinking, and volition. Consciousness is the essential aspect of the mind which is transparent and nothing in it is hidden. The Lockean view of consciousness had such a pervasive influence in Western thought that until the advent of Freudian psychoanalysis the notion of unconscious thought or perception was considered self-contradictory.

Since Descartes and Locke, the discussion of consciousness in the Western tradition has been dominated by the presumed identity of mind and consciousness on the one hand and the apparent duality between mind and body on the other. Much of the scholarly discourse of mind/consciousness was dominated by these concerns. Either the duality of mind and body is asserted or denied to be real by arguing that one can or cannot be reduced to the other.

Consciousness and the Unconscious

That some mental activities go on without one's awareness of them is a fact that no one can reasonably doubt now. Freud (1915) has shown how complex thought processes can occur without awareness and how one's unconscious may contain beliefs, desires, and feelings of which one is unaware. His studies of dreams and parapraxes (minor mistakes made in speech or action believed to be caused by repressed wishes) convinced Freud of the reality of unconscious thought and motivations. He saw meaning and purpose in unconscious material. Seemingly innocuous and unintentional acts such as slips of the tongue, forgetting, and misplacing of objects may be motivated at the unconscious level. That being so, the earlier characterization of consciousness as intentional, purposeful mental activity must be taken to apply to the unconscious as well.

With its emphasis on unconscious process, psychoanalysis showed that the unconscious is not merely the absence of consciousness but has a domain of its own. C.G. Jung, however, went further to blunt the distinction between consciousness and the unconscious. The unconscious, according to Jung, is not the dung heap of repressed thoughts and infantile sexual fantasies that Freud described; rather it is the consummate source of our collectivity, unity and creativity. The collective unconscious is

> an image of the world which has taken aeons to form. . . . [It] consists of the sum of instincts and their correlates, the archetypes. Just as everybody possesses instincts, so he also possesses a stock of archetypal images.
>
> —Jung 1954: 138

Jung was led in his later years beyond archetypal images to the concept of the archetype-as-such. The archetype-as-such, a transpsychic concept, is an a priori ordering principle by virtue of which we experience synchronistic events that suggest an "acausal orderedness". This advance in Jung's thinking from subjectively experienced archetypal image to archetype as an a priori ordering principle obscured his earlier distinction between consciousness and the unconscious (Frey-Rohn 1990). Consciousness was originally associated with a certain degree of brightness and luminosity. Jung increasingly saw that this luminosity is not limited to what is called consciousness but is also found to be in some of the unconscious contents. Jung thus came to the "paradoxical conclusion that there is no conscious content which is not in some other aspects unconscious" (ibid.: 185).

The unconscious mental events are essentially repressed, according to Freud, from reaching consciousness. There are, however, preconscious mental phenomena that are not currently in consciousness but are available for introspective awareness and reporting. Similarly, William James spoke about a fringe as well as a focus of consciousness. One's attention may be focussed on a center and around a theme, but there is also a vast surround of impressions and sensations at the periphery. The fringe is the floating backdrop of those images that are the focus of attention. "The significance, the value, of the image," as James saw it, "is all in this halo or penumbra that surrounds and escorts it" (1960: 166).

The Jamesian view of consciousness is reflected in some important respect by contemporary cognitive psychology with its emphasis on attention and the levels of memory processing. Seeking to study the place of consciousness in information processing, cognitive psychologists have attempted to determine the respect in which conscious processing differs from unconscious or non-conscious processing. It is suggested among other things that the processing of novel stimuli and voluntary responses requires consciousness. The widely held view among cognitive psychologists is that information is first processed at the preconscious level. The preconscious processing is automatic and involuntary and it can go on simultaneously to process information in a parallel fashion from different sensory channels. Conscious processing, unlike preconscious processing, is voluntary, flexible, and serial in nature. It can process only one item at a time. Information which is processed by the limited capacity central processor becomes accessible to consciousness. Only the messages to which we attend are processed for meaning. The built-in filtering mechanism prevents all other messages from reaching higher centers of the brain whose activity is essential for introspective awareness (Triesman, 1969). There is thus a close relationship between attention and consciousness. The preconscious processing is pre-attentive and conscious processing is focal-attentive. Pre-attentive processing activates the memory traces of the stimulus as well as related traces. Focal-attentive processing which requires intention for its operation and is necessary for subjective awareness, takes place after the "spreading activation" of the pre-attentive processing (Posner and Snyder 1975).

There are good reasons to believe that complex mental activity including our ability to acquire, store, and retrieve information is carried out by operations that are primarily unconscious in that they are inaccessible to introspection. Max Velmans (1991) has reviewed evidence suggesting that consciousness in the sense of being introspectively aware need not enter into the processing of information at any level, including the organization of complex activity that requires planning, reflection, or creativity. Thus, much of mental activity seems to go on without subjective awareness, which is traditionally regarded as an essential aspect of the mind.

The studies of "blindsight" and "memory without awareness" also show the limitations of the concept of mind that equates it with subjective awareness. Blindsight is the capacity among those with a damaged visual cortex to discriminate and respond to visual stimuli without being aware of them. Weiskrantz (1986), for example, carried out a series of tests with a subject whose right visual cortex had been removed. As one would expect, the subject reported that he saw nothing when the stimuli were presented to his left hemifield. However, when he was asked to guess whether the stimulus was *x* or o, the subject guessed correctly in twenty-seven of thirty trials, thus suggesting that he perceived the stimuli at some level, and that perceptions and subjective awareness of them are two distinctive processes that can be dissociated.

It is known that damage to certain midline structures in the brain can lead to serious amnesia in humans so that they were unable to remember their experience beyond a few seconds. Such an amnesia patient who just solved a jigsaw puzzle is typically unable to remember how he did it; but if he is asked to solve the same puzzle the next day he will solve it faster, which suggests that though unaware of it, he was able to retain, at least in part, his previous learning of the puzzle. There is a substantial evidence for such phenomena of "implicit memory" from a number of studies (Schacter 1987; Kihlstrom et al. 1990).

Implicit awareness, as implied in blindsight and implicit memory (which is also called paradoxical awareness because the subject is not "aware" of his awareness) is not limited to cases where there are cortical defects. Similar phenomena occur even when one's brain structures are intact. For example, positive and negative hallucinations, perceptual distortions, and analgesia that occur under hypnotic suggestion (Hilgard 1986) are analogous to the phenomena of blindsight in suggesting some kind of dissociation between reported subjective experience and the response.

Research in the area of subliminal perception has produced some interesting results. There is impressive evidence that stimuli present at low energy levels, or in masked forms so that they cannot be recalled, recognized, or discriminated from other similarly presented stimuli, can nevertheless produce detectable cognitive, affective, or other behavioral effects (Bornstein and Pittman 1992). For example, subliminal (4 ms) exposure to the message "Mommy and I are one" is shown to have beneficial effects on those undergoing psychotherapy (Silverman and Weinberger 1985). What is even more interesting is the observation that the effects obtained under subliminal conditions were greater than those obtained when the subjects reported seeing the stimulus message (Bornstein 1989).

The above observations and data lead us to reconsider the traditional notion of the identity of mind and consciousness. Alternatively, we need to expand the connotation of consciousness beyond the Lockean view that equates it with subjective reflection. So we find in a textbook on the psychology of consciousness:

> Consciousness is not the same as mind. Mind is the broader concept: It includes both conscious and unconscious mental processes.
>
> — Farthing 1992 : 5

Interestingly, however, his book which is titled *The Psychology of Consciousness* discusses in just as much detail the non-conscious mental processes as well. In effect, then, it equates the psychology of consciousness with the psychology of the human mind, once again conforming to the Western tradition of treating consciousness and mind as identical concepts that can be used interchangeably. It follows also that consciousness as a general concept cannot be limited to subjective awareness and that in a very significant sense consciousness refers to non-conscious mental phenomena as well.

Intentionality as the Defining Characteristic of Mind/Consciousness

Another feature of the Western conception of mind/consciousness is that it is *of* or *about* something. We are aware of this or aware that such and such is the case. If the mind is consciousness, intentionality is its defining characteristic. Intentionality in philosophical discourse is a technical term, and its meaning varies widely from its non-technical usage. For example, intentionality does not refer to one's motivation or intention to do something deliberately or on purpose. The philosophical concept of intentionality arose from medieval discussions that were concerned with distinguishing mental phenomena such as thoughts from physical objects like books. Physical phenomena are believed to have *natural* existence, whereas thoughts have only mental existence. To have an idea or thought is to think about something, to direct one's attention to an image or thought. Thus intentionality has come to be referred to the "directedness" or "aboutness" that appears to characterize mental existence.

The concept of intentionality has a checkered history in Western philosophy beginning with the Scholastics in the Middle Ages. It was, however, the Austrian philosopher and psychologist Franz Brentano (1838–1917) who gave it an essentially original formulation and called attention to its centrality in the philosophy of mind (Mohanty 1972).

Brentano's concern was to identify the distinguishing feature or property of mental phenomena (with which psychology deals), a feature that is not present in physical phenomena. Brentano (1973) found it in the scholastic concept of "intentional inexistence". Intentional inexistence means that conscious phenomena "intentionally contain an object within themselves". There is an "aboutness" about them. In other words, mental phenomena require reference to a context. Brentano asserted that this property of "aboutness" is distinctive to psychical states and is absent in all non-mental phenomena. Thus the act of seeing a rose is a mental phenomenon, but the object rose is not. The former is an act of representation whereas the latter is the represented object. Brentano speaks of intentionality as "the relatedness to a content" and "directedness towards an object". In an intentional situation then we have (1) the act of intention, (2) the mental representation or content, and (3) the object of which it is a representation. According to Brentano, the object can be real or imaginary, such as the one that appears in fantasy. Inasmuch as the object can be fictitious and need not exist at all, it does not enter into an analysis of the mental act. Brentano is not clear, however, as to the relationship between the act of intention and the content of cognition. In his earlier writings he seems to hold that there is indeed the intended object, content or representation, and the object of thought, the thing itself, whether real or imaginary. In his later writings, as Mohanty (1972) points out, he tended to abandon the notion of representation and not make any distinction between the object in thought and the object itself. In addition to intentionality, Brentano pointed out two more distinguishing characters of consciousness. They are (1) its self-revealing (inner perception) character, and (2) its intrinsic unity. These, according to Brentano, are characteristics that are not found in physical phenomena.

Brentano was a realist and a naturalist. His interest in the concept of intentionality was that of a psychologist. He found in intentionality a common characteristic that distinguishes all mental phenomena from all physical phenomena. Thus for him, along with self-revealing reflexivity and the binding unity, intentionality became a defining characteristic of consciousness. As a realist, Brentano could not ignore the object of consciousness as having existence independent of consciousness. As a naturalist he was committed to a causal explanation of our cognitions, beliefs, and desires. Consequently, he was confronted with the problem of relating in an intentional act, the mental act, its content, and the objects.

In this context, the following questions arise. How does the object enter consciousness? How does consciousness contain its object within itself? The object does not exist in the mind. The actual physical existence of the object outside is irrelevant because it can be an imaginary item. Then how is consciousness able to refer to its object? These questions are not answered in Brentano's discussion of intentionality. As Mohanty points out:

> If the concept of intentionality is to serve any purpose, it should be able to dispense with the content as a *medium of reference*: consciousness should be able to refer to its object by virtue of some inalienable power of its own. — 1972: 8, original emphasis

Despite the many problems in Brentano's formulation of intentionality, his thesis that intentionality is an irreducible feature of consciousness is often cited as reason to reject the notion of mind–brain identity.

It is, however, in the German philosopher Husserl (1859–1938) that we find a thorough phenomenological expression of the concept of intentionality as a consummate theory of subjectivity. Unlike Brentano, Husserl was not interested in using intentionality as a demarcating criterion for mental phenomena. Rather, his interest in intentionality is on its own. Further, Husserl has abandoned completely the causal approach to understanding conscious phenomena. Instead, he championed a phenomenological attitude, one that accepts phenomena as given. By phenomena Husserl meant "what appears as such". Philosophical thought, he felt, should be rooted in lived experience; and phenomenology is returning back to life.

Husserl saw that conscious states do not cause each other, as physical states do. The unity that characterizes consciousness consists in that conscious states imply each other; they internally refer to each other. According to Husserl, the intentional act has two functions. It does not merely refer to an object; it essentially constitutes the object. It does so by *synthesizing* the various aspects of the object revealed in different acts and by *identifying* that it is the same object intended in all the acts. The intentional act constitutes the object *qua* object involving a process of phenomenological reduction by which one "brackets" or puts aside the natural attitude and attends to phenomena as they are intended. Thus, the reduction accomplished by a transcendental mode of analysis leads one to the essence of subjective experience. Phenomenology, according to Husserl is "eidetic science" that gives the knowledge of universal essences.

Husserl (1931, 1960, 1971, 1982) shared Descartes' concern for a method to arrive at those things that are absolutely evident so that no doubt can be entertained about their existence. He considered it truly "epoch-making" that Descartes found such evidence in the act of cognition. Husserl felt, however, that Descartes did not carry his method far enough. He, therefore, proposed his own method by which we can seek what he called *apodictic evidence*, which carries with it absolute indubitability. "It discloses itself, to a critical reflection, as having the signal peculiarity of being *at the same time the absolute unimaginableness* (inconceivability) of their non-being. . . ." (Husserl 1960: 15-16, original emphasis). Further, the critical reflection itself will have in such cases the sense of indubitability, of being *apodictic*.

Fundamental to Husserl's passion for absolute evidence is his conviction that our prejudices and presuppositions generally taint our knowledge of the world and of us. Whereas we meet and exchange views and ideas concerning things about which we presumably agree, our ideas themselves seldom have universal acceptance because we are predisposed to observe and interpret those observations in accordance with our biases, intellectual or otherwise. Therefore, as Husserl observes, at philosophical congresses and such gatherings the "philosophers meet but, unfortunately, not the philosophies" (ibid.: 5). Descartes, Husserl suggests, who rightly started on the course of doubt, became a victim of his own prejudice when, for example, he equated the act of thinking with a thinking *substance, substantia cogitans*.

The essential step in Husserl's method of absolute universal doubt "is abstention from all positions that already give anything existent, must first create for itself a *universe of absolute freedom from prejudice*" (ibid.: 35). In the course of arriving at such *apodictic* evidence, one must establish oneself as a "disinterested onlooker" so as "to see and to describe adequately what he sees, purely as seen, as what is seen and seen in such and such a manner" (ibid.: 35). According to Husserl, such transcendental experience and reflection give us knowledge "intuitively", knowledge that is free from prejudice and all interpretations read into them beyond the genuinely observed. By means of such intuitions we comprehend the "essence" of objects.

Husserl's method involves a specific procedure for examining the structures of consciousness and intentionality. This procedure called *epoché* (bracketing) incorporates a "transcendental" mode of analysis. The "natural world" that we normally take for granted and the "natural attitude" of its independence from our cognitions of it are deliberately "bracketed", or put aside, so that we can closely observe the experience itself. When one does this and consciousness reflectively considers its own cognitive acts, there is then, according to Husserl, the emergence of "the transcendental ego", described as "the principle of subjectivity". Adopting this procedure to arrive at the structures of consciousness, Husserl claims that his method enables us to understand the contents of consciousness experienced internally and to see how they are generated from those structures. His method of phenomenological reduction is a way of showing how objectivity is constituted of subjectivity.

According to Husserl, the external object, the content of consciousness, and our awareness of it are directly related by the intentionality of consciousness. In fact, in phenomenology all consciousness is intentional; consciousness is always consciousness of something. Our knowledge of the world is not via the sensations we receive, but is a consequence of the logical process of intention. The common world we share with each other is not made possible by the sensations we have of them, which tend to be discrete and private, and cannot therefore reveal the universal and unitary character of their objects, but by a "constitutive function" of consciousness that intuitively grasps their essence. The constitutive function of consciousness lies in the intuiting of the essence of objects so that we may understand their significance and meaningfulness to us. The unitary character that objects have as phenomena of our experience can only be understood in terms of their essences, and not as a summation of their shifting qualities.

There are at least three aspects to Husserl's procedure. First, by putting aside the "natural attitude", an attempt is made to focus attention on phenomenal experiences instead of on the externally conceived world. Second, the internal focus is on the contents of consciousness, since consciousness is always directed to something. Such a focus is understood to give us intuitively the essence of objects experienced in consciousness. Third is that aspect in which the focus is on the enduring subject who has the experience. Just as the "constitutive function" gives us the uniqueness and sameness of objects despite the infinitely varied mosaic of "sensory states", the "transcendental" function gives us the sense of subjectivity and personal identity amidst the ever-changing contents of the stream of consciousness.

While postulating the "transcendental ego", Husserl comes close to accepting the notion of pure consciousness or consciousness as-such. S.K. Maharana (2007) traces the evolution of Husserl's thoughts on consciousness from his *Logical Investigations* to *Cartesian Meditations* through *Ideas*. Intentionality for Husserl is more than a characteristic feature of consciousness. Rather it is its very essence. How does the act of consciousness (its intention) constitute the object of consciousness? As mentioned earlier, it is by a process of synthesis in which the shifting qualities of experience cohere into "continuous thing-like unity". It is the ego function. Phenomenological reduction of experience reveals the empirical ego, the person to whom the object of intention is related in the act of cognition. As Husserl puts it, the "phenomenologically reduced ego is nothing peculiar, floating above many experiences; it is simply identical with this interconnected unity"(quoted from Maharana, 2007: 35). Clearly in this there is no room for a transcendental subject or pure consciousness. The manifest unity of experience itself constitutes the empirical or phenomenological ego.

As Maharana points out, we find a clear distinction made between the empirical ego and the transcendental ego in Husserl's book *Ideas*. The transcendental ego is the pure ego, which is "neither experience nor a process". Rather, it is "the active and affected subject of consciousness", which "no reduction can ever remove". Just as the act of cognition is directed to an object, so is the cognition related to the ego. Just as there is an enduring object revealed in phenomenological reduction among all possible changes of experiences, there is an enduring transcendental ego accompanying the varieties of experience in the stream of consciousness. This becomes explicit in *Cartesian Meditations*. In the Fourth Meditation, the ego is seen as the enduring "pole of subjective processes". As Maharana observes, "the ego is not an empty pole of identity". It is "the active and passive subject of consciousness (2007: 39). However,

> the empirical and the transcendental consciousness are not two, numerically distinct entities, but rather one and the same entity regarded from two standpoints. The "I" who lives the mental life and the "I" who experiences as "me" are the same "I" in the sense that in all acts of consciousness, there remains an identical ego. Before the *epoché* (reduction) is performed, one usually encounters an empirical ego, the ego as a "person", and a "thing" in the world. When reduction is performed, the empirical ego is bracketed, as a consequence of which one discovers the transcendental ego. — ibid.: 39

Husserl may be seen here as coming tantalizingly close to the notion of pure consciousness as *puruṣa* in Sāṁkhya ontology. However, Husserl fails to move beyond bare experience and draw the ontological implications of the concept of transcendental ego.

Others have criticized Husserl for his final step, which ended in logical abstractions, rather than staying rooted in experience, as he intended and claimed. Varela et al. (1993: 16-17) write:

> He began with a solitary individual consciousness, took the structure he was seeking to be entirely mental and accessible to consciousness in an act of abstract philosophical introspection, and from there had great difficulty in generating the consensual, intersubjective world of human experience. And having no method other than his own philosophical introspection, he certainly could not take the final move that would return him to his experience, back to the beginning of the process. The irony of Husserl's procedure, then, is that although he claimed to be turning philosophy toward a direct facing of experience, he was actually ignoring both the consensual aspect and the direct embodied aspect of experience.

Husserl's student and fellow German philosopher Heidegger (1884–1976) addressed several of these issues. In Heidegger (1962, 1982, 1984), intentionality of consciousness, divested of its theoretical and abstract look, comes closer to the practical and existential human concerns. Phenomenological reduction, which is an indispensable condition in Husserl's understanding of intentionality, is abandoned; and *Dasein* replaces the transcendental ego, the source of intentionality (Mohanty 1972). *Dasein* (literal meaning "being there") refers to human existence, the being in the world. Heidegger located intentionality in *Dasein*. His phenomenological account of intentionality is given in the context of finding the meaning of Being. *Dasein* is not an abstract or neutral being. It is in the world and yet it is outside of it by self-transcendence. "Being-in-the-world", Mohanty points out, "is Heidegger's substitute for intentionality" (1972: 129-30).

According to Heidegger there are three structural features of being-in-the-world. First is the pre-given in human experience. The second is its comprehension, which makes the world meaningful. This is the self-transcendence feature of *Dasein* and the one that bestows meaning to an intentional act. *Dasein* "projects itself to others in order to seize and manipulate them, and, in so doing, give(s) them meaning and significance" (ibid.: 130). The third is speech, which articulates. These three features of being-in-the-world together locate *Dasein* in the past, the future, and the present. *Dasein* is also characterized as "radical openness to Being". It makes it possible for beings to manifest Being. (For an in-depth discussion of the concept of intentionality in Husserl and Heidegger, see Mohanty 1972; Hopkins 1993.)

The existential philosopher Jean Paul Sartre (1905-80) also emphasizes the centrality of consciousness in the human condition. Sartre regards Heidegger's notion of *Dasein* as unsatisfactory, because it is seen as excluding consciousness. Like Husserl, Sartre locates intentionality in consciousness. He, however, questions the Husserlian method of transcendental reduction, or "bracketing", which puts aside the natural world in order to deduce the transcendental ego as a consciousness function. Sartre points out that no such ego is phenomenologically apparent. Nor is it logically necessary to account for the unity of experience. With the aim of drafting an architectonic of being, Sartre inquires into the structure displayed by consciousness. He argues that both consciousness and the objects of our consciousness are facts given in experience. They enjoy two distinctive kinds of reality. Since the very nature of consciousness is intentional, the essential characteristic of consciousness is the revelation of the thing to which it is directed. Its reality is functional and not substantive. Therefore, it cannot be described as this or that. It is not a thing; nor is it a container in which the phenomena of our experience are deposited. Its sole reality consists in its revelatory function.

Consciousness is defined in Sartre's existentialism in terms of intentionality and translucence. Like John Locke, consciousness for Sartre is self-luminous and wholly transparent; and nothing in it is hidden or opaque. Even pre-reflective awareness, according to Sartre, is transparent. Pain is pain because we are aware of it. Mere sensation cannot be an element or aspect of consciousness. Intentionality is not conceived as constituting the being of its object. Rather, the basic feature of intentionality is transcendence. By transcendence Sartre means reference to something outside of itself and also the tendency to bestow meaning on being. By its very nature, consciousness is of something other than itself. The things consciousness reveals are outside of it. Consciousness is thus distinct and distant from the intended objects. The distinctiveness, however, consists merely in intending an object, without itself being an object. Consciousness is thus nothing other than its intentional function.

The notion that consciousness is both intentional and translucent leads to his well-known theory that characterizes consciousness as signifying "nothingness". But by "nothingness", Sartre clearly does not mean complete void, but merely lack of content or corporeality. It signifies the contrast with the objective world that is "being". By "being", Sartre does not mean the phenomena of our experience that derive their significance by virtue of their appearance in consciousness. Being refers to "the in-itself" whereas consciousness is a "for-itself".

We understand by nothingness that it lacks content but not that it is unreal. Consciousness is completely transparent; it is not a substance but a form or appearance. "The existence of consciousness," says Sartre, "comes from consciousness itself" (1956: lxvi). There is nonbeing in its being, for it can transcend itself and intend an object. That is why consciousness, unlike objects of experience, is a being-for-itself.

Sartre's psychology of imagination provides a more appropriate context to understand "nothingness" better (Sartre 1948). When we imagine, for example, a book, we do not, according to Sartre, form an image of the book in consciousness. Consciousness is not a container, not a canvas on which the images are imprinted, and not a stage on which images of objects are displayed. Both in imagination, as well as in perception, the object always remains external to consciousness. The difference between the imagination of a book and the perception of it consists in the manner in which we intend the book. When we imagine something, we have an imaginative consciousness of it that reveals at once its non-presence. In perceptual consciousness of the book, we intend its presence. Therefore, the image, perceptual or imaginative, is not an entity, but merely a function of consciousness. Consciousness in signifying "nothingness" is beyond being. Inasmuch as we can go beyond being in our imagination we are able to grasp the synthetic unity and totality of the world.

It is interesting to note that for Sartre consciousness is both intentional and at the same time it has no content. How can consciousness be of something and at the same time be devoid of content? In *The Transcendence of the Ego*, Sartre answers: "Consciousness can be self-conscious only by means of which it is conscious". In Sartre's discussion of consciousness, one may find several contradictory statements. Sometimes he speaks of consciousness as if it is not an autonomous something, but dependent on the objects it reveals. On other occasions he asserts that consciousness is absolute and autonomous, which being a for-itself, cannot be derived from that of objects, the in-itself. When he asserts its autonomy and freedom, consciousness becomes the principle of subjectivity, as in Husserl.

In his introduction to *Being and Nothingness*, we find Sartre describing consciousness as "the first being to whom all other appearances appear . . . ; it is subjectivity itself, the immanence of self itself" (1956: lxvi).

When criticizing Husserl, it is apparent that Sartre falls back on the more restrictive conception of consciousness as not being absolute but dependent on objects. But he himself finds it necessary to use consciousness in a broader sense. The transcendental ego, distinguished from the empirical ego, which is the principle of subjectivity in Husserl's philosophy, is not very different from Sartre's conception of consciousness in its absolute sense. Again, Sartre's *revelatory* function of consciousness is similar to Husserl's *constitutive* function, notwithstanding Sartre's criticism of the latter. In both, it is the intentional nature of consciousness that is stressed as its essential characteristic. Both Husserl and Sartre find it logically necessary to postulate consciousness as a principle of subjectivity to account for the manifest unity, meaning, and significance of the phenomena of our experience, even though Sartre's view of consciousness as "nothingness" goes beyond the epistemological to an ontological formulation.

Our discussion of intentionality has been confined largely to the phenomenological tradition that dealt with intentionality in a metaphysical context. There are, however, other attempts to explain intentionality within the Anglo-American analytic tradition, and cognitive and computational psychology. These attempts are largely influenced by what Quine (1960) called "semantic ascent", which, putting aside the epistemological and metaphysical questions about intentional phenomena, focussed on the analysis of the way we talk about the phenomena.

The intentional view of mind/consciousness entails in some form the representational theory of cognition and knowledge. Whether it is the "input–output" model of cognitive scientists or the more traditional notion that the mind is a mirror of nature, we are led to believe that there is a pre-given world of which our cognitions are representations. Inasmuch as every act of consciousness intends something and every thought has an object, we are inescapably led to the notion of subject–object duality and the known–knower distinction. Even those who are vehemently opposed to such a dichotomy on ontological grounds have difficulty in circumventing the duality of the knower and the known. William James, for example, wrote:

> The attributions subject and object, represented and representative, thing

> and thought, thus signify a practical distinction which is of the utmost importance but which is only of a functional order and is not of an ontological order as classical dualism presents it. In the final analysis things and thoughts are not fundamentally heterogeneous. They are instead made of the same stuff, a stuff which cannot be defined as such, but can only be experienced and which can be called, if one so desires, the stuff of experience in general. — 1912/1947, : 232-33

Thus, while rejecting dualism in its interactionist mode, James locates both mind and matter, the knower and the known, in experience as-such. But what that experience is remains as elusive as the interaction of mind and matter in dualistic postulations. In fact, James is more explicit and concedes some kind of epistemic dualism in *The Principles of Psychology*. "The psychologist's attitude toward cognition . . .," he writes, "is a thoroughgoing dualism. It supposes two elements, mind knowing and thing known, and treats them as irreducible" (1890/1952: 142, original emphasis).

Again, the existential philosopher Sartre, as we noted, observed that consciousness by its very nature is consciousness of things other than itself. The objects of consciousness are characterized as being, the in-itself. Consciousness, the for-itself, is dependent on the objects for being. The being of conscious, according to Sartre, consists in its intentionality, to posit a transcendental object. Sartre wished that the subject–object duality would "disappear from philosophical preoccupations" (Sartre, 1957). But it remains completely mysterious how by being intentional, consciousness transcends itself in relating the knower and the known, as Sartre believed. In distinguishing the conscious self (subject) from the world (object), Sartre creates for himself an inescapable dualism.

The emphasis on the intentionality of consciousness in Western tradition thus highlights, on the one hand, the distinction between subject and object, whether functional or foundational, and entails, on the other hand, a disbelief in consciousness as-such, consciousness devoid of content. If consciousness is inseparable from its phenomenal content, we can have no direct knowledge of the world except through its phenomenal representations. Even those who conceived of transcendental aspects of existence, such as Kant, had to admit that things in themselves are essentially unknowable. The paradox of such veiled existence is no better illustrated than in the philosophy of Husserl.

Mind in Classical Indian Thought

The situation is very different in the Indian tradition. From the Vedic times, we find a clear distinction between mind and consciousness (Chennakesavan 1960/1991). Mind is the instrumentality, the bridge, that connects consciousness (self) and the body. Śrīdhara says in his *Nyāyakandalī* that mind is not consciousness but an instrument of consciousness. Like a jar which is not space but one that constrains space, so does the mind give shape and form to consciousness. The distinction between mind and consciousness is pervasive across the different systems of Hindu philosophy and Jainism.

The situation is somewhat different in Buddhism, as we discussed in the previous chapter, which gives no substantive status to mind and yet the culmination of life in a state of *nirvāṇa* is clearly transcendence of the mind to attain a state of pure consciousness. Intentionality is attributed to mind, and not to consciousness. Mind is that which has thought as its object (Buddhaghoṣa 1920). It is the instrument of cognition. Perhaps it is more appropriate to say that mind is a faculty that grasps an object and causes the cognitive event.

In Nyāya–Vaiśeṣika view, the mind is considered a *dravya* (thing). In both Nyāya and Buddhism, even though the latter rejects the substantive notion of the mind, cognitive activity is a cause–effect process. The mind itself is a series of cognitive events in Buddhist conception, whereas it is a substance, according to Nyāya. Through mind there is self-awareness. All the acquired properties of self are cognized through the mind. Therefore, in a significant sense to equate mind with cognitive mind will give us a truncated view of mind.

Buddhistic psychology is essentially an attempt to understand the nature of transcendence and the methods of attaining it. In Buddhism we find that normal consciousness and the psychological processes associated with it are so organized that they generate a sense of stable and enduring ego, which in turn influences, colors, and even determines our passions, thoughts, and actions. This is the cause of manifest suffering. The person in pursuit of salvation needs to transcend them by achieving a state where the psychological processes lose their ego-reference and thus attain a transpersonal state. Buddhism believes not only in the existence of such a transpersonal ego-less state but also in the possibility of attaining it by following certain practices. By describing the different stages involved in the progress from the normal to the transcendental, transpersonal states,

Buddhism provides us with one of the most interesting and pervasive phenomenologies of consciousness.

The Sāṁkhya–Yoga theory of mind is perhaps more typical of the Indian perspective than Nyāya–Vaiśeṣika or Buddhist theories. We discussed this at some length in Chapter 17. In brief, mind processes information with the available sensory apparatus. *Citta* (mind) is functionally distinguished into *manas* (the central processor), *ahaṁkāra* (the ego or self-referencing function), and *buddhi* (the executive function). *Manas* selectively reflects on the material provided by sensory processing. *Ahaṁkāra* appropriates what is processed and thus the processed material acquires self-reference. *Buddhi* then assimilates the information and reacts in an appropriate way. Up to this point all information is implicit and devoid of conscious awareness. Conscious awareness arises when the mind receives and reflects the light of *puruṣa*. Conscious awareness is subjectively experienced information content of the world of objects and events (phenomena) that are sensorily processed by the mind. It is the image of the world imprinted on the mind and reflected in the light of *puruṣa*. Therefore, the knowledge of the world mediated via the sensory channels is at best a credible image and seldom a direct apprehension of reality as such. The image is a function of the sensory system. If our senses were of a different kind, the image of the world we have would be different. The images are distorted by the processing mechanisms and biased by *buddhi*'s own state, which is influenced by past actions, *karma*, *vāsanā*s (instinctive tendencies), and *saṁskāra*s (subliminal influences). Thus, in the human condition, the way one gathers information and knows the world and of herself (phenomenal awareness) is anything but perfect. Yoga is a determined pursuit to transcend the limitations of phenomenal awareness to achieve higher states of awareness in which awareness is progressively delinked from sensory processing. Patañjali at the very outset states in his *Yoga-Sūtras* that the practice of yoga is to control *vṛtti*s (fluctuating forms) of the mind. When transcendence is achieved, awareness is successfully delinked and dissociated from sensory mode in a state of *samādhi*, which is one of mind's absorptions in consciousness. Transcendence involves achieving a state of pure consciousness or experiencing consciousness as-such. Knowledge obtained in such a state is perfect and beyond falsification and doubt. Such knowledge is indubitable and certain by self-certification. Thus *yoga* practice is believed to lead to a state of *niruddha*, complete control, and transcendence of sense processes that enables one to achieve *kaivalya* (perfection).

While agreeing with Yoga on its theory of cognition, Advaita Vedānta asserts that sensory knowledge is relatively true but not absolutely so. We have discussed this at some length in Chapter 18. Absolute knowledge is possible only when one transcends the sensory involvement and accesses consciousness as-such in a state of transcendence. At the transcendental level of pure consciousness, knowledge is free from empirical distortions. At the empirical level, knowledge is mediated. It is representational and relative. At the level of pure consciousness, it is direct and immediate. It is intuitive apprehension of reality. Here, being and knowing become one. According to Advaita, the goal of human endeavor should be one of gaining absolute freedom from the limiting conditions of empirical existence. Perfect knowledge achieved by realizing states of pure consciousness is the way. Yoga is a recommended means. It is possible to achieve states of transcendence in an embodied condition. Śaṅkara among others subscribed to the concept of *jīvanamukti*, the notion that the mind can be freed from its existential sensory bondage while being in the embodied state. *Jivanamukta* is one who has gained freedom from the constraints of the sense-bound mind and realized pure consciousness in his being.

The metaphysical speculations of Vedānta apart and also leaving aside the questions about which is real and at what level, there appears to be a general agreement among Hindu thinkers that there are indeed two levels of knowing. Knowing at the empirical level does not give absolutely true knowledge, because such knowledge is essentially variable. At this level dissociation between cognition and action, conflict between what one knows and does (as for example, when one knows that smoking is bad but continues to smoke) is possible. Knowing at the transcendental level is, it is assumed, free from empirical distortions. Since the awareness system and the response system are not involved at this level, the possibility of dissociation between their outputs does not exist. At one level, knowledge is mediated; it is direct and immediate at the other level. Freedom is the goal. Perfect knowledge is the way. Meditation is the means.

At this point, it is necessary to recognize that Sāṁkhya–Yoga–Vedānta views do not exhaust between themselves all the salient ideas concerning mind and consciousness in Hindu thought. It would be misleading to think otherwise. Even though they represent the dominant trend in the Indian tradition, there are equally important epistemological and metaphysical viewpoints. The contributions of Nyāya and Vaiśeṣika systems are specially noteworthy in this context — Nyāya from an epistemological perspective and Vaiśeṣika from a metaphysical viewpoint. Nyāya views are in the dualist tradition, but different in important respects from Cartesian dualism. (For an extensive discussion of Nyāya theory of mind and consciousness see K.K. Chakrabarti 1999 and B.K. Matilal 2002.)

In line with the Indian tradition, Nyāya–Vaiśeṣika thinkers regard mind as physical, but "physical" not in the ordinary sense of being material. It is subtle and non-materially physical. In fact, one could argue that the mind is neither physical in the sense that the body is physical, nor non-physical like consciousness and that it belongs to a third category. Different in essentials from the physical substance is the self or soul, which is non-physical. Self in Nyāya–Vaiśeṣika is like *puruṣa* in Sāṁkhya–Yoga except that it is not consciousness itself. It is the substratum of consciousness, like matter is the substratum of all qualities that physical objects manifest. Consciousness is not intrinsic, but adventitious. It is a quality of the self that manifests under conditions of self's contact with the mind. Thus unlike in Advaita and Sāṁkhya, consciousness in Nyāya–Vaiśeṣika is not a substance but an attribute of self. This is an important difference; significant metaphysical and epistemological discussions ensue from it. However, what is important from our perspective is the assertion of Nyāya thinkers that consciousness requires a non-physical substance for its manifestation and that it does not inhere as a quality of physical substance. Also, "consciousness" in Nyāya is more like empirical consciousness in Advaita, which manifests as intentional awareness. Pure consciousness, however, is entirely devoid of any empirical qualities, which are indeed adventitious and arise in association with the physical mind. Therefore, the differences between Sāṁkhya–Yoga–Vedānta on the one hand and Nyāya–Vaiśeṣika on the other do not appear crucial and fundamental to substantially alter what we have attempted to describe as the Hindu tradition.

The above observation is further reinforced when we consider Nyāya–Vaiśeṣika views on yogic perception or the supernormal abilities of *yogin*s. As Śrīdhara the author of *Nyāyakandalī* points out, disciplined and prolonged meditation enables one to enter a state of *samādhi* where one has super-sensuous knowledge. Another Nyāya thinker Praśastapāda divides yogic perception into two kinds. In the higher kind of *samādhi, yogin*s are able to have knowledge of not only of their selves, but also of others. They achieve a kind of omniscience. In them only the mind is operative and the sensory functions are held in abeyance. The Navya-Nyāya thinkers consider the *yogin* in the state of *samādhi* as one who has attained union with the Supreme Being. This does not seem to be very different from the notion of realization of pure consciousness in Advaita and Yoga. Again, Śrīdhara accepts the distinction between *samprajñāta* (determinate) and *asamprajñāta* (indeterminate) states of *samādhi*. (See the chapter on super-normal perceptions in J. Sinha 1958, vol. 1). Such a distinction clearly leads to the presupposition of pure conscious states.

Pure Consciousness and Phenomenal Consciousness

The emphasis on pure consciousness in the Eastern tradition does not preclude consideration of the intentional aspects of conscious phenomena. In the Indian tradition, as mentioned, intentionality may be considered as a characteristic of the mind, but not of consciousness as-such. The mind experiences *viṣayin* and *viṣaya* (subject–object) duality in its normal states of cognition and action. In transcendental states, however, consciousness is seen as manifesting in its pure form where there is no object to which consciousness is directed and where no awareness of subject–object duality is experienced. Interestingly, in the Indian tradition, knowledge can be obtained in both the intentional and non-intentional modes; only that which is gained in the latter is considered the highest, pure, and unbiased.

According to Patañjali (Woods 1927), the mind is a continuous stream of fluctuating modes called *vṛttis*. Conscious experience mediated by the mind via its *vṛttis* is phenomenal awareness. Phenomenal awareness involves three distinguishable aspects — (a) the subject, the one who has the awareness (*grāhī*), (b) the process of awareness (*grahaṇa*), and (c) the object of awareness (*grāhya*). All three determine the nature and content of awareness. For example, the sensory processes have their own imprint on what is known. Similarly, our predispositions, the biases and prejudices color cognitions and influence our actions. Consequently, it makes sense to think that phenomenal awareness is at best a *representation* of reality subject to all kinds of limitations and distortions, and that it cannot therefore be a true experience of reality *per se*.

Experience of pure consciousness unmediated by any mental modes is, in the Indian tradition, transcendental awareness. Such awareness is believed to be supreme in the sense it is completely unbiased. Knowledge mediated by mental functions is regarded as imperfect because the mind by its very nature has a distorting and biasing influence. Therefore, it is held that perfect knowledge can be obtained only in an experience of pure consciousness which, according to the tradition, is facilitated by voluntary restraining of all mental functions through appropriate discipline.

For example, the practice of *yoga* is believed to lead to *samādhi*, a state in which the knower progressively merges with the known. By advancing through a series of *samādhi* states one experiences pure consciousness.

Despite many important differences in their philosophical doctrines, all the six orthodox Indian philosophical systems seem to agree on the ultimate goal of all human endeavors which is one of achieving such a liberated state of perfection. They also agree that the essential means of achieving this state is one of practicing the methods described in the *Yoga-Sūtras*.

It should be noted, however, that in some systems of philosophy such as Buddhism no sharp distinction is made between consciousness and mind. But, then, in those systems various forms of consciousness are distinguished and some of the forms correspond to what is termed mind in other systems. For example, Buddhaghoṣa — whose *Visuddhimagga* is an important text of Theravāda Buddhism — defines consciousness as "that which thinks of its object". In this sense consciousness is synonymous with mind. Buddhaghoṣa also describes advanced states of meditation in which the practitioners attain non-intentional states of consciousness. Such concepts as *lokottara citta* clearly refer to non-intentional states of consciousness. Again, Nāgārjuna, an outstanding thinker of Mādhyamika Buddhism, emphasized the *Abhidhamma* distinction between *saṁvr̥tti* (empirical) and *paramārtha* (transcendental). The latter correspond to consciousness as-such where no subject–object distinctions exist. (For a detailed discussion of mind and consciousness in different systems of Indian philosophy see Panda 1994; Chennakesavan 1991; Saksena 1944.)

However, the various practices described in Buddhaghoṣa's *Visuddhimagga* are not very different from those we find in yoga (Rao 1988). There is a great deal of similarity between the meditation practices advocated by Yoga and Buddhism. The yogic *samādhi* and the Buddhist *jhāna* have much in common, including their progressive nature to achieve a transperceptual state of consciousness in which the realization of perfect knowledge and understanding is believed to be possible.

Husserl and Yoga

There are clearly some striking similarities between what is said above about the Eastern perspective and Husserl's reductive phenomenology. As we have seen, Husserl's goal is to obtain "*apodictic* evidence" which entails absolute indubitability. Such knowledge can be obtained only when one, in the words of Husserl, is in a *universe of absolute freedom from prejudice*.

We can agree that it is possible to place oneself in such a universe by practicing the procedure he described as *epoché*, which brackets the "natural attitude", and that such a practice enables one to understand intuitively the contents of consciousness experienced internally, and that the intuitive experience so generated is what gives us the essence of the object in our consciousness.

Several scholars have already called attention to the similarities between Husserl's method and yogic meditation. (For an interesting discussion of similarities between Husserl and Yoga, see Paranjpe and Hanson 1988; Puligandla 1970; Sinari 1965.)

Clearly, the *yogī* is also in search of perfect knowledge that is self-validating and is based on no suppositions. Whereas the phenomenological *epoché* remains essentially a theoretical speculation and at best a logical exercise, it is claimed for yogic techniques that they are capable of freeing one from all previously held attitudes and other hindrances and eventually leading to intuitive, direct grasp of reality. Heidegger perhaps was attempting to do something similar in advocating our going beyond "bracketing" to hidden meaning.

In addition to the three essential stages of *dhāraṇā* (concentration), *dhyāna* (meditation), and *samādhi* (absorption), yoga, as we noted, has five preparatory steps that include moral observances (*yama* and *niyama*) and physical exercises (*āsana* and *prāṇāyāma*) which enable the practitioner to control bodily disturbances, desires, and emotions that distract the mind from the practice of one-pointed concentration. The fifth preparatory state is focussing internal attention (*pratyāhāra*). As Puligandla (1970) points out:

> The function of *pratyāhāra* is to detach the sense-organ from the mind, thus cutting it off from the external world and the sense-impressions it produces on the mind. The subject's mind is now completely isolated from the world and is therefore ready to practice concentration and meditation without any distractions, bodily or mental. This preparatory stage is, the yogic counterpart of phenomenological *epoché*, the act of suspending the natural attitude. Freed from all kinds of hindrances, be they beliefs, desires, emotions, theories, or feelings, the mind now is in a position to direct full attention to any object whatever and grasp it in its primordiality. But before the subject can arrive at the imaginary or primordial intuition, he has to pass through three stages of concentration, namely, *dhāraṇā*, *dhyāna*, and *samādhi*, the last three *aṅga*s of Patañjali's yoga.

The essence of yoga is *saṁyama*. *Saṁyama* involves the triple effort of *dhāraṇā*, *dhyāna*, and *samādhi*. *Samādhi* is a state of meditation in which there is the awareness of the object alone, without any awareness of the self. With the suspension of self-awareness and complete absorption in the object of meditation, the practitioner achieves a state of being that enables one to grasp the essence of the objects of his/her focus, to know the things in their intrinsic state without the biasing influence of the senses and the presuppositions. In addition, we are told that a variety of supernormal phenomena manifest when the triple effort of *saṁyama* (concentration, meditation, and absorption) is directed at select things. These extraordinary experiences appear anomalous to those who never experienced that state. The final point of the *yogin*'s progress is, however, beyond this; and it is to achieve liberation from all constraints so that one may realize pure consciousness.

"Husserlean yoga", the *epoché*, unlike Patañjali's Yoga, falls short of reaching its logical end of realizing pure consciousness. Husserl criticized Descartes for not carrying his method of universal doubt to its conclusion. It would seem that Husserl himself did no better and became equally a victim of his own presupposition. In assuming that consciousness is always intentional, he ruled out the possibility of experiencing pure consciousness as-such. Husserl believed that the phenomenological intuition gives us the essence of things, a possibility ruled out by Kant. It is not clear, however, how such an intuition is possible on rational grounds without making some basic assumptions as in Yoga. It would seem that phenomenologists, by treating Husserl's method as a logico-epistemological tool rather than a practical method, tended to regard intuition as an intellectual abstraction, an outcome of reflection, rather than a genuine experience. By failing to appreciate the possibility that transcendental subjectivity goes beyond suspending the natural attitude, the Husserlean method stops in practice with the *pratyāhāra* stage, as it were.

Puligandla notes, "whereas phenomenology merely talks of bracketing, ideating, and performing reduction, Patañjali's yoga provides a stepwise procedure for actually accomplishing them" (1970: 33). In fact, yoga does more. It is believed to lead one to the realization of pure consciousness, a transcognitive state, which alone is regarded as capable of giving absolutely certain, direct, and self-validating knowledge. If pure consciousness exists, as the Indian theories postulate, it cannot be known through the normal sensory processes or their variants. It can only be *realized* in a very special way as the *yogins* and seers testify.

Complimentarity of Eastern and Western Perspectives

The preceding discussion of Yoga and Husserl suggests that the Eastern and Western perspectives on consciousness are not necessarily alternative approaches. They may be seen as emphasizing one aspect to the neglect of the other. Taken separately their understanding of consciousness is thus incomplete. Consciousness clearly has two domains — the transcendental and the phenomenal. Humans enjoy dual citizenship in them. In the Western scientific tradition the concern has been almost exclusively with the phenomenal aspects of conscious experience. Total confinement to this domain robs human nature of its essential aspects. The Eastern tradition does not deny our extensive involvement in the phenomenal world, which is all too obvious, but takes a stance emphasizing that it is morally imperative and epistemologically necessary that we go beyond the phenomenal realm to experience the transcendental.

Inasmuch as we actually live in the phenomenal world, our understanding of it is necessary not merely to render that experience more enjoyable but also to realize higher levels. The other-wordly emphasis in the Eastern tradition creates in a sense an artificial discontinuity between the two realms of our being. The two realms may be seen to coexist, each having a necessary function. One need not leave the body to have transcendental experience. The manifestation of paranormal events in normally functioning human beings in the so-called anomalous phenomena is an indication of such a possibility. Therefore, it would seem that a recognition of the complementarity of the Eastern and Western traditions may give us a more wholesome understanding of the nature of consciousness and its role in our being.

In fact, in some of the Buddhistic traditions we find an orderly transition without a break from the phenomenal awareness of the world to transcendental consciousness, a progress brought about by mental and moral discipline. The *Abhidhamma* text and the commentaries describe, for example, eighty-nine classes of consciousness according to their mental properties, ranging from the mundane in the *kāmaloka*, the natural world of desires and aversion, to the sublime and transcendental in the state of *nibbāna* (De Silva 1988; also Rao 1988).

For those growing up in the Western scientific tradition and interested in consciousness studies, an understanding of the Eastern perspective as complementary to their own, may, I believe, prove heuristic and may even suggest new models. The following are a few such possibilities.

The understanding that consciousness and the mind are distinct overcomes the untenable distinction between consciousness and the unconscious, as awareness characterizes both. Consciousness as awareness in the broader sense includes explicit as well as implicit awareness. Therefore, no fundamental distinction between consciousness and the unconscious can be sustained. Similarly the attempts to restrict consciousness to focal attention or reflective awareness, i.e., awareness accessible to introspection, and to regard the mind as broader to include implicit awareness and the unconscious processes (Farthing 1992) is unsatisfactory. If the mind and consciousness are synonymous, as is generally assumed in the Western tradition, the mind can have no extra connotation that consciousness does not have. Alternatively, if the mind and consciousness are separate and have distinct functions, as believed to be the case in the Eastern tradition, they are no longer mere descriptive terms to connote two levels of mentation.

The question then is whether consciousness is merely a quality of the mind as implied in the notion that equates it with focal attention or whether mental phenomena as they manifest in our experience involve an independent factor without which experience of awareness is not possible. The Eastern perspective suggests the latter and leads us to regard consciousness as that which makes awareness possible in the human condition. In other words, cortical processes alone cannot give us subjective awareness.

If consciousness is an autonomous principle irreducible to material forms, we may ask, how is it then different from the mind as postulated in Western dualistic doctrines? As pointed out earlier, mind and consciousness are not distinguished in the Western tradition, leading to the well-known difficulties of mind–body interaction. In the Eastern formulations, where a distinction is made between consciousness and the mind, we are led to a conception of mind as an interface between consciousness and the brain made possible by certain characteristics attributed to the mind that are akin to consciousness, e.g., the *sattva* component in Sāṁkhya system. This suggests that there might be some value in looking for new forms of matter and material functioning to resolve traditional puzzles of the mind–body relation. It is interesting to note that in recent years a few scholars in the Western scientific tradition, who are dissatisfied with all attempts to reductively explain consciousness in familiar physical terms, appear to be embarking on a similar course (Penrose 1994a; Chalmers 1996).

It is in line with the Cartesian legacy of mind–body duality that the Western philosophical discourse is replete with disparate conceptual oppositions and difficult disjunctive categorizations such as subject–object, physical–mental, and so on. The nature of the opposition between them is such that the assertion of one implies the negation of the other. Thus, physical implies non-mental, and mental implies non-physical; the object implies non-subject, and so on. What is of special interest is that these categorizations are shared irrespective of one's philosophical affiliations, for example, whether one is a dualist or a materialist. John Searle (1992) has complained repeatedly how this Cartesian mindset is at the base of the misunderstandings of his own ideas by other philosophers.

The Eastern conception of mind as the interface and gateway between consciousness and the objective world, I am persuaded, frees us from the compulsions of such disjunctive categorizations as mentioned above. Mind in the Eastern tradition is the instrumentality of our experience; it is our reality connection. When it connects with the objective world, we have phenomenal awareness. When the connection is to consciousness, we have transcendental realization. We make an important distinction here between states of awareness and realization. While experiencing *awareness* it is possible to have a dissociation between cognition and conduct. One may have knowledge, but that knowledge may not determine conduct. One may believe, for example, that telling a lie is bad, and still continue to lie. A state of *realization* is one where there is no room for such dissociation. Knowing and being become inseparable. The lives of true saints and those who had genuine near-death experiences may perhaps illustrate such instances of realization which have immediate transformative consequences. Accessing consciousness as-such, i.e. achieving a transcendental state, would have a remarkable impact on one's life. Such a transformational possibility has important implications for our conduct and well-being. The implications of such a claim to psychotherapy are all too obvious.

Now, contrast this with the dualism of Descartes, where mind is consciousness and is non-physical. How then do mind and the physical body interact? We all know how unsatisfactory are the attempts to answer this question. The essential feature of the mind, according to Descartes, is consciousness and consciousness is thought. Indeed it is self-evident that one cannot doubt that he is doubting; but can one doubt without the brain? If the brain is necessary for thought and awareness, how can thought be the essence of consciousness? Inasmuch as experience manifests at the phenomenal as well as transcendental levels, there is need for a concept like mind distinct from consciousness as-such, which can be the bridge.

We should keep in perspective that the Eastern model is not presented as a mere intellectual abstraction but as an empirical claim. The entire gamut of yogic tradition and a variety of psychic development disciplines in the East are based on that claim. Therefore, the question of whether consciousness as-such really exists should not be settled on mere theoretical grounds, because pure consciousness is not a logical presupposition, its existence is considered a fact of experience, a realization in one's own being. The Eastern tradition is replete with instances of those who are believed to have achieved states of pure consciousness and it is clearly an important source for finding techniques and strategies for accessing consciousness *qua* consciousness.

To conclude, we discussed two dominant perspectives on consciousness representing the Eastern and the Western viewpoints. In the Western scholarly tradition, (a) consciousness is generally equated with the mind; (b) intentionality is regarded as its defining characteristic; and (c) the goal is one of seeking rational understanding of what consciousness/mind is. In the Eastern tradition, as represented by the Indian approach to the study of consciousness, (a) consciousness and mind are considered to be different; (b) consciousness as-such is believed to be non-intentional while the mind is regarded as intentional; and (c) the goal is one of developing practical methods for transformation of the human condition via realization of consciousness as-such.

It is suggested that consciousness encompasses two different domains, the transcendental and the phenomenal, and that humans enjoy dual citizenship in them. The Eastern and Western viewpoints each seems to be directed more towards one domain than the other, resulting in a biased emphasis. Seen as complementary rather than in opposition to each other, the Eastern and the Western perspectives may give us a more comprehensive understanding of consciousness and its role in our being. Further, the Indian perspective offers significant possibilities for cultivating consciousness in human condition for enhancing human potential and wellness.

About the Contributors

Alfred S. Alschuler, Ph.D., Reich College of Education, Appalachian State University, Boone, North Carolina

Stephen E. Braude, Ph.D., Department of Philosophy, University of Maryland, Baltimore, Maryland

Jean E. Burns, Ph.D., Consciousness Research, San Leandro, California

Brenda J. Dunne, M.A., Manager, Engineering Anomalies Research, Princeton University, Princeton, New Jersey

David R. Griffin, Ph.D., School of Theology at Claremont University, Claremont, California

Michael Grosso, Ph.D., Jersey City State College, Jersey City, New Jersey

Willis W. Harman, Ph.D., President, Institute of Noetic Sciences, Sausalito, California

Thomas J. Hurley III, Ph.D., Senior Research Associate, Institute of Noetic Sciences, Sausalito, California

Robert G. Jahn, Ph.D., Professor of Aerospace Sciences, Princeton University, Princeton, New Jersey

Claiborne Pell, was US Senator and Chairman, Foreign Relations Committee, U.S. Senate, Washington, D.C.

K. Ramakrishna Rao, Ph.D., D.Litt., Chancellor, GITAM University, Visakhapatnam, India

Neil Rossman, Ph.D., F. H. LaGuardia Community College, City University of New York, Flushing, New York

Beverly Rubik, Ph.D., Director, Center for Frontier Sciences, Temple University, Philadelphia, Pennsylvania

T. M. Srinivasan, Ph.D., Svyasa University, Bengaluru, India

Charles T. Tart, Ph.D., Department of Psychology, University of California, Davis, California

Eugene Taylor, Ph.D., Department of Psychiatry, Harvard Medical School, Boston, Massachusetts

Bibliography

Achterberg, J. (1985), *Imagery and Healing: Shamanism and Modern Medicine*, Boston: Shambhala.

Adey, W.R. and Lawrence, A.F. (eds.) (1884), *Nonlinear Electrodynamics in Biological Systems*, New York: Plenum Press.

Allport, G. (1955), *Becoming: Basic Considerations for a Psychology of Personality*, New Haven: Yale University Press.

Andrews, C.S. (1991), "Promoting Health and Well-being Through a Sense of Connectedness", *Frontier Perspectives*, 1(2): 18-20. Philadelphia: Center for Frontier Sciences, Temple University.

Armstrong, D.M. (1968), *A Materialistic Theory of the Mind*, London: Routledge.

——— (1980), *The Nature of Mind and Other Essays*, Ithaca, NY: Cornell University Press.

Armstrong, D.M. and Malcolm, N. (1984), *Consciousness and Causality: A Debate on the Nature of Mind*, Oxford: Basil Blackwell.

Aung, S.Z. (tr.), (1929), *Compendium of Philosophy*, London: Oxford University Press.

Baars, B.J. (1988), *A Cognitive Theory of Consciousness*, New York: Cambridge University Press.

Balyuzi, H.M. (1980), *Baha'u'llah: King of Glory*, Oxford: George Ronald.

Barber, T.X., Spanos, N.P. and Chaves, J.C. (1974), *Hypnosis, Imagination and Human Potentialities*, New York: Pergamon Press.

Barinaga, M. (1990), "Research News: The Mind Revealed?", *Science*, **249**: 856-58.

Barker, J.C. (1968), *Scared to Death*, London: Muller.

Bernard, T. (1947), *Hindu Philosophy*, Delhi: Motilal Banarsidass.

Barnette, L. (1975), *The Universe and Dr. Einstein* (rev. edn.), New York: Bantam.

Bass, L. (1975), "A quantum Mechanical Mind–body Interaction", *Foundations of Physics*, **5**: 159-72.

Bateson, G. (1979), *Mind and Nature: A Necessary Unity*, New York: Dutton.

Baumrind, D. (1980), "New Directions in Socialization Research", *American Psychologist*, **35**(7): 639-52.

Becker, R.O. (1975), "Electrochemical Mechanisms and Control of Biological Growth Processes", in J.O. Bockris and B.E. Conway (eds.) *Modern Aspects of Electrochemistry*, pp. 289-338, New York: Plenum Press.

——— (1990), *Cross Currents: The Promise of Electromedicine, the Perils of Electropollution*, Los Angeles: Tarcher.

Beloff, J. (1977), "Psi Phenomena: Causal Versus Acausal Interpretation", *Journal of the Society for Psychical Research*, **49** (773): 573-82.

——— (1979), "Voluntary Movement, Biofeedback Control and PK", in B. Shapiro and L. Coly (eds.) *Brain/Mind and Parapsychology: Proceedings of an International Conference*, pp. 99-115, New York: Parapsychology Foundation.

——— (1989), "Dualism: A Parapsychological Perspective", in J. Smythies and J. Beloff (eds.) *The Case for Dualism*, pp. 167-85, Charlottesville, VA: University Press of Virginia.

Benedikt, M. (ed.) (1991), *Cyberspace: First Steps*, Cambridge: MIT Press.

Bernard, T. (1947), *Hindu Philosophy*, Delhi: Motilal Banarsidass.

Bhattacharyya, K.C. (1909), *Studies in Vedantism*, Calcutta: Calcutta University Press.

——— (1930), *The Subject as Freedom*, Amalner, India: Indian Institute of Philosophy.

Birch, C. (1988), "The Postmodern Challenge in Biology", in D.R. Griffin (ed.) *The Re-enchantment of Science*, pp. 69-78, Albany: State University of New York Press.

Blackman, C.F., Benane, S.G., House, D.E. and Elliott, D.J. (1990), "Importance of Alignment Between Local DC Magnetic Field and an Oscillating Magnetic Field in Responses of Brain Tissue in vitro and in vivo", *Bioelectromagnetics*, **11**(2): 159-67.

Bohm, D. (1982), *Wholeness and the Implicate Order*, London: Routledge and Kegan Paul.

Bohr, N. (1961), *Atomic Theory and the Description of Nature*, Cambridge: Cambridge University Press.

Borg, W.R. and Borg, M.D. (1989), *Educational Research: An Introduction* (5th edn.), New York: Longman.

Bornstein, R.F. (1989), "Exposure and Affect: Overview and Meta-analysis of Research, 1968-1987", *Psychological Bulletin*, **106**: 265-89.

Bornstein, R.F. and Pittman, T.S. (ed.), (1992), *Perception without Awareness: Cognitive, Clinical, and Social Perspectives*, New York: Guilford Press.

Braude, S.E. (1979), *ESP and Psychokinesis: A Philosophical Examination*, Philadelphia: Temple University Press.

——— (1983), "Radical Provincialism in the Life Sciences: A Review of Rupert Sheldrake's *A New Science of Life*", *Journal of the American Society for Psychical Research*, **77**: 63-78.

——— (1986), *The Limits of Influence: Psychokinesis and the Philosophy of Science*, New York: Routledge & Kegan Paul.

Braun, B.G. (1986), *Treatment of Multiple Personality Disorder*, Washington, DC: American Psychiatric Press.

Brentano, F. (1973/1925), *Psychology from an Empirical Standpoint* (tr. A.C. Rancurello), New York: Humanities Press.

Broad, C.D. (1963), "Two Lectures on the Nature of Philosophy", in H.D. Lewis (ed.) *Clarity Is Not Enough*, pp. 42-75, London: George Allen & Unwin.

Buddhaghoṣa (1920), *Aṭṭhasālinī (The Expositor)*, 2 vols. (tr. M. Tin), London: Oxford University Press.

——— (1923), *Visuddhimagga* (*The Path of Purity*), 3 vols. (tr. M. Tin), London: Oxford University Press.

Buber, M. (1985), *Ecstatic Confessions*, San Francisco: Harper & Row.

Bunyan, J. (1938), *Pilgrim's Progress*, New York: American Tract Society.

Burns, J. (1981), *Your Innate Psychic Powers*, London: Sphere.

——— (1986), "Consciousness and Psi", *Psi Research*, 5: 166-205.

——— (1990), "Cotemporary Models of Consciousness: Part", I. *Journal of Mind and Behavior*, **11**: 153-72.

——— (1991), Cotemporary Models of Consciousness: Part II", *Journal of Mind and Behavior*, **12**: 407-20.

——— (1993), "Four Questions About the Relationship Between Consciousness and the Physical World", *Proceedings of the First International Conference on the Study of Consciousness Within Science.*

Bursen, H.A. (1978), *Dismantling the Memory Machine*, London: D. Reidel.

Byrd, R.C. (1988), "Positive Therapeutic Effects of Intercessory Prayer in a Coronary Care Unit Population", *Southern Medical Journal*, **81**(7): 826-29.

Cairns, J., J. Overbaugh and S. Miller (1988), "The Origin of Mutations", *Nature*, **335:** 142-45.

Campbell, D.T. (1974), "Downward Causation in Hierarchically Organized Biological Systems", in F. Ayala and T. Dobzhansky (eds.) *Studies on the Philosophy of Biology*, Berkeley: University of California Press.

——— (1984), *Body and Mind* (2nd edn.), Notre Dame: University of Notre Dame Press.

Cannon, W.B. (1942), "Voodoo Death", *American Anthropologist*, **44**: 169-81.

Careri, G. (1984), *Order and Disorder in Matter*, Menlo Park, CA: Benjamin/ Cummings.

Chakrabarti, K.K. (1999), *Classical Indian Philosophy of Mind: The Nyaya Dualist Tradition*, New York: State University of New York.

Chalmers, D.J. (1996), *The Conscious Mind: In Search of a Fundamental Theory*, New York: Oxford University Press.

Cheisman, J. and Merikle, P.M. (1984), "Priming With and Without Awareness", *Perception and Psychophysics*, **36**: 387-95.

——— (1985), "Word recognition and Consciousness", in D. Besner, T.G. Waller, and G.E. MacKinnon (eds.) *Reading Research: Advances in Theory and Practice*, vol. 5, pp. 311-52, New York: Academic Press.

Chennakesavan, S. (1991), *Concept of Mind in Indian Philosophy*, 2nd rev. edn., Delhi: Motilal Banarsidass.

Chethimattam, J.B. (1971), *Consciousness and Reality*, London: Geoffrey Chapman.

Chopra, D. (1989), *Quantum Healing*, New York: Bantam.

Chopra, D. (1991), *Unconditional Life*, New York: Bantam.

Cobb, J.B. Jr. (1967), *The Structure of Christian Existence*, Philadelphia: Westminster.

Consciousness Technology: A Consumers' Guide (1990), *MEGABRAIN Report*, Spring Sausalito, CA.

Conze, E. (1954/1995), *Buddhist Texts Through the Ages*, Oxford: One World.

Conze, E. (1969), *Buddhist Meditation*, New York: Harper and Row.

Cousins, N. (1983), *The Healing Heart: Antidotes to Panic and Helplessness*, New York: W.W. Norton & Co.

Curtayne, A. (1930), *Saint Catherine of Sienna*, New York: Macmillan & Co.

Dasgupta, S.N. (1922/1963), *A History of Indian Philosophy*, vol.1. Cambridge: Cambridge University Press.

Dasgupta, S. (1930), *Yoga Philosophy in Relation to Other Systems of Indian Thought*, Calcutta: University of Calcutta.

——— (1957), *A History of Indian Philosophy*, vol. 2, Cambridge, UK: Cambridge University Press.

——— (1988), *A History of Indian Philosophy*, 5 vols., Delhi: Motilal Banarsidass (first published in 1922).

Davids, C.A.F.R. (ed. and tr.), (1923), *A Buddhist Manual of Psychological Ethics*, London: Royal Asiatic Society.

——— (tr.), (1963), *Milindapañha (The Questions of King Milinda)*, New York: Dover Publications.

Davies, P. (1987), "The Creative Cosmos", *New Scientist*, 17 December: 41-44.

De Caussade, J.P. (1975), *Abandonment to Divine Providence*, New York: Image Books.

Deikman, A.J. (1963), "Experimental Meditation", *Journal of Nervous and Mental Disorders*, **136**, 329-73.

——— (1966), "Deautomatization and the Mystical Experience", *Psychiatry*, **29**: 324-38.

Del Guidice, E. (1991), "Orthodox and Heretical Orthodoxies", *Frontier Perspectives*, **2**(2): 25-27.

Del Guidice, E. and Preparata, G. (1990), "Superradiance: A New Approach to Coherent Dynamical Behaviors of Condensed Matter", *Frontier Perspectives*, **1**(2): 16-17.

Descartes, R. (1969/1911), *The Philosophical Works of Descartes* (tr. E.S. Haldane and G.R.T. Ross), Cambridge: Cambridge University Press.

——— (n.d.), *Discourse on Method: Metaphysical Meditations* (tr. G.B. Rawlings), London: Walter Scott.

De Silva, C.L.A. (1988), *A Treatise on Buddhistic Philosophy or Abhidhamma*, Delhi: Sri Satguru Publications.

Dharmarajadhvarindra (1942), *Vedanta-paribhasa* (tr. S.S. Sastry), Madras: Adayar Library.

Dixon, N.F. (1979), *Subliminal Perception: The Nature of Controversy*, London: McGraw-Hill.

Dubrov, A.P. (1978), *The Geomagnetic Field and Life: Geomagnetobiology*, New York: Plenum Press.

Dunne, B.J. (1991), *Co-operator Experiments with an REG Device* (Technical Note PEAR 91005), Princeton Engineering Anomalies Research, Princeton University, School of Engineering/Applied Science.

Dunne, B.J., Dobyns, Y.H. and Intner, S.M. (1989), *Precognitive Remote Perception III: Complete Binary Data Base with Analytical Refinements* (Technical Note PEAR 89002), Princeton Engineering Anomalies Research, Princeton University, School of Engineering/Applied Science.

Dunne, B.J. and Jahn, R.G. (1991), *Experiments in Remote Human/Machine Interaction* (Technical Note PEAR 91003), Princeton Engineering Anomalies Research, Princeton University, School of Engineering/Applied Science.

Dunne, B.J., Jahn, R.G. and Nelson, R.D. (1983), *Precognitive Remote Perception* (Technical Note PEAR 83003), Princeton Engineering Anomalies Research, Princeton University, School of Engineering/Applied Science.

Eccles, J.C. (1976), "Brain and Free Will", in G.G. Globus, G. Maxwell, and I. Savodnik (eds.) *Consciousness and the Brain: A Scientific and Philosophical Inquiry*, pp. 101-21, New York: Plenum Press.

——— (1977), "The Human Person in Its Two-way Relationship to the brain", in J.D. Morris, W.G. Roll, and R.L. Morris (eds.) *Research in Parapsychology*, 1976, pp. 251-62, Metuchen, NJ: Scarecrow.

——— (1990), "A Unitary Hypothesis of Mind–brain Interaction in the Cerebral Cortex", *Proceedings of the Royal Society of London B*, 240: 433-51.

Eccles, J.C. and Robinson, D. (1984), *The Wonder of Being Human: Our Brain and Our Mind*, New York: Free Press.

Einstein, A. (1956), *Out of My Later Years* (rev. edn.), Secaucus, NJ: The Citadel Press.

Eisenbud, J. (1970), *Psi and Psychoanalysis*, New York: Grune & Stratton.

Eliade, M. (1960), *Myths, Dreams, and Mysteries* (tr. P. Mairet), New York: Harper & Row.

——— (1969), *Yoga: Immortality and Freedom*, Bollingon Series LVI, Princeton, NJ: Princeton University Press.

Ewen, S. (1988), *All-Consuming Images: The Politics of Style in Contemporary Culture*, New York: Basic Books.

Farthing, G.W. (1992), *The Psychology of Consciousness*, Englewood Cliffs, NJ: Prentice Hall.

Feigl, H. (1967), *The Mental and the Physical*, Minneapolis: University of Minnesota Press.

Ferenczi, S. (1956), "Some Clinical Observations on Paranoia and Paraphrenia", in S. Ferenczi (ed.) *Sex in Psychoanalysis*, New York: Dover.

Fisch, M. and T. Bergin (tr.) (1976), *The New Science of Giambattista Vico*, Ithaca: Cornell University Press (original work published in 1948).

Forwald, H. (1959), "An Experimental Study Suggesting a Relationship Between Psychokinesis and Nuclear Conditions of Matter", *Journal of Parapsychology*, **23**: 97-125.

Frank, J. (1971), *Persuasion and Healing*, New York: Schocken.

Freeman, W.J. (1991), "The Physiology of Perception", *Scientific American*, February: 78-85.

Freud, S. (1915), *The Unconscious*, in standard edition of *The Complete Psychological Works of Sigmund Freud*, vol. 14 (ed. J. Strachey), London: Hogarth.

Frey-Rohn, L. (1990/1974), *From Freud to Jung: Comparative Study of the Psychology of the Unconscious*, Boston, MA: Shambhala.

Gallup Organization (1984), "Princeton Religious Center", *Emerging Trends*, **7**(5): 1.

Gauḍapāda Ācārya and Rapheal (2002), *Māṇḍūkya-Kārikā: The Metaphysical Path of Vedānta*, New York: Aurea Vidya Foundation.

Gilinsky, A.S. (1984), *Mind and Brain: Principles of Neuropsychology*, New York: Praeger.

Globus, G.G., Maxwell, G. and I. Savodnik (eds.) (1976), *Consciousness and the Brain: A Scientific and Philosophical Inquiry*, New York: Plenum Press.

Goldberg, B. (1982), "Mechanism and Meaning", in C. Ginet and S. Shoemaker (eds.) *Knowledge and Mind*, pp. 191-210, Oxford: Oxford University Press.

Goleman, D. (1985), *Vital Lies, Simple Truths: The Psychology of Self-Deception*, New York: Simon & Schuster.

Goodwin, B.C. (1987), "A Science of Qualities", in B.J. Hiley and F.D. Peat (eds.) *Quantum Implications: Festschrift for David Bohm*, London: Routledge & Kegan Paul.

Goswami, A. (1986), "The Quantum Theory of Consciousness and Psi", *Psi Research*, **5**: 145-65.

——— (1989), "The Idealistic Interpretation of Quantum Mechanics", *Physics Essays*, **2**: 385-400.

——— (1990), "Consciousness in Quantum Physics and the Mind–body Problem", *Journal of Mind and Behavior*, **11**: 75-96.

Gould, S.J. (1982), "Darwinism and the Expansion of Evolutionary Theory", *Science*, **216**: 380-87.

Gray, C.M., König, P., Engel, A.K. and Singer, W. (1989), "Oscillatory Responses in Cat Visual Cortex Exhibit Inter-columnar Synchronization Which Reflects Global Stimulus Properties", *Nature*, **338**: 334-37.

Greeley, A.M. and McCready, W.C. (1975), "Are We a Nation of Mystics?" *New York Times Magazine*, 26 January: 12.

Greenwald, A.G. (1992), "New Look 3: Unconscious Cognition Reclaimed", *American Psychologist*, **47**: 766-79.

Grene, M. (1987), "Hierarchies in Biology", *American Scientist*, **75**: 504-10.

Griffin, D.R. (1986), *Physics and the Ultimate Significance of Time*, Albany: State University of New York Press.

——— (1988a), "Of Minds and Molecules: Postmodern Medicine in a Psychosomatic Universe", in D.R. Griffin (ed.) *The Reenchantment of Science*, pp. 141-63, Albany: State University of New York Press.

——— (1988b), *Spirituality and Society: Postmodern Visions*, Albany: State University of New York Press.

——— (1991), "What Is consciousness and Why is it so Problematic?" Paper presented at the L.E.R. Conference on Consciousness, Durham, NC: Foundation for Research on the Nature of Man. Reprinted in this volume.

Grinberg-Zylberbaum, J. and John, E.R. (1981), "Evoked Potentials and Concept Formation in Man", *Physiology and Behavior*, **27**: 749-51.

Grinberg-Zylberbaum, J. and Ramos, J. (1987), "Patterns of Interhemispheric Correlation During Human Communication", *International Journal of Neuroscience*, **36**: 41-55.

Grosso, M. (1992), *Frontiers of the Soul*, Wheaton, Ill.: Quest Books.

Guenther, H.V. (1976), *Philosophy and Psychology in Abhidharma*, Berkeley, CA: Shambhala.

Hadamard, J. (1954), *The Psychology of Invention in the Mathematical Field*, New York: Dover.

Haight, J. (1979), "Spontaneous Psi Cases: A Survey and Preliminary Study of ESP, Attitude, and Personality Relationships", *Journal of Parapsychology*, **43**: 179-203.

Hales, S. (1986), "Epilogue: Rethinking the Business of Psychology", *Journal for the Theory of Social Behavior*, **16**(1): 57-76.

Hall, J.A. (1991), "*Patterns of Dreaming*: *Jungian Techniques in Theory and Practice*", Boston: Shambhala.

Harman, W.W. (1991), *A Re-examination of the Metaphysical Foundations of Modern Science*, Sausalito, CA: Institute of Noetic Sciences.

Hayward, J. (1987), *Shifting World, Changing Minds*, Boston: Shambhala.

Hearst, E. (1979), "One Hundred Years", in E. Hearst (ed.), *The First Century of Experimental Psychology*, Hillsdale, NJ: Erlbaum.

Heidegger, M. (1962), *Being and Time* (tr. John Macquarrie and Edward Robinson), New York: Harper.

——— (1982), *The Basic Problems of Phenomenology* (tr. A. Hofstadrer), Bloomington, IN: Indiana University Press.

——— (1984), *The Metaphysical Foundations of Logic* (tr. M. Heim), Bloomington, IN: Indiana University Press.

Heil, J. (1978), "Traces of Things Past", *Philosophy of Science*, **45**: 60-67.

——— (1981), "Does Cognitive Psychology Rest on a Mistake?", *Mind*, **90**: 321-42.

——— (1983), *Perception and Cognition*, Berkeley: University of California Press.

Heisenberg, W. (1958), *Physics and Philosophy: The Revolution in Modern Physics*, New York: Harper & Row.

Helsel, S. and Roth, J. (1991), *Virtual Reality: Practice, Theory and Promise*, Westport, C T: Meckler.

Hilgard, E.R. (1986), *Divided Consciousness: Multiple Controls in Human Thought and Action*, rev. edn., New York: Wiley-Interscience.

Hiriyanna, M. (1949/1995), *The Essentials of Indian Philosophy*, Delhi: Motilal Banarsidass.

——— (1993), *Outlines of Indian Philosophy*, Delhi: Motilal Banarsidass.

Ho, M.-W. (1989), "Reanimating Nature: The Integration of Science with Human Experience", *Beshara*, **8:** 16-23, 25.

Ho, M.-W., P. Saunders and S. Fox (1986), "A New Paradigm for Evolution", *New Scientist*, 27 February: 41-43.

Hopkins, B.C. (1993), *Intentionality in Husserl and Heidegger*, London: Kluwer Academic Publishers.

Hurley, T.J. (ed.) (1988), *The Greater Self: New Frontiers in Exceptional Abilities Research*, Sausalito, CA.: Institute of Noetic Sciences.

Husserl, E. (1931), *Ideas: General Introduction to Pure Phenomenology* (tr. W.R. Boyce Gibson), New York: Macmillan.

——— (1960), *Cartesian Meditations: An Introduction to Phenomenology* (tr. D. Cairns), The Hague: Martinus Nijhoff.

——— (1964), *The Idea of Phenomenology*, The Hague: Martinius Nijhoff.

——— (1965), *Phenomenology and the Crisis of Philosophy* (tr. and ed. S. Lauer), New York: Harper.

——— (1971), "Phenomenology" (tr. R. Palmer), *Journal of the British Society for Phenomenology*, **2**(2): 77-90.

——— (1982), *Logical Investigations*, 2 vols. (tr. J.N. Findlay), New York: Humanities Press.

Huxley, A. (1945), *The Perennial Philosophy*, New York: Harper & Row.

Jahn, R.G. (1991), *The Complementarity of Consciousness* (Technical Note PEAR 91006), Princeton Engineering Anomalies Research, Princeton University, School of Engineering/Applied Science.

Jahn, R.G. and Dunne, B.J. (1984a), *On the Quantum Mechanics of Consciousness, with Application to Anomalous Phenomena* (Technical Note PEAR 84001), Princeton Engineering Anomalies Research, Princeton University, School of Engineering/Applied Science.

——— (1984b), *Appendix B: Collected Thoughts on the Role of Consciousness in the Physical Representation of Reality* (Technical Note PEAR 84001-B), Princeton Engineering Anomalies Research, Princeton University, School of Engineering/Applied Science.

——— (1985), *Variance Effects in REG Series Score Distributions* (Technical Note PEAR 85001), Princeton Engineering Anomalies Research, Princeton University, School of Engineering/Applied Science.

——— (1986), "On the Quantum Mechanics of Consciousness, with Application to Anomalous Phenomena", *Foundations of Physics*, **16**(8): 721-72.

——— (1987), *Margins of Reality: The Role of Consciousness in the Physical World*, San Diego: Harcourt Brace Jovanovich.

Jahn, R.G., Dunne, B.J. and Nelson, R.D. (1987), "Engineering Anomalies Research", *Journal of Scientific Exploration*, **1**(1): 21-50.

Jaiswal, O.P. (1999), "An Evaluation of the Nature of Consciousness in Vijnanavada Philosophy", in S. Singh (ed.) *Buddhism in Comparative Light*, Delhi: Indo-Asian Publishing House.

James, W. (1890/1952), *The Principles of Psychology*, New York: Henry Holt & Co.

——— (1900), *Psychology: Briefer Course*, New York: Henry Holt.

——— (1902), *The Varieties of Religious Experience: A Study in Human Nature*, New York: Longmans, Green & Co.

——— (1960/1909), "The Final Impressions of a Psychical Researcher", in G. Murphy and R.O. Ballou (eds.) *William James on Psychical Research*, pp. 309-25, New York: The Viking Press.

——— (1912/1947), *Essays in Radical Empiricism*, New York: Longmans, Green & Co.

Jaynes, J. (1982), *The Origin of Consciousness in the Breakdown of the Bicameral Mind*, Boston: Houghton-Mifflin.

Jeans, J. (1943), *Physics and Philosophy*, Cambridge: Cambridge University Press.

Johansson, R.E.A. (1969), *The Psychology of Nirvana*, London: Allen & Unwin.

John, E.R. (1976), "A Model of Consciousness", in G.E. Schwartz and D. Shapiro (eds.), *Consciousness and Self-regulation*, vol. 1, pp. 1-50, New York: Plenum.

——— (1980), "Multipotentiality: A Statistical Theory of Brain Function", in J.M. Davidson and R.J. Davidson (eds.) *Psychobiology of Consciousness*, pp. 129-46, New York: Plenum.

Johnston, J.R. and Millay, J. (1983), "A Pilot Study in Brainwave Synchrony", *Psi Research*, **2:** 71-91.

Jones, R.M. (1932), *George Fox: Seeker and Friend*, London: Georg Allen & Unwin.

Jung, C.G. (1954/1919), "On the Nature of Psyche", in *Collected Works of C.G. Jung*, vol. 8 (tr. R.F.C. Hull, ed. H. Read et al.), Princeton, NJ: Princeton University Press.

Jung, C.G. (1919), "Instinct and the Unconscious", in H. Read, M. Fordham, and G. Adler (eds.) *Collected Works of C.G. Jung* (vol. 8) (tr. R.F.C. Hull), Princeton: Princeton University Press.

——— (1954), "On the Nature of the Psyche", in H. Read, M. Fordham, and G. Adler (eds.), *Collected Works of C.G. Jung* (vol. 8) (tr. R.F.C. Hull), Princeton: Princeton University Press.

——— (1963), *Memories, Dreams, Reflections*, (ed. A. Jaffe, tr. R. Winston and C. Winston), New York: Random House.

Kalupahana, D.J. (2006), *Mūlamadhyamakakārikā of Nāgārjuna*, New Delhi: Motilal Banarsidass.

Kant, I. (1929), *Critique of Pure Reason* (tr. N. Kemp Smith), London: McMillan.

Kazin, A. (ed.) (1976), *The Portable Blake*, New York: Penguin Books.

Keller, E.F. (1983), *A Feeling for the Organism: The Life and Work of Barbara McClintock*, San Francisco: Freeman.

Kenawell, W.K. (1965), *The Quest at Glastonbury*, New York: Helix Press.

Kennedy, J.E. (1978), "The Role of Task Complexity in PK: A Review", *Journal of Parapsychology*, **42**: 89-122.

Kihlstrom, J.F. and Schacter, D.L. (1990), "Anesthesia, Amnesia, and the Cognitive Unconscious", in *Memory and Awareness in Anesthesia*, ed. B. Bonke, W. Fitch and K. Millar, Amsterdam: Swets-Leiflinger.

Kihlstrom, J.F., Schachter, D.L., Cork, R.C., Hurt, C.A. and Behr, S.E. (1990), "Implicit and Explicit Memory Following Surgical Anaesthesia", *Psychological Science*, **1**: 303-06.

Klemm, O. (1914), *A History of Psychology* (tr. E.C. Wilm and R. Pinter), New York: Charles Scribner's Sons.

Klimo, J. (1988), *Channeling: Investigations on Receiving Information from Paranormal Sources*, Los Angeles: Tarcher.

Konig, H.L. and H.D. Betz (1989), *Der Wunschelruten-Report: Wissenschaftlicher Untersuchungsbericht*, München: Eigen Verlag.

Krippner, S. and A. Villoldo (1976), *The Realms of Healing*, Milbrae, CA: Celestial Arts.

Kroger, W.S. (1972), "Hypnotism and Acupuncture", *Journal of the American Medical Association*, **220**: 1012-13.

Kroon, R.P. (1989), "A Mind/Matter Action", *Journal of Religion and Psychical Research*, **12**: 74-84.

——— (1991), "Mind, Matter and Psi", *Journal of Religion and Psychical Research*, **14**: 61-74.

Krueger, M. (1991), *Artificial Reality II*, Reading, MA: Addison-Wesley.

Kunst-Wilson, W.R. and Zojonc, R.B. (1980), "Affective Discrimination of Stimuli that Cannot Be Recognized", *Science*, **207**: 557-58.

Langer, W.C. (1972), *The Mind of Adolf Hitler: The Secret Wartime Report*, New York: Basic Books.

Lasch, C. (1979), *The Culture of Narcissism: American Life in an Age of Diminishing Expectations*, New York: W.W. Norton.

Lawrence, D.H. (1931), *Apocalypse*, Florence: G. Orioli.

Lévi-Strauss, C. (1963), *Structural Anthropology*, New York: Basic Books.

Levin, M. (1979), *Metaphysics and the Mind–Body Problem*, Oxford: Clarendon Press.

Lincoln, Y.S. and Guba, E.G. (1985), *Naturalistic Inquiry*, Beverley Hills: Sage Publications.

Locke, J. (1894), *An Essay Concerning Human Understanding*, 2 vols. (ed. A.C. Fraser), London: Oxford University Press.

Lövland, P. (1981), "Proposed Mental Energetics and How It Relates to Paranormal phenomena", *Journal of Indian Psychology*, **3**: 20-46.

——— (1988), "A Common Mechanism for Psi Phenomenon, Meditation and Mysticism", *Journal of Indian Psychology*, **7**: 20-32.

Maharana, S.K. (2007), "Phenomenology of Consciousness: The Husserlian Dimension", *Journal of Indian Council of Philosophical Research*, XXXIV(1): 21-42.

Malcom, N. (1977), *Memory and Mind*, Ithaca: Cornell University Press.

——— (1980), "Functionalism in the Philosophy of Psychology", *Proceedings of the Aristotelian Society*, 80: 211-29.

Masling, J.M. (1992), "What Does It All Mean?", in R.F. Bornstein and T.S. Pittman (eds.) *Perception Without Awareness*, New York: Guilford Press.

Mason, A.A. (1952), "A Case of Congenital Ichthyosiform Erythrodermia of Broq", *British Medical Journal*, **2:** 422-23.

Matilal, B.K. (1986/2002), *Perception: An Essay on Classical Indian Theories of Knowledge*, New Delhi: Oxford University Press.

Mead, G.H. (1962), *Mind, Self, and Society*, Chicago: University of Chicago Press.

Millay, J. (1978), "The Relationship Between Phase Synchronization of Brainwaves and Success in Attempts to Communicate Telepathically: A Pilot Study", Doctoral Dissertation, Saybrook Institute, San Francisco, Research Abstract International, 0402 (University Microfilms No. 00286).

Miller, J. (1981), *The Compassionate Teacher*, Englewood Cliffs, NJ: Prentice-Hall.

Mohanty, J.N. (1972), *The Concept of Intentionality*, St. Louis: W.H. Green.

——— (1993), *Essays on Indian Philosophy: Traditional and Modern*, (ed. P. Bilimoria) Delhi: Oxford University Press.

Moore, G.E. (1922), *Philosophical Studies*, London: Harcourt, Brace & Co.

Morris, R.L. (1977), "Parapsychology, Biology and ANPSI", in B.B. Wolman (ed.) *Handbook of Parapsychology*, pp. 687-715. New York: Van Nostrand Reinhold.

Muhl, A. (1930), *Automatic Writing*, Leipzig: Theodor Steinkopff.

Murti, T.R.V. (1983), *Studies in Indian Thought* — Collected Papers of T.R.V. Murti (ed. Harold G. Coward) Columbia, MO: South Asia Books.

Murphy, M. (1992), *The Future of the Body*, Los Angeles: Tarcher.

Myers, F.W.H. (1903), *The Human Personality and Its Survival of Bodily Death*, London: Longmans, Green & Co.

Nagel, T. (1974), "What Is It Like to Be a Bat?", *Philosophical Review*, **83**: 435-50.

Natsoulas, T. (1978), "Consciousness", *American Psychologist*, **33**: 906-14.

Neisser, U. (1988), "Five Kinds of Self-knowledge", *Philosophical Psychology*, **1**(1): 35-59.

Nelson, R.D., Bradish, G.J. and Dobyns, Y.H. (1989), *Random Event Generator Qualification, Calibration, and Analysis* (Technical Note PEAR 89001), Princeton Engineering Anomalies Research, Princeton University, School of Engineering/Applied Science.

Nelson, R.D. and Dobyns, Y.H. (1991), *Analysis of Variance of Random Event Generator Experiments: Operator Intention, Secondary Parameters, Database Structure* (Technical Note PEAR 91004), Princeton Engineering Anomalies Research, Princeton University, School of Engineering/Applied Science.

Nelson, R.D., Dunne, B.J. and Jahn, R.G. (1984), *An REG Experiment with Large Database Capability III: Operator-Related Anomalies* (Technical Note PEAR 84003). Princeton Engineering Anomalies Research, Princeton University, School of Engineering/Applied Science.

Nietzsche, F. (2001), *Beyond Good and Evil* (tr. J. Norman), London: Cambridge University Press.

Noddings, N. (1984), *Caring: A Feminine Approach to Ethics and Moral Education*, Berkeley: University of California Press.

O'Regan, B. (1987), *Healing, Remission and Miracle Cures*, Institute of Noetic Sciences Special Report, May, pp. 1-16.

Orme-Johnson, D., Dillbeck, M.C., Wallace, R.K. and Landrith, G.S., III (1982), "Intersubject EEG Coherence: Is Consciousness a Field?", *International Journal of Neuroscience*, **16**: 203-09.

Panda, N.C. (1994), *Mind and Supermind* (2 vols.), New Delhi: D.K. Printworld.

Paranjpe, A.C. and Hanson, R.K. (1988), On Dealing with the Stream of Consciousness: A Comparison of Husserl and Yoga", in A.C. Paranjpe, D.Y.F. Ho and R.W. Rieber (eds.) *Asian Contribution to Psychology*, pp. 215-31, New York: Praeger.

Pauli, W. (1955), "The Influence of Archetypal Ideas on the Scientific Theories of Kepler", in C.G. Jung and W. Pauli *The Interpretation of Nature and Psyche*, New York: Pantheon Books, Bollingen Series LI.

Peat, F.D. (1987), *Synchronicity: The Bridge Between Matter and Mind*, New York: Bantam.

Pelikan, P. (1983), "The Enduring Relevance of Martin Luther 500 Years After His Birth", *New York Times Magazine*, 8 September, p. 44, *The Philosophy of Nietzche* (1927), New York: Modern Library.

Penrose, R. (1994a), *Shadows of the Mind: A Search for the Missing Science of Consciousness*, New York: Oxford University Press.

——— (1994b), "Shadows of the Mind: A Preview of His New Book", *Journal of Consciousness Studies*, **1**: 17-24

——— (1994c), "Mechanisms, Microtubules and the Mind", *Journal of Consciousness Studies*, **1**: 241-49.

Polkinghorne, D. (1986), "Changing Conversations About Human Science", *Saybrook Review*, **6**(1): 1-32.

Popp, F.A., Warneke, V. and Breithaupt, H. (1989), *Electromagnetic Bioinformation*, Munich: Urban and Schwarzenberg.

Popp, F.A., Li, K.H. and Gu, Q. (eds.) (1992), *Recent Advances in Biophoton Research*, Singapore: World Scientific.

Popper, K.R. and Eccles, J.C. (1977), *The Self and Its Brain: An Argument for Interactionism*, Berlin: Springer-Verlag.

Posner, M.J. and Snyder, C.R.R. (1975), "Facilitation and Inhibition in the Processing of Signals", in P.M.A. Rabbit and S. Dornick (eds.) *Attention and Performance V*. New York: Academic Press.

Potter, K.H. (1981), *Encyclopaedia of Indian Philosophies*, vol. III: *Advaita Vedānta upto Saṅkara and His Pupils*, Delhi: Motilal Banarsidass.

Praśastapāda (1923), *Praśastapāda Bhāṣya*, Benares: Kasi Sanskrit Series.

Prigogine, I. (1980), *From Being to Becoming: Time and Complexity in the Physical Sciences*, San Francisco: Freeman.

Puligandla, R. (1970), "Phenomenological Reduction and Yogic Meditation", *Philosophy East and West*, **20**: 19-33.

Puthoff, H.E. and Targ, R. (1976), "A Perceptual Channel for Information Transferred Over a Conglomerate Disturbance: Historical Perspective and Research, *Proceedings of the I.E.E.E.*, **64**: 329-54.

Putnam, F.W. (1986), "Scientific Investigations of Multiple Personality Disorders", in J.M. Quen (ed.) *Split Minds/Split Brains: Historical and Current Perspectives*, pp. 109-25, New York: New York University Press.

——— (1990), "Differential Autonomic Nervous Systems in Multiple Personality Disorders", *Psychiatric Research Journal*, **31**: 251-60.

Quine, W.V.O. (1960), *Word and Object*, Cambridge, MA: Harvard University Press.

——— (1962), *From the Logical Point of View* (2nd edn.), Cambridge: Harvard University Press.

Radhakrishnan, S. (1923/1989), *Indian Philosophy* (Centenary edition), 2 vols., Delhi: Oxford University Press.

Radin, D.I. and Nelson, R.D. (1989), "Evidence for Consciousness-related Anomalies in Random Physical Systems", *Foundations of Physics*, **19**(12): 1499-1514.

Raja, C.K. (1963), *The Sāṁkhya Kārikā of Īśvarakṛṣṇa: A Philosopher's Exposition*, Hoshiyarpur, India: V.V. Research Institute.

Ramos, A., Schwartz, E. and John, E.R. (1976), "Evoked Potential-unit Relationships in Behaving Cats", *Brain Research Bulletin*, **1**: 69-75.

Rao, K.R. (ed.) (1986), *Case Studies in Parapsychology*, Jefferson, NC: McFarland.

——— (1988), "Psychology of Transcendence: A Study in Early Buddhistic Psychology", in A.C. Paranjpe, D.G.F. Ho and R.W. Riebu (eds.) *Asian Contributions to Psychology* pp. 123-48, New York: Praeger.

——— (1991), "Consciousness Research and Psi", *Journal of Parapsychology*, **55**: 1-43.

——— (2011), *Cognitive Anomalies, Consciousness and Yoga*, New Delhi: Centre for the Study of Civilizations and Matrix Publishers.

Rao, K.R. and Palmer, J. (1987), "The Anomaly Called Psi: Recent Research and Criticism", *Behavorial and Brain Sciences*, **10**: 539-643.

Rauscher, E.A. (1990), "Human Volitional Effects on a Model Bacterial System", *Subtle Energies*, **1**(1): 21-42.

——— (1983), "The Physics of Psi Phenomena in Space and Time: Part II: Multidimensional Geometric Models, *Psi Research*, **2**: 93-120.

Rauscher, E.A. and Rubik, B.A. (1983), "Human Volitional Effects on a Model Bacterial System", *Psi Research*, March, **2**: 38-48.

Rheingold, H. (1991), *Virtual Reality*, New York: Summit Books.

Rhine, J.B. (1953), *New World of the Mind*, New York: William Sloane Associates.

Rhine, J.B. and Rhine, L.E. (1978), "A Search for the Nature of the Mind", in T.S. Krawiec (ed.), *The Psychologists:* vol. 3, *Autobiographies of Distinguished Living Psychologists*, pp. 181-205, Brandon, VT: Clinical Psychology Publishing Co.

Rhine, L.E. (1961), *Hidden Channels of the Mind*, New York: William Sloane Associates.

——— (1965), "Toward Understanding Psi-missing", *Journal of Parapsychology*, **29**: 259-74.

——— (1967), *ESP in Life and Lab: Tracing Hidden Channels*, New York: Macmillan.

——— (1970), *Mind Over Matter: Psychokinesis*, New York: Macmillan.

——— (1975), *Psi: What Is It?* New York: Harper & Row.

——— (1977), "Research Methods with Spontaneous Cases", in B. Wolman (ed.) *Handbook of Parapsychology*, pp. 59-80, New York: Van Nostrand Reinhold.

——— (1981), *The Invisible Picture: A Study of Psychic Experiences*, Jefferson, NC: McFarland.

——— (1983), *Something Hidden*, Jefferson, NC: McFarland.

Roberts, T. and Clark, F. (1975), *Transpersonal Psychology in Education*, Bloomington: Phi Delta Kappa Educational Foundation.

Rossman, M.L. and Bresler, D.E. (1983), *Guided Imagery: An Intensive Training Program for Clinicians*, Pacific Palisades, CA: The authors.

Rossman, N. (1991), *Consciousness: Separation and Integration*, Albany: State University of New York Press.

Rossner, J. (1989), *In Search of the Primordial Tradition*, St. Paul: Llewellyn Publications.

Rubenstein, R.A., Laughlin (Jr.), C.D. and McManus, J. (1984), *Science as Cognitive Process: Toward an Empirical Philosophy of Science*, Philadelphia: University of Pennsylvania Press.

Saint Teresa of Avila (1960), *The Life of Teresa of Jesus* (tr. E. Allison Peers), New York: Image Books, Doubleday & Co.

Saksena, S.K. (1944), *Nature of Consciousness in Indian Philosophy*, Banaras: Nand Kishore and Bros.

Śaṅkara (1890), *Vedānta-Sūtras with Śaṅkara's Commentary* (tr. Thibaut), Oxford: Clarendon Press.

Sampson, E.E. (1986), "What Has Been Inadvertently Rediscovered?: A Commentary", *Journal for the Theory of Social Behavior*, **16**(1): 33-40.

——— (1988), "The Debate on Individualism", *American Psychologist*, **43**(1): 15-22.

Sangharakshita (1975), *The Path of the Inner Life*, London: Friends of the Western Buddhist Order.

Sannwald, G. (1963), "On the Psychology of Spontaneous Paranormal Phenomena", *International Journal of Parapsychology*, **5**: 274-92.

Santayana, G. (1955), *Skepticism and Animal Faith*, New York: Dover.

Sartre, J.P. (1948), *The Psychology of Imagination* (tr. Bernard Frechtman), New York: Philosophical Library.

——— (1956), *Being and Nothingness* (tr. Houzel E. Barnes), New York: Philosophical Library.

——— (1957), *The Transcendence of the Ego: An Existentialist Theory of Consciousness* (tr. F. Williams and R. Kirkpatrick), New York: Noonday.

Sastri, S.S. (ed. & tr.) (1935), *The Samkhyakarika of Isvara Krishna*, Madras: University of Madras.

Searle, J.R. (1992), *The Rediscovery of the Mind*, Cambridge, MA: MIT Press.

Schacter, D.L. (1987), "Implicit Memory: History and Current Status", *Journal of Experimental Psychology: Learning, Memory, and Cognition*, **13:** 501-18.

Schmidt, H. (1970), "A PK test with Electronic Equipment", *Journal of Parapsychology*, **34:** 175-81.

——— (1982), "Collapse of the State Vector and PK Effect", *Foundations of Physics*, **12:** 565-81.

Schmitt, F.O. (1990), *The Never-ceasing Search*, Philadelphia: American Philosophical Society.

——— (1992), A Prescription for Generating a New Paradigm in the Context of Science and Theology", *Zygon*, **4(27)**: 437-54.

Schneider, M. (1975), *Neurosis and Civilization*, New York: Seabury Press.

Searle, J.R. (1983), *Intentionality: An Essay in the Philosophy of Mind*, New York: Cambridge University Press.

Shapiro, D. (1965), *Neurotic Styles*, New York: Basic Books.

Shaw, G.B. (1951), *Saint Joan*, London: Penguin.

Sheikh, A. (1984), *Imagination and Healing*, Farmingdale, NY: Baywood.

Silverman, L.H. (1983), "The Subliminal Psychodynamic Method: Overview and Comprehensive Listing of Studies", in J. Masling (ed.) *Empirical Studies of Psychoanalytic Theory*, vol. 1, pp. 69-103, Hillsdale, NJ: Erlbaum.

Silverman, L.H. and Weinberger, J. (1985), "Mommy and I are One: Implications for Psychotherapy", *American Psychologist*, **40:** 1296-1308.

Simonton, C.O., Simonton, S.M. and Creighton, J.L. (1975), "Belief Systems and Management of the Emotional Aspects of Malignancy", *Journal of Transpersonal Psychology*, **1:** 29-47.

——— (1984), *Getting Well Again*, New York: Bantam.

Sinari, R. (1965), "The Method of Phenomenological Reduction and Yoga", *Philosophy East and West*, **21:** 255-64.

Singh, S.P. and Mukesh, Y., *Yoga: From Confusion to Clarity*, vol. 1: *Foundations of Yoga*, New Delhi: Standard Publishers.

Sinha, J. (1958), *Indian Psychology: Cognition*, vol. 1, Calcutta: Sinha Publishing House.

Skarda, C.A. and Freeman, W.J. (1987), "How Brains Make Chaos in Order to Make Sense of the World", *Behavioral and Brain Sciences*, **10:** 161-95.

Skinner, B.F. (1974), *About Behaviorism*, New York: Alfred A. Knopf.

Skolimowski, H. (1984), *The Theatre of the Mind*, Wheaton, Ill.: Theosophical Publishing House.

Skutch, R. (1984), *Journey Without Distance*, Berkeley, CA: Celestial Arts.

Smart, J.C.C. (1979), "Materialism", in C.V. Borst (ed.) *The Mind–Brain Identity Theory*, pp. 159-70, London: Macmillan.

Smith, L. (1990), *Intelligence Came First*, Wheaton, Ill.: Theosophical Publishing House.

Smithies, J.P. and Beloff, J. (eds.) (1989), *The Case for Dualism*, Charlottesville: University Press of Virginia.

Spence, D.P. and Holland, B. (1962), "The Restricting Effects of Awareness: A Paradox and an Explanation", *Journal of Abnormal and Social Psychology*, **64:** 163-74.

Sperry, R.W. (1976), Mental Phenomena as Causal Determinants in Brain Function", in G.G. Globus, G. Maxwell and I. Savodnik (eds.), *Consciousness and the Brain*, pp. 163-77, New York: Plenum Press.

——— (1981), "Changing Priorities", *American Review of Neuroscience*, **4:** 1-15.

——— (1983), *Science and Moral Priority: Merging Mind, Brain, and Human Values*, New York: Columbia University Press.

——— (1987), "Structure and Significance of the Consciousness Revolution", *Journal of Mind and Behavior*, **8:** 37-66.

——— (1988), "Psychology's Mentalist Paradigm and the Religious/Science Tension", *American Psychologist*, **43:** 607-13.

——— (1991), "Search for Beliefs to Live by Consistent with Science", *Zygon*, **26**(2): 237-58.

Sridhara (1985), *Nyayakandali*, Benares: Vizayanagaram Sanskrit Series.

Stanford, R.G. (1977), "Experimental Psychokinesis: A Review from Diverse Perspectives", in B.B. Wolman (ed.) *Handbook of Parapsychology*, pp. 324-81, New York: Van Nostrand Reinhold.

Stapp, H.P. (1982), "Mind, Matter and Quantum Mechanics", *Foundations of Physics*, **12**: 363-98.

——— (1985), "Consciousness and Value in the Quantum Universe", *Foundations of Physics*, **15**: 35-47.

——— (1991), "Quantum of Propensities and the Brain–Mind Connection" (invited contribution to the issue honoring Sir Karl Popper), *Foundations of Physics*.

Stigliano, T. (1986), "An Ontology for the Human Sciences", *Saybrook Review*, **6**(1): 33-63.

Stokes, D.M. (1987), "Theoretical Parapsychology", in S. Krippner (ed.) *Advances in Parapsychological Research*, vol. 5, pp. 77-189, Jefferson, NC: McFarland.

Tarnas, R. (1991), *The Passion of the Western Mind*, New York: Harmony Books.

Tart, C. (1967), "A Second Psychophysiological Study of Out-of-the-Body Experiences in a Gifted Subject", *International Journal of Parapsychology* **9:** 251-58.

——— (1968), "A Second Psychophysiological Study of Out-of-the-Body Experiences in a Selected Subject", *Journal of the American Society for Psychical Research*, 62: 3-27.

——— (1972), "States of Consciousness and State-Specific Sciences", *Science*, 176: 1203-10.

——— (1974a), "Some Methodological Problems in Out-of-the-Body Experiences Research", in W. Roll, R. Morris and J. Morris (eds.) *Research in Parapsychology 1973*, pp. 116-20. Metuchen, NJ: Scarecrow Press.

——— (1974b), "Out-of-the-Body Experiences", in E. Mitchell and J. White (eds.) *Psychic Exploration*, pp. 349-74, New York: Putnam.

——— (1975a), *States of Consciousness*, New York: E.P. Dutton.

——— (1975b), "The Physical Universe, the Spiritual Universe, and the Paranormal", in C.T. Tart (ed.) *Transpersonal Psychologies*, New York: Harper & Row.

——— (1976), "Studying Out-of-the-Body Experiences", in T.X. Barber (ed.) *Advances in Altered States of Consciousness and Human Potentialities*, vol. 1, pp. 579-85, New York: Psychological Dimensions Press.

——— (1979), "An Emergent-interactionist Understanding of Human Consciousness", in B. Shapin and L. Coly (eds.), *Brain/Mind and Parapsychology*, pp. 177-200, New York: Parapsychology Foundation.

——— (1981), "Transpersonal Realities or Neurophysiological Illusions? Toward a Dualistic Theory of Consciousness, in R. Valle and R. von Eckartsberg (eds.), *The Metaphors of Consciousness*, pp. 199-222, New York: Plenum Press.

——— (1986), *Waking Up: Overcoming the Obstacles to Human Potential*, Boston: New Science Library.

——— (1987), "The World Simulation Process in Waking and Dreaming: A System Analysis of Structure", *Journal of Mental Imagery*, **11:** 145-58.

——— (1990), "Psi-meditated Emergent Interactionism and the Nature of Consciousness", in R. Kunzendorf and A. Sheikh (eds.), *The Psychophysiology of Mental Imagery: Theory, Research and Application*, pp. 37-63, Amityville, NY: Baywood.

——— (1991), "Multiple Personality, Altered States and Virtual Reality: The World Simulation Process Approach", *Dissociation*, **3:** 222-33.

Taube, M. (1936), *Causation, Freedom and Determinism*, London: George Allen & Unwin.

Taylor, E.I. (1973), *Pyschological Suspended Animation*, Dallas, TX: printed for private circulation by the Essene Press.

——— (1988a), "Contemporary Interest in Classical Eastern Psychology", in A. Paranjpe, D. Ho and R. Rieber (eds.) *Asian Contributions to Psychology*, pp. 79-122. New York: Praeger.

——— (1988b), *Cyberphysiology: The Science of Self-Regulation*, Minneapolis: The Archaeus Project.

——— (1991), "William James and the Humanistic Tradition", *Journal of Humanistic Psychology*, **31**(1): 56-74.

——— (1992), "A humanistic Psychology for the Future?", *The Humanistic Psychologist*.

Teherzadeh, A. (1980), *The Revelation of Baha'ullah*, Oxford: George Ronald.

Thouless, R.H. and B.P. Wiesner (1948), "The Psi Processes in Normal and 'Paranormal' Psychology", *Journal of Parapsychology*, **12:** 192-212.

Toulmin, S. (1986), "The Ambiguities of Self-understanding", *Journal for the Theory of Social Behavior*, **16**(1): 41-56.

Triesman, A.M. (1969), "Strategies and Models of Selective Attention", *Psychological Review*, **34:** 433-39.

Tyrrell, G.N.M. (1947), "The Modus Operandi of Paranormal Cognition", *Proceedings of the Society for Psychical Research*, **48:** 65-120.

Underhill, E. (1960), *Mysticism*, New York: Meridian Books.

Underhill, R.M. (1968): *Singing for Power*, New York: Ballantine.

Vācaspatimisra (1969), *Sāṁkhyatatvakaumudi*, Bombay: Samvat.

Valentine, J.D. (1982), "Towards a Physics of Consciousness", *Psychoenergetics*, **4:** 257-74.

Van Dusen, W. (1974), *The Presence of Other Worlds*, New York: Swedenborg Foundation.

Varela, F.J., E. Thompson and E. Rosch (1993), *The Embodied Mind: Cognitive Science and Human Experience*, Cambridge, MA: MIT Press.

Vasu, Srisa Chandra (tr.), (1979), *The Vedānta-Sūtras of Bādarāyaṇa with Commentary of Baladeva*, New Delhi: Oriental Books Reprint Corporation (first published in 1912).

Velmans, M. (1991), "Is Human Information Processing Conscious?", *Behavioral and Brain Sciences*, **14:** 651-726.

Vijnanabhiksu (1909), *Sāṁkhyapravacanabhāṣya*, Benares: Vizayanagaram Sanskrit Series.

Walker, E.H. (1970), The Nature of Consciousness", *Mathematical Biosciences*, **7:** 131-78.

——— (1972a), "Consciousness in the Quantum Theory of Measurement", Part I, *Journal for the Study of Consciousness*, **5:** 46-63.

——— (1972b), "Consciousness in the Quantum Theory of Measurement", Part II, *Journal for the Study of Consciousness*, **5:** 257-77.

——— (1975), "Foundations of Paraphysical and Parapsychological Phenomena", in L. Oteri (ed.) *Quantum Physics and Parapsychology*, pp. 1-53, New York: Parapsychology Foundation.

——— (1979), "The Quantum of Psi Phenomena", *Psychoenergetic Systems*, **3:** 259-99.

——— (1984), "Review of Criticisms of the Quantum Mechanical Theory of Psi Phenomena", *Journal of Parapsychology*, **48:** 277-332.

Walsh, R. (1983), *Staying Alive: The Psychology of Human Survival*, Boulder: Shambhala.

Watson, J.B. (1928), "The Unconscious of the Behaviorist", in C.M. Child, Kurt Koffka and John E. Anderson (eds.) *The Unconscious: A Symposium*, pp. 91-113, New York: Alfred A. Knopf.

Weinstock, C. (1977), "Notes on the Spontaneous Regression of Cancer", *American Society of Psychosomatic Dentistry and Medicine*, **24**(4): 106-10.

Weiskrantz, L. (1986), *Blindsight: A Case Study and Implications*, Oxford: Oxford University Press.

Whitehead, A.N. (1978), *Process and Reality* (corrected rev. & ed. D.R. Griffin and D.W. Sherburne), New York: Free Press.

Williams, J.A. (1962), *Islam*, New York: George Braziller.

Woo, C.H. (1981), "Consciousness and Quantum Interference : An Experimental Approach", *Foundations of Physics*, **11:** 933-44.

Woods, J.H. (1927), *The Yoga System of Patanjali*, Cambridge, MA: Harvard University Press.

Woodward, F.L. (1982), *Manual of Mystic: Yogācāra's Manual*, London: Pali Text Society.

Zeeman, E.C. (1977), *Catastrophe Theory: Selected Papers, 1972-77* (chaps. 8-9), Reading, Mass.: Addison-Wesley.

Zorab, G. (1963), "Yoga and Parapsychology", *Research Journal of Philosophy and Social Sciences*, **1:** 78-83.

Index